The Well-Tempered Garden

Also by Christopher Lloyd

THE MIXED BORDER

CLEMATIS

HARDY PERENNIALS

SHRUBS AND TREES FOR SMALL GARDENS

GARDENING ON CHALK AND LIME

The Well-Tempered Garden

Christopher Lloyd

Collins   St James's Place, London

First Impression 1970
Second Impression 1970

ISBN 0 00 211929 3

Printed in Great Britain
Collins Clear-Type Press
London and Glasgow

Contents

List of Illustrations

All colour photographs are by the author

Preface

Gardening is one of those creative activities that produces an enjoyable sensation of achievement. It is so many-sided that even if we all started off with similar rectangular plots, the end-products would be completely different. Temperament decides whether we prefer to grow what we can eat or what we can simply look at with pleasure; whether we concentrate on attaining a prescribed standard of perfection in individual specimens like chrysanthemums and onions, or whether we are plantsmen, with a love of plants for their own sake regardless of size or sophistication; whether it is the arrangement of plants and relating them to one another and to their setting that fascinates us, or whether their propagation and the bringing of new plants into the world has us hooked.

There is room for many approaches to gardening and they give us the satisfaction of expressing ourselves. Ours, in its humble way, is an art as well as a craft. At the same time it keeps us in touch with the earth, the seasons, and with that complex of interrelated forces both animate and inanimate, which we call nature. It is a humanising occupation.

Gardening has been the mainspring of my life and I have been lucky in my opportunities. In this book I have exploited most of the ingredients which, in my case, combine to make for happy gardening. Sometimes the reader may be incited to exclaim: 'what a lot of trouble!' or 'who wants to go through all that?'. But however labour-saving you make your hobby, you will never get more out of it than you put in. Now and again it seems worth taking that extra bit of trouble that brings in its train some rather exciting result. You feel you have got somewhere. Effort is only troublesome when you are bored. *The Well-Tempered Garden* is for gardeners who have not been dragged into this pursuit but are here because they love it.

1. Ways and Means

Planting

Planting Precautions and Methods

Friends sometimes ask me to deliver post-mortems on their less successful gardening efforts, but it is very difficult to pronounce with any certainty when their case history has been thoroughly masked. 'I planted a dozen hardy cyclamen,' one will say, 'and not one of them ever came up.' Where are they? Heaven knows. They were not marked; they may have been planted 6 in. deep, instead of just below the surface; they may have been planted just below the surface and subsequently chucked out as so many pebbles in a trugful of weeds; they may have been planted upside-down, or they may have been virtually dead before ever they were planted.

The great wonder, in gardening, is that so many plants live. I seldom get the opportunity of watching the private gardener at work. Privacy, indeed, is their watchword. They may be demons of efficiency in running their houses or businesses, but are understandably self-conscious when it comes to being seen doing a spot of manual work in the garden. They wait till the coast is clear rather than risk the onlooker's sharp intake of breath as their trowel chaws through the heart of an unexpected bulb or the guffaw that attends the stabbing of their shoe with the garden fork. Still, the time was when I had to instruct horticultural students in the various crafts of gardening, and to see them at work was instructive to me. One got a good idea of what was likely to go wrong.

When planting, one of the likeliest faults is that the hole made will be too small for the plant going into it. Some gardeners will try to get round this by twirling the plant round so that its roots are forced in with a spiral twist. But if the roots are spread out naturally, the plant has a much securer purchase on the ground and is less likely to get rocked by wind and lifted by frost. Others push the centre of the plant into the hole and fill in quickly, while a conveniently glazed vision ignores the root tips that are left waving about in mid-air. The motto here is to fit the hole to the plant, not the plant to the hole.

Gentle handling and firm planting are two complementary precepts. The handling part of it applies most particularly to soft material, such as summer bedding: you are beseeched to bruise a plant's stems, leaves and roots as little as possible. Try to keep soil and roots intact as one unit. When soil falls away from roots, it carries with it many of the smallest but most important feeding roots. So, if you are moving a tree or shrub in your garden, it pays to be patient in lifting it and to get it out and in again with as much bottom-hamper as possible. Even with plants like wallflowers, it greatly helps to move them with a good ball of soil.

Nurseries often have to send plants out with little or no soil adhering to their roots, otherwise carriage costs are prohibitive. Particularly in the case of trees and shrubs grown in the open ground, this means that a good deal of root will have been lost. Some may have been deliberately chopped off, for ease of packing. What tends to impress the naïve customer is a handsome array of trunk and branches. A friend (why have I any friends?, I sometimes wonder) proudly showed me three trees she had bought as a job lot at a market for only £1. One of them was stone dead; the other two were dead except for the stock on which they were grafted, which was suckering. When I pointed this out, her husband congratulated her on having bought three dead trees for £1.

Another keen gardening friend wanted to make a park out of a field next to his house, and set about it in a big way a few winters ago. Perhaps 60 trees were in question and they were all ordered at the same time but from several nurseries. They all arrived about the same time, too, and, unfortunately, in the one hard spell of the winter, in January. After the frost it was wet, in February. The trees were planted in a hurry. My friend is a week-end gardener and was unable to supervise the operation. No drought developed in the spring that year, but even so, more than half the trees died, and although I never saw their root systems on arrival, I reckon, from the general appearance of their tops, that this mortality was unnecessary.

One mistake to avoid is the ordering of more at a time than you can conveniently cope with. You can help yourself by asking for staggered deliveries. This is particularly easy if several nurseries are involved anyway.

When the trees arrive, you should bear in mind that they have not only spent a long time in transit, but that they were very probably lifted on the nursery a considerable time (far too long, let's face it) before they were actually despatched. Therefore the bundles should be unwrapped immediately and the roots given a jolly good soaking. If you can't plant forthwith, wrap them up again in thoroughly wet hessian. In a cold shed, dormant shrubs— even evergreens—will keep quite happily like this for several weeks.

Never make your holes in advance. It would be nice to be able to do so, in readiness for popping the trees straight in, on arrival, but your open hole will either get too wet (swimming wet, most often) or too frozen, and so will the spoil with which you are going to fill it in. Make your hole, plant and stake your tree, all in one continuous operation. Under turf, the soil is usually in a nice friable condition even in wet weather. But if the soil is sticky and won't break down so as snugly to fill in all the gaps between the roots, take a barrow-load of fine dry soil with you on the job, or some horticultural grit.

Assuming that the trees you have received from the nursery have more tops than roots, you must steel yourself to the unpalatable but always paying task of reducing all the branches of a deciduous tree or shrub so that top and roots are equally balanced. This usually entails reducing the branches by about two-thirds of their original length. Make your cuts immediately above a bud or pair of buds. Most gardeners know that where a rose bush is in question you give it a hard pruning to remove three quarters of its top growth immediately. The same treatment applies to all summer and autumn flowering shrubs that flower on their young growth. But vigorous deciduous shrubs such as philadelphus, deutzias, weigelas, forsythias and spring-flowering spiraeas can be sufficiently helped by removing all their older, weakest branchlets, leaving the strong unbranched ones intact. If you are handling a twiggy shrub like a lilac, you should thin out about half its network of twigs.

Most evergreens have fibrous roots and can be lifted and replanted without much root loss. Those with delicate root systems such as garrya, ceanothus, cistus and the brooms will usually be pot grown anyway, so that planting presents no difficulty. Sometimes, however, newly moved evergreens do sustain considerable root losses; this is very serious in their case, because they are losing moisture all the time through their leaves. You can anticipate this danger at planting time by watering in well or even by puddling in—an operation that is not necessarily to be sneered at even in November. Then, whenever you see the plant's foilage dry on the surface, you give it a sprinkling from a can. If this is not enough to stop the leaves and shoots from wilting, there is nothing for it but to defoliate. Remove half the bush's leaves; just pick, or snip, them off. This is not nearly as drastic as it may look and immediately cuts down on the supplies of moisture which the damaged roots will need to pump into the shrub's foliage.

Firm planting is not just something you read about that really only applies to other people's gardening. All plants need it. If it was a herbaceous or bedding plant you were putting in, take hold of it, after planting, by a leaf or small shoot, and give it a steady pull. If this brings the whole plant out of the ground, it means that you did not plant it firmly enough. Every such plant should be bedded in with the back of your fists, one on each side of it, and the weight of your body behind them. In the case of a tree or shrub, your entire weight is brought to bear, in a gyrating act on one heel. The only time when you should not plant firmly is when you should not really be planting at all: that is, when heavy ground is in a state of plasticine squelch. If the deed must be done in these conditions, the best technique, after standing the plant in its hole, is to pour grit (such as is used in the John Innes composts) over the roots so as entirely to cover them before filling in with the mud pie that is passing for soil. You do not compact when the ground is very wet, because you do not want to squeeze all the air out of the soil.

However, firm planting is the general rule, and for several reasons. Frost action, for one. Frost is a great lifter, and even if you planted firmly, you will have to look over your more shallow-rooted plants, following a thaw, to see if they need pushing home again. Another reason for firm planting is so that the roots can make immediate close contact with their new soil surroundings, and, again, to prevent trees and shrubs from rocking in the wind. But here staking will generally be necessary, in addition. It may be a good plan to stake even a fibrous rooted shrub like a hydrangea, for a start, until it has had time to anchor itself with new roots.

A common error, in attempting to get firm anchorage for his new trees and shrubs, is for the gardener to plant them deeply: deeper, that is, than they were when growing in their previous positions. I shall not pretend, for didactic convenience, that this is always fatal or, indeed, always bad practice. Roses planted with their graft unions below the surface are thereby encouraged to make scion roots. When lilac is grafted on privet, deep planting is essential, because unless scion-rooting occurs, the plant will die within a short period. Further, heathers are often planted deeply in order to encourage them to make roots on the buried portions of their stems; each bit of rooted stem can then be made into a new plant. Deep planting of a clematis often prevents its loss from wilt disease. The wilt fungus usually attacks at, but not below the soil surface, killing all the plant's aerial portions. If there is some stem below ground, the clematis can react by making a new shoot from down there.

But when these exceptions have been acknowledged, the fact of a nasty condition, descriptively known as collar rot, remains. If you plant a tree or shrub so that the base of its trunk or of its lowest stems and branches is covered, it will react in one of two ways: either by making roots from these newly buried portions or, if this is not its nature, by rotting at that point. This happened to me with a strapping young bird cherry, *Prunus padus* 'Albertii'. To keep grass and weeds away from its base, I used to mulch it throughout the summer with lawn mowings. The mulch got too thick about its trunk, the rot set in and that was that.

It is not just trees and shrubs that need to be planted as soon as the ground is ready for them. The same principles apply in any sort of bed or border. Undug ground, particularly if it has been covered with a crop of sorts—summer bedding plants or weeds—tends to remain fairly workable even after heavy rain. But the moment it has been dug over it becomes like a sponge, full of air spaces that are ready to lap up quantities of water. And so, again, in a border of hardy perennials, I always find it wisest to cut down, split, manure, dig and replant—all in one manageable bite, not taking in a larger area than I feel confident of finishing off in the same day.

When a herbaceous border is looking thoroughly disorderly, it is tempting to start by laying low everything within sight that is lay-lowable. But this is unwise. Protective top growth not only helps to keep the ground dry and protects it from frosts, but when it is gone, one tends to forget which plant was which, how tall it grew and where, and whether it needed splitting.

Many gardeners get over this difficulty of identity and location by not cutting their perennials right down, but leaving a foot-tall tuft of stalk stumps. I abhor this practice. A herbaceous plant should either be cut down flush with the ground or (if it still looks pretty, even in death) not cut down at all. Stumps become hard and hollow; they are a refuge for earwigs and woodlice; they obstruct young growth in the next spring. They look unsightly; and, worst of all, they become so woody that their cut surfaces will later deal vicious, jabbing wounds to the unwary gatherer of long-stemmed flowers the following summer.

When one is planting a wet piece of ground, a wonderful lightener is the grit I keep harping on—that recommended for use in John Innes composts. You can get it from builders' merchants (such as M. P. Harris, in Kent, Surrey and Sussex) and it is usually described as $\frac{3}{16}$ horticultural grit. This is the finest sifting from ground up shingle or gravel, and is far more useful than the coarsest natural sand. Once one has developed a taste for it, there is no end to its applicability in the garden, first as a heavy general dressing, to be dug into slimy ground; then, when planting bulbs, as a protection from slugs, rots and bad drainage. Grit can also be used as a protective mound heaped, in early winter, over the crowns of fuchsias, lemon-scented verbenas, delphiniums (with slugs in mind) and eremurus. In fact, read 'grit' for 'ashes' when gardening journalists are on this topic.

Planting Distances

An experienced gardening friend—one of the exceptions to the theory that farmers make the worst gardeners—was saying to me that the problem of spacing was the most intractable of all; the one which he had never learnt to solve without first making a series of gigantic blunders. He would plant an area with shrubs that looked pathetically small, only to discover a few years later, that they were suffocated for lack of space.

We were looking, as he spoke, at a shrubbery planted 8 or 10 years previously in a large triangular corner, formed by the junction of two hedges. The most prominent object, at the front, was a bamboo that had hitherto risen to a height of only 7 ft., but whose new canes had that year soared to 10 ft. A nice, gentle bamboo, with feathery foliage and only moderately rampant habits; the one that should, I believe, be known as *Sinarundinaria nitida,* but if you wish to be understood in the world of bamboo lovers it is enough to murmur the word *nitida* and leave it at that. Behind this, one could just see an 8-ft.-tall *Elaeagnus pungens* 'Maculata'; behind that, again, I fancy there grew a 10-ft. *Magnolia soulangeana*; the rest was quite hidden.

This friend reckoned that the soundest course was to space your permanent shrubs very widely at the outset, interplanting with temporary shrubs such as short-lived brooms, tree lupins and cistuses, and with easily removed herbaceous plants, in the early years. This is what I would term a paper principle; in practice, it proves better than no principle at all, but overcrowding will never be ruled right out. You must resign yourself to the necessity of big upheavals and rearrangements from time to time, right through the years. It is obvious that close planting gives a furnished look to a border almost immediately; equally obvious that it is wasteful and expensive. A point about it that can be overlooked is the fact that shrubs afford each other very considerable protection against damage by frost and wind, if they are close set.

At any rate you should try to get the immovables permanently sited from the outset; all the legumes (members of the pea family), walnuts, magnolias, ceanothus: trees and shrubs, in fact, with fleshy, fragile roots or with deep-delving fangs, that simply will not stand being moved once they have got themselves ensconced. For the rest, one tries one's best to make as few mistakes as possible. Most trade catalogues give the approximate heights that your shrubs are likely to attain and some hazard a forecast of their probable breadth, at maturity, too. But so much depends on

soil and cultural treatment. If, for instance, shrubs are planted in
what I consider to be the worst way of establishing a shrubbery:
in individual circles cut out of turf, they have the grass to compete
with for water and food, and many of them will stand still, while
others will grow at a snail's pace. Others, to be honest about it,
will benefit from a semi-starvation diet. *Cotinus coggygria (Rhus
cotinus)* and *C. americanus* (R. *cotinoides*) for instance, make much
too watery a growth on well fed soil. They are best grown as
lawn specimens.

Assuming that soil conditions and feeding are suitable and
adequate, let us consider a few distances, starting with trees.
Cherry orchards are usually planted on a 40-ft. square with interplanting in the early years. Therefore, if you are planting a
similar cherry such as the double white gean (*Prunus avium* 'Plena'),
it should be 40 ft. from another cherry of like vigour. You could,
however, interplant with trees like ornamental or fruiting peaches,
that you expected to be fairly short lived. If the next permanent
tree to your cherry was going to be a John Downie crab, 30 ft.
would be adequate spacing. This would allow 20 ft. for the cherry
and 10 ft. for the much neater growing crab.

Never allow less than 6 ft. between large growing shrubs: as
it were a *Spiraea vanhouttei* and a *Forsythia* 'Lynwood'; 8 or 10 ft.
would be much better, but at least be firm with yourself to
the extent of not reducing below 6 ft. Now, any shrubbery that
is planned on the basis of one of a kind, right through, will look
spotty. Particularly the lower growing, 3-ft.-tall shrubs, need
grouping.

Hydrangeas look much their best for this treatment; not the
real giants, such as the 12-ft. *Hydrangea bretschneideri,* or the 8 ft.
by 12 ft. *H. villosa,* but even a comparatively large cultivar such
as Blue Wave looks more effective when, say, three are gathered
together. Caryopteris, hardy fuchsias, the lower growing hebes,
Hypericum 'Hidcote', *Spiraea* 'Anthony Waterer' and many more,
are all the better for grouping, their individual forms having
nothing special to recommend them. In this case the group is the
unit and it does not matter if individuals composing the unit
grow into each other with interlocking branches, at quite an
early age. You could thus allow 3 ft. between the individuals
in a group of *Caryopteris clandonensis,* and 4 ft. between this

and the next item—say a group of *Potentilla fruticosa* 'Katherine Dykes'.

If you get the spacing of herbaceous perennials wrong, it matters little; most of them can easily be moved and rearranged.

The bedding plants that are intended for spring flowering are usually spaced too far apart. They are planted in autumn and will make no more bulk before they throw up their flowering shoots in spring. To be effective, they need to go in thickly. Summer bedding, by contrast, wants much wider spacing than it usually gets, especially if the ground is in good heart, as it should be. In this case the plants want to be put out from their seed boxes as soon as they are touching each other and before they start to feel crowded. They will then make considerable bulk in their final quarters before starting to flower and will do themselves and you most credit if they can develop almost to their limit before joining up with their nearest neighbours.

Bedding plants are so often starved at one stage or another in their upbringing that few of us have much notion of their real potential, when given their chance. The revelation can be quite exciting. Take the ordinary sort of Busy Lizzie that is almost invariably grown in a pot on a window-sill, for instance. It is usually a stemmy plant about a foot tall and sprawling a little more across. But try it as a bedding plant in moist, well enriched soil, say in a shady, north facing border. Each plant will grow 4 ft. tall and quite as much across. A staggered row of them makes a splendid flowering hedge, and so luxuriant that people seeing it for the first time will have to blink and gasp awhile before realising that this is their old friend in almost unrecognisable guise.

When to Plant

Autumn and spring are the two great planting seasons. The tree, shrub and herbaceous plant catalogues arrive in late summer, for the most part, and the majority of nursery sales are made in the autumn period. However, following wet autumns and cold winters such as have been frequent of recent years, mortality among autumn planted purchases can be very high indeed. On heavy, water-retentive soils, which get cold early, warm up late and are frequently in a sodden condition most uncongenial to the establishing of young plants, the situation is doubly aggravated. On such soils there is, moreover, a high slug population; and even with the help of the excellent metaldehyde preparations available for slug control, it is still impossible to cope through the long dormant period with those small black slugs that live permanently underground and batten on the resting buds of defenceless herbaceous plants.

Evergreens are most popular among the shrubs. Being evergreen, they are never as fully dormant as their deciduous counterparts. The recommended times for their planting are therefore in early autumn, when the soil is still warm and they can make new roots before winter arrives, or else in not-too-early spring, when the soil is warming up again and they can go ahead without a check. My own view of this choice is that an autumn planting is too risky. It should be remembered that all broad leaved evergreens (and a number of needle leaved heaths and conifers also) come from warmer temperate climates than our own. A plant like *Osmanthus delavayi* or any of the *Camellia japonica* hybrids may be trustworthily hardy, once established for a few years; but when young and new it is all too easily killed. Its best chance will result from a spring move; then it has an entire growing season before it in which to make and ripen new roots and shoots. The only danger from a spring planting is drought, and compared with other climatic hazards this is so easily countered that it should certainly not defeat the self-respecting gardener. If you are going to risk planting, say, a camellia in autumn, do at least take the simple precautionary measure for protecting its roots, of putting over them a thick layer of about 4 in. of grit. This must be scraped aside again in spring after its duty has been done.

A number of deciduous trees and shrubs are more safely planted in spring, too. Thoroughly tough characters like the weigelas, deutzias and many philadelphus are admittedly indestructible, but lilacs will succumb to waterlogging; time and again I hear of witch hazels (*Hamamelis mollis*) that have never broken dormancy; while deciduous magnolias, with their fleshy, rot-prone roots, are notoriously ill-suited to autumn planting, yet are frequently distributed at this season.

There is a strong case, I feel, for making a practice of ordering your new trees, shrubs and herbaceous plants as early as possible, as always, but for requesting spring delivery. If there are to be winter losses, they will then occur in the nursery, not in your garden. Any general acceptance of this view would make nursery organisation more difficult and hence more expensive with a consequent rise in prices, but would be worth it by preventing the despatch of thousands of plants each autumn that are doomed to die soon after. Alternatively you can accept your order for autumn delivery but overwinter the more perishable elements in it, under cover, yourself.

The particular drawback to spring deliveries is the trickiness of timing. Where plants and shrubs have been grown on the nursery in open ground, there may be a very brief interval between dormancy in freezing conditions and, following a mild spell, growth too advanced to allow transplanting. We should not forget, though, that ours is one of the very few cool temperate climates in the world where autumn planting is considered feasible. In New England, for instance, although on average ten degrees of latitude nearer the Equator, the severe winters limit all planting to a hectic spring period.

Our kinder climate does allow us to get through a great deal of regular overhauling work in autumn. There is all the difference between moving a plant in your garden and having it sent to you from afar. You can lift a shrub or a plant like a delphinium with so much soil attached to its roots and with so little delay in the process that it need scarcely notice the change. Splitting up of herbaceous phloxes, aconitums and *novi-belgii* asters is safe enough in autumn, too. But whereas we can dare to move a delphinium or a grass like miscanthus, a dictamnus or an amellus-type aster, with roots and ball of soil intact, these and certain other herbaceous plants cannot submit to the greater disturbance of being split up, until spring. Then they can immediately make good the damage done to them, by growing, instead of just sitting about and rotting, as they would in autumn.

There is always such a rush of work in spring that we should get everything done that we can in the more leisurely periods of congenial weather during the autumn and even into winter. But where there is any doubt about moving a shrub or splitting up a herbaceous plant in autumn, the task should be deferred till spring.

That is my official pronouncement. Don't expect me to follow it myself, because I'm also a great believer in doing a job when I want to do it, and to hell with the consequences.

Summer Planting and Mid-Season Swaps

Once June is behind him and the gaps are all filled with summer bedding, the not-too-serious gardener tends to sink back on to his latest model for comfort in garden furniture, with the happy notion at the back of his mind that the ardours of spring are past and no further great efforts will be required of him for the next three months. A little gentle hedge clipping and lawn mowing; perhaps an occasional assault on the weeds that he would have gladly shut his eyes to, if officious relatives would only stop pointing them out; but nothing more. Oh, dead-heading the roses, of course, but that is a woman's job; even a guest might fairly be let loose on it.

Given this outlook, no garden will be worth looking at by mid-August. If you then go away for six weeks, all well and good, but if not, then there is every reason to go on grunting and sweating under the July sun. For one thing, the planting seasons are no longer restricted to spring and autumn as they traditionally always were. A well run garden centre will have a wide selection of shrubs and young trees, established in a varied assortment of containers, as ready for planting in summer as in the dormant season. In fact, so long as you can water your plants in thoroughly, summer is the best of times to get a shrubbery started and established, because the ground is warm (and so, incidentally, are you) and the shrubs will get rooted into their new environment and happily established within a matter of weeks.

But July is also the moment to do some switching around, in your borders, of biennial and herbaceous plants. Various early-summer-flowering plants will then, or soon, be going out of flower. If they are of a kind that does not mind being cut back and moved out of the way till brought back again in autumn, this is what I like to do. Such are the bergenías, doronicums, the early flowering achilleas such as Moonshine, and the 3 ft. *Campanula persicifolia*. Then there are the early-summer-flowering biennials to replace: sweet williams, Canterbury bells, Brompton stocks and foxgloves.

What to put in their place? It is wise to plan ahead for this moment by making late sowings of annuals, in May, that will be just right for planting out in July. Bedding dahlias sown about 1st May and potted off individually, will just be coming into bud two months later and will flower non-stop till the autumn. If seed sowing doesn't form a part of your organisation you will find boxes of late-sown annuals still available at the garden centre.

Perhaps you have chrysanthemums in your picking garden. Many varieties are fit only for picking or else for exhibiting (or for the rubbish heap), but the early flowering types that produce a mass of blossom—the so-called Koreans and Rubellums—look charming in the border and are easily moved, provided that they are gently handled, for their branches are brittle and do break off terribly easily at their junction with the main stem. Michaelmas daisies move well from the open ground, even when in full growth, and so does the cardinal flower, *Lobelia cardinalis*.

A liberal use of water is the basis of success. Several hours beforehand, soak all the plants that are to be lifted, so that the water has time to get down to their roots. Add a quick-acting general fertiliser to the site that is to be replanted and fork it over. If the ground is still dryish, then each plant should be puddled in: dig your hole, stand the new plant in it and pour a gallon of water quickly over its roots, by turning the can upside down. The roots will thus be coated with a skin of fine soil particles. As the water drains out of your miniature pond, fill the hole in and firm gently. The task can be completed twice as quickly if the ground has already been saturated by one of those cloudbursts that we frequently get at that season.

The best opportunity for turning out all the contents of your greenhouse, and giving it a thorough clean-out, usually presents itself in July. Many of the shrubby plants can be made to do their stint in the garden and, being pot-grown, there are no transplanting difficulties. One can, of course, plunge them in the border, pot and all. That is the best way with lilies, but with most things I prefer to turn them out and re-pot in the autumn. But, once again, give each plant a very thorough soaking in its pot before attempting to turn it out. Nearly always, de-potted plants should be puddled into their new positions. Fuschias are especially suitable. The Angel's Trumpets, *Datura suaveolens*, with white, night-scented funnels, the vivid orange-red *Streptosolen jamesonii* and the pale blue *Plumbago capensis* are also good as are the various kinds of abutilon and hibiscus. Any small flowered pelargoniums, such as those with aromatic foliage, are good bedders-out and so are many foliage plants.

Manuring

Manures: Animal, Vegetable, Mineral

We are probably all a little cranky in our ideas on manuring. The young man who used to collect the contents from his friends' ashtrays for later application to his roses is a case in point. Tea leaves get saved exclusively as a mulch for camellias, simply because the tea plant is a camellia species. For my part, I cast all my nail parings out of the bathroom window so as to feed the ceanothus below with hoof and horn. Since, at 20 years, this is the oldest ceanothus in my garden, and it is still flourishing, I naturally congratulate myself on a sagacious policy.

It seems a pity, though, when crankiness is carried to the pitch of eschewing all artificial fertilisers; for an adequate all-organic manurial programme in the garden will generally run you to considerable extra expense. The use of artificials by themselves over a period of years is harmful in the negative sense: you are failing to replace the continuous losses of organic matter from the soil that are inevitable on cultivated land. But if their use is combined with applications of bulky organics such as farmyard manure, garden-made compost or peat (whose nutritive value is nil), artificials are excellent. Some time in March I go over all my flower and shrub borders distributing a balanced general fertiliser, containing nitrogen, phosphates and potash, at the rate of 4 oz. per square yard, put on before the soft young foliage of herbaceous plants, roses, etc., is too prominent, so as to get the fertiliser on the ground easily without any scorching damage. During the summer, whenever I change over any sort of planting—for instance, discarding sweet williams or foxgloves for something to follow in later summer—I use another dressing of quick-acting fertiliser.

My bulky manures are spread or dug in during the autumn or winter, whenever I am getting at any piece of the garden to give it its annual overhaul. The most sought-after product is farmyard manure. This is a mixture of three main ingredients: liquid and solid excreta, and litter, usually straw. (One might add weed seeds as a fourth.) Between 80 and 90 per cent. of the manure's nutrient value is contained in the liquid constituent, and there is constant danger of this being washed away. Straw in plentiful quantities is invaluable for soaking up this liquid.

Long manure, in which the straw has barely started to decompose, is still fairly fresh from the stable or cattle yard. It is strong-smelling, though this soon wears off. It is also harmful to actively growing plants, but it is quite all right used in autumn on bare ground that is to be dug and then left fallow till the following spring. The quicker it can be transferred from cattle-yard to garden and then dug in, the better. Every time it is distributed, nitrogen is lost by volatilisation, while every bit of drying-out incurs further nitrogen losses through the operation of denitrifying organisms. Losses are at their minimum when the manure is incorporated with the soil. If it must be kept hanging around, try to store it in a compact heap under cover, so that rain cannot wash nutrients away. If it must be left on the ground where it is going to be dug in, leave it in heaps, and not already spread out. Spreading should be done only just before digging. Long manure can also be used harmlessly in the garden as a surface mulch to dormant shrubs and young trees. You will not want to dig it in, because of root disturbance.

Short manure, in which the straw is thoroughly decomposed, is of most general use to the gardener, as it is harmless, odourless and easily handled. Inevitably it will have lost a good deal of its nitrogen and potash content; but this, after all, is where the boost supplied by quick-acting artificials can easily rectify matters. Concentrated organic fertilisers can also be used in conjunction with the bulky kinds. They are slow-acting and release their nutrients steadily over a long period. Best known here are hoof-and-horn, dried blood and bone-meal.

Farmyard manure's greatest asset is in its contribution of

organic matter to the soil. This increases the soil's water-holding capacity, which is of paramount importance on hungry, free-draining sandy or chalk soils. Again, it improves drainage on heavy land, first by enabling the soil to retain a good structure that allows the passage of water through it; and second by encouraging a high earthworm population, the channels made by them in the soil also allowing a freer movement of water.

Gardeners are constantly removing organic matter from their borders in the form of dead leaves, weeds, herbaceous material at the end of the season, prunings and so forth. Its replacement is essential; but, as farmyard manure is not obtainable generally, one may have to look around for alternatives. Almost anything that is bulky and organic will do, so long as it is capable of decomposing within a reasonably short span. Garden compost is excellent. Manure from a deep-litter hen house is best of all, but it is so concentrated that care must be taken not to use too much at a time. It is powdery and dry; easy and pleasant to handle; and weed-free. Moreover, the litter content in it will generally be well decomposed, even if it started out as such stubborn material as wood shavings or sawdust. Peat contributes humus to the soil. Its sole value is as a soil conditioner.

There is currently a tremendous vogue for peat, which is so widely believed to be a panacea for every cultural problem that supplies can barely keep pace with demand and prices are rocketing accordingly. One of its great attractions is that, when wet, it looks so good; that rich dark colouring and soft juicy texture seems to be instinct with every property that any reasonable plant could desire. 'Shall I give it peat?' the customer asks the nurseryman, when buying a plant. It is usually safe for the latter to answer yes; no harm is likely to result and there will be some good. But in putting his question the customer often mistakenly hopes that by applying a little peat and gaining a nice black effect his obligations will be at an end.

Sewage sludge may be readily available in some districts, spent hops or seaweed in others. Seaweed should be stacked in the open, before use, so that rain can wash the salt out of it.

Composting and Mulching

It has often been pointed out that the gardener burns his inheritance on the garden bonfire. So convenient a method of destroying rubbish is hard to resist; but except for the roots of perennial weeds, for wood and for old cabbage stalks (which are virtually wood), all vegetable refuse should go to the making of composted manure. For those of us living near an assured supply of farmyard or deep-litter chicken manure, the fag of composting may not always be worth the labour. But most gardeners live in or near towns, and for them the compost heap, if there is room for one, is sacred indeed.

In order to decompose, all vegetable matter needs supplies of nitrogen. This encourages a build-up in the population of the micro-organisms responsible for decomposition. The other necessary ingredients are air and water. Lime also helps by preventing conditions in the heap from becoming too acid.

To make a compost heap, then, you start with a six-inch-deep layer of refuse, covering an area of up to 12 ft. square. If the refuse contains long stems such as old herbaceous plant stalks, they should be chopped up into shorter lengths, or else they will not pack down enough; the heap will be too well aired and will not heat. On the other hand, refuse like green lawn mowings packs down all too well. These should be kept as loose as possible by mixing with coarser rubbish. If mowings pack down tightly, the absence of air has the effect of not allowing them to heat properly, and you end up with silage instead of compost.

You thoroughly wet this layer and then add a proprietary accelerator (containing nitrogen and lime) before going on to the next. The stack can be added to until it is 4 or 5 ft. high. After six weeks, it should be turned so as to get the outside into the centre and also so as to admit more air, for it will have subsided and compacted considerably. Properly made in this way, the heap will be ready for use in six months. An alternative to the addition of a proprietary 'compost-maker' between layers of refuse is to add sulphate of ammonia and garden lime (which is ground-up chalk—calcium carbonate) in alternate layers. They must be kept separate in this way, because together they react on one another with a consequent loss of nitrogen.

Most of our own compost is made from hay. If you have rough grass planted up with bulbs, you will probably not want to cut it before the end of June. A rotary cutter chews up the grass into just the right length and consistency for composting. As the grass may be rather sere, it should be raked up and whisked away to the heap as quickly as possible. It will need considerable watering, not only at the time of stacking but at intervals of every ten days or so.

We subsequently cut our rough grass again in August and in October, so as to keep the turf from becoming coarse and tussocky. These later cuts can also be composted, but, as they are fairly free of weed seeds, we largely use them as direct surface mulches. All our lawn mowings are also used for this purpose; and you can mulch with bulky manure or with already made compost, with leafmould, peat, straw and so on. When the mulch is of un-decayed material such as straw or grass cuttings, you should again remember that it will take nitrogen from the soil in the process of decomposition. If put among growing plants, you should at the same time add a nitrogenous fertiliser such as sulphate of ammonia at an ounce to the square yard.

It is important never to mulch on dry ground, as this will prevent rain from penetrating. But if you can apply your mulch to wet ground, then the moisture is retained in the soil and the effects of drought are much reduced. Mulches also have the effect of building up the population of the soil fauna, including earth-worms and micro-organisms, and this is a healthy reaction. If applied thickly enough, they suppress weeds.

We have two permanently mulched areas in our garden. First, the blackcurrants: these are under straw, a few extra bales being scattered over the area every winter. The bushes' tendency to root near the surface is accentuated by mulching, and it is therefore very important not to discontinue the treatment, otherwise the currants' surface-feeding roots would be terribly susceptible to drought. The berries, of course, are absolutely mud-free, and no weeding or digging is called for.

Second, there is the rose garden. This used to be a very badly drained area, but a vast earthworm population has made the heavy soil beautifully crumbly and full of channels. Also, the permanent mulch has here practically eliminated blackspot—much to my surprise. Our rose beds are surrounded by paving. In the process of turning the mulch over, blackbirds are constantly flinging it out on to the paths, and a daily sweep-up is necessary in summer. This would be an insupportable nuisance with mown grass verges. A box-hedge edging might be one solution. No system is perfect: one has to balance the advantages with the drawbacks.

Pruning

Shrubs for Winter Pruning

Quite a number of shrubs can be pruned at the deadest season of the year. There is the rose, discussed elsewhere, but there are also many other shrubs whose pruning is the same as the average hybrid tea rose's, and which we were likewise brought up to deal with in March or April, when growth was being resumed. In fact, it seems as though they, too, can be pruned whenever it may suit us in the dormant season. It certainly suits me to cut back my buddleias good and early, because they look like so many wrecks, scattered about the winter landscape: I mean the forms of the common **butterfly bush**, *Buddleia davidii* and *B. fallowiana*. One should be severe with these, leaving no more than stumps of last summer's 6-ft. shoots. Even then, a bush will become unduly leggy after ten years or so. I decided on drastic action with one such, some years ago, and sawed it back into thick old wood, leaving a 2-ft. stump. 'If it dies, it dies,' I told myself; and, as I had another plant up my sleeve, it was easy to be philosophical.

Well, of course, having been dared to do its worst, it did not die, but grew away from the stub like an old willow. If any reader is prompted to take similar action, he can safeguard himself by making a number of hard-wood cuttings from the cane-like prunings, trimming each, top and bottom, just above and just below a node, to make sticks a foot long, which can be stuck by two-thirds their length into light soil in a spare plot. They root easily.

Any other hardy shrub that flowers on its young shoots in summer and autumn can be pruned by shortening them back in winter. But if, like a caryopteris or a fuchsia, it is none too hardy, I believe in leaving its old flowering shoots as some sort of self-protection, not clipping them over till April. One such shrub is the finest of all the **indigos**, *Indigofera gerardiana*. I have a plant quite unprotected in our mixed border, and in each of its 15 years there it has tried to fool me into thinking it has died. No shrub ever looked more passé for half the year, and it is late in spring before it gives a reassuring sign. If its top growth should be killed, it will throw up strongly from the base; but with me this has never had to happen. From June to September it is a most delightful plant, opening a succession of rosy purple pea-flowers, borne in spikelets in the axils of its no less charming feathery foliage. As so often happens in the pea family, its leaves close up and droop at night, like a sensitive plant that has just been touched.

The other group of shrubs that can be pruned in winter are those that flowered in spring and early summer on shoots made in the previous year. Chief among them are the mock oranges (*Philadelphus*), deutzias, weigelas (and the nearly related kolkwitzias and dipeltas), and the early spiraeas (for example *Spiraea vanhouttei* and *S. prunifolia*). Textbook advice would have us do them immediately after flowering, so as to let in light and air for the developing young shoots, which will provide next year's flowers. Three objections here are: that the young shoots are so tender and brittle then as to be easily knocked off; that there is so much else to do in the garden then; and that you can see far better what wants doing to a deciduous shrub when its leaves are off.

Tackling the job in winter, you should remove all the previous season's flowering shoots. You can recognise them not only from their old flower remains but because they are minutely branching. Tracing each of them back, make your cut at that point where a new young shoot arises. This will be an unbranched, wand-like stick, of warm brown colouring, and must not be pruned at all. If there is a shortage of strong young shoots to cut back to, it is either because pruning has been neglected in previous years, or because the shrub is starved. Give it a good surface mulch of well rotted manure or compost, straightaway, and a dressing of bone-meal, hoof-and-horn or dried blood in the spring.

How to deal with the pruning of **forsythias** is often a problem. The commonest variety is *Forsythia intermedia* 'Spectabilis', a vigorous shrub that is frequently planted where there is insufficient space for it. If you prune at all severely, it will react by making a forest of thick, watery young shoots that will not flower. The best way with it is to cut out the oldest branches— those which tend to splay outwards—leaving the younger, more upright growths untouched and untipped. As these old branches should be thick with flower buds (if the bullfinches haven't already got at them), I like to bring them into the house at the turn of the year, for they respond admirably to gentle forcing.

F.i. 'Spectabilis' has sported to give the cultivar Lynwood, which I consider to be a distinct improvement. The petals have not the usual narrow, starved look, but are broad, flat and prosperous. Really, though, I much prefer *F. suspensa*, partly for its soft colouring, but also because the flowers are not borne in lumps, but scattering in pairs along its slender shoots. This and its even more flexible variety *F. s. sieboldii* are the best for training against walls, and they are quite at home on a north aspect. They can be pruned hard back after flowering without prejudice to the next year's performance. Where a bush of restricted growth is required, the newish Arnold Dwarf will serve, or else the early flowering, pale yellow *F. ovata,* which, again, has none of the brashness of Everyman's forsythia.

Lilacs do not need pruning every year. Indeed, many gardeners never prune theirs or, at best, just remove the dead flower trusses. Removing the dead heads is worth doing in certain cases for the looks of the shrub, especially in the case of Mme Lemoine, whose double white flowers change to a most unsightly brown without the old petals being shed. But dead-heading does not improve the next year's flowering, as has often been claimed. This is something I have tried out and am quite convinced of.

When you decide to prune a lilac it is for one of two reasons, or for both at once: either because the shrub has become cluttered with useless, twiggy wood or because it has got into the habit of flowering only every other year. It may not be necessary or advisable to prune oftener than one year in four, and the time to choose for this is in the winter prior to one of the lilac's 'on' years: immediately, that is, preceding a spring in which the shrub will be covered with blossom. You can soon establish whether or not it is coming up for an 'on' year by cutting in half a selection of terminal, resting buds. If they contain flower trusses, these will already be clearly identifiable as such—a cluster of tiny, pale green pimples. In their absence, the bud is a barren one, and will produce a leafy shoot, only. In an 'on' year, every strong shoot will be carrying flower buds. Every weak shoot will be barren and all such shoots should be removed completely. If they're not strong enough to flower in an 'on' year they never will be. Their removal will open up the centre of the bush, freeing it from a clutter of useless twiggery, admitting light and encouraging the production of strong young shoots from this central area.

Biennial bearing (the cycle of flowering only every second year) requires special pruning tactics. At every branch's extremities you will find a number of strong, flowering shoots. One-third of these should be shortened back (selecting the most vigorous in each case) to a pair of leaf buds. This will entail removing the tip bud or pair of buds and, very often, the pair behind these also. The third pair back is almost certain to be leafy, and you want to encourage this to make strong leafy shoots on which to flower in the following 'off' year. The two-thirds of flower buds that you leave unpruned will provide ample blossom for the current season. I can vouch that this system works.

A word about the frame of mind in which you should approach your pruning tasks. Each tree or bush is a problem. If it has been left unpruned for several years, it is a knotty problem. You look at it and think 'where on earth do I start?'. You look at one particular branch, and think 'I wonder if that should come out or not? It looks rather weak but then there are others even weaker and if I take everything out that's as weak as this one, will there be any bush left?'.

Now the answer in such cases is never to collide with your problem head-on. If you find it hard to make a decision on a particular cut, turn aside for the time being and tackle the obvious cases. 'That branch must certainly come out' you tell yourself, or 'you must certainly come out', if you prefer to address the bush itself. By the time you have made a whole series of indisputable cuts it will suddenly become clear to you what the answer should be to your original problem.

I also strongly recommend discussing each problem out loud with yourself or with the patient (let's call it, rather than victim). Don't be put off by silly people telling you that talking to yourself is the first sign of madness. Pruning calls for concentration and if you talk over the intricacies of the task, it will pass off all the more smoothly.

Pruning to Meet the Case

The subject of pruning is certainly not simple. To an extent, you can boil it down into basic principles and methods, pigeon-holing your shrubs accordingly. But then you may want different results from the same species, in which case you will have to give it differing treatments. For instance, you may want your deutzia to take up as much space as possible. Space may be the overriding consideration. In that case, it will be best not to prune it at all. It will accumulate masses of weak and dead wood; its young shoots will not be very strong individually, nor the flowers very large, but the shrub will build up a considerable bulk and it will flower well enough.

You may want your butterfly bushes, *Buddleia davidii*, to flower in late June and early July, rather than in late July and early August, when you are on holiday, perhaps, or when the main season of the border in which these bushes are situated is past. In their case and, of course, in that of roses also, early flowering will be induced by no pruning. There will be other effects, such as small flowers or flower trusses, but perhaps season of flowering will be of greatest importance.

Supposing you wanted your buddleias to flower in September, though, and thus blend with a foreground of Michaelmas daisies. Somehow you must give their growth a severe check, in order to delay their flowering, and this will be done by pruning all their shoots hard back after they have already started growing strongly, in spring. This will be some time in May.

The largest blooms are often induced by the hardest pruning. Growers of exhibition roses have long known this one. They prune their bushes extra-hard, so that their energy is concentrated into a few extra-strong shoots, and these, in turn, are disbudded (which is a form of pruning) so that size is further concentrated into the few remaining flower buds. The price that has to be paid for this result is a weakening of the shrub's general vigour and health. Its life will not be a long one.

The most striking foliage effects are likewise achieved by hard pruning. *Ailanthus altissima* (*glandulosa*), the **Tree of Heaven,** is one of the most soot-tolerant of deciduous trees and hence a familiar component of the London scene. Its pinnate leaves are rather like an ash's, but longer and with more divisions. If you prune a young and vigorous plant to the ground each winter and then allow only one of its young shoots to develop in the following growing season, each leaf will be much enlarged and up to 4 ft. long, which may achieve for you just that touch of the tropical and bizarre after which you were striving. The same treatment works with *Paulownia tomentosa*, this having a hairy, heart-shaped leaf up to 3 ft. across.

Hard pruning or pollarding also makes a tree or shrub go on growing right through the summer, instead of just in spring. It is forced to work overtime in an attempt to make good the loss of leaf and branch that your pruning brought about. Here again you may be cashing in on the situation. The young leaf is frequently more attractive than the mature. Thus, in the purple **Norway maple,** *Acer platanoides* 'Schwedleri', the young leaf is a reddish-purple that looks particularly fetching when seen with back-lighting from the sun. At maturity it changes to dark green. But by hard pruning, you get a succession of young leaves being put forth right up to the end of August. It is interesting to note that, in his handbook on trees and shrubs, Mr. Hillier advocates a hard pruning every other autumn—not every autumn as one might expect, regular prescriptions being easier to make and to follow than the extra taxing of one's intelligence and memory imposed by the occasional. The reason behind this one is doubtless, again, the weakening effect of hard pruning if regularly applied.

I have found an advantage in pruning my **sweet briar,** *Rosa eglanteria*, fairly rigorously each winter instead of allowing it to grow into a natural, unpruned specimen. Its stewed-apple scent wafts strongest from the young foliage, and a stiff pruning ensures that young leaves will continue to be produced right into autumn. True I sacrifice most of its flowers and hips, but these are no great loss.

With a shrub like the **American elder** *Sambucus canadensis maxima*, the creamy flower heads borne on the current season's young shoots will be up to 18 in. across, following a hard pruning, but there are drawbacks to this method, even when applied to the right shrubs. In a windy situation (and there are plenty such in these windy islands) the very soft young shoots that result from hard pruning can easily get torn right off. And the leaves themselves, if they have a large surface area like the paulownia's, can get sadly battered.

The official advice on keeping the **Spanish broom,** *Spartium junceum*, in order is to cut it all over in spring, shortening the previous year's shoots to within an inch of the base. This means that it will not start flowering, on the soft young growth, until late July, instead of in mid- or late June, as would an unpruned specimen. Probably the delay won't matter to you. What may matter, however, to anyone gardening on a heavy clay soil like mine, or in the humid climate of the west, is the botrytis moulds that attack the lush young shoots on hard pruned specimens. They go for the flowers first and then work back into the soft green shoots, quite ruining the shrub's performance. In these circumstances, you should not prune at all. The shrub will become large and unwieldy and will need efficient staking, unless you prefer to let it lie on its side from an early age. Well, there is a certain fitness in a group of unpruned spartiums, neat though they may not be. And, when the situation gets out of hand, they are easily and quickly replaced by youngsters.

Pruning, then, is as full of traps as of rewards. It is better to do none than the wrong kind. The principles and theories behind pruning are fascinating, to my mind, but many gardeners, especially the women, will turn on your theorist snappishly with a 'don't tell me why; tell me how'. The best books will tell you how, tree by tree and shrub by shrub, as they occur alphabetically in the text. However, some of the finer points of differing treatments that can be applied to the same species can only be learned from accumulated experience, from a study of the theory of the subject and, most important of all, by using your loaf.

Cutting Back: a plea for freedom

There is a psychological distinction between cutting back and pruning. Pruning is supposed to be for the welfare of the tree or shrub; cutting back is for the satisfaction of the cutter. Some gardeners have a cutting back mentality: my father had it. No sooner did a shrub appear to be looking really comfortable and prosperous than he would declare that it was too large for its position or, if it were a tree, dangerous; or detrimental to his precious yew hedges or something else that entailed its butchery or removal. My mother and I were forced into the position of preservers; we had to gang up against him. It is always as well, in a garden, not to have too many interested parties, otherwise there are endless disputes and frictions. One can feel surprisingly embittered at an act of vandalism on a cherished plant by another member of the family. If the deed was a hired assassin's, it's not so bad. But one cannot easily give the sack to one's own parent, child, husband or wife.

Many shrubs will only look their best if allowed to grow naturally: *Cytisus battandieri,* for instance. This broom, with its silky, silver-green foliage and candles (or night-lights, rather, for they are short and stubby) of fruit-scented yellow flowers, is often planted against a wall, where, indeed, it does look well. But in no time it will have overtopped the average wall and its breast wood will reach forward 10 ft. or so. That looks marvellous if it can be allowed, but it very seldom can, the planter never having envisaged the prodigious vigour of his protégé. He has to hack back, and things are never quite the same again. All the shoots and flowers thereafter are concentrated above the wall. This shrub is usually most satisfactory as a free-standing specimen.

The **evergreen ceanothus,** on the other hand, can seldom be trusted to survive and flourish except against a wall. They, too, are tremendous growers, putting on 3 or 4 ft. in a season, when young. I am sometimes asked by gardeners who have planted a specimen only within the past year: 'What am I to do about it?' They are longing to start cutting the wretched thing back, whereas all it needs, at this stage, is to have its branches pulled in and tied to the wall, in various directions. Those that are low down and pointing straight forward should be left until after they have flowered in spring. Then they can be cut back. Any branch removed from a ceanothus in autumn means several thousand fewer blossoms next spring. If, in its maturity, you must take a firm line, to keep it close against its wall, you can even take shears to it, immediately after flowering, without serious loss of blossom in the following year, but it should never be cut in autumn and it should never be cut beyond the base of the growth it made in the previous season, for it is reluctant to 'break' from old wood, and you may easily find yourself staring at a lot of dead stubs, where your cuts were too severe.

If evergreen ceanothus will flower reasonably well after an annual early-summer cut, **pyracanthas** will not. Hence *Pyracantha coccinea* trained to a wall is magnificent in youth but practically barren once the cutting back process has started in earnest. I admired a magnificent specimen recently on a house on Kingston Hill. It was a mature tree, brimming over with clusters of orange berries, but it had a sensible (or lazy) owner who did not prune it but had allowed it first to bulge over the porch and then to billow freely up to the first floor. The timid gardener's 'mind-forg'd manacles' could never endure any such demonstration of ebullience. Returning, for a moment, to the ceanothus: a type like Cascade or Edinensis never looks so well as when it can be allowed a free treatment similar to the Kingston pyracantha's.

Many **conifers** resent being cut back into old wood. The most notorious example is *Cupressus macrocarpa*. This was planted in particularly large quantities in the twenties and thirties, to form hedges and windbreaks, but invariably outgrew its position. Desperate reducing measures caused (even more than the hard winters of the early war years) wholesale losses. Nowadays, Leyland's cypress *Cupressocyparis leylandii,* which is hardy and even faster growing than *C. macrocarpa,* is used to perform the latter's office. Evidence of its behaviour when severely cut has not yet reached me, but a specimen in the National Pinetum at Bedgebury, Kent, that had its top knocked out by a falling tree in 1943, has recovered so well that one would not now suspect an accident had ever occurred, and this does suggest that we may here have a tree that responds kindly to butchery.

It is far more satisfactory, however, to anticipate and forestall trouble. The cypresses and junipers can be kept compact and within reasonable limits if they are given an annual shave which, as in the case of the evergreen ceanothus, can go back to near the base of its young growth, but no farther.

The Pruning of Clematis

The majority of **clematis** are pruned between mid-February and late March, according to whether spring has come early or late. The prospect of the task fills many gardeners with such dismay that they prefer to think about something else until it is too late for this year anyhow. There are two good reasons for their apprehensiveness: the pruning of clematis conforms not to one set of rules but to three, and the actual operation can be lengthy, in some cases, if perfectly performed.

The first point to be clear about is the three basic types of pruning treatment, and to which clematis they apply. The early-spring-flowering clematis—that is, *Clematis armandii* and all the relatives of *C. macropetala*, *C. alpina* and *C. montana* (including *C. chrysocoma*, *C. spooneri* and *C. vedrariensis*)—need no regular pruning; and such pruning as they do need, if they get too large and tangled, consists of removing their old flowering wood and all the dead accumulations (including birds' nests) of years, immediately after flowering.

That will be about the end of May. They then have the whole growing season ahead of them in which to make new shoots. And they will flower along these shoots in the following spring. If, as so often happens, it isn't till the autumn tidying-up season comes along that you decide that 'that Montana really is beyond everything', and you give it an old-fashioned army haircut forthwith, you may be right in doing the job at the wrong time as an alternative to not doing it at all but it is well to realise that every strand you cut off in autumn and winter represents perhaps 50 or 100 potential blooms that won't be carried in the following spring. Here's a case where it does pay to act at the right time.

The SECOND group comprises all those clematis that flower at the extremities of the young shoots that they have made in the current season (young growth that may be anything from 3 to 12 ft. long). They are easily identified, without putting names to or in the other ways categorising them, by the fact that none gets into its flowering stride until after the middle of June. Examples would be Jackmanii, Victoria, Perle d'Azur, Comtesse de

Bouchaud, Star of India, Lady Betty Balfour, Mme Baron-Veillard, Gravetye Beauty and Etoile Violette, among the hybrids; *C. flammula, C. viticella, C. campaniflora, C. tangutica* and *C. orientalis* among the species. Their pruning is simple and brief, and resembles that of all deciduous late-summer-flowering shrubs, such as the common buddleia. You reduce all the previous season's shoots to within a pair of buds of the base. This leaves a stump of increasingly thick, old wood, perhaps no more than a foot high. On a well established plant it is quite safe to perform the task, and get all that unsightly top-hamper out of the way, in November. But the safe, official pruning season is late winter.

If a clematis of this type is required to cover a large area or to climb 20 ft. up a building or tree, it need not be pruned so severely.

Now we come to the THIRD, the only difficult, group: clematis (they are all hybrids) that flower on short young laterals made from the previous season's wood. They all start flowering in late spring or early summer, between mid May and mid June. They comprise the very largest flowered clematis, like Lasurstern, Lady Northcliffe, Marie Boisselot, Mrs. Cholmondeley, President, Nelly Moser, Lord Nevill, William Kennett and Beauty of Richmond; and also those with double flowers, such as Beauty of Worcester, Vyvyan Pennell, Belle of Woking, Proteus, Daniel Deronda, Duchess of Edinburgh and Countess of Lovelace.

If we gave these no pruning, as some leading nurserymen advocate, we should save ourselves a lot of trouble and worry, it is true, and we should continue to get blooms from them. But the blooms are not then well displayed; they are carried in a congested lump, wherein many individuals are crushed and concealed. Pruning aims at sorting out this tangle so that the shoots are spread over the maximum possible area.

When you come to examine one of these clematis hybrids with a view to pruning it, you will find that at least half the tangle confronting you is dead wood. This will be the case even if you regularly and conscientiously removed all its dead shoots in the previous year. It does not mean that the plant is unhealthy. A clematis that is vigorous and in good health always makes far more shoots in one season than it can carry forward to the next. Your main task now is to cut out all that is dead, for a start. Trace each shoot back to a pair of strong, juicy-looking buds and make your cut just above them. We prune in late winter rather than earlier or later, because these buds are large enough to be seen and identified, yet not so forward that they may be damaged in the course of pruning. You will trace many shoots back right to the base without coming upon any live buds. This is just some of the superabundance of growth that the clematis has made and is now casting off, and it should be removed completely.

When all the dead stuff has been eliminated, your quickest course is to plaster the living framework that remains against its support as best you can. But if perfection is your aim, you will snip between each strand so that the tendrils linking them are severed, and then train them to their supports in an orderly fashion. A clematis of the type I have been describing, whose pruning has been neglected in past seasons, calls for drastic treatment. Cut all the tangle away, live and dead together, leaving only as many stems near the base, as you can easily sort out and pin into position. It won't flower for you at the normal time, in early summer, but it may flower quite well at the tips of its young shoots in late summer and autumn, and it will certainly make a splendid show in May and June the following year.

In The Mood

As I go about my tasks in the garden, it often strikes me that I am doing this and that at quite the 'wrong' season. I will give a buddleia a hard pruning in the autumn, for instance, or split up and replant a group of irises in November—at quite the worst time to be tampering with them. But so often it's a question of now or never. If you postpone a job until the ideal moment from a plant's viewpoint, the chances are you will miss doing it when that moment arrives, for reasons of forgetfulness and preoccupation with other matters. And so, to the amateur gardener's eternally repeated question 'when should I?' and 'what's the best time to?' I've concluded that nine times out of ten the answer is 'when you're thinking about it; when you're in the mood.'

This, I realise, is the last thing he wants to be told, because it is an adult answer and the amateur, in whatever the subject, will long remain a child, seeking advice and guide-lines in the form of clear-cut, black-or-white answers to his manifold doubts. To be told that it doesn't matter is unsettling. The kind answer to 'when should I?' is 'do it on 31st March.' No shilly-shallying there.

The best policy for anyone new to gardening is to do his jobs by the calendar until he has built up sufficient confidence, experience and general understanding, to be able to break the rules cheerfully when it seems sensible and necessary to do so.

One could trace the steps in his education by his answer to questions on the much disputed subject of rose pruning. 'When do you prune your roses?' 'In the first week of April,' the novice will answer. 'Why then?' 'Because it says so in my book.' Ask him why he doesn't prune them at mid-winter and he will just look blank. But put him this same question a little later in his education and he will wax indignant: 'Prune them at mid-winter? Do you think I want to kill my bushes? have them lured into fresh growth in the first mild spell only to be hit by frost immediately afterwards?' He has been reading the correspondence in a gardening journal and feels the ground is safe.

Many gardeners stick at this point for the rest of their lives, reading the opinions that back their own practices and ignoring or resenting the rest. Others, of a more supple and inquiring turn of mind, go on from here. 'When do you prune your roses?' 'In December or January, usually.' 'Why then?' 'Because I can do the job then when there's not much else on and I don't feel tempted to skimp or rush it like I used to in spring.' 'Aren't you afraid of damage by frost after you've winter-pruned?' 'No, I haven't suffered that way.'

However, along comes a winter like 1962–63 and the answer to the last question has to be modified to 'Yes; if the weather after mid-winter pruning is really foul I may have to go over my bushes again in spring to cut out wood that's been killed back subsequently. But this is still worth my while because it doesn't take long and the largest task has been completed in the slack season.'

This sort of progress story will obviously be modified by climatic considerations and other special factors, but my point is that experience enables you to take a less rigid and bookish approach to your gardening.

When you do your pruning, planting or transplanting matters not nearly so much as *how* you do it. The majority of gardeners faced with the task of moving a well established shrub or herbaceous plant, set about it in the wrong mood. No sooner do they feel tenacious roots resisting the leverage of a spade or fork, than their eyes become bloodshot, their breathing stertorous. 'You would, would you?' is implied, if not actually uttered.

The victim is seized by its top as though a club were about to be wielded, there is a dreadful noise of tearing roots, and if the plant doesn't actually finish as two separate halves, at least the end product is a sorry mess, and all for what? Just for lack of a little patience and phlegm.

If your host kindly offers you a plant from his garden, accept for then and not for 'the right time.' Don't watch him lifting it, as your gaze will only aggravate his self-consciousness and inflame his impatience. If you possibly can, get him to let you lift the plant yourself. When he comments: 'That looks a good piece,' afterwards, don't be cowed into saying 'Yes, I'm afraid I have taken rather a lot.' A bland smile and 'Yes, isn't it?' will better suit the occasion.

Weeding

The Pleasures of Hand-Weeding

Many gardeners will agree that hand-weeding is not the terrible drudgery that it is often made out to be. Some people find in it a kind of soothing monotony. It leaves their minds free to develop the plot for their next novel or to perfect the brilliant repartee with which they should have countered a relative's latest example of unreasonableness.

Efficient hand-weeding requires that you should get down to the task on your knees: as comfortably as possible, with a soft rubber mat and a good sharp-pointed, sharp-edged, stainless steel trowel.

You will observe that professional gardeners do all hand-weeding from a standing stooping position. They pull the weeds out (or break them off) by the hair and do not use a trowel. Their standards of weeding are mediocre, but they remain men, standing proudly, if not erect, at least on their two feet, whereas you and I become animals, even reptiles. The one advantage that I must give the standing posture (having no inhibitions about crawling on all fours) is that it occupies the least lateral space and is hence less damaging, in close country.

If you are working from a path, there are no problems: but if you are burrowing into and among plants in a border, you should do as much as you can from one position, because the more often you move, the more havoc is your frame likely to wreak. So you should be sufficiently ambidextrous to be able to wield the trowel with either hand, collecting up the weeds with the other. Some weeds are notoriously wet, even in dry weather—opium poppies and chickweed in particular—so that the collecting hand gets clogged with slime and mud. Given a change of job, as trowel manipulator, it will soon dry out.

Of recent years I have had to take to gardening in gloves because of skin allergies. I never thought I could weed with gloves on. 'I must be able to feel them (the weeds) between my fingers', I used to say, and my non-glove-wearing friends still do say. A kind of mystical religious fervour enters the voice as the words are uttered. Well, I can tell you all, now, that that's just my eye. It's easy to weed in gloves and it's no less efficient. And it's marvellous, incidentally, how clean your hands keep. The one disadvantage is that the handles of whatever tools you're using do tend to get plastered with mud and that this isn't automatically rubbed off.

Weeding on your hands and knees means that your eyes are close to the ground—the scene of operations. They should always travel just ahead of the trowel point so that the unusual can be observed before it is destroyed. I never like to weed out anything that I can't identify. Not all seedlings are weeds. You may feel that life is too short to leave a seedling in till it's large enough to identify. My own feeling is that life's too interesting not to leave it there until you can identify it. Taking this view, you will very soon learn to recognise weed seedlings when they are no larger than a pair of seed leaves. The not so easily identified ones will then most probably turn out to be the progeny of some of your border plants or shrubs, and it may suit you to save and grow them on.

For instance, the elegant and feathery mauve *Thalictrum dipterocarpum*, revelling in a nice wet soil like ours, is a herbaceous plant that never needs disturbing and does not readily lend itself to division anyway. But in early summer you will nearly always find its seedlings in the neighbourhood of old plants. They can be pricked out into a seed box and, later on, lined out, and they may even, given individual treatment, carry a few blooms in their first autumn. *Mertensia virginica* is another plant with the welcome habit of self-sowing. The seed leaves are shaped like Spades in playing-cards, and are glaucous. Here again, if the seedlings are pricked out, they will develop very quickly and continue to grow long after the parent plants have died off for the season. Next spring they will be full of flowers themselves. *Dicentra spectabilis,* the Bleeding Heart, is none too easy a plant to multiply by vegetative methods, but it usually sets seeds and in some years the babies come up quite thickly around their parents. They look rather like fumitory seedlings, to which they are closely related.

Seedlings can be very deceptive. None more so than the various brands of what I loosely term the lesser willowherbs. They are the small-flowered, tall-growing species and natural hybrids of *Epilobium*: a thoroughly promiscuous crowd, and insidious, too. They have often managed to flower and seed before you have become aware of their presence, and they are abominably prolific. In winter, they make a dense basal rosette and you may be almost certain that any gardener you employ will fail to weed them, or any other rosette forming plant, out. They look precious. Quite often, they look remarkably like small sweet william plants.

When weeds are growing fast and healthily, they are always easier to extract than on a piece of ground where they have been allowed to form a dense mat and are in a half starved condition. So, generous feeding of the garden is a good plan, even if it does benefit weed growth. When visitors exclaim 'what a year it is for weeds!', (which they do, every year), I'm apt to point out that if the weeds won't grow, nothing else will. Weeds that are growing healthily will not run to seed nearly as quickly as those that are starved and this gives you more breathing space in which to get around to coping with them.

Staking

The modern no-trouble gardener, who would really much rather

take his recreation with the family in a motor car than in gardening at home, has no time for staking. He resents it as 'one more
thing'. And, of course, he's right. It is one more thing, but that's
not necessarily to say that it's not worth doing. It all depends on
what plants and gardening mean to you. If you love a plant, and
it is good in other ways, you will not grudge its staking requirements.

Plant breeders and nurserymen are well aware that the no-
trouble gardener is in the ascendancy, that he is still prepared to
spend money on plants but that they must not need supporting.
And so we now have a wide range of material within all the
popular plant categories that can accurately be described as dwarf,
bushy and compact. Picking on the first catalogue that comes to
my hand, *Antirrhinum* 'Floral Carpet' is described as producing
'very dwarf, bushy plants, uniform in habit.' That's all very fine
if carpet bedding is what you're after, but dwarfness and uniformity can become deadly. A plant's natural grace and dignity, its
architectural qualities are sacrificed. For these we must (and,
fortunately, we still can) turn to *Antirrhinum* 'Rocket Hybrids', for
instance. Instead of two flowers to a stem, as has Floral Carpet,
these will carry upwards of 40 on a 4 ft. spire (perhaps more; I'm
writing, as gardeners have to, in the winter, and haven't a spike
to check up on). But they will need staking.

The number of worth-while plants that make this demand on
our time is not, after all, very great. It annoyed me, visiting the
RHS gardens at Wisley one April, to see that *all* the plants in their
double herbaceous borders were being barricaded with brushwood. This 'to be on the safe side' attitude struck me as wasteful,
unintelligent and uninstructive. (That was some years ago, and
the criticism may no longer be valid.) If you approach the subject
intelligently and treat it as an art, rather than as a chore, all the
sting will go out of it.

The two essentials in staking are that it should be both efficient
and unobtrusive. Most galvanised wire supports, though capable
of doing duty for many years, are not unobtrusive. A popular
pattern consists of a ring with one or two supporting legs. It
always shows and it looks beastly.

For plants of an intricately branching habit like *Aster acris,
Salvia superba* or monardas, **peasticks** are ideal. Plants and twigs

interlock and form a rock-steady unit. Peasticks are also excellent with many-stemmed plants like alstroemerias. However, they last for only one season and are often not easily procured. Canes and soft string, called fillis, will do. Make sure that the fillis is man enough for its role: 5-ply will last the season in most cases. A really heavy plant like the cardoon, *Cynara cardunculus,* needs heavy stakes and insulated telephone wire, or something of comparable strength.

Bamboo canes are obtainable in a range of lengths and different stoutnesses. It is a good thing to have them in variety. Nothing looks worse than canes, new and yellow, sticking up a foot above the plants they're supporting—and crookedly at that, likely as not. On top of which, gardeners surprisingly often stick them in upside down, with the thicker end (one end always is thicker than the other) uppermost. Test your old canes that have been used in one or more previous years, before trusting them again. Try breaking them across your knee. It's far better they should break then, than later, when in use. It's the bottom of a cane that rots. Cut off this bottom bit (if you cut with secateurs at a joint in the bamboo, it won't split) and the shortened cane will be just as useful on a lower job. Don't buy British-grown canes; they're not nearly as well ripened and durable as the imported article.

At the end of the season, pull the canes out and store them, but store them clean and ready for the next season, not with lumps of mud sticking to them, and wisps of old string. All this must sound pedagogic and I can't deny that it is. But if you're tidy in this sort of way you're much more likely to be critical of the actual job you're doing with the canes in the border. However, I admit that if you're not naturally tidy, no amount of nagging will make you so.

Some people like to get all their stakes in position as early as possible, but they aren't pretty and I prefer the opposite way. In the case of delphiniums, for instance, the shape and pale green colouring of the young foliage make a handsome feature from which a forest of canes can only detract. And then, again, foot-prints on the border are an unlovely sight, so that if your staking can be combined with a first tying at a useful height, a whole set of plod marks can be eliminated. I leave the staking of my delphiniums until they are 3 ft. tall, on average. This may sound dangerous, but they put up with a surprising amount of wind buffeting at this stage, and if the position is so exposed that they get blown over when only 3 ft. high, it is unsuitable for most delphiniums anyway.

Five-foot stakes or canes are long enough even for the tallest varieties: the supports should never reach higher than the foliage. To be worth its place, the flower spike itself must be sufficiently wiry to stand a reasonable amount of wind without snapping. Delphiniums with bloated, puffy stems are useless and should be thrown out, whatever the quality of their blooms. It is quite unnecessary to devote one stake to each stem. On a moderate-sized plant I allow two stout canes and make one circuit of soft string, taking in each stem in a resilient structure that will yield before the wind. Rigid ties invite trouble: they cause a rapid vibration that is more dangerous than no support at all.

One cane to each plant is usually enough for anchusas. Staking and tying is done in one operation at the moment when the first blooms are opening at the end of May.

With many-stemmed plants like *Achillea filipendulina*, the best procedure is to knock in a number of canes round the group and one or two in the middle; then secure your string with a clove hitch round the first cane and take the free end from cane to cane, hitching as you go, until you have a cat's cradle of string that will hold the plant up without actually binding its stems individually.

With *Lychnis chalcedonica* and also *Thalictrum dipterocarpum,* the stems themselves are strong enough but they are liable to sway over from the base. Quite short pieces of cane are long enough for them, with string doing its job at the one-foot level. You soon get to know your individual plants' foibles and requirements, and where the draughty spots in your garden are.

When you're staking a newly planted tree, knock the stake in on the prevailing-windward side and make your tie for a standard or half-standard tree, just below the point where the lowest branches arise; not half-way down the trunk, because your stakes aren't long enough.

Dead-Heading

The Art of Dead-Heading

The culling of dead heads is a ploy that figures persistently in the garden in summer. We are inclined to regard it as a chore, but there is a world of difference between doing this job well and doing it badly. The first principle in dead-heading is always to cut back to something definite, whether it be to a leaf, or to the point at which another stem branches off, or to ground level. Simply to remove the dead heads is not good enough; behind them you will be leaving a forest of ugly and meaningless stalk ends. Bedding dahlias provide the most striking monitory example. It is fatally easy to whisk through them just tweaking off the heads, but the plants will soon become an eyesore if so treated, because there is about six inches of naked stem behind each dahlia. Nothing will do but its complete removal.

With many plants it is a question of experience to know how much of the plant to cut away in order to obtain the best results, and it is difficult to lay down rules. One can distinguish broadly between those plants that are dead-headed with no further object than to tidy them up and those from which we are hoping to encourage another flowering. Dahlias obviously belong to the latter category, and so do the bedding penstemons, whose branching spikes flower over a considerable period. Each of them should, when the last funnels have dropped, be snapped off as one large unit. As soon as this has been done, the plant will start making side-shoots, and will flower again on these, presently.

Salvia superba can always be depended on for a second crop, given the encouragement of removing its first spikes. Its dwarf, 2 ft.-tall cultivar East Friesland is not nearly so reliable in this respect, however. Heleniums that start to flower in July can often be induced to make a further effort. The central cluster of daisies is cut right out, while the outer daisies, which are carried on the longest stalks of the whole branching truss, are carefully shortened

Plate 1. *Above*, the pale yellow, low-growing broom, *Cytisus kwensis*.
Below, *Anthemis cupaniana*, with white flowers and grey leaves, enjoys hot, dry places.

back to vestigial flower buds, which you can clearly see when you look for them but could otherwise easily be missed. The same treatment goes for *Anthemis tinctoria* in its popular selections, such as Grallagh Gold and Wargrave Variety. This is one of the most tedious plants to operate on, as every knob-like dead head gets caught up among its neighbours, but the results justify the tedium.

A thriving and productive colony of herbaceous phloxes will often flower again from small side-shoots when you remove the central panicle, but if the clump is crowded and overdue for splitting and replanting, it will make no second effort. With Canterbury bells the correct treatment is, for once, simply to pull off the dead flowers as they shrivel. Always wear gloves for this job, or your hands will get full of tiny colourless prickles. New buds will develop immediately behind the old flowers. The same practice is equally successful with the perennial border campanulas: cultivars of *Campanula persicifolia*. *Spiraea japonica* 'Anthony Waterer' goes brown on fading; an immediate beheading will coax a welcome flush of blossom in October.

Neatness only, without ambition for further rewards, will be our aim when removing the dead heads from plants such as delphiniums, bergamots, *Lychnis* species, *Campanula lactiflora*, candelabra primulas (whose self-sown seedlings can otherwise grow too much like weeds) and *Cephalaria tatarica*, the tree scabious.

With certain lax-growing shrubs, the objective of neatness results in a combined pruning and dead-heading. The santolina tribe, *Senecio laxifolius*, *Phlomis fruticosa* (Jerusalem sage) and the holly-leaved daisy bush, *Olearia macrodonta*, all have the same manner of carrying an abundance of flower trusses in a ring surrounding a central leafy shoot. The simplest and best treatment here is to lop off each complete aggregate of flowers and central shoot, making your cut just below that point on the branch where the lowest truss of flowers arises. Your shrubs may

Plate 2. Above, the evergreen, spring-flowering *Clematis armandii* likes a warm, sheltered position.

Below, double yellow gorse will grow on the poorest soils and is twice as showy as the wild single.

look a trifle naked for a few weeks afterwards, but will soon be clothed in new young shoots and will be kept compact instead of being allowed to straggle.

It is pleasant to discover that some of the most vigorous herbaceous plants respond happily to being cut right down to the ground as soon as they have flowered. Nothing could be simpler. Such are giant chives, *Viola cornuta* and the perennial cornflower, *Centaurea montana*. These will flower again on their secondary growth. *Tellima grandiflora, Geranium grandiflorum* and *G. ibericum* will reclothe themselves in decorative young foliage within a week, but cannot flower a second time. The best treatment for alstroemerias is to yank out each stem with a sharp jerk. It will break cleanly away from the roots at about 6 in. below the soil surface, and you can then plant something temporary in the gap.

Finally, it is worth observing that there are some plants whose dead heads it is unnecessary to remove because they are a decoration in themselves. It is quite a wrench to cut down the sedums, even when we are doing the borders in late autumn. The winged pods of dictamnus are always fascinating. Sea lavenders retain a soft grey cloud till blown away by autumn gales, while cardoon and acanthus remain gauntly statuesque to the last.

2. To make more and Still More

Plant propagation can be absurdly simple at times; even accidental, as when you put a bunch of flowering currant in a vase and find when preparing to throw it away, that the branches have made roots in the water. Of all the fascinating sides there are to gardening, the making more of plants is what has given me the greatest pleasure and interest. And with the diminution in number of professional gardeners, so an ever-increasing number of amateurs have learned to 'do it themselves' and have derived an enormous thrill from the surprising and gratifying results of their efforts. After all, it is rather exciting, when you've pushed a dead looking stick into the ground, to find, a few months later, that it is making leaves and shoots. It's hard to resist the temptation to pull it out of the ground every few days to find out if any roots are forming. This wouldn't be necessary if only our eyes 'was a pair o' patent double million magnifyin' gas microscopes of hextra power' as Sam Weller put it, but being only eyes our vision's limited.

Cuttings

Summer Cuttings: Details of Procedure

There is no season when cuttings of some sort may not be made, but the busiest season is in the warm half of the year, when plants are cheerful and active and in a co-operative mood. Let us consider how to set about it, taking the bare essentials first and filling in details afterwards.

First, then, the question of choosing your material. Whenever possible, take it from a young or, at any rate, a vigorously growing bush. Cuttings from an old bush that is making little growth do not root nearly so readily. When you are actually examining the shrub to decide which bits to take, avoid anything that is too soft, lush and sappy: escallonias and forsythias, for instance, often carry a number of exceedingly watery young shoots. Conversely, avoid those parts of the shrub where growth is at a standstill and the young shoots are stunted. Something in between will be ideal, and the shoots will still be making some extension growth at their tips, in most cases. Never take flowering shoots if you can help it.

Next comes the business of removing the cutting material. Many shrubs branch near their extremities into anything from two to seven ramifications. You simply lop each branch off below the lowest of these side-shoots and go away to a comfortable place to deal with them in detail. Examples are *Daphne odora, D. tangutica, D.* 'Somerset', garrya, pittosporum, skimmia, Kurume azaleas and other small-leaved rhododendrons. Other shrubs have a more obviously leading shoot, followed up by a number of lateral shoots, all of the current year's growing. The evergreen ceanothus are typical here. Again, the whole branch can be carried away, and all but the shortest and most immature of the side shoots used for cuttings. However, if you want to detach individual shoots for cuttings from a branch (without severing the entire branch from the shrub) and are going to take them with a heel of older wood, get your thumb down into the angle made by shoot and branch, with your middle finger outside and just below the angle, and then lever gently but firmly outwards. In the case of ericas, you can just pull off the young shoots, 2–3 in. long, and they will automatically come with the required heel. The winter-flowering *Erica carnea* group are especially easy to root. They will already be clothed with flower buds, but there is no need to worry about these.

All these cuttings so far described will be taken with a heel, but there are a whole lot more, of the soft type, where you use the tip of a shoot and simply trim below a node (joint). You can pick these tips off the bushes as though you were plucking tea shoots on a plantation. Here I am thinking of. hydrangeas, lavender, santolinas, hebes, fuchsias, rock phloxes, *Lithospermum* 'Heavenly Blue', aubrietas, *Anthemis cupaniana* and *A. tinctoria, Cheiranthus* 'Harpur Crewe' and *C.* 'Moonlight'.

Always try to allow as short an interval as possible to elapse between removing cuttings from a bush and preparing them; but, if there must be a time-lag, put them dry into a plastic bag and close it at the neck. They will keep even better than with their stems in water.

Now as to preparing the cuttings. Where you have a whole branch to deal with, on which there are a number of potential cuttings, you can usually sever them there and then at exactly the right point, with a razor blade. Make your cut so that, at the point of detachment, the cutting swells very slightly at its base, where it began to join on to the branch system. A heel is no more than this: it is not a great hammer-head of a thing. Where a cutting has been taken individually from a shrub, with a larger heel of old wood, it must again be trimmed at the base, so as to leave the same slight swelling. All the leaves are now removed from the bottom half of the cutting, cleanly and flush with the stem. If the cutting is too long, and it should seldom be longer than 6 in. in summer, considerably shorter in spring, cut out the tip, just above a node. All these cuts can be made with a razor blade, although a budding knife may be handier in some cases: e.g. where leaves to be removed lie close against a stem. As regards blades, I find a one-sided type, such as Ever-Ready produce, the most convenient.

At this stage, I always dip the bottom of the cutting into and out of a jar of water, so that it cannot dry out before I am ready to insert it. If you are using a hormone powder, dip it into this now, while the base of the cutting is damp, and tap off excess powder on the edge of the carton. Most cuttings root perfectly well without, but I use it on a difficult type like *Osmanthus delavayi*. If you are interrupted at any point, put the cuttings back into the plastic bag, to keep them plump. Never let them wilt.

Fill a 3½-in. clay pot with damp cutting compost and compress rather firmly and evenly with the tips of the fingers, leaving no more than ¼-in. watering space between soil and pot rim. If you are using a plastic pot (which is just as good) then the compost will need little compressing.

Until the cuttings have made roots, the great idea is to give them as much light as possible but without ever allowing their foliage to scorch or to wilt. Individual pots can be enclosed in a plastic bag, secured with a rubber band. Or they can go into an unventilated cold frame, well shaded in the heat of the day. In a mist propagator, the brightest of light and ventilation can be admitted, since the cuttings are never in danger of drying out.

When they have rooted, they can be potted individually into John Innes No. 2 or an equivalent soil-less compost; returned to a close atmosphere but then gradually hardened off by the admission of more air.

So much for the bones of procedure. Now for the various 'matters arising'. For instance, a visitor told me that he had followed the instructions in my book *Clematis* for rooting cuttings of these shrubs, covering each potful with a plastic bag, secured, at its mouth, around the pot. He had had complete success with the easy species, such as *Clematis montana*; this was to be expected. But the large-flowered hybrids, while remaining plump and promising so long as the bag was in position, wilted as soon as it was removed. How was he to wean them and how was he to know when or whether they had rooted?

To take the second point first: nearly all cuttings, after insertion, retain a static kind of look for a greater or lesser period. They appear to be brooding, undecided as to whether they wish to live or not. They look fresh enough, sometimes even flower, but refuse to take a positive step forward. However, once they have come to a favourable conclusion, the fact becomes evident by them making new, fresh green growth. When this happens, you can be fairly sure that roots have been formed, and the process of hardening off can be begun. But the only way of making certain is to turn the pot upside-down, holding the fingers of your left hand over the soil surface but between the cuttings, not damaging them; to give the pot a gentle tap on its edge against something firm so as to dislodge the ball of soil which you can now balance on the fingers of your left hand while you remove the pot with your right. Take a look, replace the pot, reverse it, tap it gently on its bottom and you are back at the *status quo ante*. If the rooting medium is pure grit, this method won't work as the grit doesn't hold together.

The period of broodiness, in cuttings, varies enormously from plant to plant. A quick-rooting species such as *Anthemis cupaniana* will snap out of it in a matter of ten days or a fortnight. On the other hand, I find that the cuttings I take in summer of *Elaeagnus pungens* 'Maculata' are best left undisturbed until the next March, and potted off then. Some of them will, it is true, have rooted by October or November, but to disturb them then, at a time when they are in no mood to make new growth anyway, often proves fatal.

As regards hardening off, this must be gradual. The contrast between living with a plastic bag over your head and of its sudden complete removal, is too great. If you think the cuttings have rooted, make a gentle start towards their exposure to the outside world by cutting the corners of the bag and admitting just a little air. See how they take that, and if they remain turgid, gradually increase the ventilation by one means or another. When you turn the rooted cuttings out of their pot, and pot them off individually into a richer compost, the disturbance will once again call for a close atmosphere, with little or no ventilation, until they have got over this new shock.

Some plants are exceptional in resenting a close atmosphere, even when the cuttings have only just been taken. Such are those with woolly leaves—*Senecio cineraria*, for instance, and *Buddleia fallowiana* 'Alba'; also, glaucous-leaved subjects such as carnations and pinks, rue and *Euphorbia wulfenii*. A close atmosphere destroys the waxy coating to their leaves, so that they are liable to rot before they can root. However, they make up for this tiresome foible by being less liable to wilt than are most plants, and they can generally be rooted in a ventilated frame (or bag), provided there is no direct sunlight on them.

It is sometimes quite a fight to prevent certain cuttings from rotting, while they are being kept in a close, unventilated container. Clematis are a case in point, and we spray these with captan at weekly intervals, as a preventive from fungal infection. Another way in which fungi can gain entry is through the flowers that cuttings may carry, even though they have not yet rooted. If you see any flower buds at the time of making your cuttings, you remove them then. However, flowers may appear subsequently. This often happens with *Convolvulus mauritanicus, Osmanthus delavayi*, the above-mentioned elaeagnus, *Genista lydia* and eucry-phias. The flower fades and grey-mould spores pounce on this happy hunting-ground, working back from the faded bloom into the live tissue of the shoot itself. So these premature blooms must be pinched out betimes.

Camellias have a great way of flowering as cuttings, too, and in their case you should rub out the flower buds as soon as it becomes evident, from their plumpness, that they are not leaf buds. Otherwise the cutting will be putting its efforts into the wrong channel; that is, into flower formation instead of into root and shoot formation.

The foliage on some sorts of cuttings is too luxuriant and voluminous. It takes up too much room in the pot and flags too easily. Without some foliage, no soft or half-ripe cutting could root at all, but you need a balance between too little and too much. Thus, with hydrangeas and camellias it is normal to remove the distal half of each leaf, with a sharp knife or razor blade, when making the cutting. A large-leaved lilac like Fountain or Bellicent can be so treated, too. In the case of a clematis with large leaves, you can either remove the central of three leaflets or, if the leaves are undivided, cut half the leaf away. *Mahonia japonica* often has an enormous whorl of leaves on the terminal shoots that make such good cutting material. All these leaves can be reduced in length to the two or three pairs of proximal leaflets.

The striking of cuttings being, as I have suggested, a race between rooting and rotting, we, as referees, or guardians rather, have to try by every means available to prevent the onset of decay for long enough for the cutting to make a plant. The core of a young shoot is pithy and, generally speaking, this pith, if exposed at the cut surface, is particularly liable to rot. The older wood you expose when making a heel cutting is not pithy, and this will be the best sort of cutting to prepare from all those shrubs that have a pulpy core to their shoots: magnolias, brooms, elders and, in fact, most of those that make rather soft, lush young growth. Roses, too (on which see 'Growing Roses from Cuttings', page 253).

I have by me, when making cuttings, a razor blade and a sharp budding knife, so that I can turn freely from one to the other, according to which seems the more efficient for the two jobs in hand. These two jobs are the cross-cut that makes the base of the cutting and the removal of the leaves from the lower portion of the stem. This leaf removal needs to be done cleanly and neatly, so that you neither leave snags or leaf stalks sticking out, nor tear any rind off the stem of the cutting itself—conditions that are both of them conducive to rot setting in. If a leaf will pull cleanly off its stem, this is both quicker and more efficient than any sort of cut, so it is always worth testing your material to see whether it will respond to this easy treatment. Among plants that will respond to it are hydrangeas, hebes, fuchsias and euphorbias.

Euphorbias and a few other plants are apt to lose their life blood (so to speak), when wounded, by exuding the milky fluid called latex. Staunch the wounds as quickly as you can. When gathering the cuttings from the parent plant, take a little dry sand or any other fine, powdery but inert substance (peat dust will do), with you and dip the wounded surface into it. Similarly, on the cutting bench, sprinkle some dust over the bleeding leaf scars, after the leaves have been pulled off.

Half and half is approximately the right ratio of cleaned stem to leafy, for cuttings taken in summer. When you insert them, the bottom of the cutting must rest on the bottom of the hole made for it, and the lowest leaf must come just above the surface of the compost. It is worth emphasising that, if any part of the lowest leaf, or pair of leaves, is buried, you are again inviting trouble from rot. Leaves were never intended for burial.

Some very soft cutting material can get so floppy, however quick you are about whisking it from the plant to the potting bench, that it becomes awkward to handle. Just try inserting a potful of wilted *Convolvulus mauritanicus* cuttings in an orderly fashion. Here, the plastic bag should again be brought to the rescue. Pop your cuttings into it for an hour with a few drops of water, and they will emerge as plump as any partridge.

If the tip of a shrub cutting is too soft, and the material is slow to root anyway, you may get rotting from the tip backwards. *Genista lydia*, for instance, does not start making the year's new growth until after it has flowered, in June, and only in August or September is there firm enough young material on it, for propagation purposes. But the tips are still growing apace, especially in a wet season, and it is necessary to remove them at the time of making the cuttings, in order to avoid trouble later.

For general purposes, a cutting compost that consists of one part by bulk of soil to two of peat and three of horticultural grit, is excellent. The soil provides a little sustenance between the time of rooting and of potting-off into a stronger compost. The peat is moisture-retaining and the grit provides the obligatory free drainage. Some of the most rot-prone plants, however, need even freer drainage than this, while others, like camellias and eucryphias, are inclined to make a huge knob of callus, rather than roots, unless the rooting medium is exceptionally open-textured. For such as these, then, one uses grit alone, but must bear in mind that, while it is virtually impossible to overwater this substance, it very easily dries out; also it should be remembered that it has no feed value whatsoever, so that you must rescue your cuttings from starvation risks once they have rooted.

Summer Cuttings: Some Individual Cases

Taking summer as starting in May and continuing till September, I want now to consider more closely some of the foibles of individual plants or groups of plants, when they are being struck from cuttings. The idiosyncrasies of the individual often have a more general application.

One point to be alive to is that a number of shrubs propagate most easily when their shoots are still very young indeed: that is, in May. If you can get them rooted then, you will already have a substantial plant by the autumn. *Caryopteris* and *Perovskia,* for instance. Remove their young side shoots from the parent plant, with a heel, when only about 1½ in. long, in early May, and they will, if grown on without a check, make quite a display of blossom in August and September. In fact, I often use newly struck *Caryopteris clandonensis* as bedding plants for that season.

May, too, is a fine time for propagating hydrangeas from the young shoots culled off bushes in your garden. You can, again, use the entire shoot with a heel, at that early season, and probably won't even need to reduce the leaf area. By autumn the plants will be growing strongly in 5 in. pots and will each have about three well budded branches ready to flower in the following year. Don't plant them out till the next spring, though, as their growth won't be hard or tough enough to come through their first winter unprotected.

You can go on taking hydrangea cuttings right up till August, using the shoot tips. It isn't even essential to cut the base of the cutting just below a node, as they are capable of making roots from the lenticels (those funny reddish-purple scars) all along their stems.

Other shrub cuttings I take in May, though at the very end of the month, are *Lippia citriodora,* the lemon-scented verbena, from their newly sprouted shoots, and some of the lilacs: namely the cultivars of the Prestoniae hybrids (with pink, privet-scented flowers) and of *Syringa vulgaris.* The former root very readily; the latter, which are the most popular and typical lilacs, are tricky. Some, such as Messina, are much easier than others, like the double white Mme Lemoine. Take their ·young shoots, with a heel, just as they are firming up. A mist propagator makes them much easier to deal with.

Many shrubs are easily rooted from young or not-so-young side shoots at any time from May to September: weigelas, deutzias, escallonias, olearias, forsythias, philadelphus. The earlier you strike them the stronger the plant you'll have for overwintering.

The best time for taking cuttings from camellia bushes growing outside will usually be in late July or early August. Much depends on the season (dull and wet or sunny and dry) on the age of the bush (how vigorously it is growing) and on whether it is sited in the open or under trees. The stem wood wants to be supple but not soft. If the bush is making long shoots, you can make several cuttings from each, with two leaves to each cutting. Remove the lower leaf and halve the upper one. Then make a long (inch-long), sloping cut with a sharp knife, right across the wood at the base of the cutting. This cut can come well below the lower leaf bud. Both leaf buds are kept intact.

Given the advantage of bottom heat, rooting will be much accelerated, but even in an unheated frame your cuttings should have struck by the next spring. I root mine in a cold frame, but it has double walls and double glazing. The point of this is not, as some people think, to whack up the temperature by day, but to hold it by night. The walls are of 2-in. concrete blocks with a 1½-in. gap between them. The inner lights are set horizontally. These had to be made specially, to measure, by a local carpenter.

But the outer lights are of the standard Dutch type, and slope, to throw the rain off.

I take cuttings of *Garrya elliptica* in early August, by which time next season's catkins will already be present, but must certainly be removed. For preference, choose shoots about 4 in. long that are not going to flower, and take them with a heel. Not more than two or three should go into a 3½-in. pot, since the young roots of garryas are not merely fragile but exceedingly sensitive to any sort of handling, and you can easily lose newly rooted plants by disturbing them unduly at the potting-off stage. *Buddleia alternifolia* is fragile in the same sort of way, and I usually root cuttings of this singly, in 2-in. pots, but the amateur who wants only one or two extra plants will probably do better by waiting till the dormant season, in November, and then inserting foot-long hardwood cuttings straight into the ground where he wants the shrub to grow.

Skimmias are among the most satisfactory and easiest of shrubs to strike. They make nice thick, sturdy roots that show no inclination to crumble or snap. The current season's shoots are carried in a whorl of up to five, each of which, taken with a heel, will make a new plant. Skimmias should always be propagated in this way, from specimens of known sex, and one should eschew those tempting, self-sown seedlings whose sex remains undivulged for many years, until their first flowering. In any case, plants from cuttings mature more quickly than do seedlings. The related *Choisya ternata* strikes a little more slowly, but again with thick, strong roots.

Of the daphnes, the evergreen *Daphne odora* is the most amenable, rooting as easily as a skimmia. The deciduous *D. burkwoodii* (sometimes called Somerset) has to be done in this way, but is swinish. You can never be sure what results you are going to get from a batch. *D. tangutica* is rather slow, and I prefer seeds, in this case, although, again, plants from cuttings start flowering almost as soon as they have rooted, and a year or two earlier than seedlings.

Evergreen ceanothus vary greatly, as between cultivars, in the ease of their striking and in the time at which they strike most freely. Some time in August should be right for most of them, using firmish side-shoots with a heel. I usually leave their individual potting off till the following spring (as with *Elaeagnus* already mentioned), but their roots are white and super-fragile. Cistus roots drop off very easily, too, and it may be difficult, if they have made too many, to separate one cutting from the next without losing the roots altogether. They should be potted individually at the earliest opportunity after rooting has taken place. One way you can sometimes cope with fragile roots is by separating the rooted cuttings under water.

There is no need for heel cuttings with cistuses. You can use the young tips, trimming below a node. The young shoots of the related helianthemums can be rooted likewise at any time from June till September. And, while on the subject of rock plants, aubrietas come best from the young shoots that have appeared since your plants were shorn back (if you bothered to do this), after flowering. Aubrietas do not lend themselves to division. On the other hand, cuttings of their furry shoots rot very easily, and they should not be kept under close conditions for a moment longer than is necessary.

Rock phloxes present no difficulties, taking their young shoots, trimmed below a node. Your only troubles with them will occur if their shoots have been allowed to harden before being taken for cutting material.

Very few amateurs make the attempt to root cuttings of *Lithospermum diffusum* 'Heavenly Blue', although it is one of the most popular of all rock plants. I suppose the operation is just tricky enough to be off-putting, and yet nurserymen, without recourse to magic, propagate all their stock from cuttings made from young shoots at midsummer. And there is no need to use growth promoting powders or solutions. Either the cuttings will rot or, by September, they will have rooted. Pot them individually into $3\frac{1}{2}$-in. pots, in John Innes No. 2, harden them off, and by May you will have a fat little plant, smothered in blossom. Lime is the species' only hate, but the lime in a John Innes or other standard compost is not enough to upset it.

Most euphorbias will strike from cuttings, although other methods are likely to appeal to amateur gardners, who only want a few extra plants. *Euphorbia palustris* makes a hard and woody rootstock, not easily divided and I have never seen it setting seed, though I don't know why it shouldn't. Soft tip cuttings root easily however. But the young plants must make a basal bud by the time winter arrives, if they are going to come to life again in the following spring. Otherwise they just peter out. The earlier in summer you take your cuttings the better their chances of doing this.

So, too, with a number of shrubs. The several cultivars of *Hydrangea paniculata* should be rooted in June, if possible. If left till August, the young plants, however well rooted by the autumn, will generally fail to produce a young shoot the next year. *Celastrus orbiculatus* also has this little habit. You should always grow the hermaphrodite form, which doesn't need a second plant of the opposite sex in order to set fruit, and you can only guarantee to perpetuate your hermaphrodite by propagating it vegetatively. Take your cuttings by early July at the latest.

Hardy Plants from Spring Cuttings

From the middle of March, the mad spring rush is on. Even if there is still some snow to come, the somnolent span of winter, when we could catch up on autumn work at our pleasure, give or take a few months, is past. It now becomes a question of getting each task done at the exact critical moment, or not at all.

This is particularly so with cuttings of herbaceous plants. Perhaps not many amateurs want to take these, anyway. Perhaps, on the other hand, they have never wanted to because they had never thought about it. Division is the obvious and easiest method in most cases, but cuttings do allow you to increase your stock of a plant very quickly, and there are certain plants that do not lend themselves to division: those like *Salvia superba*, with long fangy roots, and those whose stems all arise from one, tough, indivisible rootstock, like perennial pinks, gypsophilas and scabious.

You want to catch your plant at the exact moment when it has first been inspired with the joys of spring but has not yet grown lush. That is to say, it no longer consists only of the sullen, shrunken basal foliage (if any) that carried it through the winter, but has put out a few new, fresh-looking leaves, on each shoot. Even in mid-March, the delphiniums and lupins will already be just as one would want them, but other plants—dianthus, salvias, oenotheras, will be right in April, and others again will come in between.

Now, as to the removal of your cuttings from the plant. Sometimes the best and simplest way is to grasp (a gentle grasp, not a bone-crushing hand-clasp) the shoot low down, between index finger and thumb, and waggle it free from its parent stem. This works excellently with all the sedums, with dianthus, gypsophilas, *Oenothera missouriensis, Aster frikartii* and *A. amellus, Heliopsis* and the yellow yarrows (*Achillea*). Put them straight into a plastic bag and, just before inserting into the cutting compost, take a very fine sliver off the base of each with a razor blade. With delphiniums and lupins and perhaps also with phloxes and *Salvia superba,* it is best to cull them by cutting across the pulpy base of their shoots with a sharp knife. If this is neatly done, there will be no need for further trimming at the potting bench—provided, that is, that the base of the cutting has not been allowed to dry out in the meantime.

Use the standard cutting compost of one part by bulk of loam, two of peat and three of horticultural grit. Insert your cuttings firmly yet without bruising them—either in pots or boxes, depending on how many you are taking. Water thoroughly, and keep in a close frame, shaded sufficiently to prevent serious wilting in direct sunlight. But the more light they get, short of wilting, the quicker they will root. Dianthus and gypsophilas should not be kept under close conditions a day longer than is necessary for rooting them. Otherwise the waxy bloom on their leaves is destroyed and they rot. As soon as you see signs of shoot extension, you can take it that they are rooting or about to root and give them air. Harden your cuttings off in the usual way and plant them out about the beginning of June, in most cases; earlier with quick ones like asters, later with slow ones like some gypsophilas.

The succulent cuttings that you take from sedums need a modified treatment, since they should never be given close conditions. Give them a compost of pure grit (which it is impossible to over-water), and you can stand them in the open, unless there is a danger of birds scattering the cuttings around. They are rather easily loosened, not having any length of stem.

The herbaceous plants that you raise from cuttings will nearly all flower the same year. In most cases they will produce larger heads of larger blooms than you could obtain in any other way. Sometimes I grow *Anthemis tinctoria* from cuttings struck in spring, simply in order to obtain a widely branching plant that yet comes all from one stem and thus needs only one stake; that will grow only 3 ft. tall instead of the 6 ft. of established clumps, and flower over a longer season than old groups.

Much the same may be said of perennial asters. The amellus types and *Aster frikartii* have woody rootstocks that do not good-temperedly divide, so cuttings are especially suitable for their propagation. So, too, with any cherished delphinium you may possess. The named cultivars can, virtually, be increased only in this way. Division is seldom feasible, though not impossible.

Half-Hardy Shrubs from Cuttings

Half-hardy shrubs would be more popular garden plants if we did not have to buy new stock after every severe winter. The genus *Hebe* (which is the sensible distinguishing name given by many botanists to the shrubby types of veronicas, as against the herbaceous and annual kinds) is a typical case in point. The handsomest, most exciting hebes in flower are also the most frost-tender. And so, after a couple of killing winters in succession, many gardeners will refrain from replacing their losses. What I am always trying to persuade them to do is automatically to take a few cuttings from each variety, each autumn, so that, if their old plants do succumb, they will not feel too badly about it. After all, a hebe is an extremely fast-growing shrub, and a youngster will in many cases flower profusely in its first year and over an exceptionally long period, from July till December.

When this bit of pleading fails to kindle any sort of response, I know that it is the question of actually taking the cuttings that is the stumbling-block. I shall here ignore the fact that many readers have glass protection of some sort, from a heated greenhouse down to a cold frame; and have available a reasonably

Plate 3. Our native spotted orchid, *Orchis maculata*, makes a splendid border plant in the garden or will naturalise in rough grass. The flowers are rich mauve in the best forms.

expert manipulator of a knife with which to take cuttings. Without any of these advantages, gardeners can still be successful in striking their tender plants, and October-November is a very good time for doing it, especially where evergreens are concerned.

Say it is a hebe we want to strike; and let us suppose it is of that most brilliant of all hebes, Simon Deleaux, with its spikes of crimson flowers. Take a terminal shoot, preferably without flower spikes on it, as these inhibit the growth of the shoot. But if flower spikes cannot be avoided—for these hebes are most of them flowering madly up till the first hard frost—then just nip them off near the base. You should be left with a shoot consisting of a terminal bud of leaves that have not yet unfolded, and three pairs of expanded leaves behind this. Pull the bottom pair off; they will come away quite cleanly.

Now, with scissors or a razor blade, cut through the stem immediately below this joint from which the leaves have been removed. The inch or so of stem that is left below the next pair of leaves is now stood in water in a clear glass (so that you can see what is happening) on a windowsill in any light, frost-free room. Provided you don't allow all the water to evaporate, roots will appear in the course of a few months and the young plant can either be potted, or, if this is a bother, kept hanging around until frost danger is past and then put straight out into the garden. A cutting that gets rooted too early in the winter may be an embarrassment, and this is why I recommend not taking them until November. If the bottom leaves do not pull off as obligingly cleanly as do the hebe's, but tear of, taking a strip off rind from the stem, then you must remove them with a blade.

Some shrubs may take six months to root in this way, but there is nothing to get worried or impatient about, as long as the foliage remains green and healthy-looking. If the water becomes murky with algae, it must be changed. Alternatively, you can add an antiseptic to the water. A highly informative article in *The Lancet* some time ago described an experiment in selecting the most effective antiseptic for delaying the decomposition of cut flowers

Plate 4. *Above, Daphne* 'Somerset', pale pink and carnation-scented.
Below, Senecio laxifolius, a grey-leaved evergreen with silver buds opening into gay yellow daisies in June.

E

in hospital wards. The conclusion was that chlorhexidine (marketed by I.C.I. as 'Hibitane'), added to flower water in the proportion of 1 ml. of 5 per cent. solution (which is the strength at which you buy it) to half a litre of tap water, nearly doubled the life of the flowers and much delayed the development of an unpleasant smell in association with decomposition. An antiseptic would be particularly useful with soft-stemmed cuttings liable to early decomposition.

Many grey-foliage plants are doubtfully hardy or downright tender. Such is *Helichrysum petiolatum* and the equally attractive *H. microphyllum*, with minute leaves. Then there are the fuchsias. They can be increased by the method I have described at any season when the parent plants are carrying young shoots. But if you want to exhibit a handsome specimen in your local flower show, in the following July or August, I recommend taking cuttings in mid-September. Pot them into 3½-in. pots in October and keep them as cold as you can without actual damage to the plants, through the winter. The thermometer can fall to freezing point but must go no further. They will start growing again strongly in March, and in April can be transferred straight to their final pots, for which the 8-in. size is suitable (remember that clay pots look better than plastic), and in these I suggest using the strong John Innes No. 3 potting compost. From the end of May you can feed once weekly with a liquid fertiliser.

Propagation by Root Cuttings

When buying plants, you are frequently faced with the problem of how many to get of each kind. Unless you are afraid of offending the nurseryman, you will probably say, with a hopeful lift of the voice: 'I suppose I shall be able to split it up quite soon?'. The answer, where most herbaceous plants are in question, is usually yes; but now and again you stumble on a type that does not lend itself to being pulled apart and messed about at all. 'Resents disturbance' is the appropriate catch-phrase for one such, and these plants are noted for the expression of mutinous obstinacy that crosses their foliage as the gardener approaches, fork in hand. They generally have deep, fleshy taproots; and if you try to move them from one part of your border to another, the operation is almost certain to be incomplete. The pieces that were taken away will sulk for a year or two while every piece of root that was left behind will make a new plant.

Eryngiums (the sea hollies) are typical, and so are seakale and the perennial limoniums (statice, or sea lavender). They will not split up; but, if their roots are damaged, the wounded surface is capable of making adventitious buds—shoot buds that occur, not where you normally expect them, but out of the blue. This faculty allows them to be propagated, in cold blood, by means of root cuttings. The task is usually left to the nurseryman, but there is no reason whatever why it should not be practised by the amateur. The dormant season is the best time to set about it.

Let us take by way of an example the hardy eryngiums, with steely blue or purple stems and domed blue flower heads, with a spiky grey-blue ruff framing each of them. Dig a plant up with as great a depth of taproot as you can extract. It will not matter if, as is inevitable, pieces of root break away from the parent crown. Collect these odd lengths, too, but lay them parallel in your trug or basket, with their top ends all pointing the same way. Now repair to the potting-bench and further subdivide each piece of root into 1½-in. lengths, cutting them straight across. But still keep their top ends all pointing in the same direction. To avoid confusion, it is usually recommended that the bottom end of the cutting should be made with a slanting cut, so as to distinguish it from the top end, made with a straight cross-cut. This, however, entails making twice as many cuts and wasting a wedge of root each time.

You must next three-quarters fill a deep seed-box with cutting compost. Prick out your cuttings into this with a dibber or widger, keeping the pieces upright and still topside up. Cover with half an inch of compost, and firm. Water; and then for preference put the box in a close cold frame. But if a ventilated greenhouse (under the staging) is more convenient, or even an outside standing-ground, that will be all right.

Some of the pieces of root used will have been much thicker than others, but this doesn't seem to matter: they will nearly all take. Shoots will appear around April or May, but one should be careful not to overwater until new roots have been put out, which happens subsequently. The young plants can be lined out in a spare plot in late spring or early summer and will be ready for the border by the autumn.

Limoniums, acanthus, perennial verbascums (mulleins) and oriental poppies can be treated similarly, as also can the plume poppy (*Macleaya cordata*) and the Californian tree poppy (*Romneya*). Most of the hardy cranesbills (*Geranium* spp.) will come from root cuttings and so will the tender pelargoniums. Japanese anemones are best taken singly in 3½-in. pots and grown on through the summer in these, planting them out in autumn. It is curious that this plant, which is almost rampant once established, is so costive in its behaviour when you try to move it in a normal way. Any thistle can, not unexpectedly, be increased from roots, including the choice alpine *Carlina acaulis*. So can *Crepis incana*, which looks rather like a dandelion until it flowers.

Herbaceous phloxes are easily split up, of course, but their comparatively fine though fleshy roots do offer this other method of increase. Commercially it is usual to propagate by root cuttings in sterilised soil. Phlox plantings are frequently ruined by the stem eelworm, whose microscopic presence you can recognise when the foliage is reduced to curiously twisted threads. But this pest doesn't live in the phlox roots, so if you propagate from these, on a fresh piece of ground, you may elude the eelworm.

Anchusas (cultivars of *A. azurea*) are always strongest in their first year of flowering, and should consequently be treated as biennials. Seed germinates uncertainly, but root cuttings, about 3 in. long in their case, are most satisfactory. You can tie them into bundles of 25 and plunge them, rather deeply (because, as Mediterranean plants, they cannot cope with the severest frosts), in a well-drained spot outside, and line them out in spring.

I have said nothing of the trees and shrubs that can be increased this way—paulownias, for instance. Any batch of seedlings of *Paulownia tomentosa* will do if you are growing this simply as a foliage shrub. But if you want the tree for its mauve foxglove flowers in May, before the leaves unfold, it is most important to get a good flowering strain. Root cuttings should be taken from a specimen that you know blooms well. All trees and shrubs with a tendency to sucker are worth trying from root cuttings; clerodendrons, for instance, and even some roses.

Layering

Putting Down Layers

Layering is the most certain of propagating methods and the pleasantest of tasks. As Mr. G. R. Wakefield observes in his excellent book on camellias, 'I like layering: there is something very satisfying about working out in the wild garden all alone with just the country sounds.'

This is a job one tends to do in winter—on some mild January day, perhaps, when nature's heart-beat is at its slowest and there is a leisurely feeling that nothing presses; garden commitments are at a low ebb. Actually, you can put down layers at any season. Another relaxing aspect of this occupation is that you don't have to do it. It is just a pleasant extra to provide you and your friends with bonus shrubs. If you are bored with weeding, you start thinking about the shrub you were weeding near or under. 'It would be rather nice to have another of that magnolia,' you tell yourself; 'here's a clean patch of ground doing nothing. I'll peg a layer into it.'

I have, in fact, a large specimen of *Magnolia soulangeana* 'Lennei' that I layer quite frequently. It lends itself so willingly. Of lax habit, its branches bend easily to the ground and it often sends up strong young shoots from its centre which, when about a year old, make ideal layering material. It usually takes two years to give me a well-rooted piece that I can detach and transplant. That would be a long wait, if you were thinking about it every day, but if you make a practice, as I think one should, of putting down the odd layer from every good shrub whenever you happen to be near it and not in a hurry, you are more likely to find yourself forgetting about a rooted layer that is ready for moving, than waiting impatiently for roots to be made.

To be sure of success, a few points are always worth observing. Make quite certain that your layers are rigid. Some gardeners keep them steady by placing a heavy stone on each, but this is less wind-proof than pegging with wooden hooks. It is not a bad idea to tie the layer to a cane, where it emerges from the ground. First, the cane will act as a marker; for a layer is easily disturbed by subsequent thoughtless hoeing or digging; second, it will steady the layer; and third, it will keep it in an upright position. It is important that the layered shoot should describe as sharp an angle as possible, at its lowest point, since this checks the sap flow and thereby encourages rooting.

You will usually find it advocated, in books where shrub propagation is described, that the layered shoot should be wounded in one way or another, at its lowest point, again as an inducement to rooting. But this is quite a tricky procedure, and often leads to breaking the shoot altogether. It is, moreover, seldom necessary. But you should select reasonably young material for layering, in most cases; second-year wood fairly near the tip of a branch system is usually in the right condition. Clematis, by contrast, never root so well as from old stems.

One shrub I have found troublesome to layer successfully is *Hamamelis mollis,* the Chinese Witch Hazel. Our plants are some 35 years old and those branches that come down to near the ground are as old as any; encrusted with lichens in fact. With them I do make a 2-inch-long, tongue-like slit, reaching into the centre of the branch, on its underside at what will be the layer's lowest point. To keep the tongue open, I slip a pebble into it at the base of the tongue. Fortunately hamamelis wood, even when old, is remarkably supple and not a bit inclined to snap. As the wood calluses and heels, it makes roots, but you must give it two years.

Some shrubs are quick rooters and, if layered in winter, will give you detachable plants by the next autumn. Roses (of suitable habit), figs, forsythias, Japanese quinces (*Chaenomeles*), clematis and wisterias are cases in point. For ease of handling later on the last two are best layered into a large (7-in.) pot filled with a gritty compost, before putting down a layer. The underground portion must always be stripped of leaves, if it should happen to carry any.

Grafting

Good and Bad Grafting Practices

Many of the trees and shrubs that we buy have been grafted. Sometimes, as with cherries, we take this as a matter of course, while with others we regard it as a nurseryman's practice designed to get him an easy sale, regardless of the probable demise of his miserable product. There is sometimes a foundation for this disturbing suspicion, and it is hence always better to deal direct with a sound nurseryman whose reputation depends on maintaining good relations with his customers, rather than with the impersonal medium of a market or chain store, where bargains so often turn out to be the opposite and there is no redress.

One should keep an open mind on this question of grafting. Sometimes it gives much better results than would be the case if the desired plant were on its own roots. *Viburnum carlesii*, for instance, is very slow from rooted cuttings and inclined to be a puny weakling all its life. How it manages in the wilds of its native land, I don't know. Perhaps the damp English air gives it asthma. Anyway, when grafted on to our own wayfaring tree, *V. lantana,* it makes a fine bush or a still finer standard. But the wayfarer is inclined to sucker, and if you think your *carlesii* is suddenly making the most splendid growth, almost doubling its size in a year, watch out! The trouble here and in a number of cases is that the stock's foliage and general appearance is too similar to the scion's. You need a 'botanical eye' to distinguish them. So too with rhododendrons grafted on *Rhododendron ponticum*. The leaves of many of the most popular hybrids are terribly close to ponticum's. Beware shoots you notice coming up from below ground level. If you fail to notice these, your first intimation of trouble will be when the ponticum suckers are already large enough to carry their mauve flowers. By then, much damage will have been done. Far better that these rhododendrons should be increased from cuttings or layers. Cuttings are, thanks to modern propagation techniques, a much more feasible proposition than they were even a few years ago, but where the demand for a cultivar like Pink Pearl is enormously heavy, we must expect to buy grafted plants for many years to come. Cuttings of these large-leaved hybrids have to be rooted in a mist propagator, which is expensive and space-consuming. Grafting, however, can be done in the field. The only expensive item is the skilled grafter.

It is always worth asking the nurseryman whether the shrubs you are buying are grafted plants and, if so, what they have been worked on; then you will have some idea of what to watch out for.

Take lilacs, for instance. Varieties of *Syringa vulgaris*—that is, all the named kinds of the traditional spring-flowering lilacs—may be bought grafted on wild *S. vulgaris*, or else grafted on privet, or growing on their own roots. If on their own roots, these lilacs are likely to throw suckers from time to time, but true to name. They make useful presents to friends. When grafted on wild lilac, suckers will again be produced, but much too freely, and all of them of the wild type, so that, if allowed to take charge, they may swamp the cultivated variety, which will then be supposed to have reverted. Lilac and privet are only partly compatible, and grafting on privet rootstocks can be fatal after a few years, unless the lilac scion is subsequently replanted sufficiently deep to be able to make its own roots. Then it will be perfectly healthy. This is a case of scion rooting, and it is often worth encouraging.

Nearly all the ornamental and fruiting cherries that we buy are grafted on a selected clone of the wild gean, *Prunus avium*. Many of the cultivated varieties flatly refuse to grow on their own roots. Some of the species will do so, but it is still almost invariable to buy them grafted. I have tried rooting the winter cherry, *P. subhirtella* 'Autumnalis', on several occasions, both from hardwood cuttings of 10-inch-long, current season's shoots, struck in winter; and from soft cuttings taken in a frame about the end of May. A fairly good percentage of them make roots by either method, but the difficulty thereafter is to get new shoots from them. Instead, they persistently make flowers, right through the summer, but no shoots and very few leaves. Occasionally one of them sorts its ideas out and behaves rationally, but this is the exception. It is a strange business.

Ornamental apples, pears, plums and peaches nearly all, likewise, get grafted on the same range of rootstocks as are used for the eating varieties. Potentially one of the most delightful of the peach tribe is the double form of *Prunus triloba*. It is hard-pruned each year immediately after flowering and then makes a 4- to 5-ft. bush of wand-like shoots that blossom in frilly pink along their entire length, the following spring. It is perfectly hardy, but in this country I have only ever seen two well grown specimens: one, trained as a wall shrub near the propagating department at the Royal Botanic Gardens, Kew; the other in a Birmingham garden, now built over. The trouble most of us experience with this shrub is that it suckers madly. Too often, it is grafted on a rootstock that is particularly inclined to suckering, and, sooner or later, the stock takes charge. But it can be grown to perfection on its own roots, and you should try to layer a branch on a newly acquired specimen at the earliest opportunity. This is the obvious course to take where sucker trouble is expected. Naturally, one must be handling a bush, not a tree, and if its branches will not of themselves approach the ground in a layerable manner, it can sometimes be replanted obliquely, on its side.

Pears are nearly always grafted on quince rootstocks, nowadays, as the latter have a dwarfing influence. Any suckering of the stock here is easily detected, as the quince leaf is soft and furry. Wild pear seedlings used to be used as stocks; we still have many of them in our garden and the suckers they throw are exceedingly spiny and uncomfortable. As a rootstock, pear produces a too large, vigorous and slow-maturing tree for the average small modern garden and the average impatient modern gardener.

Wisterias are, or should be, grafted on seedling wisterias. This is called nurse grafting. The seedling's roots supply the scion with moisture and nutrients until the latter has made its own roots, whereupon the seedling rootstock fades away. Less scrupulous nurserymen will sell the seedlings themselves. There is a ready market· for them as demand for *Wisteria sinensis,* deservedly the most popular species, always exceeds the supply of grafted plants. What makes it essential to graft, here, is that this wisteria is a very variable plant, and seedlings almost always give rise to a lot of rubbish with small, wan flowers on miserable trusses. By grafting you can be sure of using a good cultivar. Layers are another commercial alternative.

Grafted clematis are likewise nurse grafts, using seedlings of *Clematis vitalba* (Old Man's Beard) or of *C. viticella,* as stocks. A tradition founded many years ago, and still maintained in books and articles on the subject today, claims that clematis should never be grafted, and that plants so raised are more liable to the dreaded wilt disease, which strikes down so many of the hybrids. Research at the Glasshouse Crops Research Institute has now proved conclusively, however, that the wilt disease is caused by a fungus and that this has no preference for grafted plants but is indiscriminate in its attacks, though frequently entering the host where it has been damaged.

Collecting Your Own Rootstocks for Future Budding

There is a great fascination in bud-grafting one's own trees. The mechanics of budding are described, with diagrams, in every book on propagation, and there is little difficulty in it for anyone who is accustomed to using a knife for, say, taking cuttings or peeling potatoes. If any rootstocks come your way (and they will without seeking them, even) you can have a lot of fun working them with an interesting scion. There can be few gardens, even in towns, where it is not easy to find self-sown hawthorn seedlings that can be used as rootstocks. And you need not restrict yourself to budding on to them any of the numerous species and varieties of *Crataegus*, the thorn tribe. Medlars are usually grafted on to hawthorn. We have two in this garden. The older was budded on a hawthorn stem at a height of 6 ft., so that its trunk is hawthorn. This appears to have had a rather inhibiting effect on the plant, though soil probably has something to do with it. The other, worked on hawthorn near to ground level, has a medlar trunk and is vigorous. Medlars can also be worked on quince stock or on pear, the latter inducing a large tree. You could produce seedlings of either by sowing pips.

Hawthorn, again, is the commonest stock for any or all the different types of rowan. But it is better to bud a rowan on a rowan seedling, where possible; and anyone with a rowan tree in his garden is sure to find seedlings from it on numerous occasions. The other *Sorbus* group, the whitebeams, are best budded on to whitebeam seedlings. I once collected some berries of this from Cheddar Gorge—but it (*Sorbus aria*) grows wild on most of our chalk and limestone formations. The berries took 18 months to germinate, and this is normal with the rose family, to which our fruit trees all belong.

There is much to be said for raising roses for your own use, from cuttings. But some varieties won't strike or else make very weak plants on their own roots. It is easy to buy 50 or 100 dog-rose (*Rosa canina*) seedlings very cheaply, lining them out in the dormant season. They will be ready for budding in the following summer. It is an uncomfortable and prickly job.

Making your own standard roses is great fun, however, and far more comfortable, because you can stand up to it. You should go, armed with a sharp spade, on a standard-collecting expedition, at any time in the last two months of the year, but not later, because dormancy in roses is of brief duration. In coppiced woods, on patches of common land or along rough hedgerows you will find that the dog-roses have thrown up, during the past season, long vigorous and unbranched shoots, of a deep warm brown colour and heavily armed, to a height of 7 ft. or thereabouts. Dig these up and cut any other shoots cleanly away from the base. Behead each rod at about 4 ft. You will then have a straight stem terminated at its base by a thick, one-sided, knob-like swelling. There will be no proper roots, but, if it is planted as it is, roots will develop.

The rods will form a number of shoots, and these should be reduced to two or three, near the top, pointing in different directions. Then, in July or August, a bud is inserted on the top side of each of these branches, 2 or 3 in. above the point at which they spring from the main stem.

If you want a stock on which to bud an ornamental cherry, you will often find that an existing cherry in your garden is in the habit of making a few suckers where its roots were damaged, at some time. Detach these suckers with a few roots on them, in winter, and replant, heading them back to a foot from the ground. They will be ready to bud the next summer. Peaches and apricots are usually worked on a plum stock, and these plum suckers arising from a peach can be wrenched out, replanted and used for budding most kinds of plum or peach cultivars, whether ornamental or fruiting. Peach seedlings often come up under a wall peach whose fruits were not all gathered before the wasps attached them. It is seldom that these seedlings are worth growing on as fruiting peaches themselves. Far better to use them as stocks on which to bud a peach of known quality.

Seeds, Seed Lists and Plants from Seed

Saving Your Own Seeds

There is a particular satisfaction in sowing and growing seeds that you have collected yourself. Whenever you look at or think about the resulting plants, your mind flicks back to that moment when you garnered the pods and the whole act of creation was, from your point of view, begun.

Now, most seed collecting happens in one's own garden and it should therefore be simple enough to do it at the right moment. And yet it is extraordinary how often that moment slips by when your thoughts are elsewhere and then, when you do remember (in the bath, most likely), it is only to discover that the bird has flown for yet another year.

A plant I keep missing at this critical stage is the white form of *Cyclamen neapolitanum*. Cyclamen are self-fertile; they rarely get cross-pollinated and as, in addition, this particular plant grows in isolation in one corner of the rose garden, I know that all its babies will come white, too. But seed of this species is an unconscionable time a'ripening. It takes a year, all but a few weeks. If it took a full year, I should be all right, because the new season's blooms would remind me to harvest last season's fruit. I suppose the sensible answer is to lard one's diary, on acquiring a new one, with memory-jogging entries of expected ripening dates.

My earliest entry would be May Day, for the winter aconite. It might be said, why bother? Why not let them sow themselves? That is all very well in your garden, perhaps, but these aconites make favourites of some and are peevish with others, myself among them. To hope that they will self-sow is to waste most, if not all, of their seed crop. Crocuses of all kinds, whether autumn, winter or spring flowering, ripen their seeds about the end of May or the beginning of June. The pods rise from ground level on 2-in. stalks, and you must be there, waiting for them.

Had you ever thought of growing *Iris stylosa* from seed? Its fibrous-textured pods stay at ground level, but are clearly visible if you happen to be weeding among the clumps in late spring. Two plants whose moment of seed dispersal catches me napping at the turn of June and July are *Euphorbia myrsinites* and *Pulsatilla vulgaris* (*Anemone pulsatilla*). The former, a beautiful prostrate spurge, seeds freely but in my garden never produces self-sown seedlings, which seems curious. Its seeds can be stored and will germinate abundantly from an April sowing. Pulsatillas I like to sow fresh; they make plants large enough to prick out by the end of August. Cyclamen, too, should be sown at once. They germinate in a cold frame within a month or 6 weeks and will keep growing all through the winter.

But there are few seeds, on the whole, that need to be sown as soon as collected. It is a nuisance to have to look after pots and boxes with seeds in them, through the winter. Probably they will get over-watered, at some stage; then mosses and liverworts will cover the surface, and the seedlings will damp off or else fail to penetrate the blanket. In most cases it is much the best to wait till the spring, when rising temperatures and lengthening days are working on your side.

Berries are best sown in autumn, however, and left where the frost can reach the seed and vernalise it. This is a chilling process necessary to many seeds before they can germinate. You can do a little artificial vernalisation on your own account. I get magnificent germination from *Thalictrum dipterocarpum* by sowing its previous year's seed in April, watering and then putting the container in our frig for a week or two (not always a popular incursion). Hellebore seeds are apt to be slow, too, and if you can't wait for self-sown seedlings to germinate around your old plants, the best thing is to sow them as soon as ripe, sometime during the summer, and give them refrigeration. This is a good method for increasing Christmas roses, *Helleborus niger*.

Large, fleshy seeds that would shrivel in storage should also be sown immediately. Peonies are the most obvious case in point. Sow these in a deep pot and cover with an inch of gritty soil. If this gets weedy or foul, it can be replaced at any time up till March, 18 months later. Peonies germinate in two stages: in the first year they simply make a long root; only in the second does a leafy shoot appear. Wintersweet, *Chimonanthus praecox,* seeds at irregular intervals and only certain bushes then. The seed pods hang on, ripe and intact, for many months. But as soon as they are collected (and they ripen in September) they should be sown and will germinate promptly, even in a cold frame. The magnolias' fleshy seeds must not be stored or dried, either. Some species, like *Magnolia wilsonii* and *M. sieboldii,* germinate readily in the following spring. The beautiful large-flowered and lime-tolerant hybrid, *M. highdownensis,* luckily comes true from seed and germinates well. *M. soulangeana* 'Lennei' carries splendid pods packed with gleaming red seeds, but I have never persuaded one of them to germinate.

Some plants disperse their seeds as soon as ripe, with a loud report of the exploding capsule. Apropos of this, you have to be on the watch for *Alstroemeria ligtu* hybrids. Collect the pods as soon as they turn brownish and lay them on a tray in a sunny place, with one sheet of newspaper covering them so as to contain the explosions. The alstroemerias' dark brown or black seeds are useless. The good ones are a light orange-brown. They will keep for at least three years if well stored.

It may be necessary, with agapanthus, to cull the seed heads before they are ripe. Winter tends to overtake them while still green. But these, and some of the later flowering lilies and other long deliberators such as *Cobaea scandens,* may be stood in a sunny place indoors with their stems in water, there to finish off the job.

I would never bother to collect seed from the majority of annuals. It is usually so cheap to buy, and where not cheap is probably a first-cross (F1) hybrid, which is expensive to produce and from which it is quite useless to take the seed yourself anyway. Others, like strains of nasturtiums, eschscholtzias and lupins, quickly revert towards their wild prototypes, unless they are meticulously rogued as soon as they come into flower, every plant with less desirable qualities being destroyed. This, again, is no task for the gardener.

Still, there are some annuals of whose seeds it may be nice to have a hundred times as much as you would get in a packet: love-in-a-mist, for instance, and opium poppies. You might want a large colony of one or other of these. If you have a vast amount of seed of either at your disposal, you can broadcast it without any sort of preparation of the ground, knowing that only one seed in a hundred needs to germinate for you to have as many plants as there is room for. This saves trouble.

There are other plants of whose seed you may have no immediate need, but which is easily collected and might come in useful within the next few years (after you have had a rest from them in the garden). Seeds that are tough-coated and not too small will remain in good condition for a number of years, if stored in an airtight tin in a coolish place. Screw-top jars, or the sort of tins that typewriter ribbons are sold in are excellent. Smaller seeds can go into pay-packet envelopes and then be stored in a larger tin. Always be sure to label the seeds as soon as collected, and also note the year.

Choose two or three dry, windless days at ten-day intervals for collecting seeds. It saves time later on if you can clean them there and then. Very often you can just tilt them out of their pods into your palm without any foreign bodies being included, except, of course, for earwigs. You must steel yourself, before starting, against dropping seeds, earwigs and all, when this happens. Remember that the earwigs are as keen to get away from you as you from them.

If you find a lot of husks mixed up with the seeds, you can do a little gentle winnowing by blowing into your cupped palm. However small the seeds, the husks and chaff are always lighter. The seeds can then go straight into their final containers, if perfectly dry. If not, let them dry out on a sunny windowsill first.

Those of us who open our gardens to the public will know how infuriating it is to have the seed pods that we were guarding swiped by visitors—often while they were so unripe as not to be of any use to anyone. Lilies and meconopses are some of the most regular victims. We have all been subject, at some time in our gardening careers, to this temptation, and, nine times out of ten, yielding to it will be harmless. But that tenth occasion will cause great distress to the garden owner. I find that a small tag-label hung about a cherished seed-pod's neck, with 'this is being saved' inscribed in non-smearing pencil upon it, usually works.

Seedlings, Sex and Sexless Reproduction

The gardener has two principal methods of propagation at his command: from seed (sexual reproduction) or by some vegetative procedure (asexual reproduction). In the latter he is taking a chip off the old block and may do it by cuttings, layers, grafts or simply by division. Often he has a choice before him between the two fundamental methods and it is interesting to consider the factors that will incline him sometimes this way, sometimes that.

If he is a nurseryman, he will be interested in the simplest method of obtaining the largest number of saleable plants. That method may be seed, but seedlings will not necessarily give the better result in the long run. Take the case of *Magnolia grandiflora* as an example. Nothing could be simpler for the nurseryman than to raise and sell off a batch of seedlings from imported seed. The customer buys a nice looking plant and thinks he has made a good purchase. But seedlings, being the product of sexual reproduction, vary in the way they turn out—both appearance and behaviour—as much as human children will vary. And if you are unlucky with your magnolia, you may grow it for 30 years before it carries its first bloom. Indeed I know of some specimens that have never bloomed in 50 years and over.

What the gardener wants is a young plant that has been raised vegetatively from a parent magnolia that is known to flower freely from an early age. The method used will generally be cuttings. If you know *M. grandiflora* and its voluminous clusters of large leathery leaves, you will appreciate that the handling of cuttings made from them is cumbersome and that they take up a lot of space in the nurseryman's propagating house. But, although raising them from cuttings may be inconvenient, it is not difficult.

Plate 5   Paeonia mlokosewitschii (above) is not a plant for a small garden. It flowers for about 5 days in early May and is at its ravishing best for about four hours in the middle of this period. For a herbaceous peony it has a wonderful colouring and the leaves are a distinct asset.

The soft yet brightly coloured *Alstroemeria ligtu* hybrids *(below)* have the springlike freshness of azaleas, yet flower in June-July and are splendid cut flowers even in the hottest weather. After flowering they become unsightly and it is good policy to grow in front of them some intertwining plant like *Senecio leucostachys*, shown here. Its creamy flowers are pleasant but the main point of it is its grey foliage and its habit of weaving among and into neighbouring plants. See also Plate 22. Alternatively you can yank out the alstroemeria stems after flowering and plant annuals or tender bedding plants in the six inches of soil above its very deeply situated roots, for a late summer and autumn display.

There are two clones of *M. grandiflora* that are known to be particularly satisfactory. A clone comprises all the vegetatively produced progeny of one single individual. Being vegetatively propagated, they all have exactly the same hereditary attributes as the original plant that founded the clone. In this instance we have Exmouth Variety and Goliath. They will generally flower when seven years old, and I know of one case where Goliath flowered when its owner had had it for only three years.

Sometimes a desirable clone has not been given a particular varietal name by which to recognise it. *Kolkwitzia amabilis* is a relative of *Weigela* with masses of pink funnel flowers in spring. But seedlings of this shrub are apt to be very shy flowering. I raised a batch once, and up till the time they were 4 ft. or so tall,

Plate 6. Top left, Rheum palmatum is the finest of the ornamental rhubarbs: a 7 ft. giant with red-flushed leaves followed by massive panicles of tiny red flowers in May. It leaves rather a gap later. Excellent waterside plant or in any large border. *Right,* the hardiness of the April-flowering *Arum creticum* is its most astonishing asset. It is scarce because so slow to increase, but perfectly happy in rich moist soil.

Middle left, 'Escarboucle' was probably the most dramatic hardy waterlily ever produced by that French wizard Marliac, who bred so many *Nymphaea* hybrids but died without revealing his methods. This is a particularly vigorous plant, especially suited to water 5 or even 6 ft. deep but happy enough with only 2 or 3 ft. Its flowering season, from June to October, is exceptionally long. *Right,* gazanias are among the most temperamental of South African daisies, shutting up or refusing to open if weather conditions are not absolutely blazing. But there is a marvellous range of colours among them, much developed and improved by the RHS at Wisley, and the best varieties should be propagated from cuttings, though it is easier still to raise a batch from seed and treat it like an annual. They flower from May to October and can be planted out in spring before danger of frost is altogether past.

Bottom left, Crocosmia masonorum has only of recent years achieved its remarkable popularity as a garden plant and elegant cut flower.

Right, the New Zealand kowhai, *Sophora tetraptera* is excellent against a warm wall. After an initial period of several unproductive years during which it simply grows, flowering is regular, occurring on naked branches in late April and May. The pinnate leaves that follow are airy and graceful, falling only in March.

none of them ever bore a flower and I threw them away in disgust. But George Jackman's of Woking make the point, in their catalogue, of mentioning that theirs is a free flowering clone.

With the Passion Flower, *Passiflora caerulea*, we are on even more uncertain ground. No clones are distinguishable and no nurseryman that I know of claims to be able to offer a free-flowering form. Whenever I have grown this plant, it has flowered with me from the word go, but some gardeners are unlucky and have had it for years, growing rampantly, yet never flowering. The problem has not been investigated and we don't therefore know why this should be. I suspect the same cause as with *Magnolia grandiflora* and *Kolkwitzia amabilis*. Passion flowers are easily raised from the seeds in their egg-shaped fruits (which are borne only occasionally in the garden, but quite freely under glass). So it may be a question of heredity.

There are times when we are obliged to depend on seedlings and just hope for the best. Thus it is with many rhododendron species, particularly those with large leaves. They simply do not produce enough shoots on a bush to allow of propagation from cuttings, layers or grafts in sufficient quantities to meet the demand. I wanted a plant of the F.C.C. form of *Rhododendron macabeanum,* which has flowers of a particularly rich yellow colouring, in contrast to the rather washed-out cream colour that is more usual. It was, I found, not just a question of paying so many pounds for it but of joining a waiting list with the prospect of delivery only years hence. The best I could do, in the circumstances, was to accept a seedling raised from the F.C.C. form and grow it on till it might be expected to flower, perhaps in ten years' time, keeping my fingers crossed and hoping that I might be rewarded with something good. But I have no guarantee. It may throw back to some comparatively bourgeois antecedent.

There is a general tendency for the seedlings of all perennials (including trees and shrubs) to reach maturity (i.e. to start flowering) more slowly than plants of the same species that have been vegetatively reproduced. Hebes (the shrubby veronicas) are great self-sowers, but if you have ever grown their seedlings on you will know that 3 or 4 years generally elapse before the first flowering spike appears, whereas a rooted cutting would flower within the year. You can sometimes succeed in hurrying on a seedling's flowering by propagating it vegetatively as soon as it is large enough to give you propagating material. In the case of hebes, you would take cuttings from the seedling. When new roses are being bred, the seedlings are grafted at the earliest opportunity on to a briar stock. The hybridist does not wait for them to flower on their own roots. Another reason for this transfer is that the briar stock imparts extra vigour, so that scion growth is more rapid.

The mat-forming South African daisy, *Dimorphotheca barberiae*, with pinky-mauve daisies produced in succession from May till the frosts, is easily rooted from cuttings at any season and these start flowering forthwith. Out of curiosity, I once raised plants of it from seeds, which it sets only spasmodically, but they can be found in a good year. Sown in spring, they germinated rapidly and soon made great leafy plants, but never bore a single bloom till more than a year old.

Many of our most popular bedding plants are perennials that we treat as annuals, discarding them in the autumn. In the old days we should not have been able to discard them, but should have had to go through the laborious procedure of taking cuttings in the autumn and overwintering the young plants under frost-proof glass. All the best named varieties of *Antirrhinum* had to be kept going vegetatively; also fibrous-rooted begonias deriving from *Begonia semperflorens* and bedding verbenas—some of these, like 'Lawrence Johnston', we still do by cuttings. In most of these lines, however, tremendous strides have been made to produce seed strains that can be relied upon to give rise to a uniform and predictable product. Which all makes for easier gardening.

Of our most popular bedders, only the zonal pelargonium (geranium) seemed obstinately to insist on being perpetuated from cuttings. Now this, too, is at last yielding to hybridising work by the Americans and we have their new Carefree colour strains which can be raised from seed to flower in one season and give an acceptably uniform product. Perennial bedding plants that are being raised from seed do take rather a long time to reach flowering size, very often, and so these pelargoniums, as also begonias, 'annual' carnations (which are not really annuals), heliotrope, antirrhinums and a few others, need to be sown early, in February at latest, so as to have a fairly advanced and mature plant ready to put out in the garden in the spring.

Certain trees and shrubs wear quite different foliage in their youth (as seedlings) from what they do in maturity. As this juvenile foliage (as it is called) may be particularly attractive, it has been horticulturally encouraged. Eucalypts have become well known examples of this phenomenon since they were taken up by the flower arranging movement. All species of *Eucalyptus* are raised from seed anyway. The juvenile foliage tends to be rounded. In *E. perriniana*, for instance, each pair of leaves is joined to form a perfect disc around the stem. When you have a whole series of these discs gradually getting smaller as they taper towards the shoot tip, the effect is fascinating. Small wonder that the tree's maturity brings little joy to its owner, for the adult leaf is long, thin and willow-like, as is normal with most gum trees. However, juvenility can be much prolonged by treating the tree as a shrub, and constantly pruning it back at the extremities. More juvenile shoots will then be produced.

Seedling conifers also have juvenile foliage of quite different appearance from the mature leaf. In the genus *Chamaecyparis,* the false cypresses, this habit has been exploited. It was found that if juvenile shoots were detached from the parent and propagated vegetatively (usually from cuttings), they retained their juvenile characters, even into old age, making much smaller but very attractive plants, particularly suited to the rock garden. These juvenile types have sometimes been referred to as Retinospora.

There is one important advantage in the seedling over the vegetatively propagated clone, that has yet to be mentioned. Few virus diseases are transmitted through the seed and it is therefore probable that most seedlings will start off with a clean bill of health, where viruses are concerned. Virus infections are much more widespread than the layman would ever imagine. In many plants their existence has never been investigated and can only be surmised at by the appearance of typical virus symptoms. I would suggest clematis as an example here. Virus diseases are of serious concern to professional rose growers (although seldom suspected by the amateur); they are widespread among fruit trees and soft fruits, in camellias, daphnes, bulbs, vegetables and many annuals. Indeed, there are few plants not subject to them and although they do not always kill, they always reduce vigour, usual-ly to a serious extent. And so it makes a wonderful springboard to be able to raise, for instance, lilies and pelargoniums—both martyrs to virus—from seed and to start with a healthy plant.

Perennials from Seed

The great seed houses with byword names like Sutton, Carter, Unwin and Webb, have built up their reputations, for the most part, on annuals or, at least, on perennials that can be treated as annuals. But, in fact, they trade in seeds of all kinds of plants, and the gardener might well take more careful note of the shrubs and perennial herbaceous plants.

An obvious enough point that we yet need reminding of, from time to time, is that it is possible to stock a garden quickly and cheaply simply by making a judicious selection of these shrubs and perennials, and growing them from seed. Few perennial plants now cost less than 3s. 6d. each and to make a group, you need, on average, five. But for 17s 6d. you could buy ten packets of seed and raise, from these, enough plants (and to spare) to furnish ten times the border area.

Typical of the good seed strain is **Coreopsis grandiflora** 'Baby Sun'. I have long since given up growing the old-fashioned *C. grandiflora* itself, because of its sprawling untidiness, while the popular cut-flower cultivar, Badengold, is even floppier and, in addition, shy flowering on many soils. Baby Sun makes a compact, self-supporting mound, only 2 ft. tall and smothered with golden-yellow daisies, each with a bronze central zone. A little riotous, perhaps, but then we do not all want to float endlessly among silvers and greys and tender pinks, in the gentle nicotiana-laden ambient of a summer's gloaming. Some prefer a bright, brash midday glare with plenty of stuffing.

I don't think Michaelmas daisies should ever be grown from seed, because the best named varieties are far superior, and very cheap when you consider that a plant can be pulled into half a dozen pieces at the moment of its purchase and will thank you kindly for the attention. But the foot-tall, early-summer-flowering **Aster alpinus** is quite another matter. This is a modestly mat-forming plant, often used in rock gardens but equally appropriate at the front of a June border. Its daisies are proudly held on stiff stems and their lavender colouring is pleasantly offset by a large yellow disc.

A. subcaeruleus is similar but with a vivid orange disc, while *A. yunnanensis* 'Napsbury' is again similar but larger in all its parts and, growing 2 ft. tall, is excellent for cutting. These two remain in season for only a fortnight or so, but one always welcomes their return. *A. yunnanensis* goes very well with *Buphthalmum salicifolium*, a plant familiar to those who take a summer holiday in Austria, where it grows wild in open woodland. It is another composite, 2 ft. or so tall and of a stiff, wiry, branching habit, set with gay, spiky-rayed yellow daisies. It seeds itself without becoming a pest.

We have had the **maiden pink**, *Dianthus deltoides*, in our garden since before I was born. From the paving cracks in which it was originally planted, it has seeded itself over the years into other cracks and in among stemmy plants at the border margin. Its mats are green; the flowers, on 6-in. stems, quite small but very numerous, magenta, each with a thin, darker, pencilled circle towards the centre, which lends it purpose. They close at night and in dull weather. The new strain, called Flashing Light, is certainly a marked improvement, for it is several tints more brilliant, with less blue in its colouring.

A perennial that one is surprised to see as a seed-raised plant is **Salvia superba**. The strains that have long been in cultivation and are usually propagated from cuttings, are sterile, but someone has presumably gone back to the wild plant for a seed-bearing strain. Few perennials are longer in flower than this, especially if you dead-head the first crop. Another perennial you might not think of raising this way is **Euphorbia epithymoides** (*polychroma*), always a comely plant, right till October when its foliage frequently takes on warm autumn tints. In late April and early May it is bright even among spring flowers, with its mounds of fresh yellow, shot with green.

One is, naturally, gratified by a perennial that will oblige by flowering in its first year from seed. Though it carry but one flower, it is giving an earnest of its future potentialities. The **balloon flower**, *Platycodon grandiflorum*, will do just this; one flower in the first summer being about its limit. This is an excellent front-of-the-border plant, so long as it does not have to sit about for months on end in sodden, ill-drained clay. For its roots are fleshy, and all fleshy-rooted plants insist on good drainage. The species is about 2 ft. tall and not so showy nor its flowers so large as the cultivar "Mariesii". The latter comes true from seed in both its 'blue' and its 'white' versions, the former being, in fact, a rich campanula-blue and the latter a delicate French grey, slightly darker on the outside of the petals. From fat, balloon-like buds, the flowers open to 3-inch-wide stars, dished in their centres. The plants grow about a foot tall, but tend to splay outwards, which matters not at all. I realise that I grow clematis in a number of unconventional ways, but I was rather surprised, one summer, at being asked by a visitor the name of a blue clematis that was flowering on the ground in a certain part of the garden. It turned out to be this, the balloon flower. Be warned against the variety called Roseum, sometimes described as rosy pink. It is as dirty and washed-out a mauve as the equally deceptive 'pink' lavender.

Platycodons not only look as though they belong but actually do belong to the *Campanulaceae*, and fleshy roots are a feature in this family. **Codonopsis** species are similarly endowed. The stem *codon*, incidentally, occurring again here, means a bell. Botanists ring the changes between this and the synonymous *campana*, when they wish to designate a bell-flower. The codonopsis flower quite quickly from seed. They are, for the most part, easily grown but not always so easily placed. Being rather fragilely constructed plants, they must not be allowed to get crushed by hearty, extrovert neighbours. Furthermore, they are often exquisitely coloured and marked *inside* their bells, and so they should, ideally, be sited above eye-level, if that can be organised; at the edge of a retaining wall, for instance. But a rock garden will usually provide the happiest opportunities. *C. clematidea* is the best known: about 18 in. tall, carrying a succession of milky blue bells with a bold pattern inside, including orange and blue-black. A fact I feel obliged to mention is that it has a strong, foxy smell. *C. convolvulacea*, although herbaceous, has a climbing habit. Plant it at the front of a small shrub, where its fragile stems will not get accidentally destroyed. *C. ovata* is another charmer, and quite low growing. Seed of all these is available from Thompson and Morgan of Ipswich, famed for specialising in the unusual.

Incarvilleas are among the most surprising of hardy perennials. They belong to the bignonia family, and are hence cousins of the catalpa. But the flowers of *Incarvillea* 'Bee's Pink' resemble a gloxinia's and, flowering in May, they look, in the spring garden, as though they had lost their way—especially as their stalks appear to be too short for the clusters of soft pink, wide-mouthed trumpets. However, this is one of the clearest coloured incarvilleas, and by June its stems are rather longer. *I. delavayi* is seen more frequently. It makes a larger plant, carrying smaller flowers at the 2- to 3-ft. level, but they are a nasty, muddy magenta. These are all very fleshy-rooted, making thick fangs, so they should be left alone, once planted in well drained soil; and it is advisable to mark your groups, as they disappear completely from autumn till May, showing through, again, only a week or two before flowering. Seed really provides the only feasible method of increase, though it takes three seasons to get a flowering plant. In the first year, the seedlings can be pricked out into a box as soon as large enough to handle. Their roots are stumpy and shallow at this stage. They can spend the second year growing on in this box, undisturbed, and be planted out in their final positions in the early spring of their third season.

Asclepias tuberosa is a further example of a hardy plant belonging to a predominantly tropical family, *Asclepiadaceae,* of which the greenhouse climbers, *Hoya carnosa* and *Stephanotis floribunda,* are well known examples. *A. tuberosa* will flower in its second year from a spring sowing. It is another plant that comes into growth exceedingly late, and should thus be marked. Unlike the others so far mentioned, it rather seems to like my stiff soil, but will not tolerate lime. Growing to about 18 in. tall, it carries umbels of rich, deep orange flowers in July and August. The colour is singularly intense. Each flower is less than an inch across and star-shaped, but made more than usually interesting by the curiously embossed structure of its stamens. The stems are rather weak at the base, so a little discreet support at a low level is worth giving.

It associates particularly well with the intense blue spikes of **Salvia patens.** If you save your tubers of the latter tender perennial and overwinter them in slightly damp soil or peat in a frost-free place, they will flower at just the right time for the asclepias. But *S. patens* is also easily and quickly raised from seed to flower, and can be treated as an annual. In this case, however, it will be at its best in the months of August and September.

Eryngium alpinum is gradually achieving belated recognition; it is a wonderful border and flower arranger's plant. Growing 3 ft. tall, it has large blue flower heads; but instead of one rather unfriendly ruff of spiky bracts, as in most sea-hollies, it carries them in several rows, and they are lacy and quite soft to the touch. I originally grew mine from seed, and I think I am right in recollecting that it did not germinate until the second spring. Anyway, one should not lose hope if nothing happens the first year. The seed-pan should not be coddled, and needs no protection. A spell in the frig, after sowing, might speed things up.

The **alpine thistle**, *Carlina acaulis*, is another exquisite flower-arranger's plant, and is everlasting. Despite the fact that its name suggests stemlessness, it does grow about a foot tall, even in the wild. The disc, which turns pure white when ripe, is 2 in. across, and is surrounded by inch-long bracts that dry out to the colour of tarnished silver. This is a good garden plant, too, beloved of butterflies during its late-summer-flowering season. Seed germinates within a fortnight of sowing and you can propagate established plants from root cuttings, if you want to.

Veratrum nigrum was introduced from its native South European habitat as long ago as 1596, but has always remained comparatively rare because it is so slow of increase. Long-established clumps are a dramatic garden feature, and the plant is absolutely hardy. It belongs to the lily family, and makes an exciting start each spring with a bouquet of broad, pale green, pleated leaves—slightly reminiscent of a hosta's and no less popular with slugs. From these arises a stout, self-supporting, 5-ft. flowering stem that branches into a compound pyramid, clothed in scores of tiny star-shaped flowers. They are the rich brownish-purple colour of the darkest tulips. These are followed by winged seed-pods, and the whole structure dries out so decoratively that it is whisked indoors to serve another stint. *V. viride* makes a very similar plant, but is not quite so striking in flower, but *V. album*, in a pure white strain, is most effective, with larger blooms.

These veratrums seed freely, and the seeds, sown in spring, quickly put forth a root, but the first leaf does not appear until the spring a year later, and the seedlings will not want pricking out until a year after that. So they are left undisturbed in their seed pot for the first two years. Progress thereafter is still slow and you are unlikely to get a flowering spike before the fifth year. So, if you decide to buy plants instead of going through with the rigmarole yourself, don't be surprised should they seem expensive.

Melianthus major is not as hardy as one would wish, but so ravishing a foliage plant, with its large, divided, sea-green leaves, that a slight effort on its behalf is tremendously well repaid. Actually, although plants are almost invariably cut to the ground each winter, they survived the deep and prolonged frosts of 1963 in my garden without protection. But this imposes such a check on their growth that the next season they come to life too late to be much use. What you should do is to lift your plants in late autumn and overwinter them in a cold cellar or cool greenhouse, planting them out again in May. Alternatively, cover your plants *in situ* with a thick quilt of bracken or fern fronds. Established plants usually make several strong 3-4 ft. stems, but sucker mildly from the base, and one can take cuttings, in late summer, from these basal shoots. Seed is also available from Thomas Butcher of Shirley, Croydon, Surrey. It germinates well in slight heat, and young plants grow quickly. Melianthus is a fine gap-filler in any part of a border. I have liked it best when the broadly feathered leaves, which are carried in a more-or-less horizontal plane, are contrasted with the vertical spears of a dark-leaved canna—preferably the near-wild type, in which the rather narrow leaves are more important than the small red flowers.

Trees and Shrubs from Seed

One of the more eccentric lists that annually comes my way is from the Italian nursery Barilli & Biagi, of Bologna, marketing seeds of trees and shrubs. It arrives (unlike most seed lists) in autumn and one wishes that orders placed would do likewise because the seeds of many shrubs and trees quickly lose their vitality. Magnolias and peonies come to mind. By the time their seeds reach us in spring, they are dead. Then, again, other seeds need a period or periods of freezing before they will germinate and this, again, they can naturally get if sown in the autumn. Most of the rose family, from apples to cotoneasters, fall into this category, as do the spindles. However, the seeds do not arrive until the new year.

The list is mainly used by nurserymen, though there is no restriction to wholesale trade, but the seed is sold by the pound rather than by half-ounces or packets. It arrives in comely cotton bags which are found, on untying, to contain not only the seed but all the pods, husks or, in the case of conifers, the cone scales of the fruiting part of the plant. With some items the seed has been cleaned and a pound of it (for instance *Arbutus unedo,* the strawberry tree) will go a very long way.

One of the terms of business is that orders of less than 4 oz. per item cannot be accepted. This is all very well in some cases like, for instance, *Fraxinus ornus,* the manna ash, which sells at 1s. 6d. per pound. Four ounces of this will quickly give you material enough to make a plantation of several acres. But when I wanted a batch of *Indigofera gerardiana* (listed by its old name *I. dosua*), it set me back a bit to find it priced at 227s. per pound.

I should think three-quarters of the items are listed under outdated or misspelt names, and by and large, this list strikes me as extraordinarily haphazard. It includes many items that one would not have thought anybody would want and yet omits what would seem to be obvious candidates, such as *Acer griseum.* All the same, it is fascinating, as any such list must be to those of us for whom the growing of trees (especially) and shrubs from seed is a compulsive and unreasonable mania against which we can put up no kind of resistance. 'But what are you going to do with them all?' is a question to which we turn a deaf ear. Who knows but what we may not want an arbutus spinney? Imagine sauntering among their rust-red trunks, on a balmy autumn day, when the branches are laden both with fruit and with waxy white blossom on which red admirals are regaling themselves.

When you sow tree seeds, it must always be in a spirit of patience and dedication with a limpid, far-away look in your eyes. (Try to emulate the *allwissende* Erda of Wagner's *Ring*). Either everything will come up or nothing, or (a further possibility to keep you guessing) just one plant. I sowed a quarter-pound of catalpa seed (listed as *Bignonia catalpa*), and it yielded me exactly one strong, upstanding seedling. As I do not want a catalpa and have recently got rid of one from my garden, one seedling was enough. Then I sowed a quarter-pound each of *Magnolia soulangeana* and *M. denudata* (listed as *M. Yulan*). Result: one seedling, I forget of which, but anyway it later damped off. However, a nurseryman of my acquaintance got a nice batch of *soulangeana* seedlings from the same source, though in a different year. So perhaps it was just me (I'm joking, of course).

Any very hard seeds should be soaked for a day or two before sowing and it helps to chip them individually with a knife or razor blade, otherwise they are so effectively sealed off from their environment that they cannot absorb the moisture necessary for germination. Such are the majority of legumes: *Sophora, Gleditschia, Genista* and other pea-flowered shrubs. Seed of many trees that do not readily set or ripen in the climate of Britain, is much more likely to give results for having come from the Mediterranean: for instance, the Judas tree, *Cercis siliquastrum*, a Mediterranean by birth.

Never throw the contents of your seed pots away after only one season of inactivity. Keep them till all is green with mosses and liverworts, for much seed is slow to move.

Here, then, are black mulberries for your delectation, olives to make your own grove; pomegranates to press against your sweetheart's lips; gum trees wherewith to build her an arbour of odorous branches. This is heady stuff for the enterprising.

Choosing from the Seed Lists

I find going through the seed lists hard work—like playing half a dozen fish simultaneously, without getting your lines crossed. It is worth drawing on the resources of up to half a dozen firms, because their fortes will be different in each case. The difficulty always is to know what to leave out. Come the spring, we shall be as rushed as we always are. Coping with a mountain of seed packets is tough enough, but to keep up with the resulting progeny invariably ends in some getting so box- or pot-bound as to be virtually useless.

The old are as enticing as the new, when we make our choice:

plants like mignonette, which we suddenly realise we have not grown for years and long to smell again; or an old-stager, perhaps *Hunnemannia fumariifolia* (from Thomas Butcher), which has just been a name to us all our lives—something we skip because the words look forbidding, but pause at now, for once. Can a thing called hunnemannia be beautiful? It can, indeed; a sort of cross between a poppy and an escholtzia, with large, soft yellow blooms offset by lacy glaucous foliage.

Where novelties are in question, presentation on the printed page must be persuasive. On reading of 'New Improved Tetra Snaps Giant Ruffled Tetraploid,' we may not react in quite the manner intended. And it may curl us up to be confronted by 'Antirrhinum, Double Formula Mixed.' We can see that the formula got mixed, right enough, from the picture. I had not realised, before, that **snap-dragons** had entrails; but there they are, being coughed up before our eyes.

However, some of the newer tall growing strains are tempting: the first-cross (F1) Rocket hybrids, for instance. F1 hybrids are always excellent of their kind. They are the result of crossing two very pure, inbred lines, and the product has great vigour and high quality. I have two things against them, in certain cases including the present one. The seed is expensive to produce and expensive to buy; that's fair enough. But you get so few in a packet and they can be so small, that your sowings and after-care have to be desperately meticulous if you are to get any results at all, let alone value for money. The other thing against these Rocket hybrids is that they are available only in a mixture, not in separate colours. Still, there are other tall antirrhinums that can be so obtained: the Tip Top series, for instance, and as you get a nice lot of seeds to a packet I think these are probably still the best buy.

Tall antirrhinums are most useful in borders. They grow to 3 or 4 ft. and need support, but little else can give us long, hand-some spikes quite like these. A tall yellow antirrhinum would contrast well with the blue, rather horizontal lines of *Eryngium oliverianum*, for instance. Or it could help to pull together the attenuated spikiness of perovskia, again in blue.

It was always a matter of regret to me that the best coloured, dwarfest **heliotropes** (cherry-pie) were all named varieties, which had to be perpetuated from autumn cuttings and overwintered at a minimum temperature of 50° F. The seed strains, whatever their catalogue write-up, always resulted in a ragged assortment of plants up to 3 or 4 ft. high and of generally washed-out colouring. But we now have a strain called Marine that really is almost what it purports to be: a rich, deep purple, with very dark foliage and growing to no more than 2 ft. It does not have the branching habit claimed on its behalf. Its scent is weakish, as heliotropes go; but from a good-sized batch you receive an adequate waft. Here is another plant with which pale antirrhinums would contrast effectively.

The annual **rudbeckias** are a tremendously showy tribe of Black-eyed Susan, carrying enormous daisies in a continuous succession from August till the end of summer. They grow 3 or 4 ft. tall and are the better for individual staking—one cane per plant. There is a modern strain called Gloriosa daisies, described as 'fantastically huge'. They are, indeed, impressive, but, by reason of the flower being double, I missed the jet-black central cone. Many single strains have a mahogany zone around the centre, but this again detracts from the eye's fullest impact. My highest recommendation goes to Autumn Glow (from Sutton's), in which the dark eye is framed by a double row of long, golden-yellow rays.

Lilium formosanum is an extraordinarily variable species as to its hardiness and stature. The least hardy strains grow 4 ft. tall and are excellent for pot work and for raising under glass, for eventual use as cut flowers. Sutton's list theirs as *L.f.* 'Pricei'. The hardiest grow only 9 in. or 1 ft. tall, and can be colonised under trees among hardy cyclamen, for instance, or with other bulbs. Seed of the latter can now be obtained from Unwins of Histon, Cambridge and from George Roberts of Faversham, Kent, as *L.f.* 'Little Snow White'. The scent, in this species, is particularly pleasing, while the flower shape—a long trumpet—is even more graceful than the better known *L. longiflorum*. *L. formosanum* sown during January or February in heat, will carry one bloom apiece the very same year, from July onwards. Impatient gardeners take note.

For two successive years I grew the early strain of **sweet williams** called Messenger Mixed. They start flowering about a fortnight earlier than the standard types, and are at their best throughout June. The one considerable advantage in an early-flowering strain that I can see, is that you can sweep it out of the way in the first week of July in order to replace it with an annual (sown in May) for late summer and autumn display. The later-flowering strains of sweet williams scarcely give the follow-on plants enough time to make the most of themselves.

The Messenger sweet williams are a step in a useful direction but the strain needs improving considerably to bring it up to the level of its later confrères. The colour range is limited. It excludes salmon shades and the only pure and vivid scarlet flowers are borne on plants that come into flower just as all the rest are going over. This, of course, defeats the whole object of the exercise.

I have grown the 'Excelsior' **Digitalis** hybrids for many years, and consider them to be an excellent strain of foxglove. Recently, however, I have returned to the more traditional type in a Giant Spotted selection, and decided that I liked it better. The advantages of the Excelsior strain are that it flowers all round the spike and holds its blooms in a near-horizontal position, so that their speckled interiors are easily appreciated. This arrangement sounds clumsy in print, but is not so in fact. Yet the one-sided spike is more graceful, after all, and if the plants are well grown, reaching a height of 6 ft. and over, it is no effort to look into downward-hanging gloves. And the Giant Spotteds have magnificent, maroon blotches.

What curious conventions the traditionalist seedsmen display in their use of plant names for their catalogue entries. They use Sweet Pea, Wallflower, Honesty and Aster as primary headings, rather than *Lathyrus, Cheiranthus, Lunaria* and *Callistephus,* but prefer *Antirrhinum, Aquilegia* and *Digitalis* to Snapdragon, Columbine and Foxglove. Some groups find them mixed up: Canterbury Bell is listed as such rather than as *Campanula medium.* All the other bell flowers come under *Campanula,* however, but without even a cross-reference to the Canterbury Bell. Certain pinks are listed under *Dianthus* but *D. barbatus* and *D. caryophyllus* must be sought for under Sweet William and Carnation. Stocks are listed as Stock but the Night-Scented Stock finds itself in-flated into *Matthiola bicornis.*

Double daisies are sometimes listed under Daisy but oftener

under the more dignified and pompous style of *Bellis perennis*.
Perhaps this makes the identical relationship with the little flower
that is a weed in our lawns, easier to forget.

The marigolds have a peculiarly dotty treatment. Most *Tagetes*
are listed under Marigold but just a few of the small flowered
ones come under *Tagetes*. And the plant I was always brought up
to think of as the true marigold is referred to as *Calendula,* usually
spoken with accent on the third syllable. Ugh!

Surely, almost every gardener, nowadays, who can give an
alternative name to the Red Hot Poker will correctly use *Kniphofia,*
yet the seedsmen persist in the antique synonym *Tritoma*.

Raising Your Own Bedding Plants

This country has a flourishing and expanding industry in bedding
plants. Already, 280 million plants are supplied for the market
annually, and according to one survey over 40 per cent. of garden-
owning households are purchasers. It would be interesting to know
what percentage raise some, at least, for themselves. Most of us
realise that by growing certain lines of vegetables we will fare
better than on the frozen, canned or 'fresh' retail product. It is
the same with bedding plants.

The qualities that make a good bedding plant were defined by
a well known plant breeder in this genre before a packed Bedding
Plants Conference, not so long ago. It should, he said:

1. Perform well in a wide diversity of conditions

Plate 7.   Above, one of the most spectacular forms of woodland
gardening is achieved by the colonising of polyanthus, as here shown
in the nut walk at Sissinghurst Castle, Kent. Although they look so
happy and relaxed, a great deal of work is involved in keeping them
weed-free and in continually replacing worn-out or virus-infected
plants with healthy young seedlings.

Below, the snakeshead, *Fritillaria meleagris,* is a British native, inhabit-
ing water meadows. Given a stodgy piece of permanent turf, it can be
naturalised in the garden. Start off with a cheap batch of bulbs and,
provided you leave the grass uncut until late June, they will seed
themselves and make a colony. Flowering in April, the typical colouring is purple, but albinos are common and so are intermediate shades.

2. Give a long period of flower and/or foliage
3. Look attractive when sold
4. Transport well and transplant well
5. Be easy to grow and cultivate
6. Have good resistance to disease

Now let us consider these propositions as they affect the gardener. Points 1 and 5 are almost identical. The good bedding plant has got to be able to flourish as well on sand as on clay; in a dull, wet summer as in a hot, dry one; in a sheltered but grimy urban cat-run as in a salubrious seaside wind-trap. Well, that may not be a bad aim to have at the back of your mind, but a good deal more impossible of fulfilment these days than wishing for the moon. And any plant that succeeds in being all things to all gardens in this way, is likely to be a very dull plant. A gardener raising his own plants is in a much stronger position, however. He will soon find out which are likely to relish his conditions. As for the weather to be expected in any given growing season, he just takes a risk on, say, petunias, and balances the likelihood of failure against his love of the flower.

The second point, concerning the length of display, touches most of our hearts because a main reason for growing summer bedding plants at all is their extended season as compared, say, to bulbs or the majority of herbaceous perennials. Still, there is a freshness about a display of nemesias or of the annual mesembry-anthemum that the ubiquitous marigold could never match. The brevity of the former's contribution has compensations that should

Plate 8.   Above, in a good clone, *Hydrangea villosa* is the most exciting of the whole tribe. The lacecap-type flower heads vary little in colouring whatever the soil and are in season late August and early September. The large, felted leaves are rather easily damaged by sun scorch after rain, by wind and, when young, by late spring frosts, but the shrub is winter hardy.

Below, *Hydrangea paniculata* is bone hardy in every part of the British Isles. Characterised by its cone-shaped head of white flowers, it is seen at its most elegant in this form called Floribunda in which large sterile and small fertile florets are evenly mixed. As they fade, they flush pink.

W.T.G.   G not be ignored. And it is not difficult for the seed-sowing amateur to follow his June and July display of nemesias with a subsequent show from late-sown annuals.

Point 3, on the attractive appearance of the plant when sold, too often boils down to an insistence on its already being in flower when the sale is made. The customer can then see what he is getting—or at least he thinks he can. What he does not see is that overcrowding and starved conditions at the root have forced the plant into premature bloom. And once it has started blooming there is little or no chance of its going into reverse; that is, of its making a good, leafy plant of considerable substance before it starts making flower buds. To some extent the marketer of bedding plants can get over this one by displaying an attractive coloured photograph of how the subject will presently look, next to boxes of plants that are still all greenery. But there will always remain the irresistible temptation to trade on the folly of the masses.

Point 4 requires that the plant shall transport and transplant well. And yet some of the most fragile plants to handle are the most satisfactory once they are established in the garden. What future can there be for mesembryanthemums, portulacas, eschscholtzias and the related hunnemannias, for larkspurs, cornflowers, bartonias and venidiums as marketable bedders? It would be cruel, having once become acquainted with their charms, to be forever denied them.

On the desirability of resistance to disease there can be no argument from any viewpoint.

A current fashion, stressed at this conference, is towards plants of dwarf habit. The truth of this observation is quickly established by conning the names of cultivated varieties in any seedsman's list. The adjectives baby, pigmy, fairy, wee, little, bambini, thumbelina, dwarf compact and nana compacta, occur over and over again. I hope it is but a fashion. You have only to think of the front gardens you drive past in summer that are planted up almost entirely with dwarfs to realise how lacking in character and individuality they are. Such plants never get off the ground; they are mere colour explosions.

Clearly, then, if we don't want to follow the fashions, we must be prepared to fall back on our own resources, to raise our bedding plants ourselves and thus achieve the variety and range that will make our hobby so much more pleasurable.

Everyone has their own ideas on the raising of annuals, so I might as well contribute a few of mine. I have pretty well given up sowing flower seeds direct in the borders where they are going to flower. This always sounds the simplest way of doing things, but really it is nothing of the kind. You catch your soil at the right state of dryness and break it down to a fine tilth by alternately raking and treading. The seed bed you have thus made is ideal not only for the seeds you sow on it but, still more, for all the weed seeds that were there already. If you drill your seeds in rows, so as to make the weed seedlings easier to cope with, the fact that your plants are in rows never ceases to be an obvious eyesore. Another point against direct-sowing is that, if it does not rain, the sparrows enjoy dust baths on the site and you have to erect wire netting or other deterrent entanglements. If it does rain, your fine tilth pans forthwith and then bakes into a cement cake that is a long way from ideal for the development of a young seedling.

One way and another, it is best to do all your sowing under controlled (and comfortable) conditions. Even cornflowers, mignonette and eschscholtzias, disliking root disturbance, can be sown a few to a small pot, thinned to a singleton and then transferred bodily to their flowering positions.

Don't sow your seeds too early. Siren voices from the horticultural press and other media aimed at the gardening masses will constantly be urging you to hurry up. 'Half-hardy annuals should be sown without delay', they'll tell you in early March, whereas Lloyd will be sowing his in early April and with no subsequent regrets. Seven weeks from sowing to planting out is long enough for most quick-growing annuals and the ideal timing is to have the plants ready to put out at the same moment as the ground and weather are ready to receive them. That is seldom before the end of May.

The aim of the gardening trade is, naturally enough, to get their customers garden-minded and in a constructive, buying mood as early in the spring as possible. Trade lost in these early weeks of February and March is never fully recouped in the inevitable Easter rush, so the earlier the better, as far as the salesman is concerned. All this is very understandable but, as thinking individuals, we don't want to be stampeded.

The easiest mistake you can make when sowing in pots and boxes is to cover the seed with too great a depth of compost. The thickness of the seed is the greatest depth with which it should be covered. I know this well, and yet I still make this mistake myself from time to time. Recently it was with some *Salvia patens* seed. This has a way of all germinating together and lifting the entire top layer of soil like a lid, or as you might have a corps of ballet dancers balancing an enormous tray above their heads at arms' length. 'I'll teach you,' thought I, as I covered the seeds with extra soil. 'You can jolly well push your way through that lot instead of balancing it on your heads.' They didn't try.

Some gardeners go to a lot of trouble in watering their pots and boxes, by holding them in water so that the moisture gradually percolates from the bottom to the surface. I have never found this necessary. Overhead watering from a fine-rose can is perfectly adequate. But as the first and the last drops that come out of the rose are the coarsest and heaviest, always start and finish your watering with the can pointing away from the seedlings. And never let the soil surface flood for a moment through putting more water on it than it can immediately absorb. This flooding is what shifts the soil and may bare the seeds or move them around so that they are all herded together. An easy, to-and-fro swishing motion of the can will do the job gently.

Pricking out should be done as soon as the seedlings are large enough to handle: the earlier, the less their roots are damaged. Many people seem to be all thumbs when it comes to a fiddling task like this, but those who are used to threading fine needles or other kinds of precision work will have no trouble. My mother, aged 90, still does all my pricking out for me and she handles seedlings when still so small that visitors to the potting-shed protest they can't even see them. It's a question of training. Hold each seedling gently by one ear and be careful not to bruise its stem or roots when settling it in with the tip of your dibber.

Now as to spacing. The bedding plants you buy are 54 (9×6) to the box, but this is false economy for they are dreadfully overcrowded. My own standard spacing is 28 (7×4) except for small or slow-growing subjects like portulacas and leptosiphon, when you can get by with 40 to a box (8 × 5). A deep box of at least 2½ in. is best. Then, when it comes to planting out, you can detach each plant from its neighbour with a really good ball of roots on which the soil will hold.

If you raise the best possible plants by sowing at the right time, pricking out early and giving each seedling a generous spacing in the box, you will have such fine material at the end of May, that you will need only one quarter as much to do the same planting-out job as you would when they are grown the all-too-usual, starved way. Furthermore, planting out itself will not impose the check it would from an overcrowded box, and thus the young plants will be off to a flying start.

Seeds for May Sowing

The misguided enthusiast will sow his zinnia seeds in a heated greenhouse in March and be pricking them out in early April. And then what? Like many other tender annuals, **zinnias** loathe the chilly weather that is inevitable at one time or other in May. It gives them a pinched appearance, makes their leaves turn yellow and renders them prone to damping-off troubles. From a March sowing, the seedlings will be ready for planting out a month before it's safe to do so. They will just have to kick their roots in their pots or boxes under glass. Such delay is a severe and quite unnecessary check.

The first half of May is the ideal time for sowing zinnias. If you have heated glass under which to start them, well and good; the seeds will germinate in four days and be ready for pricking out a week later. They transplant most readily when small, as soon as you can handle them. If you have no heated glass, only a cold greenhouse or frame, that will be quite warm enough at that time of year. You will lose only a few days by not having artificial heat. A mat rolled over a cold frame in the evenings is most useful for conserving sun heat far into the night, when you are bringing on seedlings like this or soft cuttings.

Another seed that should be sown late is **Tithonia rotundifolia,** a relative of the zinnia. By August, if the season is good, the plants will be 6 ft. tall. Late sowings of petunias can be made, too, and will be particularly useful for replacing mid-summer-flowering

102 The Well-Tempered Garden

biennials in early July. Or, if you are making a splash with a bed
of annual mesembryanthemums, for instance, these will run to
seed in July and can be replaced by May-sown petunias or other
annuals—stocks, for instance.

You can often arrange to follow one short-lived annual by
another. Admittedly, it makes a lot of work, and you will probably
not want to repeat the performance very often; but it is such a
pleasure to grow the old favourites occasionally that you may be
prepared to put yourself out for them. You could, for instance,
sow nemesias in May to follow an earlier display of Shirley
poppies, annual candytuft or godetias. Or, if the nemesias were
sown early to make the first display, sow another seed to take
their place in late summer—China asters, perhaps, or the rich
purple heliotrope, Marine.

I always grow a lot of sweet williams and foxgloves, and it is
really rather unenterprising not to follow them up with something. Cosmos are very quick maturing; a late sowing of these
would not need to be made till mid-May. Cleome, the spider
flower, should be sown about May Day and not be allowed to
become root-bound before planting out. Like zinnias and
tithonias, it does not need stopping. The leading growths don't
need pinching out to make them bushy. These will flower well
and earlier on their leading shoots, and will, given the space,
bush out naturally.

Venidium fastuosum is another annual that benefits enormously from late sowing. Indeed, early sowings usually fail
completely, and the seedsman is unjustly blamed. It is a South
African daisy with clammily felted leaves and buds, and has bright
orange rays with a large, glistening, boot-blacked disc. It grows
about 2 ft. tall and sprawls, but needs only enough support to
start it off when planted out.

Any of these late-sown annuals that are ready for planting out
a few weeks before their places are ready for them can be kept
happy by potting them on into 5-in. stiff paper pots, and giving
them a weekly feed with a liquid general fertiliser.. The great
thing is never to let them sustain a check. Then you will have
plants to be proud of.

I used to think that the climbing annual that is usually called
Ipomoea rubro-caerulea (correctly *Pharbitis tricolor*) with the

thrillingly blue and large convolvus trumpets, was suffering from a virus disease, as one usually sees it grown. The leaves are so often distorted and yellow and growth so stunted. But no; this is nothing more abstruse than the effect of low temperatures and can be avoided in the simplest possible way by sowing and planting out when it is no longer cold. This is, let's face it, a plant that will do really well in the garden only in those rare years, like 1959, when we have a roasting summer. But it's better to sow hopefully each year than to find, too late, that you could have been successful had you but acted in time.

Another related climber requiring exactly similar conditions and treatment is *Quamoclit* (*Mina*) *lobata*. Its clusters of tubular crimson-orange-and-yellow flowers are fascinating.

The **chimney bell flower**, *Campanula pyramidalis,* is a plant that gardeners constantly forget to do something about until it is too late. When they see them in flower, in July and August, they have already missed the boat for the next year. Seed must be sown in spring and the plants are treated as biennials.

The mauve and the white strains are equally beautiful, but it is only as a pot plant that this campanula is worth growing. Then it will last in beauty for three weeks at least and can be splendidly architectural, rising to 7 ft. in a series of spires. The plants themselves are hardy and can be overwintered in their final 10-in. pots in a cold frame. The reason they are unsuccessful in the garden is because the bees pollinate their flowers, and these then fade in a matter of three days, instead of three weeks. All campanulas are similarly bee-inflicted and are well worth growing as pot plants for indoor use, wherever possible. A comparatively rare biennial species, *C. formanekiana,* can be extraordinarily effective with its sea-green foliage and white flowers; but I don't know of a seed source at the moment; it is sometimes offered by Thompson & Morgan.

Seedlings that Sprout in the Spring

There are ash trees at the bottom of our garden. A belt of them was planted as a windbreak at the time the gardens were laid out, 60 years ago. This is the silly sort of choice that landscape architects have always been liable to make, through insufficient knowledge of the plant material they are recommending. One spring evening, I weeded 807 ash seedlings out of a bed containing two dozen HT roses. In fact, the job was pleasant enough and took only a quarter of an hour to get through, because, at this stage, you need merely to tweak the tops off the seedlings without bothering about their roots. But this sort of self-sowing becomes a real nuisance in a paved garden, for instance, where paving plants preclude the use of weedkillers, or in a hedge bottom, where young ash saplings can grow to a considerable size before they are noticed; by which time, of course, it is quite a struggle to pull them out.

The ash belt runs along the garden's west side, and we are very glad of its protection, from prevailing winds, when it eventually puts on its leaves at the end of May. But south-westerlies are often prevalent in autumn, and I well remember a gale at that season that strewed the whole garden with a litter of winged ash seeds, looking like the corpses of spent locusts. If the gales blow easterly at that season, we have crops of sycamore seedlings from the garden's opposite boundary. Sycamores are regular and prolific croppers, every tree being a seed-bearer without ever missing a year. But in some seasons, ash trees set no seed at all. Furthermore, a great many ash trees carry male flowers only, and are consequently non-seeders.

A saving grace in both ash and sycamore is that their seeds always germinate in spring; so we have a whole year in which to cope with one batch before the next horde comes along. Few garden weeds show the same restraint, but the prolific little ivy speedwell, *Veronica hederifolia*, is another such. This is a softly hairy, prostrate annual with a tiny, washed-out mauve flower that has none of the charm of the majority of 'granny's eyes.' It can be a great nuisance among low spring-bedding plants such as pansies, but will have vanished from the scene by midsummer. Once established, it is hard to eliminate, but the seeds are heavy and have no special method of dispersal, so this weed can usually, with a little care, be kept to one part of the garden.

Spring, again, is the time when **violet** seedlings appear in battalions, but they can be regarded as troublesome only in a limited sense. The wild, scented violet should really be allowed more scope in gardens. Tolerant of shade, it will grow harmlessly at the foot of all kinds of shrubs, where nothing else would do. It will peer out from the bottom of a hedge or make ribbons of colour when treated as a paving plant, or colonies in rough grass. The typical violet-coloured form is the readiest to flower precociously at any moment from autumn to spring. But there is also a clear pink variety, an albino and an apricot-shaded one. These are always ready to cross, one with another, their offspring developing an infinite variety of more or less pleasing, clean or muddy shades.

The North American *Viola cucullata* is a splendid plant, and an even more reckless self-seeder than other violets. Admittedly it is scentless, but you cannot have everything. Its flowers are enormous, wider than long, giving them a prosperous, well-fed look. They are white, but enlivened with mauve pencil-marks in the throat. The plant is completely deciduous, so that gardeners not yet familiar with its ways think that they have lost it in the very first winter. But it is used to colder climates than ours, and the evidence we should look for of its continuing existence is a series of interlocking, short-jointed, fleshy rhizomes, right at the soil's surface. Both flowers and young foliage appear in early May.

The **eryngiums,** or sea-hollies, are typically a tribe of taprooted perennials, but *Eryngium giganteum* is monocarpic. A plant may take two, three or even four years to reach flowering size, depending on how crowded its growing conditions are, but, having flowered, it dies. A mass of seed is set, but this does not germinate until the spring 18 months later. All of which may sound a great trial to the peace-loving gardener. But once established, a colony of this lovely plant, popularly known as Miss Willmott's Ghost, could not be less trouble, because it does all the work of sowing and growing for you. Your part will simply be the negative one of leaving those celandine-like seedlings alone or, at most, thinning them out a little. It is a sturdily-branching 3-ft. plant (by no means a giant), with greenish flower heads shaped like a large bullet-nose and surrounded by the really showy part, a ruff of silvery bracts. This is a wonderful flower-arrangers' plant, whether living or dried.

3. Features

Annuals, Biennials and Bedding

Why We Grow Annuals

It is very difficult to stand back and take a dispassionate look at one's garden; some weed or dead head will immediately intrude and occupy the centre of one's focus. But from time to time we can at least stand back mentally, when the garden is only before the inward eye, and ask ourselves questions about it. Reading some gardening book or catalogue will start a train of thought. Mr. Percy Thrower, in his practical guide on garden flowers, gives as his main reasons for growing annuals their advantage in providing a quicker and cheaper display of colour than any other flowers; also the fact that they will thrive in almost any soil. Indeed it must not be too rich, he says, or they will make a lot of leafy growth at the expense of flowers.

As I read these opinions, it struck me that there was something missing. If this were all, none of us would be growing annuals after the first few years of starting a new garden. Many annuals have a quality of gaiety and freshness that is especially gladdening, I find. This is not to say that other flowers are not similarly endowed, but annuals most of all. 'Here we are,' they seem to say; 'enjoy us while you may. We cannot stay for long.' I think one's childhood memories of annuals are some of the strongest. I always remember, in particular, the Shirley poppies coming into flower, and how my sister and I were allowed, each June morning before breakfast, to go into the garden and each alternately to choose and pick their newly opened blooms: the radiance of those silky gauds, sparkling with dew, and with their boat-shaped night caps still perched on a petal rim, is still with me.

I should always want annuals in my garden, whether there were gaps to stop and areas in need of pepping up, or not. Of course they are not all pristine and fresh. Your African marigolds have just about as much freshness as the leather of a new football, but without the quality of being easily kicked out of the way. However, this leads me to another point I should make in favour of annuals: that you can so easily ring the changes with them. If you tire of a herbaceous plant or, worse still, of a shrub, it requires a considerable effort of will-power to make you get rid of what is, after all, an established feature. But, as you browse through the new season's seed lists, you can freely indulge all the pleasures of change and variety.

Mr. Thrower's dictum that annuals must not have rich soil needs rather heavily qualifying, I think. A high proportion of the annuals one sees in private gardens are suffering, or have suffered at an earlier stage in their lives, from under-nourishment. Underfeeding is, in my experience, far commoner than overfeeding. Even a succulent annual like *Mesembryanthemum criniflorum,* or *Portulaca grandiflora*, that looks as though a starvation diet would suit it ideally, will actually reward you tenfold if you grow it on a well-nourished piece of ground such as you would accord your HT roses. True, an annual like the nasturtium can run to leaf and hide what flowers it has beneath this canopy if overfed; but some of the modern strains, like the compact, free-flowering Jewel nasturtiums, may pack up midway through the season from exhaustion, if grown where groundsel itself would only make a few flower heads.

I haven't the time for many annuals that are at their best in July and then quickly run to seed but I have a specially soft spot for the late-flowerers, typified by the China asters. In fact, from mid-August onwards the plants in my garden that attract most interest have been raised from seed sown that spring. Yet I have only to say, following an enquiry, that such-and-such is an annual, for all curiosity to evaporate. I suppose there are still gardeners who raise their own annuals, but they seem to be singularly few, which is sad.

Most annuals need a reasonably fine summer if they are to show what they can do. A difference of a couple of degrees in mean temperatures can make all the difference to the amount of growth they will put on, while too much wet in their flowering season will convert many to a sorry mush. Fortunately, fine summers are not nearly as rare as people like to make out. The English weather is always good for a hard luck story and so much can be blamed on it. The same years that produced good claret vintages will generally be found to tally with good years for annuals: 1959, 1961, 1962, 1964, 1967 and 1969 with 1966 a respectable runner-up. Not such a bad tally, surely.

Trying Out New Annuals

Never let your gardening become stereotyped and never take a plant or group of plants in your garden for granted. Even shrubs should be put through the hoop at regular intervals, and with annuals it is a crime to grow the same kinds in the same place year after year, simply because they were a success on the first occasion.

I always try out some that are new to me in every year and I shall here make a few suggestions which have nothing original about them: they are old and long cultivated species—but I shall be surprised, none the less, if they are all familiar to the reader, unless he is one of a few professional names I could count on the fingers of my two hands.

I have already mentioned **tithonias and cleomes** (pages 101-2), but they deserve a fuller treatment. I often grow these two together. The tithonias (if you gave them a good start) can be planted 3 or even 4 ft. apart; the cleomes about 2 ft., so that you don't have to raise many plants to fill a fair-sized border. But, being luxuriant annuals on a large scale, I recommend one stout 5 ft. cane for each tithonia and a less stout 3 or 4 ft. cane for each cleome.

Tithonia rotundifolia (*speciosa*) is a relative of the zinnia and likewise hails from Mexico. It naturalises easily in the tropics and is regarded as something of a weed in those parts; but if you have not been thus prejudiced against it, it will be generally acknowledged a handsome plant. Its large, heart-shaped leaves are rough textured, coarse and flabby, but the sombrero-like single flowers are a gorgeous and glowing blood-orange shade, borne on long, inflated stalks like the candle-holders of a branching candelabrum.

This annual is easy if not mishandled. It hates cold nights in spring, and young plants turn yellow and stunted under these conditions. It also dislikes any check to its extremely rapid growth, once it is under way. Sow in early May, pot the seedlings straight off into 5 in. paper composition pots and plant out, pot and all, in late June or early July to follow some biennial like foxglove or Canterbury bell.

Tithonia seed is not everywhere available: Sutton's and Blom's have given it up of recent years but it is offered by Thomas Butcher and by Thompson & Morgan.

Cleome spinosa (*pungens*), the spider flower, is treated in exactly the same way. There are two principal cultivars: Pink Queen, a bright, true pink, and Helen Campbell, white, which looks the better in front of tithonias. The plant's foliage is in this case a great asset, since it is palmately dissected like a horse-chestnut's and is a cheerful green. But it is also armed with vicious, hooked green spines that go unnoticed until they have clawed you, so it wants respectful handling.

Cleomes have been seen a good deal in London parks of late years and are used for unimaginative bedding schemes on the Continent. But when happily placed and well grown, this is a satisfactory annual, and of such a substantial build as often to be taken for a perennial. The irregular flowers are fascinatingly shaped, while the developing seedpods are like long green sausages, carried horizontally on even longer stalks. No plant suffers more or looks so miserable as this when its growth is checked in its youth.

Among the most stately of the **tobacco plants** is *Nicotiana sylvestris*. Its foliage makes as arresting a feature as does the elegant superstructure of long, tubular white flowers. It grows to 6 ft. or more but is very stout-stemmed and only a few plants need support even after a gale. They can be spaced $2\frac{1}{2}$ ft. apart. So it is altogether an annual that is economical of labour. Its flowers go only a little limp by day. At night they exhale an exotic perfume of creamy consistency—quite different from the scent of the usual nicotianas we grow, which are derived from *N. alata* (*affinis*). The latter's is delicious but with a certain roughness in its composition.

Of this type I recently grew a large bed of the mixed-coloured strain called Sensation. They do not, as proclaimed by the seedsmen, stay open by day unless it be dull and wet. They do make a fine display as evening approaches, but what has chiefly impressed me about them is their speed of growth. They were not planted out till the first week in July (to follow sweet williams) but were already in full bloom and completely covering the bed by the end of the month. By September they were getting rather floppy.

Gilia rubra (*coronopifolia*) was new to me until three years ago. It grows 5 or 6 ft. tall, eventually, but makes a narrow column and should hence be closely and generously planted, at a 9-in. spacing. The leaves are very finely divided and of a fresh green. The flowers—sized and shaped approximately like a phlox's, to whose family they belong—begin to open in late August or early September; a most beautiful, clear, soft shade of red with paler freckles near the centre. It is pleasant to be able to examine them at close quarters without stooping, let alone grovelling on one's hands and knees as for the better-known gilias. Individual staking is the price, however; with slender 4-ft. canes.

You can treat *G. rubra* as a half-hardy biennial, sowing the seed in early September and overwintering the pricked-out seedlings under glass. This produces a stronger and, earlier flowering plant. I'm trying this method out at the moment and can only report that the seedlings, which are in an unheated frame seem to be wintering well up to mid-January 1969.

Last year I grew a hedge of **Impatiens holstii** hybrids: the plant that everyone knows and grows indoors as Busy Lizzie. The vigour of this plant when it gets its toes into good soil, took me (and a large number of visitors) completely by surprise. The hedge grew 4 ft. tall and more across and I would have spaced my plants 2 ft. apart had I suspected what they were capable of. The impatiens leaf is a pretty coarse affair, but the flowers, in a range of bright and, somehow, pleasantly clashing pink, orange, carmine and red shades, are quite undeterred by bad weather. In fact the plants seem to revel in the miseries of a dank, dark summer and autumn. It started flowering in early August and went on till the very end of October. Furthermore, it showed a remarkable resilience to strong winds. I gave the plants no support. Time and again, they would get blown sideways and show villainous gaps in the hedge and I would think 'now they really have had it.' But within a couple of days the gaps had all closed in and the hedge was solid again. One thing this plant cannot abide is drought. But, by the same token, it can be grown in a wet border that gets no sun at all.

The annuals I have suggested so far have all been rather tall growing and late flowering. By contrast, **Anagallis linifolia** 'Phillipsii' (also listed as *A. grandiflora coerulea*) is prostrate and flowers continuously from June till October. It is an excellent edger. I am always being asked its name but I never have to spit it out (it is, after all, rather off-putting). All I have to say is 'it's an annual' and interest instantly evaporates, alas. Actually it is, technically, a perennial and certainly looks like one, but it is treated as an annual. It is a vivid, deep blue pimpernel that opens in all favourable weathers and is easy to please in this and other respects. In this country it never sets seed, which is a good thing because it means it never runs to seed but keeps growing and flowering.

Cladanthus arabicus is fun. Just another yellow daisy, you might say, but I am always ready to champion yellow daisies. They have abundant individuality. This one is distinct from others on account of its masses of finely cut, bluish-green foliage and by nature of its habit of growth, which is to make several branches immediately underneath each daisy. Each branch in turn produces another daisy and branches again, so that you soon have an intricate candelabrum, all at the 1½-ft. level but exceedingly bushy. Plants can be spaced 2 ft. apart.

Experiments in Bedding

The best bedding, in a private garden, is the least obtrusive. Or so I have concluded. Small beds that have been cut out of lawns can scarcely avoid looking self-conscious and uncomfortable. The happiest application of the bedding idea, even in a formally laid out garden like our own, is to let it take its place next to and in the same borders as permanent features such as shrubs and herbaceous perennials. In this way you are less likely to overdo it. On the other hand, continuity of interest, which is the forte of most bedding, will help to counteract any dullness that may have overtaken its perennial neighbours. Indeed the effectiveness of bedding out can be heightened by a sober juxtaposition of, say, shrubs in their non-flowering season. Informal bedding is my motto of content.

One also associates bedding with bright colours, though this is really a matter of choice. Certainly the breeders, in aiming at a compact plant covered with the maximum possible number of flowers have tended to produce bright colour in powerful blobs. Brightness can be pleasing; it is the blobs that tend to repel. Consider our most popular floral interpretation of the patriotic combination: red, white and blue; red salvia, white alyssum, blue lobelia. All three plants have been bred into a repulsive squat compactness. But it need not be so. If, for instance, you grow **Salvia coccinea** instead of *S. splendens* 'Blaze of Fire', you will have a sage whose colouring is no less vivid but there is much less of it, the flowers being smaller and fewer and spaced on longer stalks. They are charming. And so is sweet alyssum if, instead of having it in a series of symmetrical humps, like puff-balls, the plant is allowed to sow itself informally into paving cracks or on to pieces of gravel where weed-killers are in abeyance.

We can win freedom for **lobelias** by growing the trailing varieties that are recommended for hanging baskets and window boxes. But give them their chance on the ground. I grew one called Blue Cascade in association with *Diascia barberae,* which is a nemesia-like plant having soft pink flowers, shaped like a pixy hood, with twin spurs at the back. The whole idea would have been and, indeed, started out to be entrancing. But the lobelias were attacked by one of those wretched soil-borne fungi that go for some annuals and not for others. One by one they were struck down until, at the end of the season, only diascias remained. I must find this excellent and obliging plant some other blue companion—*Aster pappei,* perhaps.

It is my policy, whenever I can, to get my bedding plants into adjacent groups, rather than dot them fussily among each other. An effective pairing, I was told by a friend in the seed trade, is *Verbena aubletia* (which should be called *V. canadensis*) with marigold (*Tagetes*) Petite Lemondrop (the sort of name I find hard to resist). So I tried it out, but, being unfamiliar with both components, I did not know which would grow the taller and, hence, which to plant behind the other. So, in this case, I decided to jumble them up, *ad lib.* The result was ludicrous. The verbena, with a good, stiff upright habit, grew to about a foot, which was twice as high as the marigold. Perhaps this was no bad thing, as the latter was several shades more orange than my idea of lemon and looked appalling next to the screaming magenta of the verbena. Actually I have a sneaking affection for magenta, in the right circumstances, and I can still visualise the verbena in a happy association with a really pale, almost primrose yellow.

I had greater success with an annual Chabaud carnation called **Giroflée,** grouped behind a permanent clump of *Senecio cineraria* 'White Diamond'. The latter can be grown as a replaceable bedding plant, but it is the hardiest cultivar within its species (often known, incidentally, as *Cineraria maritima*) and, since it survived the 1962–63 winter, I have regarded it as a permanency. All grey foliage plants tend to develop the best, that is, the palest, colouring on poor soils and some gardeners even assist them in this by growing them in pots where the roots are restricted and starvation diet gives the foliage an 'interesting' pallor. Without any such inducement, and even on my rich and heavy soil, White Diamond is the palest of the pale, except for a few weeks in spring after I have cut the plants hard back into old wood, and the new foliage is at first (especially when wetted by dew or rain) rather green.

Giroflée is in gentle shades of magenta, verging towards purple, described in the catalogue as violet-pink. It is warm and bright and admirably offset by grey foliage. Many of your brightest colours are most happily teamed with grey; not, however, using the latter as dot plants in a molten waste of salvias, as one has so often seen them in public gardens. The brighter the flowers, the higher the proportion of grey needed. If you had to have scarlet salvias, they would look best in small groups against a background of grey occupying three quarters of the allotted area. On the other hand, pink-and-white bedding begonias, being altogether softer-toned, could reverse the ratio and themselves be three to one of santolina or *Centaurea gymnocarpa* or whatever.

One of the most palatable ways I know wherewith to dilute the shocking pinks of the most popular ivy-leaved pelargoniums is to grow them with **Helichrysum petiolatum.** The sprawling habit of both plants suits them to window-boxes and ornamental tubs and pots, but they are no less effective on the flat, where a certain stiffness in the helichrysum stems allows them to flick upwards with the pleasing bumpiness of white horses on a choppy sea (pleasing, that is, to an onlooker, comfortable on the shore). If you want extra height here and there, nothing could be easier than to train either plant up a cane, sited wherever the need occurred. The pelargonium will then flower at a height, while the helichrysum, so treated, will make a miniature tree with leader and symmetrically arranged lateral branches. It has felted, heart-shaped leaves about an inch across.

The most popular ivy-leaved is Galilee with flowers in what has been described as tooth-paste pink, but it is quite unnecessary to battle with this raw colouring. The pale pink Mme Crousse is prolific and showy and a much more amenable shade. Into this pink-and-grey confection you could introduce mauve in the person of the **Verbena** 'Loveliness'. It has the splendid mat-forming habit and long-flowering season of the cherry-red Lawrence Johnston; it carries equally large heads of blossom that are even more powerfully scented and in a strong shade of mauve that yet has none of the aggressiveness of *V. rigida* (*venosa*).

There are some good colour strains of bedding verbenas available from seed, but further developments could easily be achieved in this line, and, at present, Lawrence Johnston and Loveliness have to be bought as plants and perpetuated from cuttings struck in September or October. There is also a dazzling red cultivar called Huntsman. It is an improvement or the older Firefly, with more strongly branching growth and larger blooms. Both derive from the prostrate *V. peruviana* (*chamaedrifolia*) that is sometimes bedded into rock gardens for the summer, and none of this group has any scent. The modern seed strain called Dwarf Compact Blaze would be an adequate substitute. One year I grew Huntsman in front of a group of *Salvia patens*. A very strong red in front of a very pure deep blue could be overpowering, but there were sufficient mitigating factors: no other bedding nearby, a background of cool juniper, much greenery in the plants themselves, and *Salvia patens* anyway dispenses its blue favours with economy, seldom more than two flowers on a stem opening simultaneously.

Sweet williams are everybody's favourite until it comes to growing them, which makes quite a lot of work. The seeds are safest sown in boxes, under glass, in early April; then pricked out, lined out for the summer and bedded into their flowering positions in autumn. If sown too late, say in June, sweet williams won't flower properly the next year; only the year after. Mixtures containing a high proportion of selfs look boldly effective whereas mixtures of the auricula-eyed types, wherein the individual flowers are already a mixture, look hopelessly jumbled in the mass. Sweet williams should be massed, to be effective, not dotted among other plants. They can, however, be thickly interplanted with tulips, to provide an early display. All should be swept aside in the second half of July to make way for a planting of some late-sown annual.

Annual Carnations and China Asters

In 1964, I saw the annual types of **carnation** used so effectively for bedding, in a friend's garden, that I realised how unfair it is to grow them hugger-mugger in a squalid corner, merely for their use as buttonholes. This florist's flower has been spoilt, for many of us, by its stereotyped development into a huge, formalised rosette from which almost every vestige of scent has been eliminated. But in the annual types, the flowers are quite large enough, without any disbudding nonsense needing to be practised, and their scent is superlative. The other serious indictment that can be levelled at any carnation is its sprawling habit. From this the annuals cannot be excepted. To be acceptable, as plants, you must first of all grow them very well indeed, so that they are bushy with a wealth of shoots. Second, it is better, though not essential, to twig them, so that they cannot flop helplessly all over the place, as is their natural inclination.

The best strains of annual carnation are the Giant Chabaud and the Enfant de Nice. To the layman, there seems little to distinguish them; perhaps the latter are rather less frilly. You can buy named varieties or selected colours. Mikado, for instance, is a remarkable off-beat mauve. But the snag here is that the colours have not been selected rigorously enough, and you will get a large number of rogues of the wrong colours. If you have to root these out, you are left with tiresome gaps. So, until the seed-producer, Raoul Martin, in south France has sorted this one out, it is possibly wisest to go for a mixture. George Roberts of Faversham, Kent, is a principal distributor of this French seed, over here.

No carnation is truly an annual; those that we thus designate differ from the rest in that they can be flowered from seed in the year of sowing. But they tend to flower late, and the earlier you start them off, the sooner will their display be initiated; and this will continue until frost intervenes. If you can coax them into opening their first blooms by the end of July, you will have had excellent value from them by October (except in a wet season, when botrytis moulds will tend to spoil the blooms). This entails early sowing. I usually (unless I forget) sow mine in October and prick them out into John Innes No. 1 Compost as soon as they are large enough to handle. They over-winter in a cold frame.

Carnation seed will germinate at a temperature as low as 40° F., and you will do almost as well by sowing in February as from an autumn batch. The sooner you can get them bedded out in spring the better: April is the ideal moment. This is one of the few annuals that benefit from early sowing.

I have yet to discover why some people should be so stuffy about the annual **China asters**, *Callistephus sinensis*. There are some beautiful strains and in great variety of colour, habit and flower form. Perhaps the most satisfactory for general bedding purposes are the Princess asters. The freely branching plants, up to 2 ft. tall, should really be given some support; but, if you are lucky with the weather at flowering time, you can get away with omitting this. The blooms are abundantly produced from mid-August onwards. They are fully double and compact, the outer rays being flat; the inner rays are long and tubular (anemone-centred). A wide range of colours both obvious and subtle is included in a mixed packet.

China asters are effective when grown as specimens in 8-in. pots. For this purpose, the more giant the strain the better. I used the Mammoth type, one year, in which the 4-inch-wide blooms consist of flat rays right to the centre. My only criticism of these was in the rather high preponderance, within a mixture, of bluish-magenta shades—what the seedsman is pleased to call 'brilliant rose.'

The most interesting aster for cutting, and equally satisfactory as a bedding plant, is the Unicum strain, with needle-fine, quilled petals in a fully double flower. These are usually obtainable in mixture only, but the similarly formed Masterpiece Edelstein is a thrilling pure white strain. If badly selected by the seedsman, however, they can revert to the ostrich-plume-type flower, without quilled petals. So often, a breeder's new and carefully selected strain of a flower or vegetable is put on the market and makes a well merited impact on the public. But then, in the years that follow, seed is grown and harvested by commercial growers without the careful and expensive roguing and re-selection necessary to keep the standard up, until the strain is a mere shadow of its original self. In this sense I must reluctantly admit that the catchwords New and Novelty (when honestly used) do often indicate a higher standard.

In a summer with a wet tail-end, large-flowered double asters tend to go mouldy; it is then that the single flowered types come into their own. You may, in any case, prefer their untamed daisy flowers. I certainly like to give them an innings once in every few years.

Learning About Stocks

I am mad about **stocks** and must be forgiven for devoting considerable space to them here. Is this a neglected flower? Does it need championing? Probably not, although I was incensed to find that Percy Thrower, in his *Practical Guide to Garden Flowers* (which was supposed to cover annuals and biennials) omitted any mention of stocks except for the little night-scented *Matthiola bicornis*. That is quite a sweetie, and I don't grudge it a mention, but, but, but . . .

No, stocks are popular but they are not often well grown, as garden plants. They need some understanding. I am only beginning to understand them myself. Certain it is that their warm, air-borne fragrance is as endearing and nostalgic as the mignonette's whereas their flowers are a great deal more lively. Even the singles have an infectious vivacity, and the stock's colour range, with its special emphasis on mauve and carmine, is yet clean and clear. And white-flowered stocks are as full of character as any.

The stock-gillyflower, to give it its full name, is so called because it grows on a stock or stem and is thus distinguished from the clove-gillyflower (carnation) and wall-gillyflower (wallflower). If you were feeling argumentative you might protest that the stock is no stemmier than a wallflower. But the true perennial stock can be a very woody plant, making a sturdy, upright trunk in the course of a few years. It is a rare native of England and Wales, growing on sea cliffs, but must not be confused with the sea stock, *Matthiola sinuata*, which, however, does enter into the parentage of the East Lothian (or Intermediate) stocks. *M. incana* is the chief parent of our garden races but *M. i. annua*, from the Mediterranean, gave rise to the annual race of ten-week stocks—so called because they can be raised from seed to flower in 10 weeks (no very great claim to fame, I should have thought).

Normal garden practice treats stocks either as annuals or as biennials. The latter can sometimes be seen to have achieved perennial status in cottage gardens where they have been left undisturbed, after flowering, from one year to the next. Sooner or later, however, they are likely to be weakened and finally suc- sumb to the spotted wilt virus disease, which is also rife among their cousins the brassicas, not to mention wallflowers. Wall- flowers and stocks will often show virus symptoms by the break- ing of their flower colouring into stripes and streaks—as in broken tulips, but less attractively.

Stocks profit from well enriched soil and no plant shows signs of starvation, by a check to its growth or by prematurely flowering, more readily. But they also have an even more important pre- ference for a light, well-drained soil. Those who garden on sand or chalk start off at a great advantage. On heavy, water-retentive soils like my Wadhurst clay, stocks are much more subject to fungal diseases and it is well-nigh impossible to over-winter the biennial types as young plants in the open. They simply rot away.

There are a great many synonyms for the various series or strains of stocks. Every nursery likes to give its own strain a glamorous and new-sounding title, although it may, basically, be just another Brompton or ten-week stock. This makes for great confusion.

The handsomest annual series for bedding purposes are usually called Mammoth or Beauty (short for Beauty of Nice) stocks. They make large, bold, bushy plants with a central spike and numerous laterals, and are altogether more telling than the small and rather characterless dwarf bedding (Park) 10-week stocks. The only advantage in the latter is that they probably won't need any supporting whereas the former will be safer if given twigs.

No stocks should need stopping at any stage in their careers, incidentally. They will be bushy by nature. If they are not, then it's because you have starved them. Column stocks, exceptionally, do naturally produce just one large spike on a plant without branches. These are grown entirely for cutting.

The greatest colour range among stocks is available in the Mammoth series. Thomas Butcher lists no fewer than 24 named cultivars. If these stocks are sown in March or earlier, the chances are that they will be ready for planting out in May, before the ground or the weather are ready for them. They will get starved in their boxes, will flower prematurely and never make the grade. My greatest success with them has been from sowings on May Day. No artificial heat will be needed then. They can be sown in a cold frame. Next I pot the seedlings off singly into 3½-in. pots. This may sound laborious but it is little more so than pricking off into boxes and it makes all the difference. By the third week in June you have a really fine leafy plant to put into the garden and the plants will flower from mid-July till about the end of September.

What, you may ask, am I to do with my borders between May, when the spring bedding is cleared away, and the middle of June? Well, then, but suppose the stocks were ready for planting out in May, they would be over by early August and you would be faced with a problem of what to do with your borders until the autumn. You can't eat your cake and have it; you can't make your stocks flower beyond their natural stint. If you feel sore about this, grow marigolds, but don't invite me to come and see them.

The best known biennial stocks are the Brompton's. You sow in the first week of August or a little earlier, plant out in autumn, if your soil and climate are congenial, and they will flower in the following May and June. If your soil and climate are heavy and cold, you must pot these seedlings individually in autumn and overwinter them under glass. Even then, you are likely to sustain considerable damping-off losses in the winter, if your glass is unheated. The other biennial strain is the East Lothian or Intermediate and it can be treated in exactly the same way. Alternatively it can be treated as an annual, sowing it rather early, in March. It takes a long time to reach maturity and hence makes large bushy plants requiring no support. Flowering starts in July and August, but I find that it can't be relied upon even then and that some of the plants will go right through to the autumn without a sign of a bloom. In the winter they get killed.

Now to discuss double stocks, as against their single counterparts. As early as 1796, C. Marshall tells us that 'the French stock is very floriferous, and most apt to come double.' One doesn't want to be snobbish about this and the singles have their own charm but the double stock is of a beautiful rosette formation. Even those who claim always to prefer single flowers to doubles can hardly say so of stocks. What's more, the two kinds don't mix very well in the same planting, as the singles make elongated, straggling flower shoots as they set seed, whereas the doubles remain much more compact.

In a normal seed strain, singles and doubles will come out about half and half. By unconscious and, still more, by conscious selection at the seedling stage, however, the percentage of doubles can easily rise to 70. Doubles tend to grow the more strongly and it is anyway humanly natural to prick out the strongest looking seedlings and discard the weakest, which are probably singles. However, we can do better than this nowadays, since Hansen's 100 per cent. double strains were first put on the market in 1951. As is now well known, you sow at a temperature somewhere in the fifties, as usual, but when the seedlings' seed leaves have fully expanded you transfer them to a lower temperature, in the forties. After about 3 days under these conditions it will be found that some seedlings have dark green leaves, and these are the singles, whereas others with pale green leaves will bear double flowers.

These Hansen strains are available for Mammoth and Dwarf Bedding (Park) stocks, and also for the biennial Brompton stocks. A difficulty arises with these last, in that they are sown in summer when there isn't a hope of getting the temperature down below 50° F. However, the colour difference will still show in the adult foliage and you must grow your plants on till the autumn and make your selection in October or whenever you do get your first cold snap.

I sometimes have selection difficulties with late spring sowings. On one occasion I didn't sow my Beauty of Nice stocks until 1st June. It did turn a little chilly about the second week of that

month and I was able to do a bit of selection by dint of a good
deal of squinting while holding the box of seedlings under a grey
sky (sunshine is very off-putting, when matching colours). Only
some 15 per cent. of singles passed through my net. Following a
May Day sowing, however, you can be certain of a cold enough
spell in the course of that month to make possible a really efficient
selection.

The Hansen strains are not available in a particularly wide
colour range and they are not quite so easily grown to perfection,
I fancy. They do not therefore supersede the mixed strains, but
they are an important and welcome adjunct.

The Time to Sow Biennials

In the kingdom of the garden the aphorism '*Le roi est mort! Vive
le roi!*' exemplifies a timely shift in loyalties which applies precisely to **wallflowers.** As the old plants are being thrown out,
towards the end of May, so the seed of next year's display should
be drilled in the open ground.

If you grow wallflowers at all, it is always worth raising your
own; otherwise you will never get enough plants of a really
decent size to be able to treat them with the lavishness they
require. The individual is of a gawky, bony structure, only too
ready to be blown sideways and twisted about by six months of
gales, from October to April, or flattened by a fall of heavy snow.
Furthermore, from the time they are bedded out in autumn,
wallflowers do not grow any larger, on the contrary, by shedding
a proportion of their superfluous summer foliage, they actually
contrive to shrink. So they must be massed, cheek by jowl, with
the most extravagant abandon, each plant supporting and being
supported by its neighbours. Against this, it may be murmured
that so dense a treatment would leave too little space for interplanting tulips. Here I would suggest that the tulips themselves
will make all the more effective a foil if grouped on their own in
lots of 12, 25 or 50, near the wallflowers, either behind or in
islands among them.

There is a general tendency to sow biennials too late, not
giving them time to make fat plants before the autumn puts a
stop to their growth. All their bulk has to be made in the first

year, for in the following spring the plants' entire efforts will be concentrated on the business of flowering. Of course there is a danger, with certain biennials, that if sown too early they will set about flowering at half-cock in the same autumn, and be weakened as plants for the next year. Such is the behaviour of Brompton stocks, pansies for spring flowering, and certain of the mulleins like *Verbascum bombyciferum* or *V. olympicum*. But others, like foxgloves, Canterbury bells, sweet williams, anchusas and wallflowers themselves, can be sown as early as you please without running into this trouble.

Many gardeners may justifiably ask themselves whether wallflowers are worth bothering about at all. They are on the borderlines of hardiness, in Britain, and liable to succumb as bedding plants to wet autumns and winters or, equally, to cold. 'But I love the warm smell of them', you will protest; 'there is nothing else that comes near it.' Well, then try this for an idea. Wallflowers are perennials, if given the chance. Give them it. They naturally grow in cliffs and old walls—castle ruins, for instance, and, given this super-drainage, are perfectly hardy. You, too, could plant a few in or (more easily) at the top of a dry wall. Other suitable situations are at the bottom of a hedge (always a very dry place) or underneath an overhanging eave. We have them on the north side of our house, among ferns. They get scarcely any sun and yet they carry on for ever and ever. They have, in the course of 50 years, reverted to something very near the wild type, but are none the worse for that, in my opinion, and very often they produce extra-early blooms in March or even in February which one can snap off and bring indoors to savour in comfort. They keep themselves going by self-sowing and the ageing stragglers can be pulled out when tottering on the verge of senility.

Technically, **Anchusa azurea** (*italica*) and its cultivars are perennial. But to regard them as biennials saves much disappointment, for they either flower themselves to death at their first effort or, at best, to a condition of such weakness that old plants are never worth saving. For the next year's flowering, anchusa seed should be drilled alongside the wallflowers in May. Germination percentage is usually rather low, and it is worth any gardener's while to perpetuate a good strain in succeeding years, by taking his own root cuttings. The wallflower seedlings will need lining out in a spare plot during early July, but the anchusas can be left *in situ* until shifted to their flowering positions in the autumn.

I find the strain called Royal Blue quite satisfactory. Nobody, as far as I know, has invented a dwarf anchusa yet, thank goodness: the plant would thereby lose the nobility in its great branching panicles. But the taller strains can be a little unmanageable. Most catalogues describe the relatively low growing Royal Blue as a three-footer. However, unless starved, it should reach 5 or 6 ft. and does require support, but not much: one cane to each plant just as it is coming into flower.

A relative of anchusas and a true biennial to sow in the open in May is **Cynoglossum amabile,** often marketed as Blue Bird. Its colouring is pure azure, much paler than any anchusa's. The plants grow 2½ ft. high and, flowering in June, blend admirably with the bright pink, foot-tall *Lychnis flos-jovis* or contrast well, sited behind a mat of the lemon yellow, double sun-rose, *Helianthemum* 'Jubilee'.

Myosotis, the forget-me-not, comes in apropos as another biennial member of the same, borage, family. Gardeners seldom buy seed of this, which anyway tends to lose its viability when stored, so that germination is poor. It should, however, be mentioned in passing that storage methods have vastly improved of recent years. In the warehouse, seed is stored and keeps perfectly in a dehydrated atmosphere and can thereafter be distributed in hermetically sealed packets. Anyway, your own old myosotis plants will shed seeds that will germinate like weeds, but you do want to remember to look after the resulting seedlings so that they have made decent plants for bedding out by the autumn. The best policy is to line them out in a spare row for the summer.

Honesty, *Lunaria annua* (it used to be called *L. biennis,* but that was altogether too logical) is one of those hardy biennials that you won't lose once you have it. It seeds itself abundantly, and the gardener's only task is to remove the seedlings from where they are not wanted. The plant is best known for its decorative seed pods. When ripe and dry they are ghostly pale, but are also handsome when used green in flower arrangements, in early summer. The cruciferous flowers are carried in dense panicles and are themselves very showy in May. But do start off as you will (whether you mean to or not) go on, with a good, rich magenta colour strain, and not with one of the paler, muddy mauve strains that are also in circulation. The variegated-leaved honesty comes true from seed. There is no need to be put off by the fact that the seedlings are often green at first, because they develop their cream variegation later. Their flowers are not a good colour, so we must consider this, in the main, as a foliage plant.

Pansies and **double daisies** intended for spring flowering can be sown in late June. They need no protection, of course, but I find it best to start them in boxes, the seeds being smallish. Accidents are less likely to occur than in an open-ground sowing. Thereafter they are lined out till the autumn.

Some gardeners may care to consider the advantage of an autumn sowing of **antirrhinums.** I make mine on September 1 or thereabouts, and this timing seems to work out about right. The usual practice is to sow in February, in heat, the temperature not being allowed to drop below 50° F. Now this is quite a high temperature to have available at that season. If you delay sowing till late March or April, the plants will not be large enough early enough. An early autumn sowing gets round all this. The required temperature for germination is automatically there. The seedlings are pricked out in October and will be hardy enough by the time cold weather arrives to remain thus, in a cold frame, throughout the winter. They can either be planted out in early April, or potted up individually into 5-in. 'Hallna' paper pots, if they have to wait for spring bedding to be removed. You will then start the summer season with large, well-grown plants that, in the bigger-growing varieties, can be spaced 15 in. apart, and will be in full flower by early June.

Bedding Foliage for Effect

The trouble with a long-established garden is that it gets cluttered up with old faithfuls, and it thus becomes impossible to make the expansive gesture, to indulge in a spot of carefree splashing about. Something would get hurt. So I shall work it out of my system on paper by describing what I should like to do instead of what I have done.

A great many of the lushest and most summery of **foliage plants** are annuals, biennials or, most frequently, tender perennials, and I should like to devote a large border—12 ft. deep, if it was one-sided, or 18 ft. across if it was an island—to them. Not slavishly to them, however, for I should not exclude flowers on principle, nor a few suitable hardies.

It will be said that this is the kind of tropical bedding already widely practised by our public parks and gardens, and that they have the amenities for raising and overwintering the plants which most of us lack. This is true up to a point, but I very much dislike the methods and the taste of most of these public bodies, although I readily admit that one picks up some excellent ideas from them on occasions. I dislike the way they will raise an island bed so that it makes a huge hump at the centre; their feverish and undiscriminating use of variegated foliage and the hectic jumble of their distribution of plants in a bed. My dogs' dinners look far more appetising than this. As to amenities for raising and overwintering the plants, I should get along perfectly well with my present modest equipment of a cellar, cold frames and a small greenhouse in which the heating is controlled so that the temperature falls to, but not more than a degree below, freezing point.

The sort of hardy perennials to allow in the border of my dream are *Fatsia japonica,* wrongly called castor-oil plant, an evergreen shrub with large, glossy, palmately lobed leaves; *Cynara cardunculus,* the artichoke-like cardoon, with handsomely dissected grey foliage; and certain grasses and bamboos; also, if your soil is well drained and the climate not too severe, the evergreen *Eryngium pandanifolium,* with sea-green, scimitar-like leaves. One fatsia would make a summer, but for the rest, whether hardy or tender, my object would be to make large groups of each kind of plant.

Among the tallest of those that are safest treated as tender, is *Eucalyptus globulus,* one of the bluest of the gums. From seed sown in February or March, it will rapidly make a 4- to 5-ft. plant and seven or eight together would comprise a telling group. An even surer treatment for this eucalypt is to sow in late summer, overwinter the young plants under glass and plant them out the following May. A 6-ft. grass such as *Miscanthus sinensis* 'Gracillimus' would look well beside this. These hardy and permanent ingredients, incidentally, would not in the least militate against your having a spring bedding display of wallflowers and/or tulips. They would just break it up a little, which could be all to the good.

Near the grass and the gum, the purple, palmate leaves of *Ricinus communis* 'Gibsonii' are well contrasted. This is the true castor-oil plant. You sow seeds in late March and, by the end of the season (if it is a warm one) the plants are 6 or 8 ft. tall.

Purple-leaved cannas are worth it for their foliage alone and some of the more vigorous of these can be expected to reach 4 or 5 ft. If they are lucky with their season, their flowers will make a very positive contribution. Wyoming, with apricot-coloured flowers and the red King Humbert are two such. A sturdy annual for where a tall feature is required, is *Nicotiana sylvestris* (see page 109) and the glaucous, pinnately lobed foliage of *Melianthus major* (page 90) contrasts particularly well with the castor-oil and canna leaves just described. In front of this, one could have some purple-leaved dahlias such as Bishop of Llandaff, whose flowers are crimson or red. A batch raised from seed gives you some interesting variants from which to select the best (retaining them as tubers in future years) and discard the duds. There are other bedding dahlias with interesting dark foliage: for instance Rocquencourt, with orange flowers.

Nearer the edge of the border I should be tempted to grow *Onopordon acanthium* and *Verbascum bombyciferum*, the former a thistle, the latter a mullein, both with silver foliage. Both are biennials, also, and will run up to 6 or 8 ft. in their second year, but there is no reason why they should not be grown as annuals, just for their rosette of foliage in the first season.

Some variegated foliage will not come amiss, as long as it is not over-busy—as are most of the *Coleus blumei* hybrids—or diseased looking like the abutilons. The variegated kales make handsome border plants; one kind is picked out in white along the veins and another in purple. The milk thistle, *Silybum marianum*, has a good bold leaf spotted with white. This is a natural variegation, not an aberration. And I have a great affection for the green-and-cream-leaved *Hebe andersonii* 'Variegata'—not, however, as an edging or dot plant, as the public gardens will use it. Two-year-old plants look best, having more substance than the youngsters, and their richly coloured spikes of lavender flowers are not to be despised.

Skeletons in the Border

There are certain plants that will always arouse differences among gardeners as to whether they should be regarded as weeds or not. Of these, the teazle, the thorn-apple and henbane are outstanding for their proud, architectural bearing and for the magnificence of the skeletons they leave us at the end of the growing season. This material is just the thing for dried winter arrangements in the house, yet one seldom sees them used.

Teazles (*Dipsacus sylvestris*) are the commonest. They are in full flower in August and will be found, mainly, in the clearings left by coppiced woodland or else by stream and dyke sides. The seedlings that will flower next year will also be in evidence, forming a low rosette of dark green leaves with stumpy prickles on their upper surfaces. If you are going to transplant some of these into your garden, always choose the very smallest, since teazles are tap-rooted and hence bad movers. But failing this, seeds are available (as they are of henbane and of thorn-apple) from Thompson & Morgan, and they germinate as easily as foxgloves.

In its second year the plant sends up a central spike to about 7 ft., and there is a pair of side branches at every joint; also a pair of long green leaves of oil-smooth texture, deeply grooved along the mid-rib, so that water collects in a reservoir where they join at the base and clasp the stem. It is rare indeed to find this reservoir empty, for as long as the leaves stay fresh and green. Even in periods of drought, a night dew falling on the cold foliage is enough to replenish supplies. One imagines that the device must be of some use to the plant, though quite how I should not care to say.

The teazle heads are conical, surrounded by a fringe of spiny, whisker-like bracts. The flowers are mauve, and the thing that has always astonished me about them is the order in which they open. A band of mauve appears first around the centre of the cone; then divides into two, narrower bands that travel in opposite directions, the last flowers to open being those at the very top and at the bottom of the cone. We are familiar with spikes of flowers that open from the bottom upwards (or occasionally, as in *Liatris* from the top downwards) and with flowers arranged in discs that open from the outside inwards, but this two-directional effort is really quite eccentric.

Throughout their flowering, they are besieged by bees, and on a memorable occasion I saw a grove of teazles in one of our woods that was attended by scores of peacock butterflies. In winter, their seed heads become a favourite feeding perch for goldfinches: there is no prettier way in which this delightful bird can display itself. So, one way and another, there is good reason for always allowing a few teazles at strategic points in the garden. There will be plenty of unwanted seedlings, but they are easily decapitated and will never come again.

Henbane, *Hyoscyamus niger,* is another tap-rooted biennial that must be moved from wherever you first spot a seedling in your garden to wherever you want it to be, at the earliest moment. It is a pale plant in its first year, the leaves margined with a few, large, jagged teeth and clothed in clammy hairs. It starts opening its five-lobed flowers at the end of the following May, and continues to carry them, one or two at a time, at the tips of its ever extending branches, right into August. They are an inch across, deep purple at the throat but otherwise dusky yellow, overlaid with a very fine reticulation of purple veins. Not showy, but a thing to look into.

The plant itself is impressive, and becomes increasingly so as it grows. It reaches to about 4 ft. tall by nearly as much across, the branches taking on sinuous curves like the tentacles of an octopus. The plant is as wicked as it looks, being highly poisonous, but I cannot imagine anyone being tempted to eat any part of it. As the leaves die off, the plant's most attractive feature—its seed pods—becomes apparent in all its singular grace. Shaped like shuttlecocks (the persistent calyx forms the feathers), the pods make chains, with one-inch links, along the top sides of branches that may be anything up to 3 ft. long.

Henbane grows wild, most usually, in shingly places near the sea. On attempting to tame it, you will discover that its seeds germinate extremely unevenly, sometimes over a period of years. Once you have got your first established plant you are all right. Then you can distribute its seeds all over the garden, by the thousand. Sooner or later, a few will germinate and, as long as you can recognise the seedlings when small, you are well away.

The **thorn-apple**, *Datura stramonium,* is similarly unpredictable. It belongs to the same nightshade family and is even more poisonous, but is an annual, and will grow well only in warm summers. Its flowers are very like a white nicotiana's, opening at night and sweetly scented. Again, however, its claim to fame rests in its seed capsules, which are the size and shape of a hen's egg and covered with thick prickles. From below the central capsule two opposite branches arise, each terminating in another capsule, from below which two further branches sprout, repeating the process until autumn ends all. The resulting skeleton is a branching candelabrum of fascinating outline.

Of all seed heads, the **opium poppy's** (*Papaver somniferum*) are among the most decorative. This is a hardy annual that perpetuates itself by liberally self-sowing in the garden. All you have to do is to thin out unwanted seedlings. Of recent years and, presumably, on account of its wicked opiate associations, this plant has no longer been referred to as the opium poppy in seed lists. It is sometimes styled as peony-flowered, sometimes carnation-flowered. How fatuous can we get?

Growing Gourds for Ornament

Ornamental **gourds** are amusing to grow and one is particularly grateful to them at midwinter, when flowers from the florist's shop look as though they had turned up at the wrong party and in unsuitable clothing. Spread out on a lordly dish, these gourds do make a handsome display, especially if you have managed to grow a varied assortment.

They have many good points. The word itself has a kind of crooning, gurgling richness, as Keats appreciated when including it with his heap.

'Of candied apple, quince, and plum, and gourd
With jellies soother than the creamy curd.'

Gourd does not rhyme particularly well with curd and it is the one wholly inedible component of the feast set out by Porphyro, but the word is irresistible.

Then there is the feel of a gourd: ponderous as a paper-weight and with the cool, smooth skin generally attributed to its cousin cucumber. Sometimes, in the Oliver Cromwell gourds, the skin erupts into bumps and warts, but they are smooth bumps and have their own harmony. Perhaps I should explain that I am handling gourds in my left hand the while I write this with my right, so that my sensuous approach to the subject is directly inspired.

Gourds are well shaped, too. The smaller ones, which are the most useful for ornamental purposes, are generally globular or piriform. Some of the larger types are more eccentric, the well-named turban gourd being one of the most curious. The colours range from white through cream and buff-yellow to orange and, in the turbans, to vivid cock's-wattles red, so that they make 'one gasp and stretch one's eyes' and wonder whether a trick is not being played.

Some of the gourds retain a green colouring for a very much longer period than others; *Cucurbita melanosperma* retains its characteristic mottled, pale and darker green throughout its long life.

One of the fascinations about a mixed crop of gourds is in watching them change and develop. For instance, one plant will carry solid, dark green, pear-shaped gourds, about 4 to 5 in. long, with just the faintest hint of paler longitudinal stripes at the time you pick them, late in October. Gradually these stripes become more distinct and change to yellow, while the groundwork is still green. But the final product is an all-yellow fruit. They are at their handsomest in the intermediate stages. Other gourds attain their finest colouring early, while still on the plant. You should cull them as this happens, and allow the plant's energies to concentrate on making more. White gourds are at their whitest, like a china egg, when first picked. Later they change to a dirty cream. The turbans can be harvested while still quite anaemic. As long as the fruits are sound, they will develop their lurid colours to the full, off the plant. One of our turbans, quite a small fruit weighing less than a pound, developed metallic green stripes next to brilliant red; this is not uncommon. The largest may weigh up to 6 lb. if, for a long time, it was the only fruit set on a large and leafy plant.

Some people varnish their gourds. This does add a certain

glamour, admittedly, but is rather like gilding the lily. And it tends to shorten the gourd's life, for it should be remembered that, until it becomes paper-light and has lost all its colouring, a gourd is a living, breathing fruit, and it cannot respire through varnish. Even small gourds, untreated, should last you through the winter without drying up. Large ones often go on much longer. I had some fruits of the 6-lb. *C. melanosperma* that lasted unchanged for three years.

Two things put people off growing gourds: they think it must be difficult or, having tried, are disappointed with the lack of variety in and dullness of the results. To take the first point first. Gourds are really extremely easy. If you have any kind of glass, use it to start them off. I sow my seeds, two to a 3½-in. pot, in a cold frame in early May, harden the seedlings off and plant them out in June. If this is too much trouble, you can push the seeds straight into the ground or into a firm, moist part of your compost or manure heap, in early June. We find a number of self-sown seedlings on our rubbish heap, every year, and they do extremely well.

Like all cucurbits, gourds enjoy rich fare. They also like full sun, in order to set and ripen their fruit properly. I let mine roam over the ground at their pleasure. Against the soil, they get the maximum of ripening sun-heat. And they get shelter from the wind, which is important in a plant with large, humid leaves. Sometimes they may be trained to ramble over neighbouring tomato plants or up a hedge, which is rather fun. The advantage of training them deliberately on vertical netting is that they take up less garden space; the gourds are not dirtied by soil nor gnawed by slugs; nor do they acquire a pale area where they were lying on the ground.

As to obtaining a rich assortment of types from one packet of seed, the importance of this is clear. Space will not allow most gardeners to grow more than a dozen plants—very probably fewer, and you do want their fruits all, or nearly all, to be different (unless you are out for oddities like the turban and bottle gourds). It is a question of ordering from a seed firm that offers a well assorted strain. You can only find out about this by trial and error or by enquiring of someone who has had good results where he obtained his seed from. On this occasion, I'm not going to stick my neck out by suggesting a supplier, as I've never been wholly satisfied myself.

Bulbs

There are many ways of spending one's money in gardening but the most tempting, at least to me, occurs with the arrival of the bulb catalogues. Bulbs seem to cry out to be planted in quantities and it is hard to remain deaf to their cry. According to their species they may be had in flower in every season of the year, and whenever they bloom, there is about them a quality of irresistible freshness.

Bulbs for Autumn Colour

Autumn flowering bulbs deserve a special place in our affection because their pristine qualities are in such striking contrast to the scene of decay that otherwise surrounds us. Not that I dislike this scene: autumn has its own charm, but these bulbs do help, emotionally at least, to bridge the chasm separating autumn from spring.

Of all the orders for seeds, bulbs and plants that we make during the year, the order for **autumn-flowering crocuses** is the one that is most likely to catch us napping. The first reminder to awaken us comes when we see an alluring display of them already in full flower in another person's garden. 'I must get some of those,' we tell ourselves; but find on consulting the catalogues that orders for these precocious flowerers must be received before 15th August. The trouble is that the bulb catalogues steal upon us in the languid days of midsummer, when the mood for planting is at its lowest ebb.

For general purposes, the easiest, cheapest and showiest crocus for autumn flowering is *Crocus speciosus*. It has large mauve flowers and a network of deeper shaded veins that more nearly approach it to blue than any other crocus. This colouring is offset by the large, brilliant orange stigma in the centre of each flower. And it is deliciously scented. The perianth tube (what the ordinary chap would call its stalk) is exceptionally long, with the result that the flowers habitually fall over on their sides on the second day of blooming. I can't see that this matters myself; they still look very charming in a Mme Récamier pose, but it apparently upsets some gardeners. Undoubtedly this habit is less noticeable in rough grass, and *C. speciosus* can cope with the roughest turf, naturalising by means of bulbils and by seeding, until it makes quite a conspicuous sward of foliage, in early spring, before real grass has started growing much. In fact, this crocus should be kept out of the rock garden or any place where small and precious plants are grown, but it is excellent among shrubs. Its flowering season starts about 10th September and runs through most of October.

The season of *C. kotschyanus* (more often listed as *C. zonatus*) is slightly earlier. It is almost as cheap, and is an easy one to grow, but the pale mauve flowers are not so bold as the larger, more intensely coloured ones of *C. speciosus*. Furthermore, I find that, although clumps of *C. kotschyanus* increase and make a lot of foliage in rough grass, they scarcely flower at all. I believe this may be a question not so much of soil (although my clay might certainly inhibit flowering) as of whether or not one is sold a free-flowering strain of the species.

One of the most fascinating of crocuses is *C. nudiflorus*, the only autumn-flowering species that finds a place in our *British Flora* (of Messrs. Clapham, Tutin & Warburg): although introduced, it has naturalised in grassland in various parts of the country. And yet the main snag for the gardener is in obtaining stock. The corms tend to be very small and, presumably, do not market well. A few years ago, it was being offered by a well known Dutch bulb merchant and I bought a dozen. I think only two grew, and I imagine that complaints from customers may have been a reason for the species shortly afterwards being deleted from the firm's catalogue. However, my slight success was enough to give me a nucleus, and the bulbs have since increased, and flower well under our bay tree, among hardy cyclamen. The colour of the flowers is a particularly clear and lovely rosy lilac.

When staying in Ulster recently, my host showed me a coloured photograph of this crocus that he had taken in his own garden, and he has two or three enormous colonies of it that must have dated back many years, but in that part of the country it does not flower at all freely. Probably it requires a summer baking. Peculiar to this species is its manner of spreading by underground stolons. In fact, if you dig up a clump in spring, as my host kindly did for me, you see more stolon than corm.

C. ochroleucus is a good white flowered autumn crocus, yellow at the base. Its blooms are small but numerous and borne on sturdy stems, mainly in November but lasting till Christmas. *C. longiflorus* has the same season. It produces an abundance of smallish mauve flowers with intense red stigmata and a most delicious fragrance, similar to that of *C. speciosus*. We have it and *C. ochroleucus* under the same bay tree, among *Cyclamen neapolitanum*. They might get lost in coarse turf and would anyway interfere with our third and last grass cutting, here.

It often happens that, when the autumn crocus corms intended for naturalising in rough grass arrive in September, the ground is rock-hard. Rather than wait for heavy autumn rains, which may well arrive too late, it is best to irrigate the area intended for planting and get the job done as early as possible. I find that, under dry conditions, a sprinkler needs to be left on for eight hours in one position before the turf is truly permeated with moisture. So the watering can well go on overnight. The job is also made much easier if a bulb-planter of only 2 in. diameter is used. The plug of soil that this extracts is large enough for most bulbs.

Colchicums often get miscalled autumn crocus, but are easily distinguished when flowering by their six stamens, whereas true crocuses have only three. There is also much more pink in the rosy mauve colouring of colchicums than you ever find in a crocus. Although colchicums grow wild in pastures, they seem less amenable to cultivation in turf than crocuses, in many soils. The cheapest bulbs are nearly always the easiest to grow. Among colchicums this dictum applies to *C. autumnale*, but even so it is more than three times the price of *Crocus speciosus,* and whereas it flowers well and succeeds in maintaining itself in my grass garden, it has failed to increase over the years.

But it can be raised from seed. It is a slow method but worth persisting in if large numbers are required for naturalising. What I do is to raise a batch of seedlings in 7-in. pots and sort them over every year in late summer, when they are still dormant. The largest I plant out, the smallest I prick out fairly thickly into pots again. This is a continuous and never-ending ritual, because the bulbs contrive to multiply even at this early and youthful stage. The more expensive and precious colchicum cultivars should not be committed to rough grass, where they are apt to dwindle. They do best in a sunny position and in cultivated or, at any rate, weed free ground, as at the edge of a shrubbery. Here, too, their voluminous foliage will not look out of place, in spring. Their flowers are meat and drink to slugs, which will ruin a display unless offensive measures are taken.

Autumn-flowering bulbs do not really like being harvested and dried off, though bulb merchants find it necessary to treat them so, in order to fit them into their routines. A bulb like *Zephyranthes candida* will remain evergreen the year through, if given the chance. Dried bulbs often fail completely. The best course is to buy it in a green and growing condition from a nursery not specialising in bulbs, and to plant it in the spring. It has an August-September flowering season and white, crocus-like blooms show up well against the dark green, rush-like foliage. A group at the front of a sunny border will be well sited. It does not mind how heavy the soil is and it will, in fact, put up with shade and still flower freely if the preceding summer months were on the warm side. Summer temperatures are the factor determining how good a season your Flower of the West Wind will have.

Crocuses belong to the iris family; colchicums to the lily's and *Zephyranthes* to the *Amaryllis*; yet in all three cases the flowers are superficially alike. **Sternbergia lutea** is another amaryllid: the smell of its broken flower stalks is just like the daffodil's, which also belongs to the Amaryllidaceae. Sternbergias must be grown in a hot, sunny border, and they are particularly successful on free-draining sandy or chalk soils. On my clay I have always been utterly unsuccessful in flowering the strain of sternbergia most commonly on sale. The narrow leaved variety called *S. lutea* var. *angustifolia* is the one to look out for. This will bloom regularly from its first year, usually from mid-September onwards. The flowers are crocus-like but of the purest yellow—a most gladdening and cheerful sight. The foliage comes in winter and dies away completely in May. That is the best season for planting, and, at the latest, before the end of August. As the bulbs can be planted 6 in. deep, one can overplant groups with a sparsely growing annual like portulaca, to obtain a summer display from what would otherwise remain bare ground.

Nerines are obvious amaryllis relatives. They look the part. **Nerine bowdenii** is a fairly hardy hybrid and few gardeners would be without it. From late September to November it carries umbels of bright (even crude) pink flowers on 2½ ft. stems. They are excellent for cutting and last for ages in winter. The flowers are basically trumpet shaped but the segments are narrow and recurve at the tips, which creates a more informal, spidery effect.

Early spring is the best planting season, just as growth is resumed and new strap leaves are pushing up. These look untidy and squalid without actually dying, by the time autumn arrives, and you can, without detriment and for the sake of appearances, cut all the foliage away at the end of August, just before the flower buds make their appearance. One is always recommended to plant bulbs 6 in. deep, where they will be the safer from frost damage. However, within a year or two you will find they have multiplied exceedingly and are all at the surface. As this is obviously where they like to be, I believe in letting them. In a hard winter they can easily be protected with a coverlet of old fern or bracken fronds. A sunny position would seem to be 'de rigueur' but a gardening friend in N.W. Scotland (not famed for a sun-drenched climate anyway) tells me that those he planted among shrubs in shade flowered the best. Probably it makes no great odds.

Bulbs for Early Planting

Autumn-flowering bulbs are not the only ones that need to be planted early. There are others that naturally make new roots in preparation for their next season, quite soon after they have flowered and seeded as a culmination of their last. Dormancy in between growing seasons is of the briefest, or even non-existent. You need to be up early to catch them at the ideal moment for a move.

The **Madonna** and **Nankeen lilies** (*Lilium candidum* and *L. testaceum*) are typical. They flower in early July and should be moved (if they need to be) at the end of the month. By August, *L. candidum* shows its active temperament by putting up a tuft of leaves which will remain as an earnest of its intent, right through the winter. Bulbs should be planted only just below the soil surface. The merchants distribute these lilies in October and November, most often, and this is far too late for their welfare. They take ages to recover and it is infinitely preferable, if you can possibly wangle it, to get hold of healthy stock at the right season from the garden of a kind and co-operative friend.

The **Crown Imperial**, *Fritillaria imperialis* is also early afoot, though not showing visible shoots until the new year. It is not cheap but it is an investment. For some reason the yellow flowered kinds from Messrs. Blom are twice as costly, at a guinea a time, as any of the browny-orange strains. Peter Nyssen, however, offers them both at 7/6d. each (as I write, but you know what prices do). Left undisturbed for a period of years on rich, reasonably slug-free soil, they will increase and make the most splendid feature in your April garden.

I must move mine: they are in front of a lilac, whose roots are altogether too greedy and pervasive, so that the bulbs have been making only leaves for several years now. The inflorescence is so spectacular and unusual that one wonders how it ever came to be: a ring of bells surmounted by a bunch of greenery in pineapple style. And one cannot resist lifting the bell flowers so as to be able to look into the heart of them where the nectaries glisten like suspended tears. Of course the plant does smell appalling—a mixture of garlic and fox that is wafted afar on the wind. But then most people's sense of smell has atrophied anyway, and one can always hold one's nose.

Those easily grown May-June-flowering bulbous **irises** called Dutch and Spanish, start sprouting in the early autumn. The English irises (not in the least English, really) flower rather later, at the turn of June and July. Their colour range is limited to white, grey, mauve and rich purple but, with their broad falls, they are showy indeed. These sprout visibly in January but their young roots are active as early as August, so the sooner you plant or re-plant any of these three groups after they have flowered, the better for them.

A few years ago I dug up a congested clump of the hoop petticoat daffodil, **Narcissus bulbocodium,** from the weed-free piece of ground where it was growing among cyclamen, and started a colony in rough grass. The moment I chose for this was in the first week of August after a heavy rain of 1.2 in. had allowed me to use a bulb-planting tool. Anyone who has seen the inspiring drift of this species in the meadow at the RHS gardens at Wisley must have been fired with a desire to emulate it. Being a miniature, this bulb most often gets planted in a rather special place in cultivated soil. But it is quite tough enough to compete with turf, provided the soil is reasonably moist.

The hoop petticoats are an interesting and variable group. The commonest of them, with foot-long, rush-like foliage in upright tufts, and dandelion-yellow flowers, is var. *conspicuus*. This is easy and cheap to buy. It has a very long growing season, and the foliage of established clumps makes an appearance quite early in the autumn. Hence the importance of getting it planted as soon as you can. When grown in cultivated ground, the bulbs multiply at a great rate and soon become so congested that their flowering performance is much reduced. If you plant rather deeply, say at 4 in. as against the normal 2 in. or so, the rate of multiplication is reduced. But the other obvious way out of the difficulty is to lift and replant every few years, which is what I do. Funnily enough, once they find themselves in turf, these hoop petticoats give up the clump forming habit and chiefly multiply by self-sowing. Their colouring and stature are so exactly like the dandelion's, that the one tends to compete with the other for our attention when both are out together in the middle of the day. But the daffodil has a clear field by the evening, when its rival has shut up for the night.

When in search of the other forms of *N. bulbocodium*, you must turn to the retail specialist and expect the bulbs to be much more expensive. One firm lists as many as 14 different types. The most important to have is var. *citrinus* (which should technically be known as *N. bulbocodium* subspecies *vulgaris* var. *citrinus*), with delightful pale yellow, wide mouthed funnels. It seems not to make clumps in any circumstances, but sets seed, and can be raised from seed to flower in about three years. The foliage is not held upright but remains close to the ground and it is almost evergreen. It has a tremendously long flowering season. Not only does each individual bloom remain fresh for three weeks—that is the case with all members of this species—but they are produced in succession from early April until the second half of May.

This is a most unusual habit, when you consider that all the blooms of any *Narcissus* species or hybrid normally open within a few days of one another.

The Pheasant's Eye Narcissus, *N. poeticus recurvus*, flowers in May, which is late indeed, but is making new roots again by the end of June. So plant or divide this one as early as you can. The earlier the better with the whole narcissus tribe, in fact, making the end of September your dead-line.

The early-planting requirements of certain **gladioli** are apt to catch us napping. One gets used to thinking of this task in spring, but some of the most graceful and early flowering types need planting in autumn. They make new shoots forthwith and may get frosted, but fresh greenery will usually push up at a safer date. Their main requirements are a sunny position with good drainage. Then they will multiply over the years, and never need lifting. Among the most worth-while are the *nanus* hybrids. There are barely a dozen of these, and the prettiest, in my opinion, is Nymph: only 18 in. tall with half a dozen blooms on a slender, arching stem that requires no support; palest pink with two carmine kissing spots, shaped like a mouth, on the lower segments. It looks like some dainty orchid and is a far cry from the lumbering monsters that win prizes at the local flower show. Amanda Mahy is a good salmon red; and a comparative newcomer that has increased prodigiously with me in only 3 years, is Robinette, a deep cherry red with white flakes. The magenta flowered *Gladiolus byzantinus,* an old cottage garden favourite, must also be autumn planted. When you have so many in your borders that some are lifted every time you put your fork in, they too should be tried in rough grass.

Snowdrops resent being dried off and harvested. Like *Zephyranthes candida,* you should try to get hold of them in spring while green and growing. If it must be autumn, then as early as maybe.

So too with **Ipheion uniflorum,** a bulb worth including in any garden. It is usually listed, the poor innocent, under *Brodiaea* or *Milla* or *Triteleia*. It carries large star-shaped flowers singly, on 6-in. stems, mostly in April but sometimes as early as February. They are typically whitish, but there are blue-tinted strains available that are very well worth having. The grassy foliage appears in early autumn and has a strong onion smell when bruised. This bulb does best in a well drained, sunny border, but is not fussy, really. I have been unable to make it survive through the years in rough grass, however.

A Handful of Onions

Anyone who set out to make a comprehensive collection of **onions** would be dotty, if pleasantly so. There are nearly 300 species, and many are quite insignificant, while others can become ferocious garden weeds. But the *Allium* tribe is extraordinarily varied and includes several charmers. According to their species, alliums (as we normally refer to these ornamental onions so as not to get them mixed up in our minds with the good smell of frying) may be had in flower from spring to autumn. They include almost all the colours—white, yellow, pink, carmine, purple and blue. For the most part they are bulbous, and some of the best of these may be bought from the bulb firms. Others should be sought from rock garden specialists, and others, again, from seedsmen catering for the esoteric. Alliums are famous seeders, and this is an easy way to raise stock of new kinds; most can be brought to flowering size in a couple of years.

There is no trouble whatever about growing alliums, as long as they are given a sunny position, and provided you remember to mark their positions. In their resting season they mostly leave a complete blank, and this is my main objection to the spring-flowering species such as *A. karataviense*. Its broad, flat, glaucous leaves are fascinating at their first appearance, but soon wither away, leaving you with nothing but the seed heads for the rest of the summer. Many gardeners seem not to notice these blanks, but you can, of course, inter-plant with annuals, or you can make a mixed planting of an early- and a late-flowering allium, so that the one takes over from the other.

Chives, *A. schoenoprasum,* makes an effective edging, if you plant the right sort. There is no need to restrict it to the herb patch. The kind most commonly seen in cultivation is a rather miserable plant with squinny little flower heads that set no seed. Giant chives, *A. s. sibiricum,* is the one to grow—a bouncing plant, good to eat, with masses of handsome flowers rather like those of a scabious. A batch raised from seed will give you a nice gradation of shades between pink and mauve. The giant chives' first flowering, in May, is spectacular. As soon as it is declining, you cut the plants to the ground with a knife, and a second crop of foliage is inches high within a matter of days, followed by a second, smaller, crop of flowers. And, by repeating the operation, a third flush can be fitted in before the autumn.

One of my favourite May-flowering onions is *A. neapolitanum,* only about 9 in. high, and of a pearly, pristine whiteness that is as fresh as anything spring can offer. May-June is the season for *A. siculum,* a splendid species both for cutting and as a garden plant. The flowers are borne on slender but strong 3 ft. stems, and, though clustered, are not globose, but nodding and bell shaped, in a subtle colour combination of cream and green with chestnut striping.

A. moly is a cheerful and obliging species, suitable for planting, for instance, along an unpromising hedge bottom, where it will make colonies and be gay with bright yellow blossoms on 9-in. stems, in June. It is one of the strongest smelling onions, and wafts a powerful garlic odour even without being bruised. When Tennyson's Lotos-Eaters were 'propt on beds of amaranth and moly,' it is small wonder that they felt a bit dazed, if this was the plant that made their couch.

The king of all the alliums, flowers in June and July. This is *A. albopilosum* (now *A. christophii*). The flower heads, carried on 18-in. stems, are perfectly globular and nearly a foot across, very stiff and wiry in all their parts. The flowers are a dusky, rosy purple; but the perianth, far from disintegrating as the flower fades, becomes quite hard and spiky. Finally, you have a globe made up of six-pointed stars, each with a capsule at its centre opening into three valves to reveal the coal-black seeds. This is wonderful material for winter decorations.

Few gardeners would be disappointed with *Allium ostrow-skianum,* available from Peter Nyssen at 8/3d. a 100. It grows only 9 in. high and carries heads of quite large, bright purplish-pink flowers in June. This is the sort of bulb you can interplant, at the edge of a border, with thin-growing hardy perennials of a later flowering period such as *Eryngium tripartitum* or *Platycodon grandiflorum* 'Mariesii', the balloon flower. A more subtle, less showy species, flowering in July and August, is *A. flavum.* Its height varies, according to the strain, from a few inches to a foot, and the small, bell-shaped flowers are soft yellow. Its whiskery bracts are a notable feature as they are in the more aggressive species *A. pulchellum,* which is 15 in. tall and has quite telling heads of pinkish-purple flowers at the same season. This self-sows pleasantly in pavement cracks or among the rhizomes of bearded irises, whose long off-season it helps to mitigate.

The late-flowering alliums are particularly useful, because they do not leave gaps but are coming along all through the spring and summer months. *A. cyaneum,* which has an August season, is a miniature variety, only a few inches high, with thread-like leaves finer than those of the finest lawn grass. If it is not to be lost, it wants a special place, such as a sink or rock garden. The flowers are pure, intense blue and saucer-shaped, I would say, though described in the RHS Dictionary and in catalogues as bell-shaped.

A. beesianum is a paler blue, with nodding, tubular flowers on 9-in. stems. It is a good doer, slowly making strong clumps, and is at its best in September. So is *A. tuberosum,* the Chinese chives, another clump-former that does not make real bulbs. The umbels of white flowers are not of the purest, being green-centred, but the plant has an erect, well-set-up bearing. It is about 15 in. tall and contrasts pleasantly with more spreading plants.

Hyacinths

Hyacinths are numbered among those plants that one would like to have, both in the house and out, in far greater quantity than one's means allow. Their very artificiality has its own attraction; their petals are so neatly curled and if the hyacinth scent is cloying, I am perfectly happy to be cloyed.

In fact, the expense does not have to be so terrific. Some wholesale bulb firms will do retail trade, and Peter Nyssen offers small sized hyacinth bulbs at 65/od. per 100, which is less than the average price you would pay for the same number of tulips from a retail firm. You can get as few as 25 bulbs of any one variety at the 100 rate, that is for 16/3d., which is extraordinarily reasonable. These are, admittedly, small bulbs; the smallest on sale. But I am not alone in preferring the lighter flower heads they carry, to the top-heavy whoppers produced by 'extra choice bulbs'. If most of us will not want to grow 25 of one variety for use in the house, it is simple enough to dispose of the surplus, either in the garden or to friends.

There is little point in bringing all one's hyacinths on to flower more or less simultaneously; it is pleasanter to have them in succession from January to March. The old white favourite, l'Innocence, will flower in bowls without any special effort to force it, in mid-January. One somehow expects white flowers to be strongly scented, but l'Innocence is disappointing in this respect. Hoar Frost is better, but a tall and unwieldy grower, as all the pale colours are apt to be.

Lady Derby has been umpteen years in cultivation but is still as fine a pink as you will find, and, again, early. The colouring is soft, non-jarring. The flowers of Delight are well described as 'blossom pink' in the catalogue; a soft and pleasing shade. The scent is good and the bulbs quite often carry secondary spikes. These may not be much use for display purposes in your bowl, but are nice for picking to use in early spring flower arrangements. Cyclop is a rather crude cerise pink; its spikes are clumsy, the scent only moderate. Jan Bos, a very popular hyacinth described as red, is an exceedingly harsh carmine.

There is no pure red hyacinth, still less a scarlet, but the best of those approaching red (and they really do look it under normal yellowish electric lighting, which cuts out the blue in them) are Van Tubergen's Scarlet (also known as Mme du Barry) and the double sport derived from it, Scarlet Perfection. The flowers are small and the plants sufficiently dwarf and sturdy to be self-supporting. Their scent is of pear drops. Magazine illustrations of 100 years ago show that double hyacinths were numerous and popular. But the only other I know to be still obtainable is General Kohler—tall (up to 18 in.), with long, lush foliage, neatly charming light blue rosettes and a good scent.

Perle Brilliante is like a single version of the last, with fine, large waxy blooms. The trouble with blue flowered hyacinths indoors is that most electric lighting kills their colouring and turns it to a nondescript grey. So too with the deep blue Ostara, but this is one of the most reliable for early spring bedding.

Salmonetta (syn. Oranje Boven) is indeed an interesting salmon shade but excessively weak in the stem. Lord Balfour and Duke of Westminster are similar lilac mauves: pale at the margin with a dark central stripe and reminiscent of a Nelly Moser clematis. They are exceptionally fragrant.

Two favourites of mine are Distinction and Indian Prince. They are much alike but the latter is far the cheaper and is classed a Cynthella. The only difference I can see between Cynthellas and ordinary hyacinths is that the former tend to have lighter spikes. These two are fairly dwarf at 12 to 14 in. and are almost self supporting. Their stalks are very dark and the flowers (which are only moderately scented) a sumptuous, velvety red-purple.

I grow my hyacinths in the John Innes compost that I use for general potting, with some charcoal at the bottom of the bowl to prevent stagnation. It is easy to stake them when grown in this medium. Bulb fibre is not firm enough and anyway has no feed value, which is all very well if you mean to throw the bulbs away after flowering, but not at all well otherwise. Watering is most easily carried out by total immersion or, at any rate, by very thorough soaking, thereafter tilting the bowl on its side to get rid of some of the surplus. But this is of no great importance, seeing that hyacinths can be grown with their roots in pure water.

It is worth keeping them in good health after flowering. They can go back to a window-sill in a cool room and from there, in March, to a cold frame. Subsequently I turn them out of their bowls, intact, and let them complete their growth in a spare place in the garden. They can be harvested in June. If the bulbs seem plump and in good condition, they can be stored in paper bags till September and then replanted in bowls to serve another turn. I have done this for three successive seasons with worth-while results. Alternatively, with cheap and common varieties, I have planted them in rough grass, where they do tend to diminish in size, but are rather fun, flowering in April among anemones and dwarf daffodils.

Plate 9.   Above, Ranunculus aconitifolius 'Plenus' carries its pure white rosettes in spring.

Below, the tulip tree, *Liriodendron tulipifera,* has remarkable foliage, turning clear yellow in autumn. This is a giant.

RUDBECKIA

The usual sort of place to find for them is in a bed or border where they will not be disturbed. Among herbaceous peonies is a specially suitable position, because the hyacinth flowers, whatever their colours, combine so nicely with the crimson of young peony shoots. At the edge of rose beds is another good site, livening up an area that is otherwise dull in March and April.

I should love to be able to afford hyacinths for bedding on a lavish scale, and two years ago I did in fact buy 250 small sized bulbs suitable for bedding, of the late, dark flowered variety, King of the Blues. I wanted a blue hyacinth because I rather starve myself of this colour indoors for reasons already explained and I wanted a late one because it would then flower when our garden is open to the public and not before. The only blue mentioned as late in the catalogues was this one.

It did flower with the required lateness at the turn of April and May; both colour and scent were excellent but, alas and alack, the stems were far too weak (even in the dry, calm weather then prevailing) to support the flower heads. As the stalks lengthened, I had to attach every one of them to a cane. Among this batch were five or six rogue bulbs of a paler blue, earlier flowering variety, and these stood up like grenadiers. I must say I cursed the nurseryman for giving no guidance on this subject in his catalogue descriptions. Indeed, there is nowhere I know of that you can turn to for full and honest details on the character and performance of the florist's cultivated varieties of bulbs, in particular of hyacinths, tulips and daffodils. I can describe in full the few that I have grown but am in no position to cover a wide field. Dutch growers, in particular, *are* in that position. But they will not come forward with an honestly critical book on the subject. They are too short-sighted, it seems, to realise that a frank exposition of the subject would engender confidence. A personal assessment of the relative merits and demerits of all the most widely offered bulbs would make such a refreshing change from the usual bla. After all, not all the varieties can be equally wonderful; we need a

Plate 10. Above, Campanula carpatica, in blue or white, is a reliable front-line perennial.

Below, Rudbeckia 'Goldsturm', the finest black-eyed-Susan, lights up a shady border from August to October.

bit of light and shade in the descriptions, otherwise they become a meaningless bore.

My King of the Blues were interplanted among aquilegias. The latter's young foliage were a charming foil at the bulb's flowering and they then took over in their May-June season. After this, I dug the whole lot up and replaced them with a dwarf strain of seedling dahlias that I had sown under cold glass in late April. Meantime the hyacinths were perfectly harvested without any effort on my part. Their bulbs were quite as large as when I first bought them and have next been planted in a blue and yellow scheme with doronicums and a yellow strain of polyanthus.

Tulips

Luckily, **tulips** do not need to be planted nearly so early as most other bulbs. And so, if you are late with your autumn work, as I invariably am, the tulip bulbs will not pursue you with reproachful glances. Stored in a cool place they will sit about quite happily till Christmas, if need be. In fact, there were some in my cellar one winter that I had overlooked until March. Naturally I had to throw out a lot that had shrivelled to nothing, but I planted the remainder at the end of the month and they were up and flowering two months later at the same time as all the rest.

November is a good time for tulip planting. A long, narrow, sharp-pointed trowel is the best implement for doing the job with the minimum of effort and of ground disturbance. I always sit all the bulbs in their places on top of the ground before starting to plant, as this ensures an even distribution. If they are being arranged in solid blocks, then 4 in. between bulbs is about right, but where they are being interplanted with spring bedding, a spacing of 6 in. is close enough.

I am particularly keen on planting tulips among sweet williams. They do not flower together, but the tulips look very well against their solid green background. Then the sweet williams take over, while the tulips finish growing unnoticed, and can finally be harvested in July in perfect condition, having completed their growth cycle without interruption.

The normal practice, when tulips are associated with wallflowers or forget-me-nots, is to scatter the bulbs evenly among the plants. The tulips then have to be lifted while in full greenery and replanted in the vegetable garden to finish growing. But however carefully this job is done, the tulips obviously hate it, and their foliage starts to wither away forthwith. As an alternative to the scattering technique, it is not a bad plan to plant the tulips in groups behind the wallflowers, forget-me-nots, polyanthus or whatever the other spring bedder may be. I think they actually look more effective when given this treatment. Also, when the setting is informal, it allows the wallflowers or other plants to be replaced while leaving the tulips *in situ* either letting them die down before lifting them, or allowing them to do another turn in the same position, in which case they can be overplanted at mid-summer with a temporary gap-filler. When the groups are of a dozen bulbs only, then the use of some expansive neighbour will do all the filling in that is needed.

Of late years, I have been using fairly large tulip groups, usually of 50 bulbs, in my 70-yard-long border of mixed shrubs, herbace-ous and other plants. The border's main season is from early June till October. But it is already rapidly filling up with lush young foliage in May; and I find that a setting of plants with bold greenery, such as delphinium, cardoon, hosta and hemerocallis, together with such early-flowering herbaceous plants as I allow, because they look attractive for a very long season—*Viola cornuta,* giant chives, *Anthemis cupaniana* and the like—makes an adequately furnished setting for rather late-flowering tulips.

They can be planted where groups of dahlias or cannas or a variety of annuals are to follow later. Or they can go among perennial groups such as Japanese anemones, that start late into growth. And if I am replanting perennials that I know will look thinnish for a year or two, I interplant with tulips. They are not usually confined to the area of the perennial that they are mainly intended to bolster, but run into any other suitable neighbouring groups.

There is a difficulty in pin-pointing varieties that one likes and that will all flower at about the same time. I picked out a number whose appearance I fancied at a Chelsea Flower Show, but little idea of time of flowering can be gathered there, where the blooms have been retarded or brought on in varying degrees so as to be at their peak at the vital moment. Bulb merchants' catalogues give only the vaguest notion of flowering seasons. Thus, the Lily Flowered tulips are given as early May flowering, but there is no indication of which among them flower earlier or later than the rest, though these differences do exist. A typical varietal description, of which I take a random sample, gives the name and then the height. That, at least, is useful. Then, 'Charming warm chinese rose Tulip of exceptional merit, a flower of perfect formation and marvellous colour, elegantly carried on a stiff slender stem. Planted in a group in the garden it produces a picture beyond one's utmost expectations'. What is one to glean from this verbiage? That the tulip is pink. Nothing more. What a waste of print. Searching through the descriptions of every tulip in one of the best known bulb catalogues, there were only two varieties, Breitner and Dillenburg, whose flowering was specified as late.

Obviously there are no absolute flowering dates that can be given, as the growing seasons are at their most variable in spring time. What one wants to know are the *relative* flowering times of the many varieties. Given the same growing conditions, this will vary by no more than a very few days in different years.

Would it not be possible for the bulb firms to publish a flowering time-scale of say, 1 to 40 days, showing the day on which each variety could be expected to start its season? The figure 1 would then follow the name of, perhaps, *Tulipa kaufmanniana*, which opens the tulip season, and 40 would accompany Messrs. Breitner & Dillenburg, opening their season 40 days later, with all the others strung out at their appropriate intervals along the intervening days.

How anyone can remain indifferent, even hostile, towards this flower, passes my understanding, yet many fastidious gardeners disapprove. The tulip is many things, not just one, and you can choose and treat it to suit your own tastes. For use in a formal setting, such as public or town gardens, it is a regimental flower, to be arranged in serried ranks. It is this treatment that puts many people off tulips. In the right place I personally like it, though I do not want it thus in my own garden. Tulips are just as amenable to an informal arrangement.

You can also choose between formality and informality in the flower itself. Darwins are the most formal tulip group. They are also the dullest in outline; rather solid, square-shouldered blobs, lacking elegance. But, although generally long stemmed, they are sturdy and remarkably wind resistant. If the flower still holds together, we shall not mind too much when the wind blows a tulip stem aslant—not in an informal setting, anyway. Tulips, unlike daffodils, are resilient. If a daffodil is knocked down by wind and rain, down it stays; but tulips are gifted with swan-like necks, which they can turn so as always to face upwards again.

The comparatively new class of Darwin Hybrids have the blood of *T. fosteriana* in them. Now this is the very early-flowering species with enormous, pillar-box red flowers—exciting in the early spring garden but undeniably vulgar. It has imparted its hectic colouring to the Darwin, in these hybrids; also its size, some of its precociousness and, alas, its frailty. I have one of the less enormous cultivars, called Red Matador, and I am fond of it; a glowing red with a subtle carmine bloom on the outer segments. But the moment the wind gets up, Red Matador's flowers are blown apart and smashed. Their weakness is near the base of the petal, and it is here that they disintegrate.

Informality in a tulip flower is often, but not always, achieved at the expense of wind toleration. The informal bloom tends to have long segments. Lacking compactness, it offers too great an expanse of sail to the ambient air. Of this type, the cottage tulip, Rosy Wings, is a sad case. A delightful salmon-pink colour and a long and shapely flower, but needing the utmost seclusion if its stems are not to heel over at the base, and its flowers not to be ruined.

Another cottage tulip, Mother's Day, is remarkably garden-worthy, however. This one I picked out on the show bench, for its sturdiness of stem and for its soft, pale yellow colouring with just a hint of green in it. Too many yellow tulips start to develop orange and red tints as they age, first at the petal margins and then over the whole flower. But Mother's Day retains its pristine pallor; only its name could put one off. The petals taper to points, as is often the way with the cottage class, thereby saving them from lumpishness. It is a mixed group, however, for in General de la Rey, the petals are broad and rounded, and the main appeal is in its subtle buff-pink colouring, green-zoned at the centre of the bowl.

Elegance of flower form is consistently achieved in the lily-flowered and parrot classes. The finely tapered segments of a lily-flowered tulip might seem to commit it, inevitably, to wind-susceptibility, but this is fortunately not always so. Perhaps the finest of all white bedding tulips is the hideously named White Triumphator. It came to me in a 'superfine mixture' of lily-flowered tulips 'of many different varieties all blooming about the same time.' Thus spoke the catalogue. In fact, it included only six varieties, and none of yellow or orange shading. White Triumphator stood head and shoulders above the rest—far too dominant for a mixture but it is strikingly handsome on its own. It has, more-over, not merely held its own but multiplied.

The most thrilling lily-flowered tulip of recent years is Queen of Sheba. Its large blooms are a hot, brownish orange, edged a lighter, clear orange and shading to sultry green at the base. It looks good at every stage, from the moment colour comes into its buds, to the last full-blown stage when the flowers are ex-panded into 10-inch-wide stars.

Lilies

Whatever the 'lilies of the field' that we read of in St. Matthew's gospel may have been (and they were pretty certainly not lilies at all), they bore, in their simplicity, not the faintest resemblance to the spectacular hybrids of today, most of them emanating from Mr. Jan de Graaff's Oregon Bulb Farms. Their glamour is not—indeed, cannot—be exaggerated even in the coloured illustrations of a bulb catalogue. And yet, when we come to grow them in this country, what do we find? A few settle down as reliable garden plants, but in most cases the bulbs rapidly deteriorate until, at the end of 3 years at the outside, there is nothing left.

It has to be appreciated that Mr. de Graaff's bulbs are grown under very different conditions from what we can or would wish to offer them. Not only are there the obvious differences of climate and soil; there is the further difference in purpose. We are growing them as permanent garden, woodland or pot plants. He is grow-ing them for sale as cut flowers or as bulbs and never sees his plants again after the second year. He changes the land on which he grows his bulbs every other year, to land that has never seen

lilies before and even then finds it pays hands down to sterilise
this new land chemically before planting.

About 99 per cent. of all lily bulbs sold in this country are
imported: perhaps two thirds from Oregon, the rest from
Holland and Japan. The customer seldom receives them before
the end of November; more often in the dead of winter
or in spring. These bulbs were lifted in the previous September
and kept hanging around not just for weeks but for months. All
their roots have dried up and died. The loose scales of which the
bulb is composed, have shrivelled.

Mr. de Graaff himself states in his book on lilies that bulb
planting should be completed by September or October (while
the ground is still warm) and that bulbs should under no circumstances be out of the ground for more than 10 days. But his own
bulbs are not on sale till the new year. The middle-men will not
handle them earlier. They insist on getting the hyacinths, daffodils
and tulips out of the way first. These, then—the shrivelling of the
bulb and its roots before the customer receives it and the generally inclement weather at the time he gets it for planting—are
prime reasons for the failure of lilies ever to get started with us.

There is one producer in this country who is raising and distributing home grown bulbs that really are in prime condition.
This is David Parsons at Baas Manor Lily Nurseries, Broxbourne,
Herts. He has been trying out de Graaff's hybrids and gradually
discovering which of them will take to the growing conditions
that we can offer them and not merely remain in good health but
multiply by self division. And he is also developing seed strains
of American origin that will flourish here. His bulbs are sent out
freshly lifted, in September.

Alas, our troubles will not be at an end when we have acquired
plump lily bulbs with their roots intact. Lilies are prey to a
complex of virus diseases and this is something we can't just
ignore but should try to understand. Some lilies, if they are not
killed outright, are yet rendered quite useless by virus diseases.
Notable among these are *Lilium auratum, L. speciosum, L. sargentii,
L. longiflorum, L. formosanum, L. candidum* and *L. regale*. Others
can have the disease yet tolerate it. Their vigour will be reduced,
but not seriously; their leaves will show the characteristic mosaic
mottling, perhaps, but they will none the less be able to flower

freely and give a good account of themselves for many years. Such are L. *tigrinum,* L. *pardalinum,* L. *henryi* and many of the hybrids.

The viruses attacking lilies are not transmitted through the seed and a seedling starts off with a clean bill of health. Mr. de Graaff's lilies are all seedlings and they probably reach us virus free. Not so the Dutch and still less, the Japanese bulbs. I bought L. *henryi* bulbs from a Dutch firm not long ago, that advertised its bulbs as 'free from Virus'. They were riddled with virus. Indeed, the mosaic patterning of pale and yellow green on their foliage was so marked as to be quite pretty. Instead of growing 6 or 7 ft. tall, as this lily should, they were only 4 ft. Nevertheless, they flowered and continue to flower extremely well, and the reduced height, when they are being used in pots, is actually an advantage.

One should, I think, try to take a practical rather than an emotional view of this question. The amateur lily specialist tends to regard virus disease with such horror that he considers it wicked not to destroy bulbs that are known to be infected. This seems nonsense to me. If you want to grow the susceptible species, then certainly you must be vigilant to throw out any suspected cases and it will be wise to eliminate or at least segregate carriers in the shape of lilies that may have the disease but not show it. But if you just want a good show, as most gardeners do, then the sensible line is to grow the kinds that put up with pests and diseases and still come out smiling.

Briefly to dispose of other lily troubles. The virus diseases are spread by aphids (greenfly). There are now systemic aphicides available which remain operative in the plants' cell sap over a period of 3 weeks or so. Aphids feeding on this sap will die within a day or so. The material I use is called Saphicol. What I like about it is that it is specific, going for the aphid and for nothing else. Other aphid sprays may include DDT and BHC, but these are materials that persist in the ground for years after they have been used and I do not believe in resorting to them. It is all too easy to become spray-gun happy. Far better to use your loaf and to attack specific pests and diseases with specific counter-measures, than to go in for all-purpose sprays, hitting blindly in every direction.

Botrytis causes the most serious fungal disease in lilies. Water-soaked patches appear on their foliage during the growing season and rapidly extend so as to kill, prematurely, a large proportion if not all of the leaves. The trouble is worst in a wet season and is aggravated by overhead watering. A protective fungicide like Bordeaux mixture, applied before the trouble starts, can be helpful but often seems not to make much difference.

Where lilies are grown in the garden, slugs are a great scourge. Especially so is the small black slug that spends its whole life (how long, I wonder, is a slug's expectation of life?) underground, nestling among the lily bulbs' scales; and especially are these prevalent on heavy, wet clay soils such as mine. Planting the bulbs in grit helps. Another excellent cultural recommendation is to add a bucketful of peat to the soil in which every lily bulb is planted. It encourages strong and active root growth, which helps to counter-balance slug damage.

Lilies in Pots

The lilies with which I have the greatest success in my clay-soil garden are those that produce roots from the base of the bulb only, such as *L. pardalinum, L. martagon* and its lovely albino form, *L. szovitsianum* and *L. testaceum*. The stem-rooters are less successful and seem to be more prone to slug infestations. The stem-rooters are those lilies which, in addition to the perennial roots they make in the conventional manner from the bottom of their bulbs, also make annual feeding roots from just above the bulb, i.e. from the base of the current season's stem. These lilies, by a lucky chance, are the easiest to grow in pots and pot culture has the great advantage of giving you complete control over slugs.

But, of course, it has other merits. It enables you to grow lilies in a garden that is entirely paved. It gives mobility. I like to group pots of lilies around our porch entrance. By bringing them on the scene as their buds are opening and removing them to their private standing ground afterwards, the display can easily be kept going from mid-June till mid-September. *Pace* the purists, who consider it cheating, I have also been known to plunge pots of lilies just about to flower, into gaps that have developed mid-season in my borders.

The season kicks off with L. 'Ruby', a rather dumpy but most obliging cultivar with mahogany red, upturned flowers on short, but weakish, stems. Nearly all pot-grown lilies need discreet support while flowering, with thin canes and thin, soft string— 2-ply fillis is the grade I use. Ruby is closely followed by Enchantment, with fiery red goblets and Destiny, soft yellow with dark spots. July is the high season for lilies and the choice is legion. Some of the turk's cap types are excellent, such as the cool yellow, freely spotted Citronella. And there are the bright orange turk's caps of L. 'Maxwill' and L. *davidii*. There is a good strain of the latter which you can raise from seed to flower in two seasons, called Red Davidii, in shades ranging from red to bronze.

I am generally less successful with the trumpets, but they can be very good. At the end of July, L. *henryi* starts its season. I never tire of its gentle apricot colouring. At the same time comes L. *auratum platyphyllum*, followed by L. *auratum* itself, but the former is much the easier to grow although its broad leaves give it a comparatively coarse look. L. *speciosum*, of the large pink, scented turk's caps, comes in at the end of August and continues well into September and L. *formosanum*, although its season is variable, is often at its best then. It has the most exquisite long trumpets and the best scent of all, wafted at night-time only, but alas it is a martyr to virus disease and needs continually replacing with fresh stock raised from seed.

I usually choose some mild day in January or February for repotting my lilies. They have spent the previous 3 or 4 months in a non-frost-proof shed where they are kept on the dry side but never allowed to dry right out. There is a great satisfaction in finding that your bulbs have retained long tresses of healthy basal roots. It gives them the best of starts to the new season. It may not be fatal to start with rootless bulbs and, as I have pointed out, most of those we buy are rootless. But if our own bulbs are in this condition, it is more often because they got too water-saturated at the end of their growing season. It is difficult to overwater potted lilies that are in clay pots and in full growth during June and July, but, as autumn approaches, their requirements fall off, whereas the tendency towards heavier rainfall increases. This is the one factor making for any difficulty in growing lilies in pots entirely in the open. If, like me, you have no alternative in the way of spare greenhouse accommodation, then it is a good idea to turn the pots on their sides when heavy autumn rains are on.

My potting compost for all lilies is John Innes No. 2, and I find this perfectly satisfactory even for lovers of acid soils such as *Lilium auratum*. The compost includes a stated amount of added lime, but this merely counteracts the acidifying effect of soil sterilisation: it does not make the compost alkaline or inimical to lilies. One sees all sorts of recipes for lily composts prescribed, but it is much simpler to use the John Innes formula whenever you can, or else a soil-less compost, in which case regular feeding must be practised.

I rub all the old soil away and re-pot with, usually, 3 large bulbs to a 10 in., or one to a 6-in. pot. Clay pots are better than plastic because overwatering is then less probable, because they are heavier and less easily blown over and because they look better for display purposes.

After re-potting, the lilies go back under the potting bench or somewhere similar and are watered once weekly or once a fortnight, according to the weather and until the shoots begin to appear. They are then transferred to a cold frame. I choose one in a sheltered position as this will be their standing ground for the whole growing season, except when actually flowering. The frame is kept covered (but ventilated) until lily shoots begin to press against it, for again, at this early stage before the bulbs are at their most active, over-watering can be rather dangerous.

Routine spraying with fungicides and aphicides are now the principal tasks, as well as careful attention to watering, as required. Feeding with liquid fertiliser is also a good plan, but I must confess that it's dot and carry with me. If a soil-less compost is being used, reserves of nutrients are quickly used up and you simply must add them.

Should you, at flowering, bring your pots into the house, don't place them in the dark sort of position that you might choose for the chimney bell flower (*Campanula pyramidalis*), for instance. The latter will be thrown away when it has flowered, so that there's no future to worry about in its case, but the lilies' foliage needs all the light it can get if the bulbs are not to be weakened and the following year's display jeopardised.

Bargains from the Chain Stores

Some of our largest chain stores have a well stocked gardening counter in spring and autumn, and it is always fascinating to see what bulbs and plants are being offered. You need to be highly critical and selective before giving in to this temptation. I wonder, for instance, how much joy those huge amaryllis bulbs, in their gaily illustrated packages, will give to their purchasers. It is not that they are necessarily of poor quality in themselves, but that they are not straightforward bulbs like hyacinths or tulips, to be put out in the garden and then left to get on with it. Yet this is seldom realised.

We start off here with a confusion in naming, because the only true *Amaryllis* is *A. belladonna,* and this is a hardy bulb that can be flowered against a baking, sunny wall. The bulbs actually being offered, with heads of large funnel flowers in vermilion, white and a whole range of intermediate shades, are **hippeastrums.** If they are to be flowered in the early months of the year, they need a good deal of greenhouse heat, but if you are content to have them in bloom about April, they can be managed in any cool but frost-free greenhouse. Where most people are likely to fall down in their cultivation is in caring for the plants during that important but boring period when they are merely putting forth their broad strap-shaped leaves.

The hippeastrum starts its growing season by flowering. Then comes the foliage; and all the time it is growing through the summer months, regular watering and liquid feeding is necessary. Once frost danger is past, however, the pots (for this is essentially a pot-plant, in Britain) can be stood out in cold frames where they get the maximum amount of sun. Towards the end of summer, you can start gradually withholding water, so that growth is brought to a stand-still, the leaves wither, and, with a sigh of relief, you can at last store the pots on their sides under the greenhouse bench.

At spring's return you will see young foliage beginning to poke out from the neck of the bulb. It must be brought out into the light again. Re-potting (a 6-in. pot should be large enough for one bulb) usually needs to be carried out only every third year, at which time there will be a number of dead roots to be removed

from among the fleshy, white, live ones. In other years, all that
needs to be done is to winkle out as much old soil as possible
from the top of the pot, using a sharp-pointed wooden label, and
replace with fresh potting compost. The main danger now will be
from over-watering before the bulb is growing strongly enough
to cope with so much moisture. This would end in a sorry mush.

Hippeastrums, then, are not difficult to grow, but they do
insist on a definite routine. What to do with them when you have
got them in flower is another matter. In the average drawing-
room a visitor from Mars would look scarcely more surprising.
One mistake we make in their respect, I think, is in always growing them singly, thus accentuating their naked artificiality. They
look more pleasing, and more exciting too, if several bulbs are
grouped in a really large pot.

Another chain store conceit that caused me to smile was the
sight of lily bulbs labelled and illustrated as the brilliant blue
agapanthus. Now the agapanthus has fleshy roots but no bulbs.
These were indisputably lily bulbs, and of whatever colour, they
were going to give the purchaser a surprise, for they could never
come blue. A more obvious deception, because they were being
sold in flower: single white arabis masquerading as aubrietas. As
far as I know there's no such thing as a white aubrieta which is
odd, when you come to think of it, as most plants have albino
forms. At least arabis is in the same family. Similarly I have seen
a potted plant of pearlwort (*Sagina*) labelled *Arenaria balearica*.
They, again, belong to the same family but whereas the former
has little green flowers, the arenaria is covered with pure white
stars on thread-fine stalks.

Another denizen of the chain store in spring is *Clematis tangutica*; dormant plants done up in plastic bags sell at 2/od. a time.
These will be year-old seedlings, and there is no reason why they
should not succeed. The most likely disappointment is from their
diminutive flower size. The pretty picture on the bag shows yellow
lanterns, but without giving any scale. Thus the imagination
depicts something about the size of a wall-bracket lampshade,
whereas an inch-long flower is actually nearer the mark. No one
familiar with *C. tangutica* would decry it on this account: it is just
a question of what you are expecting.

A large flowered clematis our local store sometimes offers

cheap is Mme Le Coultre, alias Marie Boisselot—one of the most dramatic of all hardy white flowers. These are small, growing plants, straight out of a greenhouse—a wisp of stem with pale, fragile leaves. Their chances of survival if put straight out into the garden are practically.nil. If given a period of hospital treatment followed by steady convalescence, their prospects could be bright, but the average buyer can hardly be expected to know that special treatment is called for.

On house plants of the foliage type, these stores are at their best. But the most genuine bargain buy I have made has been of a nice pot-grown plant of the broom Hollandia. This is a pink hybrid derived from *Cytisus praecox,* which is pale yellow and was also on offer: both at a mere 2/9d. each.

Bog, Brink and Water

The Pond in Spring

Spring is a rush season for the gardener; no two ways about it. And one direction in which he must look is towards the pond. If it has come through the winter badly and is in need of re-cementing, this is the time to do the job. And it is also the best season for making and establishing a new pond.

Nowadays the fashion is to use a heavy grade of black polythene as a lining for an artificial pond and also for the mud on its banks wherein your marginal plants will become established. Artificial streams are entirely lined in polythene, too. The material lasts indefinitely and is impervious to assaults by frost and ice. How did we ever get on without it?

But there is a snag that I have yet to see overcome satisfactorily. At its edges, the polythene has to come into sight. It has to make a distinct barrier between the soil that is permanently waterlogged and the soil that is not. There must be no connection between these two soil types. Otherwise there will be a permanent seepage and loss of water from the wet side to the dry. Consequently the polythene edges are allowed to rise an inch or two above the surrounding soil surface. This, to me, looks vile. Some people are apparently able to turn a blind eye to it. If you say to them, with a touch of horrified reproach in your voice, 'but what about the polythene edges?' they will reply nonchalantly, 'oh! the plants will soon conceal all that'. But the plants, in fact, never do make a complete job of it.

If the pond is part of a rock garden, you can organise flattish rock slabs to overhang the margins. This has been very effectively achieved in the Northern Horticultural Society's gardens at Harlow Car, just outside Harrogate. And it needs to be well done, otherwise you steer from the Scylla of an abominable pool to the Charybdis of an insufferable rockery.

A formal quadrangular or polygonal pond could also have its concrete or polythene margins concealed by slightly overlapping paving, but here again you do want to use the best grade available and not make do with the cheap concrete slabs (usually all of the same size and shape) that are most readily available. York stone always looks pleasing, though it is, one should remember, slippery in wet weather. Many's the time I've slid into our formal pool while momentarily forgetting this point. This paving is more readily available than you might suppose. One quotation for it that I had not long ago, from M. P. Harris, the builders' merchants with branches all over the south and east, was 37/3d. per square yard for small quantities, falling to 30/0d. for a full load. One of the paving grades offered by the Atlas Stone Co. of Rye, Sussex, makes a particularly pleasing substitute for the real thing, however, and runs out at 22/9d. per square yard. Prices will rise but the comparison should remain valid. They call it, rather repulsively, Super Hortex, and it has a slightly uneven, figured surface (the figuration varies from one stone to another like watered silk) which looks natural and was, indeed, originally obtained by making a cast against the surface of some real stone paving. The slabs are available in four different shapes and sizes and in five quiet colours, which gives a good range of possible permutations.

The water in a pond is at its clearest in winter but at its most densely opaque in spring. Ours takes on the colour and consistency of turbid coffee. This is inevitable. The light is strong, the water is warming rapidly and conditions are ideal for the development of algae, which is the cause of this turbidity and of the suppurating blobs of bubble-filled slime that rise to the surface on sunny days.

In a well balanced water community this trouble will sort itself out by the middle or end of June. There is too much light in the water in spring, but by then the water-lily leaves will have expanded, and there will be a considerable development of the submerged aquatics, which themselves compete successfully with algae. In a young pool that has not yet settled down, you may continue to get an unsightly algal display throughout the growing season. It is true that you can control it by dissolving a suitable quantity of copper sulphate crystals in the water. But the effect doesn't last: the algae soon return in force.

If about a third of the water surface is shaded with water-lily leaves (not more, or you lose too much of the pleasure of seeing the water, its reflections and its movement in wind and rain), and if there are sufficient submerged oxygenating plants and plenty of fish, your algal troubles will usually resolve themselves. Not always, though, and I doubt if there is an expert who can solve the few really intractable cases where a pond owner seems to have done everything he should and waited patiently for the algae to subside without this actually happening.

If I have emphasised the benefits of shade on and in the water, it should be understood that this must be provided by the water plants themselves and not by trees overhanging the water. Few heavily tree-shaded pools are a great success because most aquatics and marginal plants like full sun. Exceptionally, gunneras will flourish in partial shade; so will our native yellow flag, *Iris pseudacorus,* and so also will king-cups, *Caltha palustris,* and the skunk cabbage, *Lysichitum americanum,* with its bright yellow arum spathes in April.

A further drawback to the willows (or other trees) that grow aslant your pond is the baleful effect on animal and plant life of their accumulated dead foliage at the bottom. Again, all fringe trees, but particularly willows, lap up an enormous quantity of water in summer. However, if the willows (which, after all, do make a fascinating study, such is the range of them that are worth collecting) are pollarded every other year to a low stump, they are innocuous enough.

Plate 11. Lysichitum americanum is a hardy arum enjoying wet, waterside conditions. Its bright yellow spathes open in April and are followed by large glossy leaves.

Too vigorous water-lilies have much the same influence and lower the water level. Many a pond or small lake has been ruined by being planted, in the first place, with these take-over types to which, unfortunately, nearly all those with white and sulphur flowers (the pygmies excepted) belong. Water-lilies have enormously strong roots and rhizomes; once established in a pond bottom they are hard to control. If they get congested, their foliage, from early July onwards, stands out of the water in a most unpleasing way and entirely conceals the flowers, while the water itself becomes likewise obscured.

Starting in the drought year of 1959 with help from the local water-board and their dredger, we took five years to eliminate the common white water-lily from our horse pond (it still has a gravelly bottom at that point where the horses used to be led in to drink). Only then did it become possible to enjoy ourselves.

A pond can never be left to its own devices for too long. Its special weeds are astonishingly robust, but if you can once get the upper hand, it requires only one willing person (an amphibious member of the family is a great asset) to spend one day in each year (July or August is a good time) pulling out any over-exuberant plant growth, and you will remain in command. The pond garden, apart from new plantings, will require no further attention. Now I call that a very labour saving form of gardening and the rewards are far greater than can generally be expected of self-consciously labour saving practices.

Establishing Water Plants

Plants that will grow actually in water are more useful on the whole, I find, than most of those that we are recommended to grow at the waterside. If the water retreats, in summer, from plants grown in the bed of a pond, there is usually enough residual moisture available to keep them in reasonable spirits. Not so on the bank. This position is all too likely to be subjected to alternating ordeals by drought and flood.

Plate 12. *Above*, globe artichoke, Vert de Laon, decorative and edible.
Below, seakale, with honey-scented white flowers, seen on its native shore.

I have for 12 years grown the greenhouse **arum,** *Zantedeschia aethiopica,* in various parts of my garden, including the bed of the horse pond and also in pots in a formal pool. In the ferocious winter of 1962–63 all those grown in water were killed, but those grown unprotected in the open border survived. The moral here is that water is a grand protection against intense cold as long as the crowns of your plants are situated below ice level. Normally, a foot below the winter surface level would be ample for arums, but on this occasion it was not; and if your plants should get frozen into a solid block of ice, they are far worse off than in a comparatively dry border, covered by a snug snow blanket. Winters of such severity are quite rare enough to be ignored, and nothing should deter us from striving to obtain the incomparable picture of arums in a setting that does them justice, for once— their pure white, sinuously outlined blooms and scarcely less handsome foliage mirrored in water.

Late spring and early summer is the best season for getting aquatics established; the water is tepid and they will grow visibly from day to day. If you are planting them in a container (a submerged box or basket) or on the floor of a natural pond, it may be necessary to consider the question of anchorage. At the time that we cleared out our horse pond, we built a special submerged island for the arums and after the 1963 disaster, this was replanted in the following summer. These plants overwintered in great style, but no sooner had their young leaves breasted the surface in spring, than the entire plant bobbed up and floated away. The same thing happened to all nine plants. We had to start again. This time, however, we pegged the plants with a surface layer of coarse gravel, and that did the trick.

These arums have gone from strength to strength and carry upwards of 80 blooms at a time, when at the height of their season in mid-June. They are amazingly resilient plants. It takes a hard December frost to kill their foliage, but if we get a mild spell at any time during the ensuing winter, growth is renewed and new leaves appear.

They set good seed in the autumn and this can be germinated in a cold frame within a few weeks of sowing it. The plants will be large enough to flower in their second summer.

Sharing the arum's island is the **golden club,** *Orontium aquati-*

cum, which is another aroid. All its beauty is concentrated in a club-like spadix, which is yellow at the tip but white below. Dozens of them rise from the water in April and early May and then take on seductive curves as they splay outwards. Both these aroids need good deep loam in which to give of their best. You can feed them by stirring water into bone-meal in a bucket until you have a thickish paste, and then dropping handfuls of this tasty mixture on to the soil surface where your plants are growing. Any container-grown aquatic will need an annual feed of this kind.

Water-lilies are sent out by those nurseries specialising in them between May and August. The water is tepid then, and they establish quickly. Even so I prefer, where a large pond is in question, not to cast them upon the waters at once, but to grow them until strongly established in a good sized pot, placed in a small pool where I can keep my eye on them. After a month or two, they can be turned out into their permanent positions with complete certainty of success.

If I were allowed to grow only one waterlily I should be tempted to choose James Brydon. It is a strong shade of pink and the flower's shape is like a globe with the top cut off. This is an extraordinarily adaptable lily. In water 3 or 4 ft. deep it makes a correspondingly large plant with bold flowers, but plant it in 6 in. of water and it looks equally at home carrying flowers and foliage of miniature proportions. It will also put up with a certain amount of shade, although preferring full sun. Usually, it is bursting at the seams with buds and flowers but one thing I have noticed: its season starts comparatively late, not getting well under way until early July, and ends early. Those buds that are produced after the end of August never open fully, even in a heat wave.

The famous Escarboucle, by contrast, starts flowering in mid-June and is still making a brave show in October. This is a vigorous, deep crimson-red waterlily which one usually plants in about 4 ft. of water, though it can get along with less.

It is brought to bear upon the water gardener quite early in his career that a certain number of **submerged aquatic plants** are a necessity for the health of the community. One of their useful functions is to oxygenate the water. You can see them giving off oxygen bubbles, especially on sunny days. They benefit the fish and prevent the pond from becoming stagnant.

Oxygenators need no planting or establishing by any accepted method. You just drop a few pieces in and nature does the rest. Indeed, nature is inclined, in many cases (with the elodeas and potamogetons, for instance) to get too busy and to choke a pond with a dense growth of these rather dull and boorish manifestations of the vegetable kingdom.

However, there are at least two submerged aquatics for which I have a soft spot. The water violet, *Hottonia palustris*, is quite a thug, admittedly, but an engaging thug. You see it in winter, when the water is clear, rising from the deep like an emerald cloud and almost but not quite breaking the surface. It is composed of innumerable rosettes of filigree foliage. The common name of this plant is unfortunate and misleading, as is so often the case with aquatics. If it were called water primula, then we should know something about it, for hottonia belongs to the primula family and does look remarkably like a pale mauve *Primula malacoides,* when flowering. Nurseries find this a difficult plant to manipulate and market. In an old pond you will possibly find it already established, and there is plenty about in dykes up and down the country.

The water soldier, *Stratiotes aloides* (another native but rare and becoming rarer) behaves in a perfectly gentlemanly manner and is great fun. It forms large, brownish-green rosettes of narrowly tapering sword-like leaves. Big rosettes send out stolons at the ends of which small rosettes develop, so that you soon get a conglomerate colony of rosettes of many sizes. In winter they rest at the bottom of your pool, but in summer they rise so that the tips of their leaves just break the surface. It is in this position that they will carry their three-petalled white flowers, if flower they will. Mine never have.

Plants for Shallow Water

One of the nice things about water plants is that they never need watering. Another good point is that they give double value: themselves and their reflections. And they have an intrinsic freshness combined with predominantly gay colours. Furthermore their lush luxuriance contributes an appropriate feeling of opulence to the summer scene.

However, this seems an appropriate point, before describing some of my favourites, at which to consider the moorhen and its activities and our reactions to them. I am very fond of moorhens. They can get away with some pretty heinous crimes, as far as I am concerned. Time was when we used to shoot any that appeared on the scenes and eat them in moorhen pies. I well remember the needle-like sinews in their legs. We also ate their eggs which are as good as a plover's and about the same size.

But as fast as you shoot moorhens, others will come in from the neighbouring countryside. No piece of water with vegetation in and around it will be left untenanted for any length of time. All you will succeed in doing is to make them into exceedingly scary birds, on the point of disappearing even as you first espy them and always making you feel a brute—which is just about what you are. Ours, which have now remained unmolested for 15 or 20 years, are for the most part tame enough to treat us as so much garden furniture. It is a real delight to sit down by the horse pond and watch them about their business, strutting deliberately across the waterlily pads and prodding to right and to left, or marshalling their young, which are the tiniest balls of black fluff, apparently blown about the water's surface.

And a moorhen is not only a prettily-moving bird; it is extremely smart and sleek with its olive-coloured plumage, blood-red beak and white tail feathers constantly flicking up and down. Of course it is a pest. It makes not only the nest it needs but many other nests that it never uses and, to this end, it bends and breaks the foliage of plants that one would like left alone. It treads on the arums, it breaks off the shoots of the glycerias, it comes into the garden and eats the young vegetables—brassicas and lettuces in particular, so that they are hard put to it to become established.

Water voles can be equally pestilential, but they, too, are charming in action. They are particularly devastating to irises, but are disarming when you see one swimming across the pond with a green iris shoot held across its jaws like a mouth organ.

Now let us turn to some of the plants that can be grown actually under the water but rise well above it in their spring and summer season. Our native **yellow flag**, *Iris pseudacorus*, would be better esteemed if it were not so common. It makes a large plant and really needs a fair-sized pond to show it off in scale. The flowers come out in May and are bright yellow, followed in autumn by handsome clusters of·arching seed pods. The cultivar unkindly called Bastardii is pale lemon yellow, which makes a change, and there is another called, simply, Variegata, which is very beautiful in spring with its cream and pale green variegated leaves. Later they change to green throughout.

The yellow flag contrasts effectively with *I. laevigata,* which is typically a deep lavender colour. Zambesi is a good cultivar in this shade. The albino Snowdrift is also excellent. I like the reddish purple colouring of Regal, and Rose Queen comes pretty near to pink.

I. kaempferi is a much more variable and flamboyant species, from Japan, with enormously broad falls and standards that tend to flop outwards and look like falls. Generally speaking, however, it must be kept dry in winter, although it does not mind being submerged in the growing season. However, this is an awkward arrangement and it is more normal to grow it above the water level.

The ordinary **king-cup,** *Caltha palustris,* grows at the water margin and in boggy places, but Farrer's king-cup, as I always call *C. polypetala,* because he introduced it to this country, inhabits shallow water. Farrer himself gives this account of its acquisition, some 60 years ago: 'There is a romantic legend that it was for long only known in Europe in the ponds of the Vatican, whence the old Pope refused to let it go forth from that sacred seclusion into an heretic though horticultural world; but that one day some hero adventured thither on the high quest, enshrouded in a bevy of aunts, whom he discharged upon the custodians to hold them in talk, while he himself hooked out some fragments of the Caltha with his umbrella'. Unlike *C. palustris, C. polypetala* is not a clump former. Its flowering stems have a sprawling way with them, and where they sprawl they root; so it gets along and sets up a good colony in quite a short while. It is possibly unsuitable for a small pool, but not difficult to control, either. Its first flowers, coming in early April, are very large indeed. As they proliferate they become progressively smaller.

A **buttercup** with a similar flower to this is *Ranunculus lingua*

'Grandiflorus', which is just a selected form of our native Greater Spearwort. It flowers from midsummer till autumn and rises 3 or 4 ft. above the water's surface.

Another useful August-flowering aquatic is the **Canadian Pickerel Weed,** *Pontederia cordata,* with spear-shaped leaves above which rise its foot-tall spikes of genuinely blue flowers. They are small but effective and this rare colour is more than welcome in a pond. The plant spreads without effort into a good colony.

The **flowering rush** (which is not a rush), *Butomus umbellatus,* has such reed-like leaves that, in a well weeded pond, it tends to get pulled out with all the real reeds. It is a native of shallow dykes and disused canals and so attractive on account of its heads of pink, saucer shaped blooms, that it is getting a bit scarce in some places. Cattle are just as keen on its foliage and will munch it off to water level wherever they get the chance. If grown within the confines of a pot or even a large box, as one might treat it in a small pool, the flowering rush refuses to flower after the first year, unless it is split up and re-planted annually. It likes a free root-run.

There are some plants, normally found in damp borders, that surprise us by revelling in a few inches of water. At the end of their growing season, they form dense basal rosettes of overwintering foliage that remain clearly visible throughout the cold months, and eventually elongate into next year's shoots with the advent of warmer weather. One such is the **yellow loosestrife,** *Lysimachia punctata.* I had never admitted it into my borders on account of its coarse and invasive habit. But in a fair-sized pond its robust nature enables it to compete with other similar, or even more freely colonising, companions. Its dense spikes of substantial yellow blossoms are very showy.

Then there is that tantalising beauty, **Lobelia cardinalis,** the cardinal flower. We tend to treat it as a tender perennial, but there are hardy geographical races. It grows, after all, in the stream beds of some of the coldest areas of New England. I find that the smooth purple-leaved strain which I grow is absolutely hardy. It carries its spikes of glowing red, insect-like flowers in August and September.

Pond plants do not necessarily have to make their welcome

with flowers. The Japanese rush called **Scirpus tabernaemon-tanus** 'Zebrinus' makes elegant tubular wands some 3-ft. long, alternately cross-banded in green and white. **Glyceria aquatica** 'Variegata' is a reed-grass with strap leaves that are longitudinally striped green and cream. In spring, while young and still lying on the water's surface, they are pink. Eventually they rise to a height of 3 ft. This is quite an invasive plant and may need checking. It can be grown on dry land but does not look nearly so well, becoming very untidy at the latter end. As much can be said for Gardener's Garters or Ribbon Grass, *Phalaris arundinacea* 'Picta', with green-and-white-striped leaves. In a border it looks comely only till about midsummer, flopping around thereafter, but under water it remains neat to the last. This grows 4 to 5 ft. tall.

It is well worth putting **Cyperus alternifolius** into the garden pool for the summer. It is tender, and usually treated as a foliage pot-plant, but pot and all can be dropped into 3 or 4 in. of water in early summer. Indeed, it appears to relish this change of environment, for it will flower freely (just tufts of pollen-bearing anthers; nothing to get excited about), whereas on the kitchen window-sill, or wherever you may normally cherish it, flowering is unusual. The crowded, 18-in.- to 2-ft.-tall stems are crowned with palm-like tufts of foliage that are decorative in any setting and remind one of its august relative, the Egyptian papyrus or paper reed.

Gunnera manicata: A Giant by the Waterside

If your garden is reasonably free of pervasive, man-made noises— from aircraft, road traffic, radio sets and all the rest of them—one of the most relaxing ways to enjoy it is by stretching yourself out on a piece of grass, closing your eyes and . . . no, not dropping off to sleep; you will probably wake up flushed and in a temper. Just lie and listen. Let your ears take over: they are far more alert and receptive when vision is cut off. You will become intensely aware of birdsong, of fish rising (my favourite spot is near our pond), but, above all, of the various noises made by different kinds of foliage. The oaks sound like the distant sea, while the aspens are more personal. Their rustling is obviously composed of a collection of individuals in conversation. But the oddest sound, when the wind rises a little, is of **gunnera** leaves in motion. Here you might be listening to a giant shaving; the hollow quality of the noise suggests that he has reached his jaw and has let his mouth hang open.

On examining the leaves of *Gunnera manicata*, you see that it does indeed suffer from stubble trouble over the entire upper surface. On their undersides, the leaf veins are sharply armed, while the stalk is prickly enough to puncture even the palate of a hippopotamus, or whatever the animal may be that would otherwise devour it in its native Brazil. Everything about this gunnera —the largest hardy herbaceous plant that can be grown in Britain —is on the grand scale, But it is not grotesque, neither is it coarse, and those who think otherwise have clearly never lived in close proximity to one. It is a strongly and beautifully constructed plant, so well made that even in quite exposed positions it will withstand continual buffetings without being damaged. The leaves remain fresh and handsome till the day before the first air frost of autumn finally slays them.

Perhaps they are most admirable when seen in low sunlight. Where the sun catches their top sides, you notice how these undulate, the furrows corresponding with the veins, while the leaf as a whole is dished. But where the sun shines through them you are chiefly aware of the reflected light from ripples off the water's surface.

Gunneras look their best at the waterside, but their thick rhizomatous crowns must be above flood level, for they will not stand being drowned. Their roots go very deep, and so it is quite safe to plant them 3 or 4 ft. above the normal water level and to let them reach out for their own water supplies. Only in dry periods during the first summer after planting, before they have had a chance to establish an efficient root network, should they be watered copiously by hand.

They can be grown in full sun or in the quite deep shade of trees. In the latter situation, we have a plant with leaves that are 6 ft. across, borne on 7-ft. stalks. 'What do you call that? Rhubarb?' is a frequent question from jocular visitors. It jars a little with repetition. After all, the rhubarbs are strikingly handsome plants, too. In a sunny position. *G. manicata* grows only 5-ft. tall with leaves of a 4-ft. span, but it is probably happier in sun. One is not obliged to place it within sight of water. Any damp or boggy spot will do.

For winter, the gunnera makes, at ground level, enormous resting buds, protected by a fuzz of reddish scales. A thick piece of rhizome leads up to each bud and, if you want to make a new plant, you should chop through one of these with a spade, in April, just as growth is renewed. But chop far enough behind the bud, say 6 or 8 in., to include some roots, which are on the under-side of the rhizome.

Another way of increasing gunneras is from seed. I have raised a good many this way at various times, and seed is offered by Messrs. Thompson & Morgan of Ipswich, or you can save your own. But the outcome is chancy, and, in as many years as not, the seed fails to germinate. The gunnera's inflorescence is an extraordinary looking, cone-shaped affair, about 2-ft. long and made up of a large number of fleshy green spikelets covered with green pimples. Some of these turn orange, later in the season, and I gather a handful of them in autumn. They spend the winter drying out on a sunny window-sill. At the end of March I scrape the pimples off the spikelets and sow them. What the best conditions are for germination, I have not discovered. I can never get them to germinate in darkness. And it is usually not until July that the first seedlings appear. By then the seed pot is stand-ing in the open. The seedlings can be potted off individually as soon as large enough to handle. They should be overwintered in a frost-proof frame or greenhouse and can, if large enough to fill a 5-in. pot, be planted out in the following June—the best time for establishing them in the garden. If not large enough, hold them over for another year.

A great danger for gunneras of any age is from a late spring frost on the young foliage. In severe winters, and in the vicious sort of frost pockets where you are most likely to want to plant gunneras, because of the availability of water, established crowns may get killed. Immediately following the first frost òf autumn, you should always fold the old, frosted leaves back over the centre of the plant, by way of protection.

It is worth noting that there are two quite distinct strains of *G. manicata* in cultivation in this country, but with nothing to differentiate them in the nurserymen's catalogues. The one which

I have, is altogether larger growing than the other, with broader, solider leaves and with wider, plumper looking, flowering cones. This is the one to try and get, but you will have to recognise and choose the plant yourself, because you are unlikely to obtain outside help in doing so.

Shrubs for Boggy Places: Dogwoods and Willows

Gardeners are sometimes confronted with the problem of how to treat an area of boggy ground so as to have it looking presentable with the minimum of effort. If it can be drained, then obviously a great range of trees, shrubs and herbaceous plants will immediately suggest themselves. But drainage should not be looked upon as a first necessity in every case. Even without seeking beyond certain dogwoods and a great many willows, we can do some very satisfactory gardening with a boggy area just as we find it.

The **dogwood** with the brilliant carmine stems is *Cornus alba*. *Alba* seems a bit of a misnomer, but could be justified, I suppose, either on the basis of its small dingy white flowers or of its scarcely·more conspicuous white berries. This is a fine plant with which to colonise boggy ground. The glistening bark of the young wood makes a vivid display from leaf-fall right up till early April, especially effective, of course, in sunshine but also, if sited near a drive, when the beam of your car headlights momentarily lights it up at night, and also when reflected in a pond.

The shrub is easily increased from foot-long pieces of year-old stems, stuck by two-thirds their length in the ground where you want them to grow. That should be done in autumn. Alternatively, they come from seed, and self-sown seedlings often establish themselves along a pond margin.

This dogwood needs fairly regular pruning just before growth is resumed. It is a great temptation to postpone the job from week to week. It seems such a shame to cut away those still lovely stems. Then, suddenly, the shrubs are in full leaf and you realise that it is too late to set about them, for the shock and set-back would now be considerable.

Pruning consists of shortening the shoots back to a stump within 6 in. of ground level. It is best not to cut all the shoots back every year, because this has a cumulatively weakening effect on the shrub as a whole and also reduces its stature beyond what is likely to be desirable. Cut them back every third year, choosing the oldest, stoutest shoots as your victims each time the job comes round, and leaving two-thirds of the bushes untouched. The point to bear in mind is that the youngest shoots are the most brightly coloured. Dogwood treated in this way will make a thicket 7 ft. high.

In this garden we have the common form of *C. alba*, but if we were starting again from scratch I should make a point of acquiring the even more brilliantly coloured Westonbirt variety, sometimes listed as *sibirica*, sometimes as *atrosanguinea*. Alternatively, the yellow and green variegated-leaved form called Spaethii would strongly recommend itself, where it could be given a good dark background. The dogwood leaf is normally as uninteresting as a leaf can be, but this one's variegation is most telling, and its winter stems are as bright as ordinary *C. alba*'s. Or there is Variegata, which has a white and green variegation.

Another bright-barked dogwood that should be associated with *C. alba* is *C. stolonifera flaviramea*. It has much the same habit of growth, (though it suckers freely) and is treated similarly. But its bark is a light greeny yellow. From a distance it looks bright yellow. Probably the most spectacular planting, on a landscape scale, ever made of dogwoods in this country is at Hurstmonceux Castle, Sussex, where there are broad alternate plantings of the carmine and the yellow against a background of silver birches. That really is something worth looking at through the winter.

The **willows** are fascinating and so diverse in their habits and uses that I wish a botanically minded horticulturist would devote a book to them. Unfortunately it would not sell, since most willows lack the necessary S.A. (shrub appeal) for the general gardening public. For initiates, their attractions can be grouped under four main headings: shrub or tree form, leaf colour, stem colour and catkins (pussies). Really one should add leaf shape as a fifth. Where stem colour is the main draw, catkins may have to be sacrificed. The best bark colour comes on first year shoots and these must be cut back to a stump in early spring. If the willow flowers early, and before you need cut it back, so much the better. But if not, pollarding must take preference.

The bark colouring on young stems is extraordinarily varied. Occasionally our attention is forcibly and beneficially drawn to this feature by an exhibit such as Messrs. Hillier and Sons of Winchester staged in the RHS Hall one early March, a few years ago. *Salix alba* 'Chrysostella' is well known as the brightest orange-red-stemmed willow, though more familiar under the style of Britzensis. In *S.a.* 'Vitellina', the stems are a golden yellow. *S. daphnoides* has them in a kind of dusky violet, the twigs being overlaid with a bluish, waxy bloom. In the tea-leaved willow, *S. phylicifolia*, the young stems are brownish-purple, like a birch's, but highly polished. The leaves, too, are polished, rather like a camellia's and similar in shape. In the hybrid *S. ehrhartiana,* the polished young stems are pale buff, offset by black leaf buds. In *S. purpurea* 'Eugenei', the stems are pale green, lined with litters of slender pussies. *S. rehderiana* is a rich olive green, strong growing and eminently suited to hard pruning.

S. glandulosa 'Setsuka' is shown quite often. This is a 7-ft. or 8-ft. shrub of wide-spreading habit that is cultivated in its male form, which has the more telling catkins, and these bloom in March or even earlier (unless, as sometimes happens, the birds strip them first). However, the shrub's particular attraction is its natural propensity for carrying fasciated shoots. It makes a positive virtue of the habit, and a large proportion of the young branches are flattened and broadened in opposite planes, and often curled and twisted into distorted and distracted shapes that will appeal to flower arrangers, and all lovers of the grotesque.

S. cinerea 'Tricolor' is a willow of naturally restricted habit that appeals on account of its pink-cream-and-white-variegated foliage, but to my taste the distortion of the leaves gives them an unpleasantly diseased appearance. There are a number distinguished for their soft grey foliage colouring throughout the summer. The hoary willow, *S. elaeagnus* (*incana*), is particularly fetching, and worth a place in any shrubbery, even where water or bog are absent. It is sometimes listed as *S. friesiana*, sometimes as *S. rosmarinifolia,* the latter giving a good notion of its leaf form which is long and almost needle-like. The colouring is dark green above, grey beneath and the shrub grows 6 to 8 ft. tall at most, without pruning, but is wider spreading. In *S. alba sericea,* the leaves are very pale silver all over. I have planted this in my main mixed border of shrubs and plants as a foil to the golden elm. Its vigour is modest and a great deal of pruning is unnecessary.

As fillers in this bog shrubbery one could use meadow-sweet, *Filipendula ulmaria;* meadow cranesbill, *Geranium pratense* and rosebay willowherb, *Epilobium (Chamaenerion) angustifolium.* These make a spectacular trio of cream, blue and pink in the wilds of Derbyshire, in July, and will all get on well together, though the geranium should be given the driest spot. Neither should one overlook the possibility of making a major feature with a group of gunneras, as also with the royal fern *Osmunda regalis,* while the North American Sensitive Fern, *Onoclea sensibilis,* can be allowed to ramble as it pleases, for it spreads far and wide in boggy ground by suckering.

Plants for Wet Soils

Many of us, on clay soils, have unpromising beds of wet stodge with poor drainage. I want, here, to discuss the splendid herbaceous material with which these can easily be filled; coarse but handsome plants, most of them, with huge leaves that so cover the ground as to give weeds no chance at all, except in early spring before growth has got under way. They are good in shady borders but equally at home in the sun, providing they do not dry out. They all do well for we who garden in the dry south-east, but thrive the better the farther one travels north and west, so that by the time one gets to the really wet districts, they will be happy on any soil or site, well drained or not.

First the **ligularias.** These are cousins of *Senecio,* which is probably the largest genus of all, so the RHS *Dictionary* informs us, comprising some 1,3 ᴐo species (which include groundsel and ragwort). *Ligularia* is a half-hearted splinter group that often refuses to splinter, so you must look for it under *Senecio,* too. *L. wilsoniana* is one of the tallest (but self-supporting, as are all the plants to be mentioned), with flattened, heart-shaped leaves, about 1 ft. long and fresh green. Its broadly columnar spikes of yellow daisies rise to 6ft. and more, in late summer. It self-sows abundantly and also spreads by short underground rhizomes, and so should be allowed plenty of space. *L. veitchiana* is rather similar. *L. clivorum* can be had in a number of cultivars, one of the best being Desdemona. Here the leaves are broadly heart-shaped, almost kidney; of varying size, up to 18 in. across. They start purple all over and change to dusky green on the upper surface, with purple veins, but remain purplish on the underside. The deep ochre-yellow daisies are carried in broad panicles throughout late summer and autumn on 3 to 5-ft. stems and are exceedingly popular with butterflies.

L. przewalskii (try pronouncing it pritz-vulski) is a comparative newcomer. Its long, slender flower spikes are beset with small, spidery yellow daisies, but what catches the eye are the black stems. Black and yellow always combine well. And the plant's foliage deserves equal honours with the inflorescence. The leaves are palmate, up to 18 in. across, but very deeply cut into many narrow segments. They are dark green with purple veins. A burst of sunshine turns them pitifully limp and flabby, however wet the ground, but come the clouds or evening, and they hold themselves proudly again. This plant grows 6 ft. tall, when established, and, again, self-sows.

Senecio tanguticus, another six-footer, also has conspicuously cut leaves and likewise wilts in the heat. But it is really a very distinct plant. For one thing the leaf's outline, while broad at the base, comes to a point. And the spidery yellow flowers open in August and September and are carried in broadly pyramidal heads. As the seeds ripen they change to palest grey and make ornamental 'deads'. Underground is where trouble tends to occur. Fat whitish tubers—rhizomes, actually—are made in the style of a potato, but they travel deep and wide and the plant quickly builds into a huge colony. Splendid if you know what to expect and site it correctly but devastating if there are less aggressive neighbours.

Rather like the senecios and ligularias is **Buphthalmum speciosum,** a rank grower to 6 ft., with broadly ovate, mid-green foliage, up to 18 in. long. It carries stately candelabrums of 3-inch-wide, yellow daisies, with large discs and narrow, twisted rays. A nice feature, especially in the buds, is the involucre of green bracts. It is as though the plant were flowering twice: first green, then yellow. It self-sows prolifically and has made a handsome, unplanned feature in the gardens at Chatsworth.

Some of the **rhubarbs** should be included in this community.

An outsizer, even among giants, is *Rheum officinale,* with immense green leaves and a greenish-white flowering spike that rises to 10 ft. If this plant is a trifle unnerving for those who have been reared on a diet of white alyssum and blue lobelia, then R. *palmatum* will be preferred. Its leaves, especially when young, have a dusky reddish bloom on their under surface, which reveals itself in titillating glimpses, like petticoats, where a breeze lifts them. The inflorescence is pinkish red and only 6 ft. high.

Coming down to the border margins, a planting of various rodgersias would be interesting and beautiful. *Rodgersia aesculifolia* has compound, palmate leaves divided into 7 or 8 fingers, like a horse-chestnut. R. *podophylla* is the best for spring colouring—a delicious bronze when its leaves are young. The five leaflets, splaying out from a central stalk, broaden towards their trident-shaped tips. In complete contrast is the perfectly circular disc-leaf of R. *tabularis,* in pale green. In too sunny or parched a position this scorches rather. R. *pinnata* is, like the others, well described by its specific name, with 3 or 5 pairs of green leaflets on either side of a central stalk. The group as a whole is a bit dot-and-carry about its flowering, but R. *pinnata* is pretty free. Most commonly the inflorescence of tiny flowers in an elegant panicle is white; but one should make an effort to get a pink flowered form and the finest of all is the cultivar called 'Superba' with flowers verging on red.

All rodgersias gradually spread by their rhizomes and lend themselves to division but, when they flower, can also be successfully raised from seed.

Rodgersias belong to the saxifrage family and have close affinities with the **water saxifrage,** *Peltiphyllum peltatum (Saxifraga peltata).* This, again, is usually stationed by the waterside, but thrives in any damp border. It carries exceedingly pretty heads of pink flowers in spring, before the leaves emerge, and you do want to be sure of getting a strain of a good shade of pink, not washed out. The leaves subsequently rise to 3 or 4 ft. like wide-mouthed funnels, a foot across with deeply lobed margins. What with a dense network of rhizomes and a dense canopy of foliage, these are efficient and exclusive ground coverers. The leaves on my plants turn brown as soon as signs of mortality become evident in autumn, but in some gardens, notably at Inverewe in Wester Ross, where there is an avenue of peltiphyllums, they go a marvellous red, I am told.

Still in the saxifrage family we have the moisture loving **astilbes.** There is a much wider range of these than one might suppose. *Astilbe rivularis* grows 7 ft. tall and spreads in a more aggressively subterranean manner than one expects of an astilbe. It has good foliage and a graceful plume-like inflorescence of greenish white flowers—not spectacular and soon past its best, but a good space filler like the better known *Aruncus sylvester* (*Spiraea aruncus*), whose creamy panicles are more telling but are turning brown within the week.

A bold and vigorous astilbe of fairly recent introduction is *A. taquetii* 'Superba'. It grows 4 ft. tall and has a powerful personality. The inflorescences are more than usually vertical in their alignment, whereas the much dissected foliage is contrastingly spreading. The flower colouring is a vivid and uncompromising mauve (bright purple rose, to the nurseryman). If you cannot take it, well, there it is, you cannot, but to me the plant is in all respects magnificent. I have grouped it (and here we come back to where we started) in front of the tallest ligularia in my garden; *L. hessei:* a seven-footer with great kidney-shaped leaves of oily smoothness and heads of brass yellow daisies, arranged in broad columns.

Wild Gardening in Grass

Untidiness in the garden does not matter as long as the owner is aware of it and does not mind it himself. But there is a kind of congenital untidiness, lasting the year through, that worries the owner without his ever being willing to face its implications. The work required is more than he is prepared to supply, and so the garden becomes a burden and gardening a chore. Such a pity, because he could probably halve his work by making a few simple, uncompromising decisions. To grass over the beds in his lawns, for instance; to eliminate those bits of rockery that need so much hand weeding, or else plant them over with heathers that will suppress the weeds themselves. Again, to do without bearded irises, those great harbourers of weeds, or else to attack them with a weed-killer based on simazine, that will kill the seedling weeds as they are germinating.

One of my favourite branches of gardening, in rough grass, has the particular attraction that you can give it much or little attention as you feel inclined. The only essential is to cut and pick up the grass two or three times a year. Also, your nerves must be strong enough, in face of criticism, to delay the first cut until early July, when all your bulbs, wild orchids and other plants have had the chance to complete their growth and shed their seeds. The sward's dishevelled appearance for three or four weeks before the first cut is a perfectly legitimate, planned untidiness, and only temporary.

The gay colours of bulbs and other brilliant flowers are most charmingly displayed against the soothing coolness of a grass sward. However mixed the palette, a pleasing effect is gained, as long as there is no kind of regularity and all appears to be natural. It is difficult, if not impossible, to get a professional gardener to plant bulbs informally. Either he does them in tight clumps around the bole of a tree, or else they come out in straight lines. You must do the job yourself. Only by varying the planting distances between bulbs can you be sure of avoiding straight lines.

A dark background to a sunlit area of grass is the most flattering, and can be provided by trees or shrubs, and in particular, by evergreens. But the sward itself is best not interrupted by large or solid obstacles. A few small and widely spaced deciduous trees will allow the eye to travel freely, while the grass and its contents will not become unduly shaded. An orchard of standard trees provides an admirable setting, provided the orchardist's good husbandry does not rise above an annual tar oil wash, applied in early winter, and a no-fertilisers programme.

Where the grass has to be sown, the mixture is unimportant. Whatever one starts with, the end product will be the same, those grasses and other plants dominating which are best suited to their environment. Where turf was already present, but unduly coarse or weedy, it is necessary to keep it mown very tight for a year; so tight that after a few cuts a lawnmower can be used on it. Only at the end of this period should anything be planted.

Normal treatment thereafter will consist of three annual cuts: the first in July, the second at the end of August just before the colchicums start flowering, the last in late October or early November, after the autumn crocuses and colchicums have flowered but before the daffodils' noses have pushed through far enough to be damaged. On light soils you may be able to dispense with either the second or the third cut. In each case the grass is raked up and removed for composting.

It may be wondered why more than one annual cut should be needed at all. It is to prevent the turf from becoming coarse and tussocky. Even the bouncing cocksfoot can be kept reasonably subdued if cut thrice annually. Moreover, the second cut allows autumn bulbs to be seen and appreciated the better, while the third makes certain that the lowlier spring bulbs such as hoop petticoat daffodils, crocuses and orchids, do not compete too strenuously for a living.

To allow seeding before the first (July) cut is very important, because your plan will be to establish colonies of those plants, mostly bulbous, that, once given a start, will naturalise and thus do your gardening for you. Your main task will be to start them off and to encourage them the way they should go. If your rough grass is on a slope, start your crocuses, squills, narcissus species, snakeshead fritillaries, Apennine anemones and other self-seeders at the top of the incline. Their seeds will tend to bounce downwards, thus rapidly increasing the rate of colonisation. This happened most conspicuously in our garden, where a piece of moat had been drained, leaving a hollow shaped like a giant's bath. We planted only the sides, but the bottom, where we thought it too waterlogged for anything to thrive, is now a mass of bulbs.

Whatever we may consciously introduce into our grass garden, its brightest colour effects, displayed over the longest period, will be provided by wild flowers. An alpine meadow, unspoilt (aesthetically) by use of fertilisers or of weedkillers, is the classic example. A similarly neglected British pasture, left for hay, can be quite sumptuous too. On our heavy and rather wet soil the main displays are made by three species of buttercups (*Ranunculus bulbosus, R. repens, R. acris*), red clover, hawksbeards (do not ask me which) and moon (or ox-eyed) daisies, *Chrysanthemum leucanthemum*. The population of these last fluctuates widely every few years depending, I suspect, on soil moisture content in spring and early summer. Earlier there are celandines, dandelions and, in moist spots, Lady's Smock (*Cardamine pratensis*) and Goldilocks (*Ranunculus auricomus*). I mention these background plants, which often make huge colonies to splendid effect, because one can sometimes initiate them by looking round the neighbouring countryside for ideas and trying out likely takers.

Nearly all planting can be most conveniently done with the help of a bulb planting tool. This takes out a plug of soil up to 6 or 7 in. long and not more than 2 in. in diameter. Avoid those tools which extract a larger plug, as they are quite unnecessarily hard work. If a plant or bulb is more than 2 in. across, a few more nibbles with the bulb-planter round the edge of the primary hole will quickly enlarge its circumference. I always have by me a trugful of old potting compost, 2 or 3 in. of which goes into the bottom of each hole in place of yellow clay.

Daffodils are the most obvious candidates for naturalising. It is, in fact, the only painless way you can grow them without noticing the slow and hideous decay of their foliage after flowering. Most hybrid daffodils will compete happily with grass, as long as there is abundant moisture available in April and May when they are growing. Indeed the performance of most bulbs in any given year can usually be traced back to the weather in the previous spring. Dry springs will cause blindness in the next year and a series of dry springs can cause bulbs to die out completely. On light soils it might well be worth while to irrigate, during the growing season.

As they are tall, daffodils should be kept in the background of any grassed area that is viewed from one side, or in the centre of an island patch. If you have more than one grassed area, I recommend massing the daffodil hybrids in one of them, using snowdrops and crocuses for earlier displays, while keeping the other area for small-growing narcissus species and other lesser bulbs and plants flowering in April or later. The latter will not then be swamped by too close juxtaposition with the former.

You can often buy cheap mixtures of daffodils expressly intended for naturalising but in fact they look more effective if the different varieties planted are kept in separate groups, not all mixed up in a scrambled-egg jumble. The **summer snowflake,** *Leucojum aestivum,* has much the same habit as daffodils and associates well with them. The name is deceptive, as this bulb actually flowers in March and April.

Crocuses are in an altogether gayer range of colours and to see the Dutch hybrid types expanding to the warmth of March sunshine is one of the happiest signs of spring returned. The earlier *Crocus chrysanthus* hybrids and *C. tomasinianus* are good in turf, while in autumn *C. speciosus* (see page 132) is especially rewarding, sowing itself around abundantly. *Colchicum autumnale* is for this season too.

What do you do with your Darwin **tulips** in the course of years? Line them out in the vegetable garden, and they will become embarrassingly numerous in a little while. The grass is the place for them. There they take longer to build up flowering sized bulbs, but if enough are planted this does not matter and the fact that the flowers, when they do come, are small is a positive advantage in a natural setting. The yellow flowered, sweetly scented species *Tulipa sylvestris* naturalises so well in grass that it has had to be included in British Floras. It has a stoloniferous habit and spreads efficiently in this way without any effort on the gardener's part.

We have several old and ever-increasing colonies of **snakes-head fritillaries** (*Fritillaria meleagris*), both the checkered purple and the albino forms, and there is no more delightful feature in the April garden. The bulbs are cheap to buy and, although they soon die out on sandy or chalk soils, colonies should be started wherever they can get their toes into their favourite wet clay or alluvial stodge.

Gladiolus byzantinus, with its vivid magenta spikes, never looks so well as in a setting of cool grass stems, and at the same May-June season the bulbous Dutch **irises** start into bloom, to be followed by the purple, grey and white English types. Of the **anemones**, our native windflower is certainly not to be despised. It thrives equally in sun or in shade and has several good garden variants such as the double white Vestal and the pale blue Robinsoniana. *Anemone apennina*, in shades of blue and pinky mauve, makes itself very much at home by self seeding.

The **Spanish bluebell** is an indestructible old cottage garden favourite, that multiplies into fat clumps and flowers at a useful time, towards the end of May, when many bulbs in rough grass have already passed out of bloom. At the moment it should, I believe, be known as *Endymion hispanicus*, but is most often listed as *Scilla campanulata*, obtainable either in its pale blue, pink or white forms. **Grape hyacinths** (*Muscari*) hold their own well in grass and their intense blue colouring contrasts strikingly, in April, with the yellow of hoop petticoat daffodils. The Siberian squill, *Scilla siberica*, is earlier still and an even more intense blue. It keeps going in grass but does not increase much, and I usually plant another 100 each autumn. Still in the bluebell/squill family one has the quamash, of which the species listed as *Camassia esculenta* has the strongest colouring. It grows about 15 in. tall and carries spikes of star-shaped flowers in May. They always attract attention and I'm not surprised. The star of Bethlehem, *Ornithogalum umbellatum*, is safe in no other part of the garden, but well-behaved and radiant here.

Of the primula family, cowslips, primroses and old polyanthus plants which have done their turn as spring bedding, should all be freely mixed. The mixture will become freer still as they cross and intercross. The summer season ends with blue meadow cranesbills, *Geranium pratense*, still in flower when the grass is cut in July. Meanwhile there have been hardy orchids in flower from April till June, but they deserve a separate discussion (see below).

If your grassed area is rather thin, in parts, on account of being shaded by trees and if the soil is pretty moist here, this will be the spot in which to grow winter aconites, *Eranthis hyemalis;* snowdrops and the dog's tooth violet, *Erythronium dens-canis*, whose nodding mauve flowers with reflexed petals come out in March and are followed by richly mottled foliage. Doronicums do tremendously well in this sort of situation, too. Their clumps will last indefinitely without being split up, as would be necessary in a border. Their yellow daisies contrast well at the 3 to 4 ft. level with the white froth of cow parsley, otherwise known as Queen Anne's Lace.

Hardy Orchids in Grass and Garden

Woven into the fabric of flowering grasses, buttercups, daisies, clovers and hawksbeards, our tapestry garden displays, in April, the boldly contrasting spikes of early purple orchids (*Orchis mascula*); of the cooler purple green-winged orchis (*O. morio*) in May and, greatest spectacle of all, the spotted orchis (*O. maculata*) in June. The last is a variable and ubiquitous plant, but if you get a good strain of it (we had to look no farther than the woods surrounding us), it grows 2½ ft. tall and carries long spikes of flowers that vary in colour from almost white to rich mauve. We leave one corner of rough grass uncut until the end of August, so as to give it, here, the chance of ripening and scattering its dust-fine seed. Out of curiosity, I recently counted the number of plants of this orchid—seedlings of all ages—in a square foot of turf in this corner: there were 37. It has become, in fact, the dominant plant in the area. Seedlings turn up in borders (among bearded irises especially) and pavement cracks in every part of the garden and I have purposely made a border grouping on the north side of a wall with *Lilium hansonii*, of the orange-yellow turks caps. Here the orchis has made fat clumps of 12 and more spikes in only 2 or 3 years. It has not the slightest difficulty in holding its candle for comparison with the exotica of that early summer season.

To have these native orchids—even when of the less spectacular types such as the green tway-blade—flourishing and forming colonies in one's garden, is a great thrill: a sort of compliment from nature, one feels. Their fascination needs no explaining: it is generally experienced by all who see them. And for this very reason the rarer and more local species always stand in danger of extinction. The bad old days when an 'orchid foray' could be organised by the local Women's Institute are over, indeed, but it is still common to see individuals carrying bunches of decapitated orchid spikes.

Nevertheless there are times, I should say, when it is perfectly justifiable to dig up and transplant wild orchids to one's garden, where they are locally prolific or where there seems strong evidence that a colony will otherwise be destroyed in any case.

It is a useless waste to try to establish orchids that naturally grow on soils basically different from your own. On our Sussex clay, for instance, the pyramidal and fragrant orchids of chalk downland would never take, although in gardens with a high lime content they might well prove the most adaptable species. For similar reasons, I should not normally expect the greater butterfly orchis, *Platanthera chlorantha,* to last for many seasons here. They usually grow on chalk and limestone soils. A few years ago, however, we heard of a colony in a wood only two parishes distant, which was in imminent danger. The wood, which had consisted of mixed deciduous trees, had been planted with conifers, and the carpeting undergrowth and weeds, including the orchids, were in process of being trashed then I arrived on the scene.

Here was a case where I had no hesitation in helping myself, and because the butterfly orchids were growing in soil so similar to our own, I had high hopes of succeeding with them. Eight years later it can be said that they have held their own in the grass, though without increasing. I wish now that I had tried them in thin turf under trees and also in a cool border without any competition from other plants. This is very often the best way to work up stock and one can then experiment with it in more competitive situations, once a healthy nucleus is assured.

In retrospect, our colonies of the green-winged orchis take on the appearance of a rescue act, although it did not look that way nearly 40 years ago when they were first introduced. In this neighbourhood they were locally abundant on old pastures, but changes in farming practice, whereby the plough visits every field at frequent intervals, have led to their widespread extinction.

Orchids have a curious way of shifting their territory. Scarcely any of the early purples are where we originally planted them, although they have made extensive colonies elsewhere, while the green-winged orchis has chosen to establish itself, among other places, in the few inches of soil covering our underground reservoir, a good 150 yards from the nearest planting. The little white lady's tresses orchid, charmingly named *Spiranthes spiralis,* is so capricious that it will suddenly appear, often in a mown lawn, flourish for a few years and then as suddenly vanish. It is utterly fruitless to play at taming so wayward a character as this.

When moving an orchid from the wild into the garden, a fern trowel is the most effective tool. Any time when the plants can be seen is suitable, and if they are actually in flower you can choose the best forms—an important consideration with such variable species as the spotted orchis. The tuberous roots of orchids seldom grow more than four inches deep and can readily be extracted intact with a lump of soil surrounding them, so that, followed by a generous watering-in, the transplanting need cause no sort of a setback.

A few hardy orchids are obtainable through the nursery trade, which is encouraging in these days of garden centres and the standardised product. Perry's of Enfield, Middlesex, offer a hardy orchid collection which includes our native fragrant, spotted and green-winged orchids as well as three foreigners. J. A. Mars of Haslemere, Surrey offers half a dozen hardy cyprepediums, including the rare native Lady's Slipper, *Cypripedium calceolus.* This has a very good chance treated as a border plant in a cool, shady spot. I have also had *Orchis elata* from Colonel Mars, and this is multiplying by self division in a most gratifying manner. It comes from North Africa but is hardy. I first saw it in the late Mrs. Renton's garden in Perth. Built on the same lines as *O. maculata,* its flower spikes are a rich reddish purple shade. An excellent border plant, this, as also is the closely related *O. foliosa (maderensis)* in a slightly paler shade.

The Woodland Garden

The Daemon of an English Wood

Few of us are in the happy position of coming into a piece of woodland that can be gardened, but it does happen from time to time and perhaps not so very seldom, on a small scale. Even one large tree may invite a kind of woodland gardening in its proximity. So it is interesting to consider what opportunities a wood holds out to us.

Types of woodland vary a great deal according to soil and climate and a basic question to consider at the outset is how far to go in civilising it. If you like your wood as it stands, then it will be a mistake to alter its character out of all recognition. But if it has little original personality, then it will be sensible to treat it mainly as a vehicle; as a provider of shade and shelter for exotics, notably for rhododendrons.

Let us first assume the former case. Your wood has character. Each spring the floor of it is thickly patterned with anemones, primroses and bluebells and you wish to treat them as a dominant theme on which to embroider.

These early flowering bulbs and herbs will tolerate a good deal of shade, because they make all their growth before the trees are in leaf and while the wood is still quite a light place. Spring is surely the most delectable season in woodland, followed by winter, autumn and summer, in that order. But even in spring, even your native plants will be inhibited by a too dense overhead canopy of branches.

The first consideration in your wood must be for the existing trees. They are probably too thick and they probably include a number of runts. Twisted or leaning trunks are often beautiful, but some specimens will be plain scruffy. The time to judge is in winter, when you can see a whole tree's outline and examine it from every angle for its faults and virtues. Don't make up your mind in a hurry and do not feel that all the thinning has got to be done at the outset. Not so. Just a little will probably be desirable in every winter. Sometimes it will only be low branches that need removing, so as to preserve a feeling of spaciousness and better to reveal the outline and texture of a tree trunk.

As to the existing shrub layer in your wood, most of this probably will be meaningless, scenically, and want removing; brambles in particular. They can be treated with a hormone killer, as can nettles. Do not automatically assume that all the hawthorns should go. They may just need cleaning up and could be excellent vehicles for clematis, celastrus and honeysuckles. Cherish any spindles (*Euonymus europea*) there may be. With a little extra light, they will take to berrying freely and you can add one of the more spectacular cultivars such as Red Cascade, for which the natives will act as useful pollinators. Hollies always look good in woodland; 'sombrely cheerful' as Gertrude Jekyll wrote of them. The high gloss on their leaves prevents drabness, and the trunk of a mature specimen, if kept clean by the regular removal of odd shoots, is a splendid feature.

Unpretentious additions to a wood whose character you want to preserve will mostly be low-growing bulbous plants and herbs. Coloured primroses will look appropriate and will hybridise with the natives. Our windflower, *Anemone nemorosa,* has a vigorously colonising cultivar called Robinsoniana, with large, pale bluish

flowers while Vestal is pure white with a neat double 'anemone'
centre and a latish flowering season.

Then **violets**: not only the sweet scented *Viola odorata* in its
white, pink, apricot, mauve and violet forms, but the deciduous
North American *V. cucullata* and *V. septentrionalis,* with larger,
later flowers. All the dog violets are worth looking at and to this
group belongs *V. labradorica,* sometimes listed as *V. l. purpurea,*
in which the leaves as well as the flowers are purple.

Winter aconites, *Eranthis hyemalis,* are most easily colonised
under trees, where they don't have to compete with thick grass.
If you are lucky, they eventually make a huge carpet of yellow.
Their flowering is quickly followed by the common snowdrop's,
now generally reckoned to be indigenous, and essentially a woodlander. Anyone who has seen a snowdrop wood will look back on
it as a thrilling experience. Do not attempt it on a light, dry soil.
The idea of buying snowdrop bulbs in order to get started, appals
me. Being harvested and dried off is a hateful set-back to them and
most gardeners must surely have access, from an established or
neglected garden, to a fat clump of growing bulbs. They should
be lifted, split and replanted immediately after flowering, in
March.

In introducing **daffodils** to wild woodland, do avoid the highly
bred, giant modern cultivars with huge thick stems, broad leaves
and brassy flowers of prosperous, well nourished appearance.
They look all right as the Dutch use them, under trees, in their
vast open-air exhibitions, but this is a kind of bedding out and
does not pretend to be anything else. It has nothing to do with
the daemon of an English wood. Visitors to the R.H.S. gardens
at Wisley, in spring, will have envied the colonies of *Narcissus
cyclamineus* among the trees of its wild garden, but this, alas, is an
expensive species. Our own native Lent Lily, *N. pseudonarcissus,*
is one of the best for our purpose: it is a natural woodlander
although equally happy in the open. The Tenby daffodil, *N.
obvallaris,* is as suitable. It is often listed as *N. lobularis* and can be
obtained as such quite cheaply from Peter Nyssen.

The **dog's tooth violet,** *Erythronium dens-canis,* is dearer than it
seems because its claw-like bulbs shrivel badly in storage and are
usually in poor shape when received from the nursery. They
should be planted immediately on arrival and a fairly high mortal-

ity expected. But they are worth it. Among dead leaves under deciduous trees is ideal, or in thin, leaf-strewn turf. But the soil should never be too dry. Other erythroniums are worth attempting. Once you can get them to set seed, stock can be dramatically (if not rapidly) increased, and they will also multiply into fat clumps by their own offsets. *E. tuolumnense* is bright yellow and so is the more vigorous hybrid Pagoda, derived from it. This grows to 18 in. and is not unreasonably priced for what it is.

The **crocus** 'par excellence' for natural woodland is *Crocus tomasinianus,* with thick clusters of slender mauve flowers in February. The shading varies a good deal. This is a prolific self-seeder.

Trilliums should certainly be attempted, in particular the Wake Robin, *Trillium grandiflorum,* with conspicuous white flowers of triangular outline. It is worth preparing a bed for these in a moist, partly shaded position, comprising a high proportion of leaf soil and peat. These unusual plants bear a distinct resemblance to our native Herb Paris, of alkaline woodland, to which they are actually related. They would keep good company with Solomon's Seal, the rather similar *Smilacina racemosa,* and with lilies-of-the-valley, which are grand woodland colonisers. And of the many ferns that could be included I should also give preference to those that spread by exploring rhizomes and make a colony of fronds. The evergreen *Blechnum tabulare* is especially good in this respect.

Many ideas can be culled from **wild flowers.** I shall always remember the shining yellow of kingcups, *Caltha palustris,* growing in woodland on the edge of the Yorkshire moors, near Kirby Moorside. They are quite happy under trees, where the soil is wet. There are various components of chalk and limestone that will make themselves at home on a wide range of soils. Woodruff (*Asperula odorata*), for instance, makes carpets of white and freshest green, in May. The stinking iris, *Iris foetidissima,* can be a bit dowdy as to its foliage, but its brilliant orange seeds in autumn are ample compensation, and there is an excellent variegated leaved form on the market. One should also establish a colony of *Iris japonica,* for its elegant sprays of light mauve butterfly-like flowers, in May. The hellebores are all calcicoles and our own *Helleborus foetidus* is one of the best. Any of them will look right in a wild woodland setting, especially the *H. orientalis* hybrids, called Lenten Roses.

The **marbled arum,** *Arum italicum* 'Pictum' will contribute its snaky foliage from autumn till June, and this is the season for *Cyclamen neapolitanum,* at first for its flowers, then for its mottled leaves, which die off in May. The scented *C. repandum,* with gay magenta flowers in spring, is also worth attempting in a 'choice spot' as we garden writers put it, rather in the language of house agents.

Some herbs are evergreen; among them, the **epimediums.** Their foliage is discreet and the young leaves are often a beautiful bronze shade. The old leaves become shabby and should be cut away, in spring, shortly before the young foliage and flowers unfold. These plants are improbable members of the berberis family but if I had to compare their flowers with a well known group it would be the thalictrum's. They have the same nodding elegance and are carried on thread-like stems. Best known is *Epimedium pinnatum,* with primrose yellow flowers in April. A tough and undemanding plant this, only a foot tall. There are about a dozen species and varieties available, in shades of yellow, orange, pink, mauve and white. They could make an interesting collection.

Bergenias are too coarse and heavy for this kind of woodland but another member of the saxifrage family, **Tiarella cordifolia,** will be in its element. Its low, evergreen foliage grows in tufts and spreads by short overground runners. Well named foam flower, it does just that, in April and May, with masses of branching panicles carrying tiny white flowers. The related *Tellima grandiflora* is a clumpy plant, but it does increase by self-sowing. Its 3 ft. racemes of green, bell-shaped flowers are discreetly charming; almost too discreet in the garden but just right in the unpretentious sort of primrose-bluebell-windflower wood we are considering. The plant's main attraction is in its shell-like foliage that turns bronzy in winter, darkest along the veins. *T. g.* 'Purpurea' has an even more emphatically tanned complexion.

The introduction of ground cover plants to this kind of woodland should be allowed only after stringent soul-searching. I do not mean the modest sort of colonisers like lilies-of-the-valley and the fern *Blechnum tabulare,* already advocated, but the real take-over bidders. Their far-flung evergreenery can be altogether too oppressive. Such is the Rose of Sharon, *Hypericum calycinum,* and the giant periwinkle, *Vinca major.* Furthermore, although they grow well in shade they flower much more freely in sun and are more suitably sited on some hot and difficult bank of exposed sub-soil.

Variegated sports from green-leaved plants are less muscular, however, and have a leavening influence on shaded areas. You might excusably be tempted by a few of the variegated ivies (as ground plants) and periwinkles. In the really difficult dry shade of a beech, for instance, you will have to resort to something like the variegated dead-nettle, *Lamium galeobdolon* 'Variegatum', to *Pachysandra terminalis,* whose leaves are at least a nice fresh green, or *Euphorbia robbiae,* whose leaves couldn't be darker but are off-set in spring by light green inflorescences. These are thugs.

Our native **wood spurge,** *E. amygdaloides,* is altogether better behaved, being a compact, low shrub without running proclivi-ties. It has a pleasing variegated form. A few specimens of E. *wulfenii* or *E. characias* will not look out of place, either. They are taller, at 4 ft. or so.

And there are three **daphnes** I should want. Our native, calci-colous Spurge Laurel, *Daphne laureola* always looks quietly pleas-ing in its evergreen dress and *D. pontica* is similar, about 3 ft. tall with clusters of green flowers in May giving off a powerful air-borne fragrance at night. True, you may not enter your wood at night. *D. mezereum* will scent the air at all hours, whenever the weather is mild, from February to April. Some people object to the typically not very clean mauvy purple colouring of its clustered flowers, but it looks perfectly appropriate in its season and this setting.

The **butcher's broom,** *Ruscus aculeatus,* is quaint rather than pretty, but has risen in the social scale since being taken up by the flower arrangers. If you can get hold of plants of both sexes (this is another native of calcareous woodland) it carries very handsome carmine-red berries on its dark, spiky branches. A close relative and a far more attractive plant is *Danaë racemosa,* somewhat resembling a bamboo in appearance. It grows to 3 ft., is clump forming and a delightful fresh green the year round. Old branches should be cut down to ground level in spring, as the young ones sprout.

Mahonia aquifolium used to be planted as cover for pheasants and, unlike the bird, this exotic looks singularly at home in English woodland. It makes low thickets by suckering and is always presentable. Its glossy, pinnate foliage becomes bronzed in winter. Tight clusters of scented yellow berberis flowers are borne in spring.

Perhaps, in conclusion, I should make brief reference to the rabbit. Your scope will be strictly limited if two or three rabbits are liable to gather together in order to thwart you. The wiring of individual plantings always looks hideous, and this is a serious indictment where an attractive scene is of the essence. Some plants are rabbit proof, but it is difficult to give a list. For one thing I have had no personal experience of rabbit appetites since the advent of myxomatosis 15 years ago. For another a rabbit's tastes can vary: it may leave wild foxgloves untouched, yet eat the tame ones you introduce. However, a good many rhododendrons appear to be exempt and I have never heard of them touching snowdrops or daffodils.

Woodland Gardening with Rhododendrons

In the type of woodland we have just been considering, the idea has been to elaborate without destroying its character and spirit as we found them. Questions of hardiness and shelter have not been so much as mentioned. All the plants used have been bone hardy. And all, except *Pachysandra,* have been tolerant of lime. Many, indeed, are natives of calcareous soils but are amenable to a wide range of soil types.

We now enter into a different world: the world of the **rhododendron** and its satellites; the kind of woodland gardening that is most widely practised in Britain, especially where acres are in question rather than a smallish spinney. The basic explanation of these gardens is that their owners have caught the rhododendron bug. They want to collect and grow as many of the best or most fashionable rhododendrons as they can assemble or afford. The spirit of camaraderie and friendly competition is strong among them. You should visit the R.H.S. hall at lunchtime on the first day of a rhododendron show, to get the flavour of the game: not necessarily to look at rhododendrons but at the bowler-hatted gentlemen assembled there. Here is dedicated passion indeed.

It has been said, with some truth, that the collector's mania for rhododendrons greatly changed the pattern of gardening in Britain, resulting in a host of exotic but formless woodland 'gardens'. Well, but plantsmen, of whatever leanings, have always tended towards formlessness in their gardening. They comparatively seldom combine an eye for a good plant with a pictorial eye.

We can nevertheless take off our bowler hats to them for their patronage of a genus that includes some of the most beautiful of shrubs. Many of the loveliest are slow to reach maturity. You may have to wait for 10 to 40 years to see them bloom for the first time. This requires a degree of patience that is rare indeed, but you certainly find it among the rhododendron fans. And it is rare to find so much pertinacity in breeding work as has been practised, largely by amateurs, on the rhododendron, often with the meritorious object of combining the simplicity and natural dignity of two parent species in a more easily cultivated and robust hybrid offspring. Hybridising does also often aim at greater size and 'flower power' (to borrow Mr. Haworth-Booth's odious but expressive phrase) in the progeny, but there is room among rhododendrons for all tastes.

Indeed the range and variety that one discovers in this genus, which includes all the azaleas, are impressive. You can look to the rhododendron for special interest in tree form, bark colour and texture, leaf colour, form and texture, autumn foliage colouring, a flowering season spread over eight months of the year at least, flower colouring that excludes only the purest blue, flower size and shape and, last but not least, scent. Several of these points of attractive interest are likely to be combined in the variety of your choice. On the other hand, I wish the rhododendron enthusiasts were more critical: the paeans of praise are a little too united. Rhododendrons have major faults like other plants. Their frequently lugubrious foliage can be deadly and some of the most popular and blatantly colourful azaleas should be judged by the same standards as the modern marigold—but more stringently, because the marigold may look reasonably appropriate in its formal garden setting, whereas the hotting up of an informal wood by azaleas is just a bit too much.

Now to consider the conditions for woodland gardening with rhododendrons. The wood in its own right ceases to matter. You can and will probably want to do without any of its natural contents except for the trees, which are allowed to stand in just the right numbers to provide enough but not too much shade. The choicest rhododendrons need shade and shelter. Shelter from wind, whatever the quarter of its origin, is essential. If the air in the bottom layer of your wood is still when a gale is raging in the treetops, then you can hope to grow *Rhododendron sinogrande* and other large-leaved species successfully; otherwise not. So the boundaries of your wood must be thickly planted with tough wind-absorbing shrubs such as R. *ponticum,* cherry laurel, yew and certain other conifers like sitka spruce, some of which will become trees in time.

The soil must be acid and preferably light. If peaty, so much the better, but full use must otherwise be made of fallen deciduous leaves and of bracken. Leaves can be swept from paths and other vacant spaces and massed around the rhododendrons as a deep mulch. If the wind is liable to blow them away again, they must be kept in position, preferably by bracken fronds, which stay put and themselves act as a mulch. This mulch has the effect of keeping the rhododendron roots cool and moist right through the summer. As they are near the surface, they can be ruinously affected by drought.

Ideally the woodland rhododendron garden should present the beholder with a series of pictures, the material flatteringly arranged so that he never feels hemmed in or that he is endlessly slithering through high tunnels of vegetation. The chain of lakes in Sheffield Park Gardens, in Sussex, are both foil and mirror to the rhododendrons, conifers and other trees along their margins. If we cannot manage water we can have open glades or clearings with, perhaps, a floor of wild daffodils and the stems of a few silver birches past which we can look at a frame of rhododendrons.

Always try to arrange your material so that it can be seen to advantage. Too close planting is a highly probable mistake, but is by no means fatal because, fortunately, rhododendrons have a fibrous root system that enables them to be moved successfully even when large and long established. Provided you are prepared to re-shuffle your pack as the need arises, there is no cause for alarm.

Another point to realise about the more interesting rhododendrons is that many will flower well for you only in alternate years, even if you conscientiously dead-head them immediately after flowering—and this is certainly a good thing to do if you can find the time. For this reason, and also because the shrub, even if it flowers regularly, will do so only for one month in twelve, surely one of the most important points in choosing rhododendrons is to go for a good leaf that will give you pleasure during the whole year.

The large-leaved species will certainly do this: they have great dignity and make very large specimens in time. Give them the most sheltered places you have. Two reasonably easy ones are *Rhododendron falconeri* and *R. macabeanum*. The latter's leaves are pale grey underneath, being woolly felted. They are up to a foot long, but the size of leaf depends largely on climate: the moister the larger. The flowers, opening in March, are bell shaped, pale yellow with a purple blotch inside.

R. falconeri is one of those stunning species with a bright rust brown indumentum (hairy covering) on the underside of the leaf. Its early spring flowers are white with a blotch. Similar as to its leaf but much smaller is *R. mallotum*. This has dark red flowers. Another rusty-backed rhododendron, none too hardy and needing good shelter is *R. arboreum* 'Sir Charles Lemon'. It grows to 20 ft. or more, is of upright habit and the young foliage points obliquely upwards so that you can with especial ease admire the warm colouring of its lower surface. The flowers (not freely borne) are white.

In complete contrast to this kind of leaf are the rhododendrons whose foliage is rounded, smooth and often waxy with a glaucous sheen. The waxiness may vary a lot as between clones and it is advisable to see plants in the nursery before making your choice. This blue colouring is generally most apparent in the young foliage, but *R. concatenans* wears a specially effective blue rinse right through the year. It makes a good spreading bush about 5 ft. high, clothed in fairly small, rounded leaves. The flowers, in April-May, are trumpet shaped and a warm apricot shade. This is closely related to R. *cinnabarinum*, which has flowers of similar shape, typically orange-red but including some smashing cultivars in various dusky or glowing shades of red, pinky red, coral, yellow and salmon. Names to look out for here are Roylei, Royal Flush, Lady Roseberry and Lady Chamberlain. Their leaves are not so strikingly coloured but a nice shape, and they are aromatic.

R. *thomsonii* goes in for this sort of leaf, too, glaucous when young. Its blood-red bells come out in March. This grows into a tall, stemmy shrub with very beautiful, smooth reddish bark. It associates charmingly with *Corylopsis glabrescens,* a 12 ft. deciduous shrub flowering before the leaves, in March, with pendant yellow, lemon scented racemes. One of the best yellow rhododendron species comes in apropos, here, as a relation of R. *thomsonii*, with heart-shaped leaves, blue on their undersides. This is R. *campylocarpum*; it carries its wide mouthed, soft yellow bells in April.

R. *williamsianum* grows only 2 ft. tall and has 'petite' rounded leaves, coppery when young and carried attractively on a well furnished shrub. It needs a reasonable amount of light in order to flower well, and then bears nicely spaced clear pink bells. It is one of the most exquisite of all rhododendrons. R. *orbiculare* is like a larger version of this, about 6 to 8 ft. tall, but its flowers have too much mauve in their pink. There are some splendid hybrids between these two species, and they are easy garden plants.

Foliage apart, I tend to look for rhododendrons that flower particularly early or particularly late and for those that have a sweet and fruity scent. But I can't pursue the subject without the tail wagging the dog.

Azaleas under Restraint

What is an **azalea** ? We all think we know what we mean by one but try to define the word and we're in trouble. The fact that anything we are pleased to call azalea is, botanically, a rhododendron, cannot be ignored. But the word azalea is beautiful in itself and will never drop out of popular usage; rhododendron, alas, is cumbersome and plodding.

Azalea seems to combine the aerial grace of bird, butterfly and flower. For the shrub to live up to the promise of its name, the flowers should not be small, congested and niggling, but of moderate size, well-spaced, of clear colouring and spangled over a bush on which the leaves have not yet unfolded or are still quite small and a brilliant green. The species that most successfully lives up to these requirements is *Rhododendron schlippenbachii*. Can you beat it? Man's ineptitude is inexhaustible. Still, better to be saddled with Baron Schlippenbach than some bromide like Pink Perfection.

This species is, in fact, a clear soft pink. It looks fragile and does actually need woodland shelter if its April flowering is not to be spoilt by late frosts. The foliage takes on a rich variety of autumn colouring. R. *albrechtii* has vivid carmine flowers at the same season on a comparably large, open, deciduous shrub, and is remarkably fresh. So, too, is the lavender coloured R. *mucronulatum,* but this is out in February or even earlier. It is not an azalea within the botanists' definition of the term, but looks every inch of one to you and me. It is a hardy enough shrub but flowers of such delicate texture are easily frosted and a protected site is essential. One is prepared to take risks with this sort of plant, when the rewards in a mild spell are so heartening. The shrub itself and its foliage are undistinguished.

R. *praecox* is rather scrubby, too. It has the 'merit' of being evergreen, which is what most gardeners in this country demand, but would look better were it deciduous. All the same this is an excellent and reliable shrub, its pinky mauve flowers opening, in most years, before February is out. It looks the better for being grouped in a reasonably large planting and does not need the overhead protection of trees except as a buffer against frost at flowering time.

Similar, but with a mauvy pink flower colouring in this case, is Tessa. One is particularly grateful to these early spring heralds. I accidentally have Tessa under-planted with the vivid orange *Crocus aureus*. The effect is excruciating. I keep telling myself I really must do something about it, but remain fascinated and inactive. R. *praecox* is one parent of Tessa, R. *moupinense* the other, but the best cross made from the latter is R. *cilpinense* (with R. *ciliatum* as the other parent). This is a compact, dome-shaped 3 ft. evergreen bush whose pink buds open in late March to large pink-white bells. It is a real beauty, but we are drifting from azaleas.

The bulk of these are May-June flowering. They are much abused and overplanted shrubs. First, the evergreen azaleas. The Kurume varieties are apt to be low-growing and so packed with blossom in May that not a leaf or twig remains visible. An artificial flowering shrub could hardly improve on them. Too many colours jostle and vie with one another. My favourite, here, is the parent of them all: R. *obtusum amoenum*. It makes a spreading shrub, up to 5 ft. tall but more across, clothed with dark, sulky foliage against which vivid magenta flowers glow vindictively. Seen under trees and divorced from others of its kind, this is good. Indeed, there are several sorts that are worth while if only they are grouped in a quiet context and not herded like bedding plants in a frenzied mixture of all the shades. Hinomayo, for instance, is a clean and pleasing pink and makes, in time, a 5 ft. shrub of character. The best of this type of azalea throw long straight, vertical shoots which mushroom out at the top and save the shrub from undistinguished chunkiness. R. *kaempferi* is a good parent for imparting height. It grows 8 ft. tall itself and its flowers are orange, opening rather late. Palestrina is a tall white that does not look out of place in a bluebell wood.

The large leaved deciduous azaleas are grouped under a number of strains: Ghent, Mollis, Knaphill, Exbury, and again they are easily overdone, though charming when used with restraint. Their heavy, sweet, slightly putrid scent is a great attraction to those with a weak sense of smell, but overbearing to my way of thinking. It derives from R. *luteum* (*Azalea pontica*), a shrub of such merit with its yellow blossom in spring and brilliant autumn colouring, that it is readily forgiven any shortcomings. It is no bad thing to get back to the antecedents of these popular hybrids. How seldom, for instance, does one see R. *arborescens,* a dignified azalea growing 15 ft. tall, clothed in glossy green leaves that are glaucous underneath, and cream coloured, scented flowers in a usefully late June-July season.

Ferns

Gardening with Hardy Ferns

Before long now, I think hardy ferns are likely to make a major break-through as popular garden plants. Popular, that is, with the more discriminating sort of gardener who doesn't insist on riotous colour everywhere and all the time. Once again it is the flower arrangers whom we have largely to thank for making us look at ferns again with a critical and appraising eye. Their forms are very, very beautiful, whether in the young unfurling stage or as fully expanded fronds. And so many of them are native British species, or cultivars derived from these, that their successful cultivation is no great problem.

The hardy fern has long exercised a fascination on the amateur gardener cum botanist and the fern trowel was a weapon in the armoury of many of our grandparents. Moreover, when we visit old gardens that may have become hopelessly derelict and over-grown, we shall again and again be delighted to find ancient specimens of ferns that were clearly introduced in the gardens' heyday and have managed to survive every subsequent vicissitude, thanks to an iron-tough constitution.

There are, it seems to me, two main brakes on their wide acceptance and planting, here and now. In the first place it is quite difficult to know and find out what hardy ferns there are available, what they look like and which are the easiest and most suitable for general use. Tender ferns, yes. These make good pot plants and are frequently shown. But how delightful it would be to see a display of hardy ferns at the Chelsea Flower Show, for instance. Perhaps the R.H.S. will be able to stage this for us one day. Any fern that can thrive in the naturally arid conditions of Wisley should stand a good or better chance in the gardens of the rest of us.

Second, and linked with this obstacle, there is the difficulty of getting one's bearings among ferns at all. Their names, in the main, are formidably offputting and have suffered more than most groups of plants from synonymy.

Let us suppose that some gardener, who is attracted to but

rather ignorant about ferns, wants to make a small collection. With which should he start and how should he accommodate them? To look, first, at some of the commonest. In my own garden I have as many as 8 species of wild ferns that have just arrived on the wind: three species of spleenwort and the common polypody are in steps and walls; bracken, the hart's tongue and male ferns have sown themselves under the greenhouse staging as well as being widely distributed in other parts of the garden; the lady fern, *Athyrium filix-femina* is wild on a damp bank underneath trees and has also sown itself behind a garden seat in a shaded yew embrasure.

Ferns, then, do not necessarily need to be allocated special places. If they put themselves in an awkward spot they will, of course, have to be treated as weeds. The common **male fern,** *Dryopteris filix-mas*, is the most likely to do this. Apart from bracken, this is far and away the best-known fern. It is one of the glories of the Scottish countryside in June, clothing the dampest, steepest hillsides with sheets of vivid green fronds. And what makes it so much more effective than bracken to look at in the mass, is that the fronds do not arise sporadically from creeping underground rhizomes, but are always in a circle about a crown. Thus, even when seen by the thousand and at a distance, each crown of fronds retains its individuality.

My father made a border of this fern against the front of our half-timbered house, which faces north-east. He reckoned that a quiet, restful feature was needed here, and I have certainly never felt inclined to alter a satisfactory arrangement. The ferns continue in beauty right until December but, being deciduous, they eventually have to be cut away.

The air must be thick with this fern's spores, for it sows itself everywhere, especially in wet summers. After 1954, for instance, young plants appeared in the paving cracks in the hottest, driest part of the garden. But then paving always provides a congenially damp, cool root run.

The next commonest fern that no garden should be without (and few established gardens are) is the **hart's-tongue,** *Phyllitis scolopendrium*. Its long, leathery, strap-shaped fronds make it easy to recognise and are an invaluable foil to the featheriness of the majority of ferns. It is practically evergreen, the old fronds dying in March and April just as the young crop is unfurling. At this time the old ones do become rather unsightly and are best removed.

The hart's-tongue will sow and maintain itself in the driest of walls, but is quite a pygmy in such situations. Moisture and shade are necessary if you want long fronds. It has given rise to dozens of cultivars, many of which are crested: that is to say the frond, instead of tapering to a fine point, proliferates near the tip into a multiplicity of crests. Some enjoy this sort of aberration; others feel that it spoils the balance and poise of the frond, and I personally feel that it is inappropriate in the hart's-tongue, whose svelte simplicity is its particular charm. But there are some delightful cultivars available in which the margin is waved, as in Undulatum, or more tightly crimped, as in Crispum.

Dry walling or steps with a north facing aspect are ideal situations both culturally and for display purposes, for many ferns. In steps you won't want anything bulky that projects and gets in the way. The most co-operative here will be the **maidenhair spleenwort**, *Asplenium trichomanes*. It has very neat, simple pinnate fronds with a black stem, and makes 3 in. tufts. Similar as to habit and structure but of a bright green colouring that is retained throughout the year, is the green spleenwort, *A. viride*. A slightly bulkier fern that is suitable for a wall face is *Polystichum lonchitis*, unsuitably nicknamed holly fern. It has pinnate fronds that are long for their width and often have a seductive twist to them.

For a real wall coloniser that will gradually spread its rhizomes through the cracks between the stonework, we have **common polypody**, *Polypodium vulgare*. It will also colonise on the mossy, horizontal upper surface of any old tree stump or branch you can offer it. The fronds are up to about 18 in. long and remain green throughout the winter. They become brown and shabby in spring, however, and it is late May before any young fronds begin to show themselves. The crested form of this is nice.

The **soft shield-fern** *Polystichum setiferum* is a widely distributed native species but has given rise to a large assortment of particularly beautiful garden varieties. The one I have is Acutilobum. It is practically evergreen (in common with all polystichums), the old fronds dying as the young crop unfolds. These fronds arise obliquely in a circle about a central crown. They are bipinnate, with elegant, narrow divisions and the frond itself has a twist to it as though caused by a slowly revolving motion about a central axis. There are other cultivars such as Plumoso-divisilobum, with even more finely and intricately cut divisions. Acutilobum is one of several forms of soft shield-fern that develops little bulbils along the frond's midrib. If you pin a mature or ageing frond horizontally on to the surface of a box filled with cutting or seed compost, and keep it in a close frame, these bulbils will develop into rooted plants and can presently be separated and treated as individuals.

The **royal fern,** *Osmunda regalis,* is so striking a species as to be in danger of extinction as a native. But it is easily raised from spores and young plants can be bought cheaply. In time its short, thick rhizomes make massive clumps from which the deciduous foliage rises to 4, 5 or 6 ft., according to the dampness of the situation. Although *O. regalis* likes a boggy spot, it does not respond happily to being completely submerged under water at any time of the year. It is perfectly happy in full sun, which is useful in a fern.

Onoclea sensibilis enjoys much the same conditions, the boggier the better, short of being actually flooded. Its rhizomes travel far and wide sending up handsome, broadish pinnate fronds to 2 ft. or so, at fairly wide intervals. They wither at the first breath of frost in autumn which earns it the name of sensitive fern, but it is absolutely hardy.

The **maidenhair ferns** must be protected from scorch. Indeed, they look altogether too fragile to stand up to garden life, but there are, in fact, two reliably hardy exotic species, both deciduous. A distinctive feature of maidenhair ferns (rather like the black tongue of a chow) is the glossy blackness of their stems and main veins, in striking contrast to the delicate green leaf colouring. This is especially noticeable in the foot-tall *Adiantum pedatum,* from North America. Its fronds are arranged in an arc that is almost too good to be true. Of slighter build is *A. venustum,* said to hail both from Canada and Kashmir and certainly an accommodating and delightful species. Even as I write, in February, its now brown fronds have retained their shape and are almost as pretty as in summer. It is a runner, making a complex of rhizomes near the surface and eventually covering a considerable area of ground. The fronds are 6 to 12 in. tall and composed of fan-shaped segments in the manner so characteristic of maidenhairs.

Many ferns have a running habit, like the last, and some make quite a sward. Such another is *Gymnocarpium dryopteris,* the **oak fern,** a native of acid soils in the north. Given a cool root run it makes a carpet that is rather less than a foot tall. The fronds are broadly triangular in outline and look so fragile and delicate that you feel they must wither if touched.

One of the more popular species is *Matteuccia struthiopteris,* the ostrich feather or **shuttlecock fern.** The shuttlecock arrangement of its fronds is most easily appreciated as they unroll, in spring, or (at maturity) when viewed from above, so that you are looking down the craters. Sideways on, one shuttlecock tends to merge into another. This deciduous fern again runs freely, right at the surface, so one must beware when weeding. With me, in a too dry and sunny position, it grows only 2½ ft. tall, but it can double this height.

A fern of distinctive and bold appearance is **Blechnum tabulare,** from S. America and the Falkland Islands. Its fronds with me rise obliquely to a mere 2 ft. at most but I have seen them twice this height in Scotland and Ireland. They are leathery of texture and dark of hue (though coppery when young), pinnate without further subdivisions. This is yet another runner and altogether a fern of character that lends itself to cutting. The old fronds last till spring unless caught by severe winter frosts, from which a little overhead protection as from a deciduous tree, will save them. *B. penna-marina,* from New Zealand, is a fascinating pigmy, but very robust. It is a ground-covering evergreen and one might call it mossy were it not so obviously ferny. The sterile fronds are almost horizontal, and copper-toned when young, but the fertile fronds are rich deep bronze and rise vertically to 5 or 6 in. I have this fern growing with *Cyclamen neapolitanum* but it has also spread into the neighbouring lawn and is competing successfully with grass turf.

So many of the ferns I have described have synonyms that I have omitted the lot, but readers should be able to track them down all right with the help of a Flora and a gardening encyclopaedia. One of our greatest authorities on hardy ferns is fortunately also a nurseryman and supplier of them and he has lately written a useful and enjoyable book called *Hardy Ferns*. It is by Reginald Kaye who is at Waithman Nurseries, Silverdale, Carnforth, Lancs. Other valuable suppliers are Hillier's of Winchester and Perry's of Enfield, Middlesex.

Ferns in a Mixed Border

I have already suggested various positions in a garden where ferns can be made happy. They can most of them put up with difficult situations but it is always pleasantest to have your plants looking as though they could scarcely be enjoying themselves more. In general it would be true to say that ferns will thrive more readily in the damper climate of north and west Britain than in the south and east; better in a moisture-retentive soil than in one that is excessively free-draining and liable to dry out.

On the whole they prefer free drainage but they do like a soil rich in humus: leaf mould and peat, for instance. They are predominantly at their best in shade, and there are many and many positions in London gardens that can be made wonderfully congenial for them, provided irrigation is available. Even better than overhead watering will be a perforated pipe laid as a permanent fixture just below the soil surface in your fern bed and connected at one end to a water supply.

Ferns will grow well under not too dense trees in many cases but are even better off if they can receive the dappled shade from trees in the heat of the day, without actually being underneath them. Right underneath may have two disadvantages; the roots of many surface feeding trees like cherries and birches can make the soil here exceedingly dry in summer and the drip from trees may be dirty—especially in towns and especially underneath the common lime on whose foliage honeydew secreted by aphids becomes black with sooty moulds and then drips off, even in dry weather. This sort of trouble will spoil the appearance of the ferns' fronds. However, they are excellent under deep-rooted trees like oaks or laburnums.

Suitable ferns for a border could include male and lady ferns: *Dryopteris* and *Athyrium* species; *Matteuccia, Osmunda, Polystichum setiferum* cultivars, *Blechnum tabulare* and, essential for contrast, a hart's-tongue, with its smooth, glossy, undivided leaves. To

have nothing but ferns in the border would be unnecessarily to
deny oneself the many possibilities of varied foliage patterns. And
further contrasts can be provided by certain flowering plants that
like it cool.

We can have **hellebores** in variety, both the evergreen, shrubby
types such as *Helleborus corsicus* and *H. foetidus* and the herbaceous
H. orientalis hybrids. Solomon's seal is inimitable, and one cannot
think of this except in association with lilies-of-the-valley. Both
these are runners however, and their invasiveness would need to
be watched.

Some say that the **dragon arum,** *Dracunculus vulgaris,* carries
its wickedly fascinating purple flowers more freely in sun than in
shade. That may be so in the cooler parts of the country, but with
me, in the south-east, it is free in shade. Other hardy arums could
include the marble-leaved *Arum italicum* 'Pictum', the yellow-
flowered *A. creticum* (if you can get it) and even the florists' arum,
Zantedeschia aethiopica, if you don't consider it too flamboyant,
which it would certainly not be in an urban setting.

Some of the hardy **orchids** are hard to locate or expensive
when located but are much to be desired. One could hardly do
better than start with our native *Orchis maculata*. Foreigners to
look out for are *O. elata* and *O. foliosa*. The lady's slipper orchid,
Cypripedium calceolus is far more amenable to garden culture than
is generally realised; likewise the N. American *C. reginae,* to which
the main drawback is its price. These and half a dozen species of
Trillium, the N. American wood lilies, are obtainable from Perry's
of Enfield.

Hostas in variety are, of course, obvious companions for ferns,
if strong (even violent) contrast is your aim, but there is perhaps a
more subtle relationship to be brought out with astilbes, whose
own foliage is remarkably fern-like. Except on a limy soil, one
should include *Kirengeshoma palmata,* with its handsome palmate
leaves and delicate primrose-yellow flowers in early autumn.

For more solid fare, to match the evergreen hellebores, you
could have the glossy, bamboo-like *Danaë racemosa* and one or
other of the sarcococcas, whose insignificant but sweetly scented
flowers provide a welcome bonus, in late winter and early spring,
to their wands of elegant foliage. Small bulbs like erythroniums,

scillas, chionodoxas, snowdrops and miniature daffodils should be freely interplanted and allowed to colonise by self-sowing.

Plants for Tubs and Ornamental Pots

Inhabitants of northern climates tend to snatch at every oppor-tunity for living *al fresco,* and nothing is then so delightful as to be embowered on one's own terrace or patio, in a tropical array of plants. The adjunct of a spacious heated greenhouse is, of course, a tremendous help towards developing a Mediterranean illusion, because you can then fetch out your oranges and lemons, your potted bougainvillæas, hibiscuses, agaves and cordylines—returning them to safety again in the autumn. If you further require something to look at in the winter, you can grow a set of hardy conifers and evergreens, and drop their pots into the larger containers that have now been vacated. This pot-within-a-pot idea is good when you are aiming at a succession of interest, but one has to remember that most china or earthenware containers are themselves susceptible to frost damage. Concrete is safe and can be presentable. But my own inclination is to go all out for a summer display with suitable bedding plants and a few easily managed shrubs, and to let the winter months take care of them-selves. Large containers, even in a small area, give scope for much the most dramatic and telling effects, and they do not dry out so alarmingly fast.

Most kinds of **fuchsia** flower continuously for four or five months. Combined with other types of plants, they tend to get swamped; but you can mix different kinds of fuchsia together, keeping the trailers near the margins and the upstanding sorts where height is required. At the end of the season they can be stored, container and all, in a cold but reasonably frost-free shed or cellar, and kept on the dry side, being watered perhaps once in ten days. Then, in late April, they are brought out again, cut back by about one-third, turned out, with most of the soil knocked off their roots, and replanted preferably in fresh John Innes No. 3 compost. If you can then start them growing again in a cold green-house, so much the better; but a sheltered place outside will be all right, provided you can fling some protection over them on a frosty night. One should water the plants rather sparingly until they are growing strongly, but, generally speaking, most tub plants will need watering right up to the rims of their containers every day, in hot weather. As this leaches their nutrients away pretty quickly, they also need a liquid feed from mid-summer on-wards each week. Another sub-shrub that can be treated like the fuchsia is **Solanum aviculare,** with large mauve potato-flowers, hem-stitched at their edges, and with contrasting yellow stamens. It is best to dead-head them once a week, otherwise they expend their energies on berry production instead of making new buds. Their orange berries are handsome in the flashy style of costume jewellery, but very slow to ripen. It is better to go all out for flowers.

The not-quite-hardy evergreen **Geranium maderense,** from Madeira, makes a splendid tub plant. It needs plenty of root room to do itself justice, so the tub must be large and given over entirely to one geranium plant. You will not regret it. Grown simply for its foliage, this will be one of the star features in your garden. In its first year, then, this cranesbill (for, although tender, it is a true geranium, not a pelargonium) makes a stout, woody trunk from which springs its intricately cut-leaved foliage, borne on long stalks, the whole making a dome about 3 ft. high and 4 ft. across. The plant may go on growing like this in its second year, too, if it hasn't built up enough substance to flower. But eventually it will cover itself with magenta blossoms, will set seed heavily and may die, for the plant is short-lived.

Its foliage is not winter hardy except situated under a south wall in a mild locality, but you can overwinter the whole plant, tub and all, in a cold greenhouse or lean-to or in a cellar that receives just a little light from a dusty window. I cannot find this species in any of my seed lists and the only supplier that I know of is The Plantsmen, at Buckshaw Gardens, Sherborne, Dorset.

Requiring similar treatment to fuchsias is the shrub called **Angel's Trumpets,** *Datura suaveolens.* It can be allowed to drop its leaves in winter, as long as its stems remain sound. This needs a large pot or tub to give the best account of itself, and will then carry huge white trumpet flowers over a long season. They are powerfully odorous, with an exotic fragrance, at night. The more you feed the plant the more will it persist in flowering. It is a terrible martyr to red spider, of whose multiplication you may not be aware until the datura's leaves have already been sucked dry, are yellowing and about to drop off, even at the height of its growing season. The trouble is much worse under hot, dry atmospheric conditions and can be largely prevented if you make a practice of frequently syringing the foliage with water. Frankly, this plant is as coarse as they come, but it flaunts with a flourish and one loves it for that.

Oleanders are frequently grown in tubs and large pots and need merely to be kept from freezing in the winter. I advise concentrating on the single-flowered types for a start. The doubles can be a flop if botrytis moulds get a hold on them, attacking not only the open flowers but working back from them to the buds as well.

The battering effects of wind and rain make it difficult, in this country, to grow plants with large fragile blossoms in the open. But in a really sheltered courtyard, for instance, you can succeed with the giant, frilly-flowered petunias, both single and double, the latter being often deliciously scented in the evening. Likewise, salpiglossis are useful where height is required. They grow to about 3 ft. and need staking. Related to the petunia and with a similar trumpet flower, their colours are less brilliant but far subtler, with veins that pick out the dark and light areas. On my clay soil, I can't really manage these salpiglossis as border plants and they are worth-while only when I give them shelter and individual treatment. The seed need not be sown till April to give you a full-sized plant in a 7 or 8 in. pot by July and August.

At the same time you should sow one or other variety of **ornamental maize,** with variegated foliage. *Zea japonica* 'Quadricolor' is exciting in theory with stripes in various colours among which pink predominates, but it can be fearfully disappointing, and just come green. I have had best results from Thomas Butcher's seed; from the seedlings you raise you must select the most promising and pot them on into 7 in. pots. Better and more striking is a strain of the same species called 'Gracillima', which is striped in green and cream. It makes quite a bushy, branching plant and a 6 in. pot is large enough for it. Some of these grouped in front of a porch or on a patio (most fashionable word) look well with salpiglossis or with *Lilium henryi*.

Convolvulus mauritanicus is a wonderful ornamental-pot

trailer with clear, sky-mauve flowers. It should flower non-stop for five months, but, if insufficiently fed, may take a rest in mid-season. It is a nearly hardy perennial, and old plants should certainly be kept going from year to year. Its colour is a marvellous blender. You might plant it with the shrubby **Mimulus glutinosus,** with apricot-coloured flowers or with its variety 'Puniceus', whose flowers are copper-bronze. This mimulus tends to grow upright, sideways and downwards. It needs a sheltered place, for its branches are very brittle, and those that you wish to grow upright should be staked. Again, it is almost hardy and old plants go from strength to strength.

Then there is a bewitching daisy listed variously as **Dimorphotheca ecklonis** 'Prostrata' and *D.* 'Wisley Hybrid'. Neither name has any validity but the plant remains undeterred. It is of the South African fraternity, opening or closing in response to changes of temperature and humidity. Not quite hardy, probably because it tends to grow so fast and lush that its water content is too high for hardiness by the end of a growing season. On the other hand, I have planted out young specimens in February, and had them frosted and snowed on most brutally without any ill effects, and on light soil or in really well drained positions it comes through many winters. It has a matted habit of growth and will, on the flat, make a circle three feet in diameter in the course of the summer. Flowers are carried with ever-increasing abundance,

Plate 13. The cleomes are so strongly constructed that it is quite difficult to think of them as annuals. The commonest varieties are pink or white flowered. They are seed strains of *Cleome spinosa* (*above*), the spider flower. No annual looks more miserable if starved or checked before planting out. Well grown specimens are a joy, however, the horse-chestnut-like foliage making a fine setting for the broad spikes of flowers which open in continuous succession from mid-summer till October.

Below, this mixture in my own Long Border shows the herbaceous *Clematis recta*, with quantities of tiny white blossom in June; the single flowered shrub rose First Choice, raised by Mr E. B. LeGrice, and the Astolat strain of Pacific hybrid delphiniums with pinkish mauve flowers. My great idea is to have the border looking full throughout its show season, which I try to prolong in one way or another from early June till late October.

continuously from early May until the first autumn frosts. The daisies are 3 in. across, glistening white with a deep blue disc. On their underside the rays are dusky mauve. Cuttings are exceedingly easy to root and need not be taken until the end of September or even later.

Only the shunners of white flowers ever fail to fall for this beauty. One plant on either side of a large tub will amply cater for the container's perimeter and sides. The centre could be filled by one or two plants of **Pelargonium kewensis**. This 'geranium' is not everybody's plant. Its petals are narrow and the flowers spidery. In wet weather their colour verges on magenta. In fine spells, however, they are warm cerise, and at all times they are carried abundantly, making a voluminous display. *P. kewensis* is one of the many zonal pelargoniums that tend to run to leaf when they find themselves in a border with an unrestricted root run. Tub life suits it, but liquid feeding is still advisable.

Another pelargonium that I have successfully tubbed up with the daisy is Crimson Unique. This one is everybody's idea of a pelargonium, its slightly hooded crimson flowers carrying heavy darker blotches. But its blooms are far smaller than the average regal pelargonium's, and this is what makes them weatherproof. A good many regals have a more extended flowering season than is generally attributed to their race. After a heavy flush of blossom in spring and early summer, they will make new growth and flower again quite handsomely from August onwards. But their petals tend to be so fragile that even moderate rainfall starts them rotting. In the gardens of Sissinghurst Castle, Kent, they have found Lord Bute (syn. Purple Robe) to be the only large-flowered variety that has succeeded outdoors. This is a very old regal with single flowers of firm texture, dark maroon with rather paler purple margins. It is difficult to place so as to show up well.

Plate 14. My *Euphorbia wulfenii,* shown here, is in a shady position and hence flowers only every other year. Sun makes it more regular. The season is very long, from March till June, after which the old flowering stems should be cut right down, making room for the young shoots. This is an evergreen shrub and always looks smart except in frosty weather when its leaves shrivel and become utterly dejected.

The oak-leaved *Pelargonium quercifolium,* with its crinkly, fresh-smelling leaves, needs a richer diet than most and will then make a handsome plant, studded with clusters of small cherry-red flowers, darkly blotched.

Zonal pelargoniums are apt to have startling qualities of flower and foliage colouring which makes it easy to overdo them in massed bedding. Now that the floribunda rose is taking over this dubious role, we are enabled to appreciate geraniums more easily for their better attributes. Maxim Kovalesky is a typical example of the good-servant bad-master relationship. It is usually inappropriate to mass it, yet as a beacon shining out of a grey sea of *Helichrysum petiolatum,* it has no peer. Actually, its impact varies markedly with the season. In the cool of spring and autumn, it is a soft, clear orange, but in the heat of mid-summer it becomes hotter itself, and verges on scarlet.

Many would-be gardeners without gardens but only a paved area will want their tubs to cheer them up in spring as well as in summer and autumn. They will stuff them with wallflowers and forget-me-nots; polyanthus, pansies and double daisies; hyacinths, tulips and daffodils. Indeed, with the specially treated bulbs now available, they can have daffodils and tulips flowering in the depths of winter.

All this is very understandable. The one snag, as I see it, is that the spring flowers tend to be either short-stemmed or upward growing or both; they do look somewhat foolish and out-of-scale in a large container, like a big half-barrel, that will be ideal in the summer when some of its contents consist of plants that spill over and outwards. The spring contingent looks happiest in fairly low containers like troughs, while longish window boxes, perhaps slightly raised on a shallow plinth or on piers, also look well at or near ground level. Such low troughs and boxes can still be successfully occupied in summer by ivy-leaved pelargoniums, petunias, trailing lobelias and the aforementioned indispensable *Helichrysum petiolatum.* None of these are outrageously water-demanding.

Hedges, Herbs and Edgers

Hedging: Evergreen, Deciduous and Flowering Hedges

More glaring mistakes must be made by gardeners on the subject of hedges than in any other gardening department. And they are so distressingly long-term in their outcome. For example, it is easy to underestimate the space a hedge can or should be allowed to occupy. Height is easily determined and controlled, but thickness must be allowed for from the outset. For most hedges, which will be 7 or 8 ft. high, a thickness of 5 ft. should be allowed at the base, and the hedge clipped with a batter—a gradual inward slope, that will ensure light reaching its entire surface area and prevent it becoming thin at the bottom. Hedges always grow most strongly at the top, but a solid foundation is what they require more than anything, and this the gardener must encourage at the earliest stages.

He should give thought to the source of supply. If it is a hawthorn hedge that he wants, the source will not be important and cheapness will be the main consideration. Hawthorn makes a really good barrier; it looks pleasant, and even in winter its network of branches is thick enough to prevent a feeling of being spied upon. And it puts forth new leaves in earliest spring. But it needs clipping at least twice in the course of the growing season, and really three times would be better still. Hedge clipping is a bore, unless someone else is doing it. For days on end you have to look inwards at a barrier that allows no view, and your attention must not wander, or you cut your cable or botch the job.

In my part of the country—that is, in Sussex and Kent—**hornbeam** is one of the best hedging materials. It grows wild and is the commonest component of the undergrowth in our woodland. I would not need to buy plants, but would help myself to seedlings from any piece of wood that had been coppiced a couple of years earlier. Before myxomatosis, there would have been nothing to help oneself to, but even now, the return of the rabbit is only partial and seedlings abound. Hornbeam is locally called beech; beech itself being unknown in the Weald except where planted. Both materials make a tough hedge on any soil. They hold their withered leaves in winter, which is usually quoted as an asset, but to me at any rate, seems a dismal feature.

> 'Keen, fitful gusts are whisp'ring here and there
> Among the bushes half leafless, and dry;'

Brrrrr.

Most people prefer an evergreen hedge. When you have only a narrow space at your disposal, it is worth considering **ivy** as your material. First you have to erect a fence: chestnut paling is cheap and effective. Then you grow ivy up this and by the time the fence has rotted, the ivy will have made a self-supporting barrier, for its stems become tough and woody in time. It can be clipped once or twice annually, like any other hedge. The large-leaved *Hedera colchica* is the best species for this purpose, and you could intersperse it with an occasional plant of its variegated form to add spice and variety. Ivy thrives as well in shade as in sun, hence there is no need for an ivy hedge to be broad at the base.

Lonicera nitida remains as popular a hedging material as ever, despite its drawbacks. A really well kept lonicera hedge does look extremely smart, but it needs constant attention and should be clipped four times a year. And it must not be in an exposed position, which generally means that it cannot be used as a perimeter garden hedge but only as an inner, subdividing encloser. Of course, it is wonderfully easy to propagate: any bit stuck into the ground will root. And it is quick to make a hedge. But once a piece has been allowed to go back and become unsightly, through not being regularly attended to, you had better scrap it and start again.

Box hedging could be used more. *Buxus sempervirens* is one of our few native evergreens and starts off with the advantage of being attuned to our climate. It is not necessary to confine its use to low, foot-tall hedges, for demarcating a compartment or flower bed. There are several species and strains available, of varying vigour. The strongest, Handsworthensis, will make a hedge 12 to 15 ft. tall, if you require it to. The smell of box has a nostalgic charm for many people; perhaps, also, for snails, It is, alas, no fiction that snails abound wherever you find box hedging.

Never plant a hedge of common **holly** unless you invariably do your hand-weeding and planting in stout gloves. Its dead, dried leaves blow all over the garden and are wickedly painful to encounter.

One or other of the **conifers**—yew or cypress—is the most popular evergreen hedging material. And here it is exceedingly important to acquire good stuff, furnished with branches down to ground level. As to size, I would go for the small, 1½ to 2 ft. plants. They will need no staking and will get established more quickly than larger, more expensive specimens. Spring planting— late March or April—is undoubtedly safer than autumn, provided you can cope with the eventuality of a spring drought. With regard to planting distances, I advise doubling whatever was recommended by the nurseryman. Thus, the 18 in. recommended between plants of yew, I would make 3 ft. However, there is room for more than one opinion on this matter (mine being right, yours, if different, wrong). I prefer the long view. Plants set as close as 18 in. apart are going to starve each other, by the time they are mature. But the wider spacing will entail waiting longer for something that looks like a hedge. Without question, however, you should start clipping a year after planting, so as to obtain dense, compact growth. If clipping is delayed until the plants have achieved the bulk you so much desire, they will have become hopelessly loose and open.

You can vary the texture or colouring of a hedge by mixing your materials a little. Purple beech mixed with green looks well, and the proportions of each don't seem to matter: you can have ten of purple to one of green or ten of green to one of purple or two thirds/one third or half and half. Golden privet mixed with green doesn't blend too well as the gold is so vivid, without a scrap of green in its make-up. On the other hand one or other of the variegated or golden forms of *Euonymus japonicus* mixes well with the common green type-plant. This is a good coast shrub and the gloss on its not-too-large leaves prevents it from looking dull or coarse.

A subtle and effective blending could be attained with **Griselinia littoralis** (a pale and lively evergreen that looks cheerful at all seasons) and its variegated form. But the latter is so delectable that you might prefer to have it as a solitary, unclipped specimen. Griselinias are often reckoned to be on the tender side, but if established in spring they are perfectly hardy, provided always that they are grown on well drained land. They are listed by James Smith at Tansley, Matlock, Derbyshire, and if they survive in that cold midland nursery (all their produce is grown under field conditions) they will be happy enough in most gardens.

James Smith's range of trees and shrubs are mainly of the bread-and-butter type, but they are astonishingly cheap and exceptionally good value. It is an old family firm that never advertises (thus keeping down costs); its connection has been entirely built up on the grape-vine principal. Any prices I quote may be out of date before they're printed, but they will give the reader a basis for comparison. Griselinias: 1 to 1½ ft. specimens (remember, there's no point in getting them larger) are 5s. each, 52s. per dozen. These are what one would normally regard as wholesale prices but are here available to retail customers.

You could mix a holly such as the green-and-yellow Golden King in a one to ten ratio with the plain green cultivar known sometimes as Polycarpa, sometimes as J. C. van Thol. Both these have the great advantage of being almost devoid of prickles. Golden King, having less green about it, would be the slower growing, so you would need to watch out that it was not smothered by its neighbours while the hedge was forming. James Smith offers Golden King at 11/6d. each (they would be 30/od. from a posh nursery), J. C. van Thol at 10/3d. each, 97/6d. for ten (as against 19/-d. and 170/od.

Supposing you wanted a large, evergreen barrier or boskage, rather than a hedge: something that required no clipping but had plenty of elbow room in which to develop at its pleasure. Griselinia would be fine in this role and contrasts admirably with the very dark foliage of laurustinus (*Viburnum tinus*) in a mixed planting. The appearance of all the larger-leaved shrubs benefits if they are not clipped, so the cherry laurel and Portugal laurel would come into their own here, while a screen devoted to the highly tolerant *Rhododendron ponticum* is not to be despised, though its leaves are somewhat lustreless for much of the year. Being distasteful to cattle, it could be planted hard against a fence adjoining pasture-land. Actually, although cattle won't touch rhododendrons in those parts of the country where they are very common, self-sow extensively and are familiar to them, yet they will eat them if they don't know them. This is what makes it so very hard to recommend animal-proof plants, as I have already pointed out in respect of woodland gardening.

If you wanted a large formal hedge, you could not do better than plant the **holm oak,** *Quercus ilex,* commonly called ilex for short, though this is confusing as *Ilex* is the generic name of the hollies. Ilex is a popular hedging material in Mediterranean gardens and it is, in fact, a native of those parts; certainly not to be recommended for the coldest inland districts of Britain, but reliable anywhere in the south and west, and particularly tolerant of coastal conditions. We have a hedge of it that is 15 to 18 ft. high and nearly as much through. Luckily it needs clipping only once a year, and in order to get at the top, a ladder has to be thrust through the middle of the hedge.

Ilex transplants badly except when young, so you have to start with small, pot-grown plants and the early stages seem slow, but established plants make a good 18 in. of growth each year. The units in our hedge are rather unevenly spaced in a staggered row, about 10 or 12 ft. between plants seem to be a good average and obviates overcrowding at a later date. The leaf colour is a soft olive-green, almost grey on the underside.

Cypresses and the rather similar thujas (*Thuya plicata*) are popular evergreen hedging materials where speed is of the essence. Gardeners have gone off macrocarpa (*Cupressus macrocarpa*) now that they realise that it can't abide being cut back into old wood and is not so very hardy anyway. The great favourite now (although it is by no means new) is Leyland's cypress, *Cupresscyparis leylandii,* and its price is still suffering from an enormous demand. It certainly does the sheltering job required of it with great aplomb, but is a coarse looking plant. One or other form of Lawson's cypress will give you a dense hedge of more pleasing texture. The blue colouring of Allumii is fearfully depressing in winter. Jackman's (of Woking) Green Hedger is one of the most cheerful and satisfactory or, if you're not in a hurry (that'll be the day) Fletcheri, with dense but feathery growth. This requires very little clipping at any stage in its career.

Now let us turn to hedging materials that we can plant mainly for their flowers and I will come back to yews, in their various clipped manifestations, later.

If the hedge is to be of much use as a hedge, as a barrier to wind and to vision; and if at the same time it is not to occupy an exorbitant amount of lateral space, it will have to be clipped annually. This will stop a whole lot of shrubs from flowering noticeably. Hawthorn, for instance. You never see a hawthorn hedge laden with blossom—just a few white specks here and there.

But there are other shrubs which do manage to flower profusely in spite of—even, in some cases, because of—an annual clip, provided this is given at the right moment. A common rough hedging material, rather in the style of hawthorn, is the cherry plum or **myrobalan.** You seldom see a myrobalan hedge that has more than a scattering of flowers and this is because it has been given its annual brushing in winter, which is the time one normally chooses for this sort of job, when the ground is too hard or snow-covered or wet for other tasks. However, if you could change your habits a little and delay cutting your hedge until late April or May, it would be a sheet of white blossom in early spring. The majority of flowering hedges should be cut immediately after flowering.

The myrobalan, *Prunus cerasifera,* is so vigorous that it will make at least 3 ft. of growth in a year, probably a good bit more. So, if you want its flowers you must give it space. There is no spring blossom fresher than this in my opinion, except the later flowering blackthorn. But a more popular flowering hedge is the myrobalan's purple-leaved variety, best known as *Prunus pissardii,* though correctly *P. cerasifera* 'Atropurpurea'. It is just as vigorous and cannot be kept much below 8 or 10 ft.—before pruning, that is. Even more striking, because its foliage is more determinedly purple, is *P. c.* 'Nigra'. If you want the same effect on a small scale, you should plant the hybrid *P. cistena,* which is only 4 or 5 ft. tall before its annual cut, and cannot be regarded as any sort of barrier. This plant is a bit of a mystery, though, because on some soils it refuses to make any headway and one is at a loss to know why. Of the cherries, *P. incisa* is of twiggy habit and makes a delightful hedge of more than head-height, if required to. The flowers are white, pink in the bud. However, a hedge of this would cost the earth. You need to know of a stock plant from which you can take cuttings and raise your own.

Osmarea burkwoodii would not come unduly expensive, especially if you gave it a 3-ft. spacing, as I should recommend.

It has evergreen leaves shaped like a privet's, but neater, tougher and more substantial. This is a hybrid and, like its parent *Osmanthus delavayi*, its freedom of flowering is at least doubled by an annual clip-over in late May. The clusters of swooningly scented, tubular white flowers are carried in the axils of every leaf on the previous season's shoots, in April. Osmarea will grow to 7 or 8 ft. in time; it is hardier than *Osmanthus delavayi*, and hence more suitable for hedging, though I should prefer the latter where the soil was good and the hedge properly looked after, for its leaves are much more attractive. *Osmanthus ilicifolius,* with small holly-leaves, is also a good hedger. It flowers in October but you would scarcely know it except for the airborne scent, which is just like that of a philadelphus.

Then, **Berberis stenophylla.** An excellent and not too prickly evergreen, as barberries go, and covered in swags of crocus-yellow flowers in April. Again, it must be pruned immediately after flowering. This will make a 6- to 8-ft. hedge with ease, but sometimes looks top-heavy, having become thin at the bottom. Be firm with it from the start and clip so as to get a broad base.

For summer flowering combined with a good dense habit, we must turn to **escallonias.** The small-leaved, 'cascade' types are the most reliable in inland gardens subject to a good dose of frost. Their whippy branches spray outwards like a fountain, and they are in full blow with countless starry flowers from mid-June for a month. Then they (and other types) should have their cut, so as to give them time to make new shoots before the autumn. The palest is Donard Seedling in shell-pink and white; next comes Edinensis, a fairly obvious mid-pink; then Langleyensis, which is rosy red. Probably the best effect will be gained from mixing all three. These hybrids are not truly evergreen, but make such a network of branches as to become quite impenetrable. By no means allow less than 3 ft. between plants and 6 ft. through the hedge.

The larger-leaved escallonias are not quite so hardy but truly evergreen, and they stand up to seaside conditions better than any. *Escallonia macrantha* is the one you see so much as a windbreak in Cornwall, but there are more interesting hybrids, of which Crimson Spire is one of the finest, with a sufficiently upright habit to make it a neat hedger.

The shrubby *Potentilla fruticosa* will make the longest flowering dwarf hedge at the 3- to 4-ft. level, supplying a succession of yellow or white blossoms, like miniature single roses, from May till autumn. It can be clipped in winter. A mixture of, for instance, the yellow-flowered Katherine Dykes with the white Veitchii, would look well and make a much neater and more permanent feature than lavender. This is used a lot in Sweden, which is evidence of its hardiness.

Yews for Hedging

Yew is generally accepted as being the most satisfactory hedging plant for country gardens (it dislikes a polluted atmosphere). Dark, sober and dignified, it makes a dense buttress effect and its small and numerous leaves create a heightened impression of solidity. It gives a good account of itself on sand, clay and on its native chalk, and it can rightly be described as labour saving, because it requires but one annual clipping. If this is performed in August, the hedge will retain its architectural sharpness of outline right through the next nine or ten months.

Our garden is subdivided into compartments that are mainly outlined in yew, and I have no regrets on that score. You may almost be said to build with yew hedges. It is an architect's plant, and here it links the house with the various old farm buildings that are scattered through the gardens. Formality in country-garden design is not particularly fashionable at the present time, but a formal outline does not necessitate formal planting. My practice here, in fact, has been to plant entirely informally within the framework. Nor do yew hedges need to be straight; one of their most effective uses, here, has been in broadly scalloped curves around a semi-formal rose garden.

The chief criticism levelled against yew hedging is its slowness in reaching maturity. There is something in this, but the yew's very slowness is what makes it labour saving. *Lonicera nitida* or privet will give you a cheap hedge in a very few years, but needs clipping at least three times annually, which comes expensive in the long run. Yew is not as slow as all that: it will provide a sound hedge in eight years and look mature and of an indefinite age in ten. The slowest period is in its earliest years, when still in the

nurseryman's care, and this explains why plants of the same height
—say 1½ to 2 ft.—will cost eight times as much as privet.

In the old days all yews were raised from seed—which does not
even germinate till the second spring. Nowadays they are sometimes struck from cuttings and you thereby get a standardised
product, all plants having the same vigour; and several specialist
nurseries have selected their own strain of yew with the accent
on vigour. These can be expected, on decent soil, to make 9 or
12 in. of growth in a year. Of course one has to be strong-minded
and reduce this by half in order to build up a compact hedge. An
interesting feature in a hedge of seedling yews is that the young
shoots, in May, are different shades of bronze and green on the
different plants; and so, at that one time of the year, you can
clearly see, even in the oldest hedge, just where each plant comprising it begins and ends.

Another grumble against yew that is sometimes voiced by
stock-conscious gardeners is that every part of the plant, except
for the red pulp surrounding the seed, is actively poisonous, and
not merely poisonous but sweet and toothsome, thus luring cattle
to their doom. Well, doubtless if you put your beasts in a paddock
hedged by yew, there would be trouble. This garden, like any
other in the country, has suffered numerous crises at one time
and another through horses, pigs, cows and sheep breaking in.
They have mostly had a taste of yew without suffering from after-
effects. On one occasion I saw, from a window in our house, a
flock of sheep browsing on the yew topiary set in one of our
lawns. In a great state of agitation, I descended on them rather like
that poetic wolf on the fold—not the best way to marshal a flock
away from the scene of undesired action. They scattered in all
directions, and I found myself chasing small groups round and
round the topiary bushes, while those that were temporarily
unchased eagerly renewed their browsing. However, I did finally
succeed, with calmer tactics, in ushering them out, and none
were any the worse for their poison snack.

One or two cultural points are worth mentioning. Good
drainage is essential: my father laid tile drains under all our hedges
but they were 2 in. tiles and this was not a large enough bore.
Three or even 4 in. would be better, on heavy soils, and less
liable to get blocked. In the wet autumn of 1960 we lost a section

of hedge through waterlogging. An old practice that saves laying drains is to plant your hedge on an artificial ridge.

Yews have invasive and greedy roots and I have always been grateful for a provision against these made by my father at the time of planting. Wherever the hedge abutted on a cultivated piece of ground, 3-feet-wide sheets of galvanised iron (bent double at the top so as not to leave a sharp edge) were sunk into the ground as a barrier. They have lasted effectively for 60 years.

Any quality hedge that is habitually clipped will need to have its losses made good by feeding with a slow-acting fertiliser. Bulky manures and garden compost are not very satisfactory as surface dressings, because the birds will keep scratching them aside on to neighbouring paths and lawns. Bone meal is probably the best stuff to use, applied in late winter.

Yews for Topiary

Two words that one constantly hears when **topiary** is encountered in a garden, are 'quaint' and 'old-world'. And, shudder as one may at their remorseless repetition, they are undeniably apt. But there are other people who think of topiary as merely childish. It repels them as it attracts the first type. Those whom it offends may have some bee in their bonnet against formality in gardening. Certainly this was the case when formal gardening was universally (speaking, parochially, of Europe as the universe) swept aside in favour of the 'natural' garden. Taste in gardening, however, is nowadays such a hotch-potch that many widely diverging styles are simultaneously acceptable. No, the man who disapproves of topiary is generally, I think, a rather solemn type, accustomed to taking himself and to be taken seriously, and not caring to feel that he is being trifled with.

Topiary is not solemn. It is, indeed, a kind of vegetable 'folly'. 'Let's have some fun', somebody says, and topiary results. The popular notion that it must be difficult to maintain is quite unfounded. Anyone of the meanest intelligence, provided he can handle shears—and they can just as well be power driven—needs but to follow the outline in front of him and remove the current season's soft shoots. The peacock's tail may grow more bulbous with the years, its beak less sharp, but this will matter little. A greater difficulty may be experienced in keeping the specimens healthy over a long period. This, as with hedges, is largely a question of feeding and of keeping self-sown ivy at bay, and also of starting as you mean to go on—with a wide-based shrub that tapers gradually and has plenty of light reaching all its surfaces. A broad base will also provide a substantial and well balanced plinth on which to work out your decorative motif. If the plants you buy at the outset are well provided with feathery branches right to ground level, you need never have worries, whether they are to be used as hedging or for topiary.

Yew is the best material for topiary work; a good dark green, of solid texture when regularly given the one annual clipping that is all it requires, and with small leaves that do not look mauled and unsightly as can bay and the various laurels when trimmed with shears. Furthermore, if a neglected yew has to be cut back into old wood, you can reduce it to a skeleton and it will 'break' forthwith, producing a forest of young shoots from an umpromisingly dead looking trunk. Box is good too, for smaller-scale work, but box is softer textured and it is not so easy to keep your figures shapely using it.

Both yew and box are among our few native evergreens, and so our climate is admirably suited to their use, for whatever fanciful purpose. But the old-worldliness of topiary is more a matter of tradition than of the actual years that a given specimen is likely to be carrying. Nearly all the topiary that was so fashionable in the early eighteenth century was swept away in the ensuing landscape movement. Levens, initiated around 1701, is one of the very few survivors. Packwood House, in Warwickshire, is another and dates back to mid-seventeenth century puritanism, when its owner set out to illustrate the Sermon on the Mount. As his focal point he used the mount which had been a feature and viewing point in gardens since Tudor days, and of which there was already one at Packwood.

But most of the long-established-looking topiary that you see is really of quite recent date. Without knowledge of its history, it is extremely difficult to estimate the age of any example you may happen upon. The topiary at Compton Wynyates, Warwickshire, for instance, was planted only in 1895. Thirty years later (we have photographs that my father took of it then) it looked, already, very much as it does today. 'The Multitude' at Packwood could, from their superficial appearance, be anything from 30 to 300 years old. But the notion that yew is slow growing has no foundation in fact. Nor do you save time by planting large specimens. My father, who was extremely keen on yew both for hedging and topiary, kept records of the results of his experiments in planting, and found that he got best value from nursery stock that was only 1 ft. tall. This caught up the 3 ft. plants in the course of nine years. From specimens that were 6 ft. tall at planting time, mortality was between 30 and 50 per cent. But the point I want to make is that a 1 to 3 ft. yew, planted in good soil but trimmed hard each year to make it solid, could be trained in 30 years to a mature looking, 20 ft.-tall cone, indistinguishable from any of the 300-year-old multitude at Packwood.

The Packwood yews are symbolic rather than representational. The multitude, the apostles and the evangelists are stepped up in size according to their importance and to their proximity to the Mount itself, but they do not pretend to look like human figures. This is unnecessary, for in a curious way topiary, into whatever shapes it may be cut, does people a garden. I am not being fey, I hope, in claiming that it creates an atmosphere of company. And this owes more, even, to the shadow than to the substance. The shadows in and around a topiary garden as they lengthen in the evening, are the stage props for a world of fantasy—sometimes grotesque, indeed, and yet with an air about it of companionable homeliness.

The most basic design, in topiary, is a simple cone, such as composes the entire Packwood multitude. This can be varied to form a cylinder, pyramid or tetrahedron. The next simplest design is to superimpose a ball on top of the cone. When the cone has reached its required height, you tie a tuft of strong, upward growing shoots together, at the top, and treat these as a unit. If it is a bird you wish to delineate, then the tuft must be separated into two units: one to form the bird's neck and head, the other to make its tail. These are directed by tying them in to stout wire, the tail wire being shaped in a loop to which the yew shoots are tied in. Unwanted shoots that cannot be trained in the right direction are cut away. How to elaborate the design will usually suggest itself as the work progresses. But it is important not to be finicky. Too much detail is not merely difficult to keep in good shape; it looks fussy and lacks dignity.

For the rest, all you need is the right temperament to get started. There are plenty of good potential topiarists among keen amateur gardeners. Often all that deters them from starting is the idea of its being too difficult, which just is not true. Much of our best topiary, in the past, has been associated with cottage gardens. The few basic requirements in temperament that those cottage gardeners possessed were a reasonable degree of patience and a settled outlook; a love of plant materials and its handling; and that certain quirk which spurs us on to make figures, whether out of Plasticine, clay, wood, or yew and box.

Lavender, with Aromatic Alternatives

Lavender is our most popular aromatic plant, and very convenient for enclosing formal or semi-formal compartments within a garden. The smell is sure to be one of our earliest memories and is grippingly nostalgic, while the flowers themselves, even in the modest old English lavender that makes no claim to strong colour, are nearly always charming. (I exclude the so-called pink lavender, which is a poor and washy mauve.)

But one has to consider shrubs in their off-season. They have greater responsibilities than herbaceous plants, because the latter are visually non-existent for a large slice of the year. Better, after all, not to be there than to be present and forlorn. The lavender's forlorn season is all too long, lasting from the time its flowers fade, which is in early August for most varieties, till a flush of new growth arrives in the following May. It is one of our most cherished eyesores, only less drab than the beds of thorny sticks that it so often encloses.

The most we can do for lavender in its nine sad months is to keep it looking neat. Yet, even here, it is uphill work. The plant, for one thing, dislikes heavy soils, which abound in this country. It does not dislike them quite enough for us to give up growing it, but odd gaps are constantly liable to appear. The disease called shab—it sounds like sheep on waterlogged marshland—is rife. A branch dies, then half the bush. Seldom the whole bush, mark you. Always enough living tissue remains for us to live in hope.

On light soils, lavender behaves much better and looks reasonably presentable the year round.

Another problem is whether we care more for a strong aroma and a silvery leaf coupled with insipid flower colouring, or for sumptuous, purple flower spikes with only moderate aroma and a leaf that is neither green nor grey and practically folds up in winter. Hardiness is yet another question. The more desirable, dwarf lavenders are less to be relied upon than the tall and angular old English lavender, *Lavandula spica*. Were it not for

Plate 15.   FOLIAGE PLANTS. *Top left, Stipa calamagrostis* is one of the prettiest grasses when fluffed out at its flowering season in July. But it also dies very gracefully, gradually changing to pale fawn and remaining presentable until late autumn. *Right,* the oak fern, *Thelypteris* (or *Gymnocarpium*) *dryopteris* is a native of acid soils, usually found in rocky places. It gradually spreads by its slender rhizomes and then makes an exhilaratingly fresh green sward of fronds, about 9 in. tall. Given cool, moist peaty conditions, it cannot fail, but is easier to make happy in the north and west of our islands than in the drier south and east.

Middle left, Blechnum tabulare is a stout evergreen fern from the Falkland Islands and Terra del Fuego. It spreads freely and makes good ground cover of an unusually handsome pattern. It is also useful for cutting. In a sunny position this fern will do well enough but grows only 9 in. tall, whereas in moist shade it can reach up to 3 ft. *Right,* the sea green, pinnate-leaved *Melianthus major* is a magnificent foliage plant, although its hooded, bronzy flowers can be interesting, in spring, on plants that have not died back in winter. The foliage contrasts well with the prick-eared leaves of a purple canna, as shown here.

Below left, Adiantum pedatum is one of the maidenhair ferns, but hardy. It is a clump former and can be increased by division of its slowly creeping rhizomes, although it would be a crime to disturb an established clump like the one shown here, which grows at Keillour Castle in Perthshire. The fronds are arranged in a fan-shaped arc while the stems are black. A gorgeous creature when well suited but it scorches in sun and likes cool, peaty shade. *Right,* one of the variegated forms of *Aralia chinensis* growing in a foliage border at Crathes Castle in Kincardineshire. The leaves are enormous but subdivided into numerous leaflets. The plants are grafted on the plain green species, and they are expensive. Never dig around the roots, since this induces suckering.

its tenderness except in the freest draining of soils, I think my lavender choice would be *L. lanata*, whose foliage is so silvery as to be almost white. As it is, I settle in the main for the dwarf purple Hidcote, otherwise known as *nana atropurpurea*. A nursery that ought to know better lists it as Hidcote Blue.

For something different I grow *L. stoechas*. This species has a reputation for tenderness that it deserves little more than do the majority of lavenders. We lost most if it in 1962–63, but then lavender in general was decimated that winter. *L. steochas* has its main flowering quite early, in May. The flower heads are square, in cross-section, and the flowers, which are deep purple, are lined up on the corners of the square. At the top of the flower head is a perky tuft of come-hither-ish purple bracts, that stand up like plumes. The shrub is quite neat and dwarf, only 2 ft. tall; not domed, as are most lavenders, but spiky, like the Dolomites.

Lavender cuttings can be taken at any season, but midwinter is just about the most convenient time, as it is a job you can do under cover when the weather is uncongenial for outside tasks. Pieces of any size will root, but you will get the best shaped plants by taking small, single shoots, some 3 in. long. Trim the base of each shoot with a sharp razor cut, and insert the cuttings into a box of gritty compost. You can pack as many as 60 cuttings into one standard seed tray. Water them in and keep them in a ventilated cold frame. By June they will show that they have rooted

Plate 16. Above, if you plant the violet-coloured *Viola cornuta* next its albino form, they hybridise and self-sow giving a whole range of intermediate shades as seen here. Their season is very long, especially in heavy, wet soils and they have a delightful habit of weaving into and among neighbouring plants and shrubs. *Below*, a border mixture reaching its peak in July, with shrubs and herbaceous plants of varying colours and textures. In the foreground, the bronze *Potentilla* 'Mons. Rouillard' with scarlet *Lychnis chalcedonica* behind and the purple spikes of *Salvia superba* near it. The pale lemon *Viola* 'Landgren's Yellow' is at the margin. In the middle distance is the late-flowering *Euphorbia sikkimensis*, which needs support in this context, and *Clematis* 'Mme. Edouard André' on the wall behind. Pink and white hydrangeas (Hamburg and Mme. E. Mouillère) in the distant corner, carry on right into October.

by making new shoots, and can then be lined out in the open. The next move will be to their permanent sites either the same autumn or a year later. If you have no frames, the cuttings can be rooted in the open, on a light piece of soil; but it will be advisable to cover them with cloches.

Plants may also be raised from seed. This way takes a year longer to get the same sized product and the plants will vary in size and shape as also in leaf and flower colouring. Such differences are pleasant in their way.

If we could only bring ourselves to use lavender less formally it would, in many cases, be a very good thing. Imagine a large circular bed set in a lawn; what, in my family, we know as an open jam tart. Well, anyway, there it is, and the normal treatment for this appurtenance is to fill it with roses (an umbrella standard waving about frantically in the centre) and girdle it with lavender. It would surely look more relaxed if we allowed the roses to reach the margin at certain points and gathered the lavender bushes into small flocks that penetrated inwards a little from the perimeter. In this way we could make use of different kinds of lavender of varying vigour, and any gaps that developed through untimely deaths could be repaired, piecemeal, without drawing attention to themselves. Or we could here and there make use of various alternatives to lavender.

Even as a formal hedge we have a persuasive competitor in **Santolina incana,** which used to be called lavender cotton but, by one of those strange transpositions, is nowadays oftener known as cotton lavender. It is pleasantly aromatic and looks well throughout the winter. In spring (April is soon enough) one must be strong-minded and cut it to the bone, otherwise, as a hedge, it falls to pieces. But that entails a mere two months of unsightliness, as against the lavender's nine. If one were treating the santolina informally, as I suggested treating lavender just now, then I should prefer *S. neapolitana.* It has longer, lacier leaves, a freer habit and whiter colouring. Indeed, under grey autumn skies it can appear to have been given a blue rinse. Again it should have an annual cut in spring.

Then there is **rue,** *Ruta graveolens,* of which the most effective form is Jackman's Blue. It has a remarkable steely colouring that looks stunning, even at a distance, and the leaves are elegantly subdivided into rounded leaflets. It will make a low formal hedge, again requiring a hard spring cut, but looks even better grouped, say at the head of a promontory in an informal bed.

Incidentally, all forms of low edging hedges have a tendency to collect weeds. You may consider lavender, rue and santolina to be a bit of a nuisance in requiring to be replanted every five, six or seven years, but this does at least give you the chance to make a wholehearted onslaught on any perennial weeds that have taken shelter among them. Rare is the box hedge that has not accumulated within it a nucleus of ground elder, bindweed or couch, and from there these weeds make incessant forays into the adjacent beds themselves.

Why is not **rosemary** planted a great deal more? Because its beauty is untamed, and in that tamed section of our society that goes in for gardening, rosemary is uncomfortably nonconformist. It sprawls, yet cannot be severely hacked. The sprawliness of rosemary is actually its principal charm. There is great dignity in the gnarled contortions of an old specimen, jutting out from a rotten old wall, perhaps; only a few wisps of greenery remaining on it but these still carrying their quota of pale blue flowers each spring.

One of the most satisfactory ways of using rosemary is in a large planting with shrub roses and junipers of umbrella form (e.g. *Juniperus media pfitzeriana*). Get all three components into bold groups and you have achieved something that has substance as well as colour. Lilies can be worked into this planting, too. But I think I have never seen rosemary displayed to greater advantage than when planted along the top of an old retaining wall. In course of time its branches cascade over the wall face.

There are many forms of rosemary of varying habit, flower colouring and hardiness. *Rosmarinus officinalis* is the commonest and still, in many ways, the best. I have a particular fondness for R. o. *angustifolius* 'Benenden Blue', which I always call R. *corsicus* because this was what V. Sackville West called it when she gave me my original cuttings years ago. The leaves are very slender and deep green, the aroma even more pungent than usual and the flowers an intense, rich blue. But it is not quite so hardy as the common type. You should always play safe with any rosemary (as with lavender) by planting it in the spring. Tuscan Blue is well coloured also, with a broader leaf. Miss Jessup's Upright is for those who cannot countenance the rosemary's natural sprawl, but its flowers are washy. The prostrate rosemary is particularly tender but Severn Seas, with branches that rise to 2 ft. and then spread horizontally, is good and flowers freely with light blue but well-defined colouring.

Herbs Without Herb Gardens

Herbs in the garden can be pretty or useful or both or neither. Because of this last possibility, herb gardens, in which large numbers of herbs are gathered together, are generally a mistake. Their olde-worlde affectations are examples of gardening at its least spontaneous. They are a pose and look it, being rarely justified in the outcome. What justification, for instance, can there be for growing in the garden a miserable looking plant like woad? If we pretend that its stain can still be useful to us today or that it is an amusing plant to grow, we are merely wading deeper.

When it comes to the practicalities of tending a herb garden I can speak from bitter experience (funny, how experience is invariably bitter). For it should be understood that every honest herb is a weed at heart. The moment you turn your back on them, the whole lot have ripened and scattered a billion seeds, and the next thing you know is that you're stuck on your hands and knees, winkling out each seedling, individually, from among those delightful herb paths that you use as a means of dividing the beds (instead of mundane grass or paving), just like they did in Good Queen Bess's day.

In the herb garden that I am harking back to, some paths were of **penny-royal** (*Mentha pulegium*), others of creeping peppermint (*M. requienii*) and others again of double **camomile.** 'I can't think why we don't do this sort of thing more often,' visitors would croon ecstatically, if they happened to see them on the right day of the right year. I will tell why. Gardeners have, nowadays, a wonderful range of selective weedkillers wherewith to minimise the labour of keeping grass turf free of interloping broad-leaved weeds. But in a camomile or mint path, it is a killer working in exactly the opposite direction that is needed, and this doesn't yet exist. Camomile and the rest of them do not make a dense sward and the weed problem is demoniacal.

Furthermore, the mints either grow too strongly and invade the neighbouring paths and beds, or else they die out. The camomile rushes into flower, which is very pretty, but the moment of truth is revealed when it has to be cut. It then sulks and large patches disappear. Nowadays there is, admittedly, a non-flowering camomile available, but surely the main point of camomile is its flower.

As I see it, there are two kinds of herbs that are worth growing: those that look sufficiently attractive to take their place in the garden proper, with plants that are not herbs, and those that are constantly required in the preparation of food and should be grown unselfconsciously, near the kitchen.

The pot-herbs do not need to be assembled all together in one bed. After all, they have varying habits and requirements. Everyone should have a **bay**. It can be in a tub but, if space allows, looks handsomest growing freely as a tree. Giant **chives** are exceedingly pretty in flower and just as good, leaf-wise, as the insignificant ordinary chives. The only **savory** one need grow is the perennial, shrubby winter savory, *Satureia montana*. It has a dwarf variant called Caerulea that carries bright lavender flowers in autumn and deserves a place among rock plants. **Thyme** has a similar, but more scented, flavour and is not so good, in my opinion. *Thymus vulgaris,* the garden thyme, is the most useful, growing about 1½ ft. tall. It will colonise dry walling very charmingly and has a mass of pale mauve flowers in May.

The flavour of **sage** is coarse and masterful, while the shrub is plain dull, seldom flowering in the culinary type. There are, however, a number of variants that have purple or variegated foliage and abundant purple flowers, and these are worthy garden plants. **Tarragon** (*Artemisia dracunculoides*) is preferable in the French rather than the Russian type. It is less hardy than most herbs, should be frequently divided, in spring, and never have its old growth cut away until the spring. Purple **fennel** is so pretty in the mole colouring of its young foliage that one might grow this, rather than the green, but both of them seed outrageously.

Mints are for the most part terrible rampers, and while many of them have interesting aromas, they are scarcely worth their nuisance value. Concentrate on spearmint (*M. spicata*) and apple mint (*M. rotundifolia*). These make the best eating. The variegated form of the latter is a must for its looks alone, and is only a foot tall. The golden form of **marjoram** is one of the best foliage plants of its kind, a foot tall and retaining its colour throughout the growing season. It makes good flavouring too. In too sunny a position its foliage scorches badly.

Lovage (*Ligusticum scoticum*) is a 7-feet-tall herbaceous perennial akin in flavour (and related) to celery. I love to snatch and nibble a leaf, as I pass it. It contributes well to a green salad.

Evergreen Edge-Breakers

The hard line of a border margin, whether straight or curved, always tends to be a bit of an eyesore. If you edge it with prim plants such as dwarf Michaelmas daisies, dianthus, catchfly (*Lychnis viscaria*), London pride and thrift, you will be no better off because none of these lap over. They keep themselves to themselves. Herbaceous plants with spreading foliage, such as hostas, will do a good job for you from May to October, but will then retire for their annual snooze, leaving the edge as before or (if mown grass is the adjacent feature) a good deal worse with large dead patches scalloped out. Aubrietas and rock phloxes would serve at a pinch but are really too low growing to be suitable even at the front of a border.

What one would like best of all are rather coarse, **mat-forming evergreen plants** or shrubs. The grey, filigree-leaved *Anthemis cupaniana* is just the sort of plant I mean. It asks for nothing more than sun and good drainage. I find it as well to thin out its mats in June, after their first main flush of white daisies has gone over. If you trace their flowering stems as far back as they go and cut them out, nothing but young shoots are left; the plants are rejuvenated and will reward you with a pleasant sprinkling of blossom for the rest of the summer and autumn.

There is an old-fashioned group of erigerons that make evergreen mats, and I only wish they were not so rare nowadays for, unlike all the other herbaceous members of their tribe, they emphatically do not flop and need support. Furthermore, they never stop flowering from June till October. Elsie, Ernest Ladhams and Elstead Pink are names to look out for, and they mainly derive from *Erigeron glaucus*. Their daisies are in soft mauve or pinky mauve shades. If they are looking too stemmy by the time April comes around, give them a severe cutting back and they will quickly fill out again.

A third daisy plant that can be treated in like manner to the above is *Dimorphotheca barberiae*. I cut it back only if I must because unshorn plants start flowering in May and go on till the frosts, whereas the trimmed mats will not get into their stride until July. This is a South African daisy with bright pinkish-mauve flowers and the usual habit of shutting up in uncongenial weather, but surprisingly, it often seems to like a partially shaded position better than one in full sun.

The mats of *Campanula poscharskyana* are admittedly a good deal more voluminous in summer than in winter, but it is a singularly adaptable plant. Some gardeners class it as a weed, but that is because they have put it in the wrong place. On a rock garden, for instance, it would quickly dispose of all its neighbours. But at the border margin it will compete on equal terms with the majority of its probable companions. Its starry flowers are a very pale, washed-out mauve, and you should acquire one of the richer-toned cultivars such as Stella. In sunlight, the flowering stems, which grow a foot or more long, take on a bright red colouring. But this species is just as happy in deep shade. If dead-headed after its July flowering season it will often carry a sub-sidiary crop in autumn.

In a mid- or late-season border, *Arabis albida* would scarcely be appropriate, but associated with other spring flowers, whether herbaceous or shrubby, it is just the sort of plant we are looking for. The single-flowered type of plant seems pretty until you have met the double. Thereupon you must swallow all those principles and scruples that formed a basis for your much publicised pre-ference for the simple, single, natural flower as against those blowsy, double, man-made monsters. The rosettes of the double arabis are the more charming. The one advantage of single arabis is that it makes a neater plant.

If there is a whiter flower than this then it is candytuft, *Iberis sempervirens*. Out of season it is a particularly sombre evergreen mat-maker that I should be inclined to associate with something grey. Obviously the sun roses (*Helianthemum*) are made to measure —especially as you can trim them more or less or not at all, to suit their exuberance and your own temperament. Then, *Hebe* (*Veronica*) 'Autumn Glory' is an excellent edge-breaker and seldom out of flower. Another very different sort of hebe, which flowers extremely little, is *H. salicornioides* 'Aurea'. This is grown for the cheerful, yellow-green colouring of its foliage. It is never more than 15 in. tall, always remains compact enough not to need trimming and is undeterred by bad weather.

Where a lawn edges your borders, the mat-formers I have suggested will all eat pieces of it away. This margin dividing lawns from border can become a contentious frontier in many gardens. One person, the woman of the house, most likely, tends the border and would like its contents to spill informally over the lawn. Another interested party—the insensitive and practical male—sees the problems in terms of easy mowing and edging. I dislike whiskery edges as much as anyone; where edges exist they must be neat. But there is something profoundly depressing about a long, unbroken cliff of lawn edge. It should be interrupted at frequent intervals and this does not, as is sometimes claimed, make mowing impossible. A little trimming will have to be done with hand-clippers to round the job off; that's all. Far more satisfactory, of course, if you can organise it, to have a paved margin to your lawn, dividing it from the borders, In that case, do make the paved strip wide enough—about 3 ft. Most of it will quickly vanish beneath the edge-breakers.

Wall Shrubs and Climbers

Shrubs on South Walls

The character of a south-facing wall is something of an enigma. It at once offers golden opportunities and tempting risks. If we ask ourselves what we can grow on a south wall that would not do as well on any other aspect, the answers are numerous, but always with the rider that they may fail in one way or another: fail to flower freely enough or at all; fail to grow properly through repeated maiming by hard winters or through being killed outright. Many gardeners, thrilled at the idea of a south wall to plant against, are yet mortified at losing any valued plant on which their hopes were pinned. In fact, it is really much easier to write about a north aspect, where hardiness will be a *sine qua non* and the only consideration is a plant's capacity for thriving in the absence of sunshine.

However, let us turn bravely to the south but bear in mind, while doing so, that if our nerves are weak, it will be wiser to plant the shrubs and climbers that would be equally happy on a west or east aspect and even against a north.

If losses do not cause us sleepless nights, or if we are prepared to insure against them by protecting the doubtfuls or by propagating from them so that replacements are handy, then the south wall is an unalloyed joy. We should remember, too, that a sudden large gap caused by the death of a fremontia or a ceanothus, can be clothed within a matter of weeks by a couple of plants of *Cobaea scandens* or *Eccremocarpus scaber*, treated as annuals. They will hold the fort until a more permanent replacement has had time to make its mark.

A south aspect may be the windiest in the whole garden, but that seldom matters unless, like a caesalpinia or *Robinia kelseyi,* the shrub is exceptionally brittle. Its sovereign asset is in its wood-ripening capacity. Both direct sun-heat and the heat radiated off the wall's own surface will have this ripening effect which, in broad terms, may be described as inducing in the plant a high ratio of carbohydrates to nitrogen, this being the condition most propitious for flower-bud formation. In Scotland and in other parts of Britain where sun strength and sunshine totals are markedly lower than in the south and south-east, it may be necessary to give a south wall to things like the flowering dog-woods, the Judas tree, camellias and forsythias, in order to cajole them into carrying worthwhile crops. Such examples of coddling come as a surprise to us southerners, yet a gardener needs only to cross the Channel in order to be immediately aware of the still more favourable ripening conditions that obtain there. Almost anywhere in the French lowlands you would expect *Campsis chinensis* to open luxuriant crops of its broad terracotta tubas, whereas here one is really showing off by planting it at all. The most recent occasion on which it opened its buds freely was 1959.

What W. J. Bean wrote—that there are more shrubs than actual climbers that will particularly benefit from a south wall—is very true. Even the common Passion flower, *Passiflora caerulea*, will flower freely on an east or west aspect if you start off with a free-flowering strain. It would appear that shy-flowering passifloras have an inherent weakness in this respect, independent of their cultural treatment. This Passion flower is all very well in its way; its blooms are fascinatingly constructed. But it is not nearly as handsome as several species that need cool greenhouse treatment. It never really makes a show, seldom carries more than six or eight blooms simultaneously, each one lasting for only a day or so, and the plant is excessively untidy for half the year. One dares not prune it until spring.

I have known **Solanum jasminoides album** to flourish on a west wall, where it was sheltered in a courtyard but, failing such protection, one would naturally face it south. Unlike *S. crispum,* it is a true climber. If its growth is only slightly reduced by winter frosts, it starts flowering in May and carries through without pause to November. Its pure white potato flowers, each with a bright yellow eye of stamens, are carried in sprays, elegant and coolly fresh, with none of the hearty coarseness of some among this tribe. The only thing I dislike about it is the rather sour smell which the plant emits when handled. This albino variety is far preferable to the skimmed-milk washiness of the type plant.

It is said that the fascinating pink and white colouring in the otherwise green foliage of *Actinidia kolomikta*, a twining climber, is encouraged by a sunny position. I find this hard to believe, in view of the splendidly coloured specimen at Crathes Castle. Situated in north-east Scotland, it can receive only limited sunshine at the best, while in its actual position it catches only the morning sun.

Moving on from the few climbing shrubs that might not do equally well on some other aspect, let us now pick out some of the non-climbers that will benefit in their every twig from all the south sun they can get. Many of them grow bulky at maturity. Therefore, if the wall has a border at its foot, this should not be too narrow; if a path, let this be wide enough to accommodate the shrub's *embonpoint* as well as your own.

The **pomegranate,** *Punica granatum,* has brilliant flowers in the cleanest, clearest shade of scarlet. Petals, sepals and all that portion which would develop into a fruit if our climate allowed, are of this intense colour. They are seldom carried in such quantities as to make a show, but appear over a long period of three months, from July, and they are nice to pick. Our shrub is about 40 years old. It was once cut to the ground by a hard, war winter, once by a careless gardener, and half of it was once carried away by the wind, but it is apparently superior to every disaster. Its leaves are neat, deciduous, and the bush has grown about 7 ft. tall: there is, however, a miniature form available only a few inches high. You can easily raise plants from pips taken from a shop-bought fruit, but seedlings are tender while young and you never know till time has shown, whether you have got hold of a hardy or a tender strain. If you keep pruning your pomegranate hard back, to keep it into the wall, it will be very shy flowering.

The **lemon-scented verbena,** *Lippia* (*Aloysia*) *citriodora,* is deciduous also (most tender plants are evergreen) and rather an unprepossessing shrub with long, untidy shoots and rasping foliage, but its scent, when crushed, is so satisfying that one cannot do without it. I never protect my plant, and therefore expect to lose it every few years, but I know of one specimen, in Norfolk, that came through the 1962–63 winter with no more protection than a south wall afforded. It roots extremely easily from soft tip cuttings in summer, and young plants grow so quickly that this is the precautionary measure I adopt. The plant benefits from pruning to keep it tidy. You can shorten its last year's shoots, in April, almost back to where they started.

I suppose the **common myrtle,** *Myrtus communis,* must be my favourite south-wall shrub. The rich, spicy fragrance of its bruised leaves is etherealised, at flowering, into an air-borne scent that comes to meet you. Its flowering season, in August and September, is particularly useful and the white blossoms, with their pouffs of creamy stamens, are borne in thousands on a mature plant. The variety *tarentina* has smaller, neater foliage, but flowers too late and too little with blossoms that are themselves rather mingy.

Throughout the poppy family one meets flowers having the refinement and delicacy of translucent porcelain. **Dendromecon**

rigidum is no exception. This fast-growing shrub is clothed in short, leathery, spear-shaped leaves whose glaucous colouring appropriately sets off the months-long succession of clear yellow poppy flowers, each about 2 in. across, borne singly at the end of every sideshoot. You seldom see it more than about 5 ft. tall, and it is an easy winter victim, but well worth swaddling in a plastic surtout. Cuttings taken of short side-shoots are not difficult to strike in late summer or autumn, but the roots are extremely fragile and it is best not to pot them off until the following spring.

Another yellow flowerer, **Fremontia californica,** is less refined but very showy and reminds me, in its blossoms, of a substantial evening primrose. Its leaves, with their rounded lobes, are another striking feature. Its worst fault is in not shedding its calyx, which is the showy part of the flower but fades to brown and persists. Seeds are freely set and germinate readily. This is a tall, second-story shrub, but not bulky. I first met it in the garden of Mr. Norman Edyvean-Walker, a well known personality in Rugby, when I was a schoolboy more than 30 years ago. I mention this because it shows in what an unpromising and cold part of the country you may meet a tender, exotic-looking shrub, when its owner is an enterprising gardener.

It is worth trying many of the large-flowered **fuchsias** as south-wall shrubs, because in this position they may no longer behave as herbaceous plants, as they do in the open, but make stout stems, up to 6 ft. tall, from which young shoots will start to flower in very early summer, continuing till the frosts. The grey cut-leaved *Senecio leucostachys*, normally grown as a 2 to 3 ft., half-hardy sub-shrub among herbaceous or bedding plants, will rush up a warm wall to a height of 12 ft., especially if it can weave its way through the branches of another shrub. An evergreen ceanothus makes a congenial host.

The florist's **mimosa,** *Acacia decurrens dealbata* is worth trying between the windows of a 2- or 3-storied building. It grows at a great pace and its feathery, greyish-green leaves are pretty at every season. If you are lucky, or clever, in procuring a precocious strain, it will flower as quite a youngster. Its vanilla-scented, yellow pom-poms become apparent near the branch tips in autumn, so that you subsequently have six months of pleasant if anxious anticipation before they expand in March. A really severe winter will certainly finish your tree, which is too large to protect after the first year or two, but you are likely to have had much fun from it in the meantime.

Cestrums, a group of solanaceous shrubs with clusters of tubular flowers, are usually grown in the cool greenhouse but are worth risking on a warm wall. They grow 6 or 8 ft. tall and rankly. The main thing, in winter, is to protect the bottom 'part of the shrub. If that survives, it will quickly make good its losses and flower on the young shoots. Hillier's list 4 species of which *Cestrum newellii*, with red flowers, is one of the best known.

The flower shape in **Abelia floribunda** is of the elongated Bach-trumpet style. This is far and away the most spectacular of its tribe, the colouring being a dashing magenta. The flowers come in clusters and are borne over a long midsummer season.

A not-so-hardy **Viburnum** that deserves wall space is *V. macrocephalum*; well named, for it does indeed carry enormous snowball heads as much as 9 in. across, of dazzling white flowers in late spring and early summer.

Carpenteria californica is a shrub that I find rather irritating in its long off-season. It is much hardier than some gardeners suppose, but receives repeated set-backs, in winter, which make this evergreen shrub look more and more tramp-like with the passing years. All is forgiven in its midsummer flowering season. The blooms are 2 or 3 in. across, cup-shaped, white, with numerous yellow stamens. Even on a wall, it seldom exceeds 4 or 5 ft., but bulges forward.

Azara microphylla is not all that tender but its cream-and-green-leaved form, Variegata, is much trickier. It is one of the most entrancing variegated plants in existence, the leaves quite tiny but displayed on fan-like branches. Like the type-plant, its inconspicuous but strongly vanilla-scented flowers open in March and April.

Another foliage shrub for a warm wall is the evergreen loquat **Eryobotrya japonica.** With its huge foot-long leaves, this is a show-off plant, intent on being noticed. It has its points but is really a coarse thing. Among the best foliage shrubs for a wall position are the **pittosporums.** Most of them will not demand south. *Pittosporum tenuifolium,* for instance, will be safe as a free standing small tree in many gardens. All the same, it looks well when treated as a wall buttress, and clipped regularly. The clippings, which are quite long, come in useful for flower arrangements. The tender and more striking *P. tobira* really does need your kindest protection. It has large, glossy leaves and there is a silver-variegated form.

I dote on **Olearia semidentata** and it is maddening to see it growing so uninhibitedly in seaside gardens. To be able to grow this and *Senecio rotundifolius* without protection would be among the few lures that could drive me to living by the sea. Hailing from the Chatham Islands, this olearia has pleasant lanceolate foliage, grey on the under-surface. There is a continuous succession of its bold daisy flowers, in summer. They are borne singly and are a good strong mauve enhanced by the most unusual feature of purple disc florets.

Hebe hulkeana comes from down under and really prefers the sea, too. It is the queen of its tribe—the shrubby veronicas—blooming in May with open panicles of mauve speedwell flowers arranged in innumerable spikelets. The shrub itself is low and sloppy. If you get it right up against a wall you can sometimes give it a little not too ostentatious support.

Last, a plant that is sub-shrubby: it dies back in winter to a woody rootstock at ground level. This is the **Coral Tree,** *Erythrina crista-galli,* a member of the Leguminosae flowering in autumn with long spikes of large, brilliant lobster-red pea flowers. It always looks splendid at the front of its high wall in the Savill Gardens but one must, I fancy, start with a good free-flowering and reasonably hardy strain. I had no success with a couple of plants I raised from seed.

Clothing the North Walls

The tally of wall shrubs and climbers that may be grown with a north aspect is quite surprisingly high, especially if they can be provided with some nearby or middle-distance shelter from north and north-east winds. Some of them actually prefer a sunless aspect; others will do equally well however orientated but, since they will oblige without sun, we are inclined to take advantage of the fact and keep the basking walls for those that really demand them.

Something that we easily forget is how dry it can be under a north wall—under any wall, come to that, for walls lap up moisture. But north being shady, we somehow imagine it must be damp, whereas north winds, when they do blow (and in the present climatic conditions they blow pretty frequently) are habitually dry, unless you live near a north-facing coast. Apart from the obvious implication, here, that our north-wall plants will need extra water to make them grow, some of them also need it in their early years for another reason, I fancy. This is guesswork on my part, actually.

The self-clinging climbers have a habit, when young, of refusing to cling. As we had bought them largely for that property, this can be infuriating and we swear at the nurseryman for having sold us a pup. However, after two, three, or four years, the shrub decides that it is, after all, the sort of climber we were expecting and all is smiles once more. I believe that these climbers will snap out of their non-clinging phase much more quickly if they have plenty of water at the root, and that the reason they eventually get the idea of their own accord is that by then their roots have reached out far enough from the wall to find the extra water they need. Another way we can help is to plant a foot forward from the wall, where the ground will not be quite so bone dry.

Self-clinging climbers must always hold a special place in the affections of those of us who do not enjoy monkeying about with nails, vine-eyes, hammers, thumbs, wires, lattice and other such accoutrements. Actually, some of the modern plastic netting such as Nettlon or the 8-in. Weldmesh, is excellent and so light that one reasonably handy man can erect it without disaster or assistance.

Particularly interesting among the self-adherers are the **hydrangea, pileostegia, schizophragma** sorority. They all belong to the hydrangea family, are all white flowered and their aerial roots will, if presented with a suitable tree, take them up to 30 or 40 ft.

Hydrangea petiolaris is the best known, with lacecap-type inflorescences opening in June. In their moment they are charming, especially in the way they will light up a heavily shaded corner, but the display is over within a fortnight. It is followed by *Schizophragma integrifolia*, which is rather showier and interestingly unconventional. Within each compound inflorescence,

which may be as much as a foot across, the groups of small fertile
florets are each supported by one large elliptical bract, some $3\frac{1}{2}$
in. long and half as wide.

Pileostegia viburnoides is an imposing evergreen, with bold
foliage. It is hung with a mist of flowers in September. They have
no special distinguishing features but add up to a pleasing massed
effect. All your never-never-land sort of gardeners yearn for an
evergreen, self-supporting, flowering climber, and here it is. But
the flowers are white and that, to them, is as useless as no flowers
at all. They should emigrate to the lands of the bougainvillea.

Quite as colourful and interesting as flowers, in their way, are
the leaves of some **variegated ivies.** And these are evergreen.
Indeed, *Hedera canariensis* 'Variegata' also known as Gloire de
Marengo is at its best in winter. Its normal variegation in white
and several tones of green is enlivened in the cold season by
pinkish purple tones, especially at the leaf margins. The leaves
can be damaged in severe frost but the plant can generally be
accounted hardy. Its foliage is mostly fairly substantial and in
H. colchica 'Dentato-variegata', although there is a great range of
leaf sizes, the largest leaves are very large indeed. Here the
variegation is of greens with primrose yellow; sometimes very
little yellow, sometimes a good deal and sometimes taking over
the entire leaf. This shrub is a top-notcher whose virtues it would
be hard to exaggerate. You can keep it under control by cutting it
for the house, where its trails of young shoots and chunkier
mature, flowering shoots are each of inestimable value in their
different ways.

Where your north wall space is limited I can recommend the
little cultivar called Jubilee, with a yellow flash in the centre of
each small triangular leaf. On this one you have to watch out for
reversion, and remove the green-leaved shoots when they appear.

There are two more evergreen self-clingers that deserve mention. **Euonymus fortunei** (*E. radicans* it used, more helpfully, to
be called) exists in several cultivars and can be used in the open
as ground cover, but takes to climbing to considerable heights

Plate 17. *Yucca gloriosa* is the largest hardy species in this genus, and
makes a bold formal feature. When suited, it blooms regularly, though
sometimes rather late in autumn. Its bell flowers are white and waxy.

when it finds itself near a wall and is most striking in its variegated form. **Ficus pumila** (*F. repens*) is best known as a ground
cover plant under greenhouse staging, but is reasonably hardy and
will hold itself exceptionally close against a wall surface. It is dark
green.

The **Virginia creeper** tribe now belong to the genus *Partheno-
cissus* and any of them will do on any aspect but the best for a
north wall is *P. henryana* (better known as *Vitis henryana*). The
leaves are of only moderate size and palmate (divided into fingers).
In a shady position the veins are picked out in a pale, silvery shade
throughout the summer, giving a marbled effect. In autumn it
flares up and blazes with the best.

Of the climbers for north walls I shall deal with the honeysuckles separately. **Berberidopsis corallina** is beautiful and unusual but temperamental. I have had it for three years and it
makes no growth at all but is still alive. It gets absolutely no sun
and this is according to the doctor's prescription. When pleased it
carries pendant clusters of glowing red flowers resembling a
berberis.

The even more unusual-looking **Schizandra rubriflora** is far
more co-operative. It twines up wires to a height of 20 ft. and
will spread as far across. In May its flowers, which are borne
regularly from an early age, open from buds resembling cherry
stones into crimson saucers composed of seven almost circular
petals. There is a prominent green centre on which the carpels are
clustered. My plant is a female. I need a male in order to see it
at what is, by all accounts, a handsome fruiting stage. I hope I'm
on the track of a husband. This belongs to an obscure branch of
the magnolia family and is a plantsman's plant: fascinating and
gay at close range but not contributing a staggering display.

Next, two herbaceous climbers. **Tropaeolum speciosum** the
flame nasturtium, is best known in the cooler, wetter parts of our
kingdom, but will thrive in the southeast if given a cool, moist
root run in acid soil. Walls are apt to have bits of alkaline mortar

Plate 18. Above, prickly but decorative annual thistle, *Silybum
marianum.*

Below, Hosta undulata has green and cream leaves with a subtle twist
to them.

scattered in the soil around them, which is tricky. The chaplets of dark red flowers are really spectacular. They open over a long summer season and are followed by blue fruits. The plant, if happy, spreads by fleshy rhizomes and can become quite a weed.

Aconitum volubile is a climbing monkshood growing readily from seed but the flower colouring varies between a good deep blue and an indeterminate non-colour, so you may have to make more than one try. Seedlings will flower in their second summer. I have seen it looking particularly effective mixed up with the yellow flowered *Clematis tangutica*.

Clematis are good north-wallers, as we are coming to realise more and more. It is not so much a question of enumerating suitable varieties as of warning against the few that are unsuitable. Ernest Markham, Lady Betty Balfour and Huldine all want sun and so, in most cases, does Ludlow and Sheriff's form of *C. orientalis* with the thick yellow sepals, like lemon peel. Otherwise these make quantities of foliage and no flower buds. The slightly tender *C. armandii* would also seem to demand a hot spot. Apart from these, it is merely a question of tempering the wind to the shorn lamb. *C. montana* will take anything from the north, but the large-flowered hybrids need rather more shelter; while the evergreen, fern-leaved *C. calycina,* although notable for its tolerance of a sunless site, will never carry its small green, brown-speckled blossoms in late winter and early spring unless its shoots have been protected from wind and severe frost throughout the preceding months.

White flowers show up particularly well on a shady aspect and the large white clematis Marie Boisselot is excellent, here. You might combine it with the vigorous white-flowered climbing rose, Mme Alfred Carrière, well known as a successful north-waller. White with white is terribly chic, didn't you know? Oh but, my dear, you cannot expect white flowers to do themselves justice except in a white *milieu*. And the walls should be white, too. A symphony in white. There are so many shades of white; an infinity of *nuances*. Such a pity we cannot do away with all those green leaves.

Of the non-climbing shrubs that are suitable for training against a north wall, I shall discuss two cotoneasters in an autumnal context and shall dismiss the popular *Pryacantha coccinea* 'Lalandii' for this reason. It is a vigorous shrub and soon reaches a size that obliges you to cut it back. Cutting it back removes all the flowering wood and you find yourself with a sombre, bulging evergreen monster, full of roosting, nesting, squabbling sparrows, plastered with their droppings and never a berry in sight.

The **winter jasmine** is suitable, though; you can go over it with clippers in the spring, and the shoots it makes during the summer will be lined with gay yellow flowers in the following winter. Forsythia can be given similar treatment but be sure to choose yourself the right one: *Forsythia suspensa sieboldii.* It makes wand-like growths on which the flowers are strung out, not congested into lumps as in the more popular forsythias.

The **Japanese quinces** (widely known as Japonicas) can be grown practically anywhere in any garden unless it is viciously chalky, but will flower well on a north wall. Shorten back those long unproductive shoots, in winter, to where you can see next spring's flower buds developing. **Morello cherries** are nearly always relegated to a north wall and can look charming, here, in spring, with their wands of snow-white blossom tied close into the wall's surface. Pruning a healthy specimen that has not had its buds stripped by bullfinches is a satisfying task because there's something to show for it at the end. Cut out the weak, straggling old growths for a start and then tie in the productive young shoots fan-wise, so that no one shoot crosses another. Start at the outside of the fan from the right and from the left and work up to the centre.

Camellia reticulata and its cultivars have the biggest, blowsiest and most eye-catching flowers of the entire genus. But they are less hardy than *C. japonica* and their natural habit is somewhat straggling, so that from both points of view and also because they thrive in shade, a north wall is the answer. **Garrya elliptica,** with the long green catkins in January, likes a wall for protection and is indifferent as to sunshine. Do not give it too prominent a position as its evergreen leaves are dull at best and objectionable for a good deal of the year being subject to damage by frost and also by a fungus disease that spots them badly. This also makes a successful free-standing bush, 10 or 12 ft. high in any reasonably sheltered position.

The Climbing Honeysuckles

Next to clematis, the **honeysuckles** are the most popular group of climbing plants. They are particularly useful in their preference for shade, and can either be trained on north walls or be allowed to grow through trees and large shrubs like lilacs, which will themselves provide all the shade that they require.

In some seasons they are subject to infestation by black aphids which can quickly bring all growth to a complete standstill. It is important to watch out for this trouble and spray with a systemic aphicide before the damage has been done. May is usually the danger month. A satisfactory systemic spray against aphids (greenfly, blackfly, or whatever you like to call them) is Saphicol, a Plant Protection product based on menazon.

Starting with the scented honeysuckles, our own native woodbine is *Lonicera periclymenum*. There are two cultivars that are commonly used in gardens on account of their heightened colouring. The early Dutch honeysuckle, *L.p.* 'Belgica', carries a great display of carmine-tinted blossom in late May and through most of June. It does not flower again much in the autumn; berry formation seems to take up most of its energies then. The late Dutch honeysuckle, *L.p.* 'Serotina', gets into its stride in late June and is at its best in July, but it flowers generously through to September and October, coinciding very prettily with the second crop of the large, white-flowered clematis, Marie Boisselot. The outsides of the flowers of the late Dutch are a deepish red.

This type of honeysuckle carries its flowers in terminal whorls, and another in this category is *L. splendida*, June-July flowering in pastel shades of pink and cream, but whose chief glory is in the wonderful grey colouring of its young shoots and leaves. This is, however, a pernickety species and no one seems to know quite what treatment to recommend so as to ensure success. It is hardy enough and grows well at Crathes Castle in east Scotland. The finest specimen I know is on the tower at Sissinghurst Castle in Kent.

The other popular group of scented climbing honeysuckles is based on *L. japonica,* a vigorous, more or less evergreen species. The fact of its being evergreen is no particular asset, as it is a shabby tangle in winter. The flowers are carried in pairs in the leaf axils, which is not such an effective manner of display, but they smell strongly by day as well as (and even more strongly) by night, although the quality of this scent is less pleasing than in *L. periclymenum*. The flowering season is continuous from midsummer till November. *L. japonica* is carmine-tinted on the outside of its smallish flowers; white within. *L. j.* 'Halliana' is even more popular and is cream and white throughout. You can prune this species hard in spring, to keep it in order, without much loss of flower. But an unpruned specimen is the most effective in our garden, rising through the branches of an old wisteria, and then crowning it with a floral bonnet. Another well-known cultivar in this group is *L. j.* 'Aureo-reticulata', in which the green leaves are heavily veined with gold. I doubt whether many of those who acquire this one realise, till later, that it is a very shy flowerer. You must content yourself with the foliage effect. Its trails are valuable for flower arranging.

A favourite of mine is the hybrid *L. americana* (syn. *L. grata*). Its pinkish-yellow flowers are carried in the greatest profusion, not only in terminal whorls but also in the axils of the leaves along the last foot or so of each shoot, so that you get the effect of sprays of blossom flying off in every direction. This is charming grown as a pillar shrub and is quite happy in sun. A word of warning: young plants do sometimes take a year or two to settle down before they start flowering. *L. etrusca* is one parent of the last and behaves similarly in its manner of flowering, in its great vigour and in taking time to settle down. It lacks the pink blush of *L. americana* and is yellow right the way through.

Once you have got a scented honeysuckle or two in your garden, there is no need to despise the scentless types. They are complementary to the others, being very much more glamorous in appearance. *L. brownii* 'Fuchsioides' is a brilliant scarlet red. Its flowers are borne in terminal clusters and are at their best in May and June. They are of only moderate size, and narrowly tubular along their entire length. The colour is something you cannot ignore. This is a hybrid of American parentage and is known as the Scarlet Trumpet honeysuckle.

L. tragophylla is the largest flowered of all hardy honeysuckles, with clusters of 3½ inch-long blossoms that open, at the mouth, to

1½ in. The colouring is clear yellow and shows up well in the shady position that the species prefers. Again, it flowers in early summer, and so does the hybrid of which it is one parent: *L. tellmanniana.* This carries abundant clusters of orange flowers, calculated to make anyone who is strange to them fairly jump with excitement. And it is an easy plant to grow, in shade. If you want to prune it, you can cut out shoots that have flowered, immediately their season is past, but no regular pruning is needed.

The Great-Flowered Magnolia

Property agents will occasionally seize upon some vegetable feature in the garden of a house they are advertising, because certain trees and shrubs possess a cachet, a glamorous aura that helps to sell the establishment to which they belong. Figs, catalpas and tree peonies are in this category and so are the more spectacular magnolias, especially the evergreen **Magnolia grandiflora.**

This tree from the S.E. United States is nearly always at its best, in Britain, as a wall shrub. In countries bordering the Mediterranean you see it as a giant, free-standing 60 ft. tree of broadly pyramidal habit. But here, although hardy enough to take this treatment, unprotected specimens are usually of scraggy appearance. The group in the R.H.S. gardens at Wisley is a notable exception, but even this would probably flower more freely against a protecting wall.

Such a wall will automatically belong to a house, and an old-fashioned house at that, for the magnolia likes to spread itself over two and even three stories. It is the kind of shrub for whose sake any outmoded old parsonage, however riddled with dry rot and beetle, should be acquired with enthusiastic pride. If the owner starts enquiring 'how should I prune my magnolia?' a preservation order, to include every twig, must be served on him forthwith. He should be grateful for being allowed. to live in permanently darkened rooms, when the darkness springs from so august an umbrage.

For those with the true *Magnolia grandiflora* spirit, the rewards are great. Of all evergreens with a laurel-like leaf, this is probably the most lively, because its upper surface is very highly polished and light-reflecting. On its underside the leaf is sometimes brown-felted, as in Exmouth Variety, and it is worth seeking out this attribute.

The species has a great many clones in circulation. When raised from seed, which is the simplest method of propagation, they are unlikely to flower for 15 years at least; probably not for 25 and I know one specimen that must be quite 50 years old which has never flowered. Exmouth Variety and Goliath are reliable clones, perpetuated from cuttings. They can usually be expected to flower in seven years.

Your great *M. grandiflora* years will follow one when the summer was hot and ripening. Such was 1965 following on the vintage year of 1964. When a tree is really laden with buds and blossoms, a great waft of lemon scent blows off it continuously, day and night. For those who do not own a plant it is a great treat to be given a bud that is on the point of opening. It must be at this advanced stage, otherwise it generally fails to open in water.

This expansion from bud to open flower is as rapid and almost as dramatic as in a night-blowing cactus. The petals unfold in a series of jerks, until in a matter of two or three hours, the blossom has fully expanded into a cream-coloured bowl, 9 in. across. The stamens are creamy, too, but as they begin to fall, they reveal crimson bases and look like a heap of doll's match-sticks.

Although we may envy the tree specimens of warmer climates, our conditions do have one advantage. For, whereas theirs bloom all at once, at midsummer, come August there are only seedpods to remember them by. The season here is less certain but far more prolonged, reaching from late July till some time in October, when cold weather puts its seal on the last unopened buds. But if you want flowers you should try not to prune. Not that the magnolia minds being pruned, but the mass of soft leafy shoots that it will throw in reaction, will take years to settle down to the firm woodiness that goes with flowering.

Roses

Modern Wars of the Roses

The rose continues in its triumphal progress. Never have its praises been more highly sung. You only have to show a new rose to have the crowds pressing about you all agog, as if around the latest model of a motor-car. And there is money in the business: returns on roses sold fall not so very far short of the returns on all other trees and shrubs taken together. Furthermore, roses are about the only shrubs in the nursery trade that lend themselves to mass production methods such as are used for potatoes and bulbs: mechanised planting, pruning, lifting and so on. This means that, compared with any other bush, they are remarkably cheap. While a rose will cost you 6/od., a *Daphne mezereum,* for instance (a shrub of comparable size) will cost perhaps 16/od.

But what of the rose itself? Does it justify all the ballyhoo attendant on its promotion? Undoubtedly the industry's prosperity makes for an impressive breeding programme, both in America and in Europe. The new varieties being brought out are legion. They have to be, to hold the public's interest. Some, like Peace, Super Star and Iceberg, are so good of their kind that they can stay the course, even under killing pressure, over a number of years. Most, though good in one way or another, drop out of the lists pretty quickly.

Thirty or forty years is a long time in rose history nowadays. How different from clematis, for instance. Many of the finest hybrid clematis that are grown today were brought out between 60 and 100 years ago. They appear to have suffered little loss of vigour in the interval. But where is the HT rose Mme Butterfly, today? It headed the popularity polls of the early thirties but is now—outclassed? Yes, partly. The bloom, at its best, is as charming as ever but there are roses now of far greater vigour than Mme Butterfly ever commanded.

When I recently saw a bed of this old favourite at Kew gardens I could only exclaim 'you poor thing!' The bushes were decimated with mildew. We never used to be worried by mildew on Mme Butterfly in the old days. It is the same story only worse with Frensham, the red floribunda that everyone was planting only 15 years ago. Its vigour and freedom of flowering seemed irrepressible, then, but nowadays this rose, too, is generally weakened beyond redress by mildew.

This is but one of a list of troubles that beset the rose today as never before. In our great love of the flower we seem to have been

unable to avoid giving it the kiss of death. I rather cherish this
hand-out from the representative to a firm of pesticide manufacturers: 'I feel sure gardeners, especially rose growers, will
remember 1966 as a year in which black spot was more serious
than ever before, resulting in some cases in bushes being almost
devoid of foliage by mid-summer. It is reasonable to assume that
with the amount of disease inoculum present, a severe outbreak
can be anticipated next season and it is all the more important
therefore to prepare a spray programme well in advance'. I was
then recommended to start spraying in mid-May and to continue
at fortnightly intervals till mid-October.

Thus, at the start of each season, we are spurred on to make new
resolutions and fresh efforts. 'This year it will all be different', we
think. But at the end of the year we find that it was no different
unless rather worse. 'It must have been the spray application I
missed when we took our holiday in August', we think, in order
to explain our failure (for explanations are never far to seek). 'Next
year we won't go away till it's safe to, in November.' Thus can
the practice of gardening founder beneath the load of this kind
of negative tyranny. Of course the pesticide manufacturers are
doing á good job in their way but it is sometimes difficult not to
see them in the light of parasites who not only feed upon our
misfortunes but help to create them. If we can't grow decent
roses without spraying them a dozen or more times through the
growing season, then the answer surely is to grow something else.
I don't mind taking trouble over a plant I love if it is constructive trouble like sowing seed at the right time, potting on frequently at the right time, feeding and tying. But if I feel that
I am starting off with an inbuilt invalid that has been bred to be
susceptible to every passing ailment, then I am inclined to rebel.

Making up an unholy trinity with black spot and mildew we
have rust diseases of roses. I have known rose rusts for as long
as I can remember. Betty Uprichard, a Hybrid Tea rose that was
in the forefront around 1930, was always prone to rust but never
seemed much the worse for it. And you frequently see rust on
wild dog roses. It is only of quite recent years that rust has become
serious; so serious that in bad attacks it can wipe out entire rose
gardens, as happened to a keen rose growing friend of mine in
the next village. So he scrapped his collection of, perhaps, 200

HT rose bushes and replanted with new ones. And what should he run into then, but **Specific Replant Disease,** sometimes called Rose Sickness, in this plant.

This is the latest of the rose's troubles to make news, and it is serious. I was first made aware of it through reading as follows from the notes in E. B. Le Grice's rose catalogue. '*Never plant new roses in old rose soil.* An old rose bed should have the soil removed for at least 15 in. and be replaced by fresh soil in which roses have not been grown (i.e. Kitchen Garden). When filling up old beds with new bushes take out a cubic foot of soil where the new bush is to go and refill with fresh earth.'

It is a mysterious soil-borne disease whose existence has been known about for over 200 years but whose causal agents have yet to be identified. It is called Replant Disease[1] because if you replant a piece of ground with the same species of plant that occupied it anything up to seven or more years previously, the replants will suffer from severe stunting. Only certain species are affected and most of these, on present evidence, are trees and shrubs. Apples followed by apples are severely affected; so are cherries followed by cherries, peaches by peaches, citrus by citrus. Plums are less seriously affected, and some rootstocks more than others. Pear and quince are less severely affected.

Among roses, *Rosa canina* (dog-rose) seedlings (which are the most widely used stocks in commerce) are fairly seriously affected but *R. multiflora* (another fairly popular rootstock) is resistant.

It is all very strange. The original plant on the site may have been the picture of health, yet its replacement will immediately show symptoms of acute stunting. The root system is weak, small and blackened; above ground there are no symptoms apart from reduction in vigour. After this initial check the affected plant (if not killed in its weak state by secondary causes) will make a gradual recovery and a return to almost normal growth, but will never entirely make up lost ground.

The disease does not spread in the soil, and so a replant made immediately next to but not actually on the site of the previous occupant, will not be affected.

What is to be done? Commercial rose growers are seeking a way

[1]See *Specific Replant Diseases* by B. M. Savory. Commonwealth Agricultural Bureau 1966.

out by partial sterilisation of the soil with fumigants releasing methyl isothiocyanate. But this is still hazardous even where a rose monoculture is practised on a field scale, because replanting cannot take place until the soil is clear of the fumigant and, at present, residues do still tend to hang about, even after repeated cultivations. In the garden, the method seems to be even less practical.

The development and use of resistant rootstocks, however, does seem to have distinct possibilities and is a far more attractive and constructive approach to the subject than soil sterilisation.

Virus diseases of roses are little heard of by the public at large but are a matter of concern to those who realise what a weakening effect they have on roses and how widespread is their occurrence. With fruits like strawberries, raspberries, black currants and, nowadays, apples, great care is taken to propagate from virus-free stocks, but no such control is exercised over the propagation of roses. And so virus disease is propagated on the nursery as quickly as are the roses themselves. It makes an important contribution to the loss of stamina that is so often noted in popular cultivars over the years.

These diseases: mildew, black spot, rust, specific replant (or rose sickness) and virus are the rose's worst enemies. But there are also a number of serious pests: aphids, leafhoppers, frog-hoppers, thrips, scale insects, capsids and red spider are all ardent feeders on rose sap. Various grubs and caterpillars such as those of leaf-miners, rose slug sawflies, tortrix moths, leaf-rolling sawflies and winter moths, to name but a handful, are waiting in the wings. Chafer grubs will eat the rose roots while the adult beetles feed on leaves, shoots and buds, and the leaf-cutter bee makes quaint rounded gashes in rose foliage as though it were playing at cutting paper patterns as we did as children.

It is ironical that the beginner in rose growing is often the most successful grower. He starts off, in many cases, with a clean piece of land and (let us hope) with clean, healthy bushes. Gradu-ally, however, troubles begin to hedge him about. He buys in black spot and the spores thereafter remain in the ground beneath his bushes and thus ensure re-contamination at the start of each new growing season. He decides to change one variety of rose for another and runs into rose sickness. The leaf-rolling sawfly finds his bushes out and remains on the site from then on. I need elaborate no further.

The question is how are we to react while still keeping our reason and a sense of proportion? True, we can become spray-gun-happy and go all out for our enemies with every chemical in the pesticide manufacturers' armoury. We can even find an omnibus spray that combines a variety of chemicals so that, without really knowing what we're spraying against or with, there is some hope that one of the ingredients will do something to control one of the what's-it's that are getting at our bushes. 'Some of the foliage is looking a bit hippy; I think I'll give it the Combined Spray, *to be on the safe side.*' Thus the triumph of blind un-reason.

Many of these chemicals, especially insecticides like DDT and BHC, are extremely persistent. They reach the soil under your plants and there remain, for years—indefinitely, in fact, gradually building up in strength, there, as you keep adding to them. They are taken up by the soil fauna, including earthworms. Then by birds and other animals, feeding. The birds are rendered sterile by a too high concentration of the chemical and it may also affect their nervous systems. From birds to man is no great step.

A complete spray programme on roses is anyway such a bind that one looks around for other ways out. One way is to grow fewer of them. There is a danger in any sort of monoculture because it provides the ideal breeding ground for specific pests and diseases. The bigger the crop, the more easily these parasites can build up. Don't, if you can help yourself, make a whole rose garden within your garden or even commit yourself to beds of roses that cannot easily be changed over to other occupants. If you can let your roses take their place in the garden with other shrubs and plants, a serious build-up of their special pests and ailments is less likely to occur.

Where you do have beds devoted entirely to roses, consider the possibility of keeping them covered, the year round, with a thick mulch. I have discussed this in the chapter on composting and mulching. It has the effect of smothering and destroying black spot spores. I see very few signs of black spot in my rose garden (which is under a mulch of grass clippings) until right at the end of the growing season, when it does not matter anyhow. Gardeners who live in areas of atmospheric pollution by industrial fumes, will not get black spot anyway. They may get bronchitis instead!

Rust seems to be more prevalent and serious where rose beds are heavily manured and growth on the bushes is soft and lush. Do not over-manure them. There are plenty of other departments in the garden that will benefit, instead.

Touching the subject of mildew, avoid those rose varieties that are known to be particularly susceptible. Others will get it badly in one garden but not in another. To an extent, you must experiment. When you do find that a rose gets it badly, don't struggle on with it. Be ruthless and chuck it out.

That will land you up with replant disease troubles. Now, we know that certain rootstocks are more susceptible than others and it follows that some cultivars grown on their own roots are likely to be less susceptible than others. If you can grow your roses from cuttings, you can experiment in this department, too. I find Super Star an excellent replant rose, grown on its own roots. So is Peace, and there are many floribundas.

With a bit of give and take and as long as we are not too fussy, it should be possible to grow reasonably healthy roses from year's end to year's end without any spraying at all. They may have their bad moments: we all do, but, like us, they will get over them.

Roses on their Own Roots

In that last long chapter about the difficulties in keeping up with the roses, I said nothing about the curse that afflicts every rose grower: that of suckering rootstocks. Once a plant develops this woeful habit, it continues in it to the end of its working days. Among the last dozen HT roses I bought (all of one variety), nine were already throwing suckers from their roots before ever I planted them, even.

The rose industry, it seems, expects us to accept the inevitability of suckering and the gardener must therefore take his own defence measures. If he can learn to root roses from **cuttings,** he is well on the road to success.

Half-ripe rose cuttings may be taken at any time from the end of June till early October. But it is a case of the earlier the better.

Cuttings struck at the beginning of July will already be strong plants filling a 5 in. pot with roots, by the autumn. Taken in late August, however, they will not have reached the same size and strength until the following May.

It frequently happens that you see the rose that you most desire in the world in a friend's garden. 'May I beg a cutting of that gorgeous rose?' you say. 'Why, certainly: remind me at the right moment and you shall have as much as you want.' Now this is fatal. Either you or your friend will forget which plant your rose was flowering on, and your graphic descriptions of the paragon will elicit an expression of blank incomprehension; or else the next time you see him will be in your own home and he will forget to bring the cuttings; or else it will be the wrong time of year again, or he will bring the wrong kind of material. When offered a plant or a cutting, pounce at once. Delaying tactics can be reserved for the plants you don't want.

When you see and are attracted by a rose bush in full bloom, the moment is, in fact, just right for striking half-ripe cuttings from it. We usually wait until its blooms have faded, but this is simply that we may eat our cake and have it. The essential point is that the cutting should be taken before any of the eyes within the leaf axils below a flowering or faded rose have started sprouting. As soon as a rose is dead-headed, these eyes will make new shoots. But usually they are all dormant at and just after flowering time. Rosemary Rose is exceptional in that the eyes shoot while the wood that carries them is still quite immature, which makes it difficult to find suitable cutting material on this particular variety.

When removing the cutting material from a bush, you want to take not only the flowering (or just-flowered) shoot, but also the bit of older wood from which the shoot arises. The first thing I do when preparing a cutting is to remove all its thorns. This is chiefly for my own comfort. The thorns will break off cleanly if the stem is of the correct ripeness. Then I remove unwanted leaves (which have spiteful prickles on the backs of their mid-ribs). The prepared cutting will be about 6 in. long and needs only one or two leaves on it. Now one can start trimming the base of the cutting with secateurs, at the juncture of the young wood with the old. But the job is finished off with a knife so that the old wood left amounts to no more than a slight broadening of the young shoot at its base. Anyone who is not too good either at sharpening or at handling a knife can make a very good job of this final trimming with a razor blade. The top of the cutting is trimmed off just above a leaf. The cuttings go in, to half their length, round the edge of a pot filled with cutting compost which, in case you've forgotten, consists of one part by bulk of loam, two parts peat, three parts sand ($\frac{3}{16}$ in. horticultural grit). They are watered and put into a closed frame, where the atmosphere is kept humid and their foliage not allowed to scorch. The old leaves will gradually turn yellow and drop off naturally, but in the meantime new shoots will form and roots develop in three to four weeks—or less, in a mist propagator.

Now, to take heel cuttings from a rose may entail the removal of a considerable portion of the bush. And if, as is likely, it is from a friend that you are begging the material, he may be a trifle disconcerted at the brusque reduction of a cherished specimen. Of course, if you can get away with it, by all means take your cutting material with heels, but do it with an air. Brandish the bouquet of greenery in your donor's face and, with a 'Thank you kindly, old boy; I've taken the opportunity of pruning your bush for you while I was about it,' lead him firmly away from the mangled remains. However, if relations are in danger of coming under strain, it may be wise to take your chance on nodal cuttings, these being less drastic to the bush from which they derive. When you have made a sharp razor cut just below the lowest node (or joint), you can then winkle out the blob of pith that has thereby become exposed, with the tip of a knife. For the pith does not run continuously right through the length of the shoot, but only from node to node.

Gardeners who favour winter pruning (not later than January, for this purpose) can use the prunings to make hardwood cuttings. Take strong, well ripened young shoots about a foot long, trim them to a node at each end and insert them, outside, in a plot of light soil, so that only an inch or two of the cutting remains above ground. The site should be such as to receive shade from the midday sun in summer, otherwise the cuttings will tend to dry out. Furthermore, they will need good waterings in dry spells. By the next autumn they will be well rooted and movable.

Cuttings are an excellent method of propagating nearly all the larger types of shrub roses. Here I have, for instance, an 18-ft. hedge of the hybrid musk Penelope, struck from cuttings about 15 years ago. There are six plants in a staggered row, and the compact habit of this variety makes it especially suitable where one can afford to let it grow 5 ft. high by 6 ft. from front to back, but does not want huge wands of growth, such as Buff Beauty would produce, waving about all over the place.

All the floribunda roses are excellent from cuttings and so are many of the more vigorous hybrid teas. When you have a nice nine-month-old HT or floribunda rose growing and flowering in a 5-in. pot, it is tempting to think that it is already as strong a plant to put in your garden as a maiden bush bought from a nurseryman. This is not so, however. The nurseryman's product is a year ahead of yours, for his had been grafted on to a stock that had already been growing for a season and has a two-year old root system to support it by the time it reaches the customer. Bush roses from cuttings do need rather more cosseting in their first two years. In the second of these they can be grown on in a spare plot or in large (6-in.) pots before being asked to compete with established roses in their final quarters. It is sometimes claimed that roses on their own roots are not as long-lived as grafted plants. As a general statement, this has no validity. Sometimes it is true, sometimes not, and when it is true this may well be on account of a specific replant disease.

Pegging and Layering Roses

One of the most charming ways to grow the more old-fashioned hybrid perpetual and Bourbon roses is in open beds, where their cane-like growths, 6 to 8 ft. long, are **pegged** down horizontally. By this method they are induced to flower along the whole length of each cane, instead of just towards the top, as they would if left growing vertically. A third alternative, appealing no doubt

Plate 19.　Above, Centaurea gymnocarpa, with lacey grey foliage, can be hardy on well drained soil.
Below, the waterside giant, *Gunnera manicata* from Brazil.

to the tidy-minded, would be to prune all those long shoots back, as though the shrubs were just ordinary roses. But in this way you would get very few flowers and a great excess of unproductive shoots.

We have two beds filled mainly with Mme Isaac Péreire (a cabbage rose whose scent is, to my way of smelling, unparalleled), Grüss an Teplitz, Hugh Dickson, Ulrich Brunner, Mme. Ernst Calvat and an old ivory-coloured rose whose name has long been lost but whose vigour after 60 years appears to be unquenchable. It is really essential, with this type of rose, to complete pruning as early in winter as possible, even before the leaves are all off, otherwise the young shoots abrade one another so destructively each time the wind blows that they get quite worn through.

Pruning consists of the complete removal of last year's pegged branches, back to the point where a young cane arises, or else to ground level—whichever comes first. Then comes the pegging, and this can be done by a variety of methods. Some gardeners simply tie a shoot near its tip (the last foot or two of which would be removed, as with raspberries, because it is too soft to be useful) down on to the branch of a neighbouring plant. Others use iron hoops to tie the branches to at several points. Iron is durable but apt to look clumsy. You can make hoops of hazel wands (maiden shoots from coppiced hazels). These are very pliable and good for a season, if you can get them. I gather pegs from ash stubs in the second year after coppicing, when the young wood has branched sufficiently, but not too much, for the making of good stout hooks. Whatever you use, don't let it be willow, because, even when inserted upside-down, willow pegs always take root. I also prepare a number of Y-shaped forks from the same ash stubs. With some rose canes you will find, on pulling them down to a peggable position, that their noses are burrowing in the mud. If a fork is inserted immediately beyond and outside the hook, the rose branch can be lifted on to it and is then held rigid.

When roses are grown for pegging, they cover a lot of ground and can be spaced about 4 ft. apart. There is quite an art in peg-

Plate 20. The wild unspoilt *Cyclamen persicum* of the Levant is strongly scented. It has far more grace than the winter-flowering potted cyclamen derived from it.

ging each bush so that its wands run parallel with, but do not cross over, those of its neighbours.

Pegging can also come in useful on shrub roses that have been planted in an exposed position and have taken to rocking in the wind. Nothing could be worse for a shrub than to work a deep, smooth-sided, water-collecting hole around the junction of stem and roots. The short answer is to cut all the shrub's branches hard back, but this is just what one does not want to do, when the rose is required to make a large shrub. If its branches are not so inflexible that they snap off if you try to bend them down (Queen Elizabeth is an obvious example), a series of long pegs attached to young branches all round the perimeter of the bush will hold it absolutely rigid.

Roses making long, whippy canes are good subjects for **layering,** where you want a few extra plants, and this is merely an extension of the pegging system just described, and can be done at the same time. In this case the peg is fairly short and must be pushed right in, so as to bring the cane down to ground level. The stem of the latter is then inserted into a slit trench at as sharp an angle as you dare, without breaking it, and should emerge again as nearly vertical as possible. This distal portion of the stem can be held rigidly in position by tying it to a stake. In a year's time the layer should be well enough rooted to be severed from the parent plant and moved. In this way, if the parent was a bad suckerer, you can get the rose on to its own roots and throw or give away the original: a riddance that will give you much relief.

The Use and Abuse of Roses

By the end of June one might conclude that England—at any rate south of Trent—was one vast rose garden. The image is no longer as delightful as it would have been over 30 years ago. Till then, the colouring in roses was often bright but seldom crude. Perhaps the tooth-paste-pink of a Caroline Testout or of Dorothy Perkins was a trifle obvious, but the general impression was one of cosy softness. With the arrival of the geranium's red pigment into the rose all this was changed, and the change was accentuated by the development of bedding roses that are scarcely out of bloom from early summer till autumn. They produce a riot of colour and this term is often used as a triumphant achievement, worthy of emulation. Yet, as Mr. Edward Hyams has pointed out, a riot is as ugly in the garden as elsewhere; the triumph is of bad taste.

Fortunately the rose has so many facets that it can cater for all tastes. Ruskin said that a man revealed his character through his art; that he may hide and misrepresent himself in every other way, except in his work, but that there his character is intensified in all its noblest and meanest delights. Few of us are artists, but it is a solemn thought that we may be just as freely giving ourselves away when practising the gentle pursuits of flower arranging or gardening. And I believe that in his choice and arrangement of roses in the garden, alone, one can read a man's character in this sense of Ruskin's.

Many people are pitchforked into gardening. There is a piece of land attached to the house that has been bought, and their first reaction will often be that, whereas they may not have a clue about what to do with or plant in the garden, one thing they must have, and that is roses. After all, the rose is a flower they can recognise, which makes a reassuring anchor when one is quite at sea in a subject. So, roses are bought by the dozen or the hundred, and are planted in specially prepared beds, on their own. The beds usually bear no relation to their surroundings. They are cut out of the lawn and will probably be rectangular when the lawn has curved margins, or circular, kidney or liver shaped if the lawn is formal and straight edged.

But while it is easy to be scornful about other people's abuse and maltreatment of roses, it is not such an easy plant to accommodate successfully oneself. Take the **hybrid tea rose,** for instance. It carries exquisitely shaped blooms on a hideous or, at best, shapeless bush. The flower is the thing, and probably the most logical course to adopt with the HT rose is the way my friend in the next village has organised them: planted by the dozen, each variety in a rectangular bed, rather like a cemetery arrangement of graves, with intersecting grass paths. The plot is out of the way; it is not overtly intended as a garden feature but is easily looked after, and there are enough plants of each rose variety to allow a bowlful at a time to be picked for the house. Therein lies their greatest service.

The roses that he really cares for as flowering shrubs, rather than for their individual blooms, are sited nearer the house in a large, informal planting, wherein great mounds of rugosas such as Frau Dagmar Hastrup, Roseraie de l'Haÿ, Scabrosa, Blanc Double de Coubert and Pink Grootendorst jostle with hybrid musks such as Buff Beauty, Penelope and the white flowered Moonlight, whose young foliage is so wonderfully bronzed, together with R. *sericea* 'Pteracantha', placed so that the westering sun glows through its huge, young, crimson-shaded thorns, and other older roses like Reine des Violettes and Boule de Neige— badly shaped shrubs in themselves, but borne up and their faults disguised by their ebullient rugosa neighbours. Some of the rugosas are flowering by mid-May and their season, bolstered in several cases by a glamorous array of hips, carries right through till autumn. Their scent comes at you in great wafts, and is persistently abetted by the musks. Yet my friend tells me that, to many a rose enthusiast, these do not count as roses at all. 'Here are the roses,' he says, to which the mystified reply is 'Roses? Where?'

To return to the hybrid tea roses: I dearly love them, and as we have a formal rose garden I grow them in it; but my trouble is that there are so many varieties I want to grow. If you can be strong-minded enough to limit your range of varieties, and if you mean to make a garden feature of them, then I think there is no more effective treatment than to group them by height and colour in beds, whether formal or informal, with a few plants of each kind. Mistakes can be rectified, or desired alterations made by piecemeal methods (*pace* replant troubles), without necessitating a great upheaval. The beds, in fact, can go through a continuous process of gradual alteration while always retaining an appearance of settled maturity.

Shrub Roses in Mixed Borders

Shrub roses have become very popular with the more intelligent kind of gardener who is prepared to think how they can play their part with other components in a garden setting. They do not so readily lend themselves to common herding in rose beds and rose gardens.

There is nothing hard and fast separating this genre of rose from others. It cuts across the different sections but the general implication when we speak of shrub roses is that they can grow and will enjoy growing freely and expansively, requiring little pruning apart from the removal of old and weak shoots. They often make large plants but not necessarily. And often, again, one will be enough; two or three at the most.

Some gardeners, it is true, will be content to allot the shrub roses a border devoted to a mixed collection of them alone. This has to be carefully done, if it is to be a success. Roses are rather formless shrubs and their leaves, *en masse*, are often bitty: so a thoughtlessly mixed collection is generally a mess. However, it can be well planned, if certain varieties are included for qualities other than or besides their flowers. *Rosa sericea* 'Pteracantha', already mentioned for its thorns; or R. *rubrifolia* of the dusky purple leaf. This is a great setter-off to other colours, particularly yellow, and it carries heavy crops of hips in the sunnier parts of the country. In the typical rugosa roses, the leaf, at once glossy and rough-textured, has just that quality of substance which roses most need.

But where the type of rose naturally makes a shrub that is either stiff or straggling, it can often be best accommodated in a mixed border. There you can admire the flowers without being unduly conscious of the plant, and how rewarding it is to be able to associate other flowers and foliage with the roses. Blue delphinium spikes are an ideal foil, for instance, to cabbagy pink roses, or to a large, pale yellow rose like Peace or Buccaneer. I sometimes have the Crested Moss rose flowering behind a group of *Campanula persicifolia* 'Telham Beauty'. This rose is said not to be a true moss, but whatever its parentage, its calyx is as mossy as you could wish and with that spicy fragrance, when bruised, that I find so unexpected in a rose. The flower is fully double, flannel-petticoat-pink and richly scented. The campanulas are about 3½ ft. tall, roughly spiky in habit and a gleaming blue.

A hot-coloured, modern shrub rose in my main border is First Choice. The blooms are more or less single, vivid orange-red, shading to yellow at the centre and fading, alas, to crimson. The young foliage is purple and the bush is about 5 ft. tall. These modern rose colours are striking but distinctly difficult. However, they are here embedded in the creamy froth of *Clematis recta* and pastel-shaded delphiniums, and the rose's high colouring does stand out well.

Perle d'Or is a good mixed border rose if you can keep an eye on its welfare when young, so that neighbouring plants do not swamp it during the luxuriant season. Our two oldest plants are aged 35 years and are 5 to 6 ft. tall. Yet the flower is like a miniature tea and, on a young specimen, gives the false impression that the plant will be miniature too. The colour is buff-apricot at the centre, unlike the purer pink of Cécile Brunner, with which alone it might be confused. Cécile Brunner is not so vigorous, but Bloomfield Abundance, which is more often sold you in its stead than not, has tremendous vigour, showers you with roses throughout the season, and is an excellent mixed border candidate. You can always identify it by its prominent and somewhat leafy calyx lobes that protrude beyond the petals in both bud and flower.

Apart from the contribution that can be made by dahlias, there are few flowers of substance with a strong red colouring in the late summer border. For this purpose I can recommend an old floribunda rose, Florence May Morse, that grows 5 ft. tall and flowers with exceptional freedom. The individual blooms are rather globular and could not be called elegant, but for overall effect, this one is hard to beat.

By contrast R. *spinosissima* 'William III' is dwarf (2 ft.) and flowers for a few weeks in early summer. This is typical of the burnet roses, as is the way it suckers and will make a low thicket. The flowers are double and a brilliant magenta with a marvellous airborne fragrance and I have it (or hope to have it, for it is establishing slowly) contrasted with the lime green plumes of *Alchemilla mollis* and the white of *Viola cornuta alba*.

The Appeal of Flat-Faced Roses

Most of the old roses are flat. When they are double, the petals in the bloom's centre are arranged in folds, like the re-entrants on a contoured map, and this gave rise to the not altogether appropriate description, 'quartered'. Actually, there are more often five folds than four, and there may be six or more—or fewer. The point, however, is that this conformation does give the rose a very interesting appearance, so characterful that one naturally thinks of it as a face.

Flat-faced roses were unfashionable for many years, while the HT rose, with a high, pointed centre, reigned supreme. The exhibiting enthusiast will long continue to think of this as being the only kind of rose that is worthy of his attention. When a giant exhibitor's rose splits its centre, he will be furious, whereas we, who grow them simply for cutting or display, will scarcely rate the aberration as a defect.

Of recent years there has been a swing back into favour of the flat-faced, many-petalled rose. Breeders have not given them a lot of attention, but the signs are that they are slowly becoming aware of this change in their public's taste; of the fact that gardeners are rather weary of the perfect bud that tumbles into a shapeless mess on opening, and that there is scope for more roses that are at their best when full blown. These new flat-faces are to be found mainly among the floribundas.

Rosemary Rose was one of the earlier and is probably still the best, with a 4-inch-wide bloom of broad, swirling petals in brilliant cerise. This colouring is emphasised by the plum tones of the shrub's young foliage. The flower has a strong, fruity scent and Rosemary Rose is a thoroughly good grower, except for a liability to mildew in some seasons. It is not, however, a rose to lose your head over because, when massed, the cumulative impact of cerise flowers and purple foliage is oppressive. It needs the alleviation of other colours.

Plentiful is a clear, strong pink, so bright as to become aggressive in the mass, but again, a charmer when used with discretion. It has a very full flower, little scent and mildews badly in some circumstances. You could mass Geranium Red to your heart's content without danger of overdoing it but, alas, this heavenly rose is a weak grower and needs the best of everything. It is worth it. The flower is molten red, deepening and acquiring purplish tints with age, and the bloom, instead of being cupped in its outline as are Rosemary Rose and Plentiful, is out-curving, as though it were spilling over with its quantities of petals. I have worn it as a buttonhole and been complimented on the splendour of my carnation. And the scent, though different, also deserves this tribute. Edwin Murrell of Shrewsbury offers this rose and many of the less usual kinds.

There is a paler fieriness in the obviously modern colouring of

Allotria, a red that changes with age to a pinkish-purple tone that I personally like (you find it, too, in Independence) but is not to everybody's taste. Allotria is very free and its rosette flowers are gathered into huge, dense trusses. It has a splendid constitution and its lead-green foliage is singularly disease-free. Other flat-faced red floribundas are Europeana, a deep, clear shade, unadulterated by blue, and City of Nottingham, a vivid, lighter shade of red.

Brownie is not as full of petals as those so far mentioned. It is a rose about which you must have strong feelings one way or the other, being of an extraordinary mixture of biscuit, shading to mauve-pink. It is as unimaginatively named as the glorious Magenta. I certainly believe in calling a magenta-coloured flower by this unpopular word when it applies, but see no point in bravely grasping a nettle when, all the time, it is a dock. Magenta is a good mauve—a typical lilac colouring, in fact, large for a floribunda, flat, most excellently scented. Its only fault, assuming that you like its colour, is in its habit. The flower trusses are carried on long stems that are too weak to bear their weight. Above all, this is a flower arranger's flower.

Turning briefly from the new to the old, Magenta is only a few tones paler but in the same colour category of the purplish old-rose shades of Belle de Crécy, Reine des Violettes and William Lobb. Purely as to bloom, these three roses are remarkably similar. Belle de Crécy is the smallest, about 3 in. across, out-curving and very full. Its stems are covered with small, harmless prickles. This makes the best bush of the trio. Reine des Violettes is of straggling habit with smooth stems, and is best grown among other shrubs so that it can flop at will. The flat rosette blooms are composed of incurving petals. William Lobb is a moss rose with the usual fuzz of mock prickles on stems and calyx, aromatic when bruised. The 4-inch-wide blooms are packed with petals but in a haphazard fashion. Again, and as with other mosses, it is of scrawny habit and should be allowed to mingle with other shrubs or plants.

Agnes is a modern shrub rose classed as a rugosa hybrid but having even more obvious affinities with the double Persian yellow, which also figures in its parentage. This makes a spreading, 6 ft. bush and is at its best at the turn of May and June with gorgeous butter yellow blooms tightly packed with petals. Although it has a second crop in late summer, this is no more than a selling point.

Planned and Unplanned Garden Effects

Starting a New Garden

The question will often arise, when a new garden is taken over, of whether the owner is to cope with its lay-out and planting himself or whether he will get in a professional to help him. I must at least presuppose that the proprietor has a great interest in the project and an interest in and love of plants, however untutored. Gardens that are made to order, even when the cleverest consultants are called in and paid the largest fees, will be spiritually dead from the outset, if the owners are not involved and do not want to learn. A consultant can certainly be very helpful in suggesting where trees, borders, shrubberies, paths, lawns, areas of rough grass and so on might be sited. But after that, do try to cope with the planting side—the clothing of the skeleton—yourself.

Far better to make your own mistakes and thus be enabled to savour your own triumphs. Of course, you must take advice, but at least work for it. Read books and catalogues; visit gardens and flower shows. Make notes on plants that attract you. Then consult a nurseryman who really knows about plants and conducts his business on a personal level. These people do still exist, and they will not advise you to grow a plant just because they've got stocks of it they want to sell. They want a continuing and satisfactory relationship with their customers as much as their customers want and need it with them.

But, for mercy's sake, do not waste more of the nurseryman's time in detailed correspondence and prolonged conversation than is necessary. Otherwise his business will founder beneath time-consuming details and become so expensive to run that he will be inclined to throw in his hand and leave the field clear for the impersonal but paying mass-production methods as epitomised by the modern marketing concept of the garden centre.

The Planner and the Muddler

There are two principal ways in which you can set about the planting of a new border. The first is to get it down on squared paper, carefully planning your groups and the exact numbers of plants to go in them; then to assemble all your material and organise a grand planting ceremony. The other way is, immediately you have the ground ready, to start putting in bits and pieces from friends' gardens and from other parts of your own, as well as plants you have long wished to possess and feel you can now buy, as there is a place in which to put them.

I don't see why it should be said that either method is right or wrong. Which of them he adopts largely depends on the gardener's temperament. Either way, mistakes will be made, improvements thought of, and the process of alteration will go on indefinitely. The second, piecemeal, method will appeal to the plantsman. It will give a cottage-garden effect such as, in a limited area, can be wholly appropriate. But it can easily look too spotty, and the initial mistakes made will be numerous. The border will take longer to settle down. The process of trial and error is being worked out on the ground, empirically, and this is slow.

A friend who is a most successful gardener on a fairly small scale started a new border of this kind a few years ago. He included anything he fancied: cannas, hebes the variegated form of New Zealand flax (*Phormium tenax*), grasses, herbaceous plants, grey foliage, roses and sundry shrubs. Dissatisfied with results, he showed me the border and, not very surprisingly, it included a fair amount of bare earth although the month was July. He had had to plug the gaps with bedding plants, and as, like many another, he has not the time to raise these himself, they were the spindly kind of miseries that get established only by the time the first frosts are about to sweep them away. The gaps were caused by plants that had let him down, notably the hebes, of which he is (as I am also) inordinately fond.

But other things were flourishing: notably a clump of the zebra grass, tall and graceful with arching foliage, a specimen of the rich purple-leaved *Cotinus coggygria* (*Rhus cotinus*) 'Atropurpurea', and some lavender cotton, *Santolina incana.* None of these had anything in particular associated with them, but it did strike me that they formed a nucleus of good materials round which to build. Many people find it hard to visualise how a plant or association of plants will look until they see them actually growing in their own gardens in their permanent positions. Well and good. Let them make a start with something, anything. By the time climatic and soil conditions have taken their toll and other plants have revealed their unsuitability in one way or another, there will still remain a number of plants that are obviously going to be worth fostering. If wrongly placed, they can be moved and, by a process of inclusion and elimination, other good plants will take their places, so that after a period of quite a number of years, a delightful effect will have been achieved. That this can happen is perfectly evident from the older borders in this same friend's garden. He has a basic requisite for ultimate success in his love of good plants. The plants themselves make the decision of which of them are good for him.

It may, however, be objected that this is a case of muddling on and, as such, wasteful. The planner will still make mistakes, many or fewer according to his experience, but he will probably possess one tremendous advantage: the capacity for visualising how his plan will look when it materialises. This capacity will have been won by his having acquired the habit of observation, so that he can apply the details of what he has seen and liked in the past to what he is going to create in his own garden. In this way he can take many short cuts to success. Planning, moreover, goes with a penchant for bold and generous grouping, as also for repetition, in order to emphasise an effect.

The most impressive example of a planned garden that I have ever seen in Britain is at Crathes Castle, near Aberdeen. It gets frequent mention in this book. Each of its main sections has been designed to give expression to a theme. Thus, when I was there, a June-flowering herbaceous border was at the height of its glory: double-sided, straight, with the castle closing the vista at one end and a gazebo at the other. Borders for the later summer were ready to take over. There is a garden for the 'greys' and along the garden's east side there runs a border devoted to plants and shrubs with interesting foliage forms and patterns (described in a later chapter); and in the pond garden next to the castle the dominant motif is of purple and pale yellow or lime-green colour harmonies. The gardens are full of horticultural interest, and yet the plants are, for the most part, subservient to the design. To stick to such principles requires great strength of mind and a certain detachment, which I, for one, do not possess. With me, the plant comes first, but this is a bias that must, I realise, prevent one from attaining the first flight in garden artistry.

Planning before Planting

Planting can and does go on the year round, but most of it is done in spring and autumn and of those two seasons I think the feeling of beginning again is strongest in autumn. This might well be considered the gardener's new year, so I shall suggest an appropriate resolution that can be taken afresh at the approach of each new planting season.

With every new plant the gardener gets or old one he moves, let him take thought about how it will look with its immediate neighbours. Will they contribute one to the other or will each be operating in its own little vacuum?

When you are planning or altering a bed or border, whether of shrubs, plants, bulbs, bedding plants, annuals or a mixture of all these components, be strong-minded about making some big bold groupings. This is more easily achieved in a new garden that hasn't already become cluttered with personal treasures than in an old one. I know how easy it is to collect the things that fascinate and that you want to live with on close terms, until in even a quite large garden there is hardly room for more than one of each, and even then it is difficult to find a place for newcomers.

You must be firm with yourself and leave room for some large groups, some broad effects. The interstices can then be harmlessly filled in with your special pets: things like the toad lily, *Tricyrtis,* with freckled purplish flowers suggesting an upturned martagon lily's. You peer at it from a distance of inches and enter into a toad lily world that has no bearing on anything around it. Which is very pleasant, but only one side of gardening. And even a toad lily will look better leaning over a patch of pink-mauve colchicums (for both are out in autumn) than flowering in a waste of dying or diseased iris foliage, for instance.

Another necessary aspect of planning is for a succession of features to take you right through the seasons. In the tree and shrub garden, you must think in terms of camellias, rhododendrons, heathers and various kinds of spring blossom followed by shrub roses, brooms and cistuses, to be followed in their turn by hydrangeas and more heathers; these by autumn colour and finally a basic framework of evergreens, pleasing deciduous outlines and coloured or interestingly textured bark. Among herbaceous plants you plan for your main effects with poppies, peonies and lupins followed by delphiniums, then phloxes and lastly michaelmas daisies. Bulbs should start contributing in January with crocuses and *Iris histrioides* 'Major' as well as snowdrops. Lilies will take over from Dutch, Spanish and English irises in June and July, while in autumn we shall have crocuses again and colchicums, sternbergias, nerines and *Zephyranthes candida*. A fascinating succession can also be worked out with annuals, biennials and tender bedding plants, varying the materials used every year. Even a hardy plant like *Bergenia schmidtii*, which flowers in March, can be used as a bedder and extends the season.

Spring and early summer are almost certain to grab their share of every garden without any conscious planning being exercised. Planting for the April to June period is instinctive; it is the late summer and autumn that require our special attention. I have a theory that if you plan for July to October, the rest will look after itself.

Planning for the Autumn

There are two ways of planning for the autumn garden. The first is with trees, shrubs and plants that will make almost their entire contribution at that season; the second is with plants that have already been performing before autumn's arrival. Among trees, for instance, some flower prettily in spring and colour up before leaf-fall in autumn. Here, however, I shall consider border plants that reach perfection in the autumn but have already been contributing handsomely to the garden scene from way back in summer.

Many **grey foliage** plants are at their most luminous in autumn and look especially fine when decked with heavy dews. Moreover, they contrast strikingly with the predominantly warm colours of that season, *Santolina neapolitana* is whiter and more filigreed than the common lavender cotton, S. *incana*. *Senecio cineraria* 'White Diamond' looks like those enlargements of snow crystals that one sometimes sees. *S. leucostachys* will have done its usual weaving trick among the stems of neighbouring plants. *Centaurea gymnocarpa* displays the most beautifully cut foliage of any, arranged with the panache of ostrich plumes. *Helichrysum splendidum,* the name to which this hard-used shrub has uneasily settled down after shuttling between *H. alveolatum* and *H. trilineatum,* is gratifyingly hardy. Always rather tatty in spring, it is by now a solid 3-ft. hill of stiff grey spikelets, surmounted by clusters of small yellow everlasting heads. This goes marvellously with a sumptuous purple such as cherry pie or *Verbena bonariensis*. *H. petiolatum* is the most indispensable of tender bedding plants grown for their foliage. The heart-shaped, felted leaves are well spaced along indefinitely rambling shoots that fashion lacework patterns of infinite variety.

Still on the foliage theme, the **castor-oil plants** (*Ricinus communis*) sown in April will now be 6 to 8 ft. tall, in a decent season, and the variety Gibsonii, with purple leaves, is the most telling. Some of the **grasses** look splendid, too, especially those in the genus *Miscanthus* (*Eulalia*). *M. sinensis* 'Gracillimus', 7 ft. tall, makes an efficient and graceful partition between one piece of garden and another. *M.s.* 'Variegatus' is another good one, with arching foliage striped green and white.

The bold leaves of **cannas** can be enjoyed, even if our weather does not suit their fragile, silken blossoms. They mix well with other border plants, and the purple-leaved sorts are outstanding. I like to see generous groups of **dahlias** in mixed and herbaceous borders, too. They may be easier to manage on their own, but are invaluable for giving substance to a border in its latter days. Some people are rather repelled by dahlias, but it is the types often chosen and the way in which they are often grown that are repulsive rather than the dahlia itself. There is such variety of flower form and colour that there must surely be dahlias to suit every taste. One of my favourites is the cool, greeny-yellow

Glorie van Heemstede, with flowers of water-lily type. It looks nice behind a grouping of *Perovskia atriplicifolia,* in blue and grey.

On this subject of tender perennial bedding plants, many **salvias** are worth including. Best known is the rich, velvety blue *Salvia patens. S. ambigens (caerulea)* can be treated as hardy. It grows 3 to 4 ft. tall and has spikes of deep blue flowers. I have orange nasturtiums near it. **Nasturtiums** are emphatically not to be despised, as long as you remain their master, and they are not allowed to take over the whole garden. They flower on and on and have the habit, productive of many beautiful surprises, of sending forth their shoots through other plants and then flowering in a completely unexpected setting. Thus they may peer from 6 ft. up a yew hedge or flame out among a *corps de ballet* of white Japanese anemones.

These last flower for more than two months, from early August. All they ask is to be left undisturbed. **Rudbeckia speciosa** 'Goldsturm' has much the same season and is particularly effective in lighting up a shady but damp spot. These black-eyed-Susans could be grouped in front of the purple-flowered, 3-ft. *Lobelia vedrarensis,* which is generally hardy. A number of **sedums** flower in autumn, but Autumn Joy takes the prize, because it is so arresting at every stage from bud to seed. And it is such a gloriously robust plant. Two **verbenas** of similarly vivid purple colouring flower on for four months, and both should be started from seed. *V. rigida (venosa),* 2 ft. high, spreads by runners. It may die out in hard winters, but can be relied on to start again from self-sown seed. *V. bonariensis* sows itself all over the place, and one leaves just those plants that are not in the way. Six foot tall and very stemmy, but with its own appeal. *Dianthus* 'Allwoodii' and a number more of **hybrid pinks** are scarcely ever out of flower, but the price of this prodigality is a short-lived plant. They should be renewed from cuttings taken in April every two or three years.

Hardy **fuchsias** are worth exploring by every gardener. He will soon find out which best suit his conditions. Best of all is *Fuchsia magellanica* 'Versicolor'. Its leaves vary in colour from pink to ash-powdered green, while the red flowers are abundant. Other shrubs to flower non-stop for month upon month are the tree mallow, *Lavatera olbia* 'Rosea', *Hypericum* 'Hidcote' and *H.* 'Rowallane Hybrid', the clear blue plumbago-like *Ceratostigma willmottianum*, the shrubby potentillas and the pinky-white funnel-flowered *Abelia grandiflora,* the only reliably hardy member of its genus. And there are the majority of the most exciting hebes.

Training a Critical Eye

The human faculty for turning the mind away from uncomfortable thoughts is oil in the wheels of life, and so it is with things around us that we choose not to see. In gardens, it is so much easier to spot other gardeners' rubbish, making as it does a fresh visual impression, than to attack the eyesores we have got used to living with.

In a well-organised herbaceous border that I visited, I particularly admired and wanted to photograph some clumps of the 4-ft. white form of *Campanula latifolia*—frequently dismissed for general garden usage as too coarse, and hence relegated to the woodland, but really very telling as a border plant. However, the picture was spoilt by the peasticks that were still all too visible. Now peasticks have the great merit of being efficient and yet unobtrusive, but only if cut to the right length. The beginner uses them far too short. He is putting them in when the plants are still less than half grown, and fails to anticipate their needs when mature. The professional, on the other hand, will not be caught out like that. He is lavish with long pieces of brushwood, but with the consequences just described. If you cannot gauge your various plants' exact requirements at the time of supporting them, it is a simple matter to cut out protruding sticks just before flowering starts, but you must bring a critical eye to bear on the subject at the right moment.

Labels, too, can make a hideous impression. I wanted to photograph an elegant group of the striped grass, *Glyceria aquatica* 'Variegata', but there was no getting away from its four-square plaque and, the plant being in the middle of a pond, I could not get at the label, to remove it temporarily. I freely admit that this is an iniquitous practice, and that people who pull out labels will, usually, either fail to push them back in again securely or put them back in the wrong place. In fact, photographers as a genus are a menace, trampling about where they should not tread, cluttering the place with their ugly apparatus. I only wish I could give up being one of them myself. But at least it must be said that if you take photographs of plants in your own garden you are more likely to become sensitive to visual features in it that jar.

On colour effects and juxtapositions the last word will never be said. I recently saw a striking combination of *Lilium* 'Enchantment' and pink *Alstroemeria ligtu* hybrids. My host seemed rather apologetic about it but, given its terms of reference—and it must be conceded that this lily, which was present in great quantities, is of a particularly brilliant and uncompromising colouring, orange with a dash of pink in it—the mixture was thoroughly effective and successful. 'They clashed well' as a one-time gardener of ours used to say. The fly in the ointment, however, was some pinkish-purple, self-sown foxgloves, in the vicinity, then at the tail-end of their flowering season but still capable of a perfectly vicious contribution.

I went home and found a similar lapse staring me in the face. How does one miss these things? A self-sown, apricot-orange primula leaning into a planting of pinky-mauve dimorphothecas. It took but a moment to yank the primula out, but I should have done so two or three weeks earlier.

Cultivating a Catholic Taste

Where flowers are in question, it is strange and interesting how tastes change and develop in one direction—if they don't remain forever static, that is. Would a devotee of wild gladioli and of the dwarf or small-flowered hybrids ever desert them in preference for the heavy, showy spikes of the Grandiflora types? Transfer his affection from miniature daffodils and *Narcissus* species to the thick-stemmed, broad-leaved cultivars with waxy, overlapping segments and enormous frilly cups or trumpets, all of unparalleled symmetry and muscular hybrid vigour? Or from single dahlias to the massive structure of the Giant Decoratives?

A change of taste will always be in the opposite direction, away from the gaudy and towards something simpler, more informal and relaxed. It is yet another 'back to nature' manifestation; a reaction against the trappings and panoply of civilisation, and the splendours of man's works as epitomised, for instance, in the modern marigold, so uniform in height and dwarf compactness of habit; so uniform, too, in its brilliant unwinking colouring, with an unremitting succession for at least four months of enormous, crinkly double globes, guaranteed to maintain their display in every sort of weather. Who can wonder at their great and ever-increasing popularity?

Any kind of revulsion or rebellion on the gardener's part is at his peril and is likely to land him in a mess. I remember seeing a group of orange marigolds of the type I have just been praising next to a group of gazanias. Now, the latter have brilliant colouring too. They are much more varied and each flower is so subtle that it invites a closer examination. But there we were on a dullish windy day, and the gazanias, with rolled-up petals, were scarcely visible. Even if they had been fully expanded one could hardly have hoped that they would have held a candle to their neighbours.

And what happens in the rarified world of rhododendron addicts, when a devotee turns in disgust from the indestructible hybrids of never-failing reliability to the species from which their development began? It is true (at least, many of us think it is true) that the species have qualities of elegance and charm that tend to be lost in the hybrids, but the price of returning to their cultivation is a collection of invalids. The chances are that they will flower only in alternate years or at rarer intervals; that their blooms, when they come, will be excessively susceptible to frost damage and that the plants themselves will be habitually teetering on the brink of annihilation by frost, wind, sun scorch or drought.

And yet, every once in a while, you meet with a success—your own or (more likely) someone else's. And standing, for instance, before the specimen of *Rhododendron hodgsonii* cradled in its sanctuary of hard-won shelter at Inverewe in north west Scotland, you will sway before it with glazed eyes in an ecstacy of gloating appreciation, and murmur 'this is it' or 'here we are' or something equally banal, but knowing that you have arrived.

The basis of good gardening must always be a love of plants, and this love, when found, shines out for what it is and communicates with other plant lovers. Naturally you are likeliest to find it in private gardens, but it is quite frequently discoverable in public gardening too. You will unexpectedly come across an unstereotyped use of colour associations or plant juxtapositions or a varied and exciting use of plants themselves, as in London by Mr. S. M. Gault in Regent's Park or of shrubs as by Mr. Hilliar in Holland Park. But then in another park you will all too frequently come upon a motley and undigested jumble of tender greenhouse plants, bedded out for the summer months, many of them good of their kind and yet planted without a first thought of how to show them to advantage but with just the one idea of colour (and also, no doubt, of getting the greenhouses and frames emptied).

There is really nothing wrong with the ever-popular rhododendron hybrids, with hortensia as against lacecap hydrangeas. Even the less strenuous African marigolds have acceptable manifestations. Tastes that can embrace them all are most to be admired and a realisation that sympathetic treatment and proper care for the well-being of plants are what ultimately count.

Trees in their Wrong Places

The trees that should never have been planted are always a subject of fascination to me on a car journey. And I emphatically do not mean or refer here to tree-lined roads; nothing could be more refreshing to the driver on a hot summer's day than to plunge into a cool tunnel of green after the glare of the open road. The charming Sussex village of Burwash, 14 miles from where I live, has a narrow street with a row of limes along one side. They have fat trunks and no branches at all. In summer, they put out tufts of leafy twigs which are removed the moment autumn arrives, and for the next 8 months, the street is disfigured with this phalanx of mutilated monstrosities. Now, I know nothing at all about the local policies or pressure groups in Burwash but I do know that if common sense prevailed those trees would be removed and none would be put in their place because, with this example before them, it must be quite obvious to anyone with eyesight that there is no room for trees in this narrow street.

In other situations, a rational policy (or vandalism, according to how you look at it) would insist on removing large street planes whose appearance has to be ruined by pollarding. They should be replaced with trees that can reach maturity without needing to be butchered. These do not have to be flowering cherries.

Trees are often chosen unsuitably for gardens, too. It is true you can plant a vigorous tree in the knowledge that it will grow too large in time and intending at the outset to remove it when that time comes. This sounds sensible and gives you the pleasure in its youth, of some tree you would not otherwise plant. But when the time comes to be firm you may well find that you are no longer your own master (or mistress). '*You can't!*' (modern equivalent of 'thou shalt not') will resound and echo all about you.

The common spruce, *Picea abies*, constantly features in front gardens as a scraggy specimen, 30 to 50 ft. high, with a few dead or dying branches half-way up a top-knot of sickly yellow-green. One knows that it started life as a sweet little Christmas tree, which the owner could not bear to throw away on Twelfth Night. So he planted it out. Perhaps it would do another Christmas. Perhaps it did. But then it got too big or lost its lowest branches and ceased to look attractive. And there it stands to this day, un-happy symbol of a happy Christmas long ago. Just as well that most Christmas trees are sold without roots these days.

There are three conifers that I would not plant, even in a large garden that gave them room to do themselves justice in. The Douglas fir is one. Not only the tree but a pest disfiguring it came to us from the New World: a kind of aphis, *Adelges cooleyi*, that infests every Douglas fir I have ever seen, covering its foliage with waxy white blobs. Whether on this account or for climatic reasons, large pseudotsugas (for *Pseudotsuga* is its name) in this country are seldom shapely.

There is a kind of romance about a tree that can claim, however spuriously, to live for ever, and this may be one reason for the fairly general planting of *Sequoia sempervirens,* the Redwood of California. It is hardier in Britain than you might expect, and its yew-like foliage is pleasing, but severe winters do tend to cripple it so that ageing specimens increasingly bear the scars of numerous setbacks and invariably look moth-eaten. So do monkey puzzles. They are hardy but, in general, our climate is too dry for them and they lose their lowest branches. A mature monkey puzzle arrayed with branches sweeping down to the ground is a fine sight, I cannot doubt, but I have yet to see it.

Weeping willows are the most misguidedly planted of trees to-day. They look so confoundedly pretty, when young, that there is no resisting them. Pretty when old, too, as along the Backs at Cambridge or by any lake-side. But they do grow very large very quickly and should be nowhere near a house. They have a voracious and wide-spreading root system that is difficult to garden near. The best thing, if you are saddled with willows and can wangle it, is to get seed of the parasitic toothwort, *Lathraea clandestina* (common on the Cambridge willows), sow it around the roots of your own trees and hope that it will take hold. I have known gardeners succeed in this. The clusters of brilliant purple flowers appear like crocuses in early spring. There is no foliage.

A fungus attacking certain willows, the weeping ones among them, has been particularly virulent in the last few years (though not in 1968, so it may be that the phase is passing). It is called *Marssonina salicicola,* and it attacks the leaves and shoots especially in spring, often defoliating and making them most unsightly. This is having a deterrent effect on willow planting, which could be a merciful dispensation in some cases. The charming fastigiate twisted willow, *Salix matsudana* 'Tortuosa', is unfortunately subject to the same troubles. A forester acquaintance advised me to cut mine hard back, to within a few feet of the ground, in winter, and to protect the young shoots that developed subsequently with a copper fungicide. I keep meaning to.

Tapestry Gardening

The best gardening, as I see it, achieves a tapestry of plants. All the units touch or intermingle and no canvas shows through.

Others will have a different viewpoint. They will define good gardening as the cultivation of 'perfect' blooms. Perfect has to go into quotes because the prize chrysanthemum at a flower show would be a nightmare to the flower arranger, whereas the spray of spidery blossoms with spoon-ended quills that the flower arranger can revel in would scarcely be recognised as a chrysanthemum at all by a specialist grower of this florist's flower. So too with dahlias, gladioli, delphiniums, carnations and orchids. The grower of 'perfect' blooms is a monoculturist; his aims and methods are similar to those of the grower of prize pumpkins. Each plant must be separate from its neighbour, so that its development is not inhibited by competition; it must be specially fed and disbudded, so that all its strength is concentrated on the prize product.

Tapestry gardening, however, is all competition. The charming smile of insouciance that it turns upon the world is bogus. 'Here is a garden,' we tell ourselves, 'where the plants are evidently enjoying themselves,' Nothing of the kind. If a plant can be said to enjoy itself in the manner of a human, then its enjoyment is in the human category of wanting to be top dog and killing off its neighbours in the process.

It is the gardener's stiff task to control his ruthless jungle without its appearing to have been controlled; to guide his troop of beautiful savages without their seeming to be guided. Neither is the guiding all in one direction, for the sensible gardener will take lessons from his plants. Their behaviour is often unexpected and unplanned and yet successful, and he must then swallow his pride and allow them scope to go their unpremeditated way.

Take the case of **aubrieta.** Often you see it in stiff, smug blobs, adorning the holes in a stretch of concrete walling. And thus, because it is sometimes insensitively used, the plant is often sneered at by the superior gardener. This is quite undeserved because, given its chance, aubrieta is wonderful. On finding itself near some low shrub or other mat-former like sun roses, candytuft, snow-in-summer (*Cerastium tomentosum*) or the broom *Genista lydia,* it will thread its way through them and mingle with their blossom if its season coincides. For instance, the deadwhiteness of candytuft, *Iberis sempervirens*, is wonderfully leavened by an aubrieta of whatever colouring. And it will climb into deciduous shrubs like *Cotoneaster horizontalis* with a nerve that is quite surprising. One of my prettiest chance effects is where a self-sown purple aubrieta has climbed into the white flowered lilac, *Syringa persica* 'Alba'. This is a shrub with slender, whippy branches, seldom more than 5 ft. tall and casting little shade so that the aubrieta beneath it has a fine time, making a mat at ground level and climbing about a foot into the lilac's stems. They flower together in May.

Lithospermum diffusum 'Heavenly Blue' is a plant that gardeners find quite irresistible. Show them a flowering specimen that is for sale in a pot and they will fall for it every time. It is the colour that gets them. The plant itself makes a rather stemmy mat, though it can be kept neat if clipped over after flowering. On its own, as is usual with blue flowers, it looks scarcely half as attractive as when combined with a weaver. Matching of vigour is important when you take it upon yourself to plan a tapestry design. If you tried to blend this lithospermum with a vigorous sun rose such as *Helianthemum* 'Wisley Pink', it would be a case of the sow overlaying her defenceless piglets, whereas the sparse-habited single-flowered Red Orient or the double pale yellow Jubilee would do the job admirably. I actually have it with the double Cerise Queen. A great advantage in these double helianthemums is that they hold their petals so much longer than the singles; also they do not run to seed and hence have a longer season and they look cheerful even on a dull day when the singles are sulking.

Another good partner for the lithospermum is **Cheiranthus** 'Moonlight', a mat-forming, perennial wallflower of the Siberian type, and with the same Siberian wallflower scent. This, again, is sulphur yellow, only 9 in. tall; a two-year-old plant on light, well-drained soil may be as much as 2 ft. across, but after three years plants generally fade out and must be replaced by cuttings taken of young shoots in July. One plant leads to another: this cheiranthus looks very pretty in a sea of **Viola cornuta,** either in its typical violet colouring or in its albino form or in any of the intermediate shades that occur when these two interbreed and self-sow.

Viola cornuta is a true perennial and a superb blender. Backing one patch of it, I have a specimen of the grey-leaved shrub, **Senecio laxifolius** and the viola interlaces with this, flowering with its companion's grey foliage as a foil and looking its best in May. After that I usually do a bit of slashing, feed the plants and water them, and off they go again, flowering profusely in the autumn. In a really damp and shady position, however, the viola, especially in its shining white form, gets better and better right through the season without any treatment. It can be allowed to seed and establish itself with any herbaceous plant or low shrub of equal or greater vigour near a border's margin and the viola will sometimes climb 2 ft. in order to find the light. Another example of where the white viola·has put itself is with the dwarf, 3 ft. bamboo, *Arundinaria auricoma*, whose foliage is striped yellow and green. As both plants have a slightly creeping habit, you can't say where one begins and the other ends.

Some of the hardy **geraniums** make stems of indefinite length for months on end. Our own native bloody cranesbill, *Geranium sanguineum*, is of this kind, and its most effective teaming-up in my garden has been with the pale lemon yarrow, *Achillea taygetea*. Magenta and yellow? Daring, perhaps, but not dastardly; it seems to work. A group of the cranesbill and a group of the achillea are planted side by side and where they touch the cranesbill pushes through its neighbour so that they are interlocking when in flower.

The most wonderful cranesbill weaver, however, is *Geranium wallichianum* 'Buxton's Blue'. Its five-pointed, sharply toothed leaves are made particularly lively by the spots of paler green that occur at the re-entrants behind each major spur. The general effect is of a dark green surface with lighter speckles. The flowers are carried singly on long stalks and are beautifully rounded, with widely overlapping petals. The colour varies from soft mauve to a bluer tone, the central zone being paler, and against this the ten stamens stand out boldly, being crowned with deep purple anthers. The plant never stops growing and, as it grows, fresh flowers are continuously produced, from July till November, It scrambles up to 2½ ft., sometimes, through the branches of the ever-grey *Helichrysum splendidum,* which itself carries heads of small yellow buttons right through the summer and autumn.

Annuals that sow themselves from year to year can be of great assistance in giving the tapestry effect. Many of their seedlings will inevitably get weeded out, either because they are too crowded or because they're in the wrong place or simply because you cannot do your weeding without a certain amount of destruction to seedlings you would as soon leave. But there will always be enough left as long as you do the weeding yourself and are thoughtful about what you're doing.

In one sunny spot I have purple pansies, which have been self-sowing for 10 or 15 years, mixed with an annual that should be better known: *Cuphea miniata*. It does well in every season, blooms for three months without pause and makes solid little foot-tall bushes covered with bright rosy-red, interestingly irregular-shaped flowers. Another place where it did a nice blending trick was against a plant of the true-blue, plumbago-like *Ceratostigma willmottianum*. Behind this were the spikes of *Physostegia virginiana* 'Vivid'—a somewhat vicious rosy mauve, but contriving somehow to be striking and not repulsive; while to one side of the blue patch was the dwarf yellow dahlia called Bambi with small, anemone-centred flowers. They made their part of the border look very interesting in September and it was largely thanks to the cuphea having thought itself into where it was. Love-in-a-mist (*Nigella damascena*) is another of the least troublesome and most co-operative self-sowing annuals that will blend with anything.

As I said at the start, however, the gardener has to retain his vigilance if a promiscuous exchange of embraces is not to end disastrously for the weaker partner. With tears in his voice, a friend related to me how a *Clematis alpina* 'Columbine' had killed his *Pyrus japonica* (*Chaenomeles speciosa* to those who can keep pace with its name changes). At first they had looked so pretty to-gether: the pink of the pyrus and the blue of the clematis. But now this had happened and nobody had warned him.

I was not unduly sympathetic. It's no good looking at your plants just when they're blooming and then forgetting about them until another year has elapsed. My friend could perfectly well have observed the bit of thuggery that was going on under his eyes and, at the least, have pulled some of the clematis off the japonica during the strangling season. His best course, however, would have been to prune the clematis quite hard each year, in late May, as soon as it had finished flowering, leaving only a few bits of naked stem, low down. These would break into fresh growth very quickly and flower on the young shoots in the follow-ing spring, yet without smothering the host shrub.

The same lachrymose friend said that his pyracantha had been likewise killed by a *Clematis macropetala*. I thought he sounded somewhat absent-mindedly distraught about this fatality, and small wonder, because a pyracantha that has to be clipped so as to keep it into a wall, is a dismal object; its death is a happy release for the owner. A climbing rose is the ideal host for the average clematis, so long as the latter is of manageable vigour. They look well together; they like the same fruity soil conditions, and the rose can usually grow away from the clutches of the clematis.

Naturally one is bound to make mistakes, but they are usually rectifiable before any serious damage has been done. If you cannot satisfactorily restrain a clematis in the position allotted to it, you can move it, even at an advanced age.

Plants either surprise by their toughness and endurance or by their lack of toughness or endurance. There is one large piece of my border in which a running battle has for years been going on between its various components. It started, after the last war, as a sea of white Japanese anemones, this being one of the great survivors of years of neglect. Among these were opium poppies, which self-sow from year to year. They flower in June, have handsome glaucous poppy-pods in July and after that I root them out to make way for the anemone's August to October season. I added oriental poppies, so as to have colour in late May and early June. After flowering, these can be cut to the ground without objecting. Then montbretias somehow got in; small-flowered orange and red ones. Common though they are, I like them and they go well with the anemones. My last component is snowdrops. You never dig among Japanese anemones and so this was an ideal spot in which the snowdrops could colonise, by self-sowing, and they get through all their business before the other plants have got the sleep out of their eyes.

Now, 20 years later, everything is flourishing except, alas, the anemones themselves, which are gradually dying out. I did not know they could. As an ancient apple tree died here of honey fungus about 1957, I cannot help suspecting that this may be the cause, but it may just be that I've given the anemones too many competitors.

Patterns of Foliage

More and more, as the years go by, I find myself giving preference in the garden to plants with good **foliage.** I do not think that one can, should or would want to forgo the obvious effects produced by certain flowers *en masse*, but a diet based on hand-some foliage is the most sustaining in the long run, and for two very good reasons. Leaves last longer than flowers—anything up to two years, in an evergreen—and leaves tend to be consider-ably larger than flowers, and can thus produce bolder patterns, although their colouring is more restrained. The larger your leaves the greater their opportunities for producing shadows, one against another. It always seems a little sad that so much garden visiting, in summer, should take place in the early after-noon, when the lighting is flat, white and glaring. From about 6 p.m. onwards for another three hours, the light mellows and shadows achieve increasing importance, accentuating the third dimension and giving depth to the scene. One of the inbuilt charms of Scottish gardens is the fact that the light scarcely ever glares, while the evenings float on interminably. Visitors to the Scottish National Trust Gardens, at Crathes Castle, Banchory, some 20 miles from Aberdeen, will remember the foliage border there. It faces west and catches all the evening sunlight.

Being hardy there, it can be assumed that, given reasonable shelter, these foliage plants will be hardy anywhere in Britain. Among the larger shrubs are various buddleias with grey foliage. I think perhaps *Buddleia fallowiana* 'Lochinch' is the hardiest and most effective of these, its flower spikes being substantial and an excellent lavender shade. *Hydrangea sargentiana* and *H. villosa* were both being grown for their foliage. We, in the south, need to remember that the enormous, woolly, oval leaves of the former are apt to scorch when sun follows rain. The shrub is hardy but gives best value in a damp, sheltered position with dappled shade from nearby trees. *H. villosa* is the more adaptable and telling garden plant.

Then, *Viburnum grandiflorum*, which one would normally think of merely as a valuable winter-flowerer, but the red colouring of its leaf stalks and young stems is surprisingly vivid in early summer. *Mahonia japonica*, another winter-flowering shrub, carries leathery pinnate evergreen foliage. It is this rather heavy kind of greenery that one needs so essentially as a foil for the more exciting foliage of the variegated fraternity. Of these, the largest and most striking at Crathes is *Aralia chinensis* in one of its variegated cultivars. Each leaf, in green and cream, is upwards of

3 ft. long, but compoundly pinnate, and thus so sub-divided as to display a wonderful airiness and grace. This is an expensive plant. A correspondent tells me you need to shop around for it as the price may range from £3 to £9 each. It has rarity value, being tiresome to propagate, for it always has to be grafted and is, I think I am right in saying, done entirely by the Dutch and then imported. But it is certainly worth the struggle to obtain. There are two colour variants, Aureo-marginata and Albo-variegata, in gold-and-green and white-and-green, respectively.

Among variegated herbaceous plants, they have, at Crathes, *Hosta undulata*, and this is contrasted with the leathery evergreen leaves of *Bergenia cordifolia* and again, elsewhere, with the pinnate foliage of astilbes. The red- and carmine-flowered astilbes have rich plum-red leaves when young, changing to green later on but always remaining darker than the pink- and white-flowered sorts. In yet another part of the border, the hosta is seen against *Kirengeshoma palmata*, whose leaves are reminiscent of a maple's. But this 3-ft. herbaceous perennial is really a member of the saxifrage family and, in England at any rate, is carries sprays of primrose-yellow, shuttlecock-shaped flowers, in September. In Scotland it is sometimes apt to mature so late that winter overtakes it before the flowers have opened.

Brilliant spots of yellow are supplied by golden-leaved marjoram; glaucous tints by rue and by *Hosta sieboldiana*. Veratrums are there, with their great bouquets of broad, pleated leaves and, in total contrast, the long thin straps of hemerocallis, which always look so particularly fresh in early spring. *Acanthus* is represented by *A. spinosus*, which is more dissected than *A. mollis* and also freer-flowering, but I, personally, prefer the soft-leaved species. It is nicer to handle and I like the soapy smoothness of its great flabby leaves.

Alchemilla mollis is well served by its glaucous, inside-out-umbrella leaves that catch the rain drops in their centre and hold them like gouts of mercury. Its lime-green flowers are brilliantly contrasted in another part of that garden against rich purple sumach foliage, *Cotinus coggygria* (*Rhus cotinus*), in one of its dark-leaved cultivars.

Features in Lawns and Wide Open Spaces

Specimens and plantings to interrupt wide open spaces allow endless scope for the imagination. There is no more flattering method of displaying and drawing attention to a tree, shrub or plant, than by this kind of isolation that allows it to be seen from every side, from far away and close to. I want to concentrate on the lower growing material here; lower than trees anyway.

Kniphofia caulescens is so individual in appearance that it is inclined to look out of place if mixed up with other shrubs or plants in a border. But on its own it makes an exciting incident. I know of one effective planting where a broad gravel walk is interrupted at intervals along its centre, by groups of *K. caulescens*. It is of shrub-like habit and makes spiky rosettes of broad, evergreen glaucous foliage, rather like an aloe. The poker-flower-spikes, if and when they come, in autumn, are a pleasing but inessential condiment. Exotic-looking evergreens such as this are hardy if drainage is perfect and, of course, in a gravel walk this condition is met.

At Dundonnell House in Wester Ross, **yuccas** are treated in the same way. The walled garden is entered by double iron gates, and one is immediately confronted by an axial vista leading up to an enormous and ancient yew. But at this point of entry, where feet tread and wear more concentratedly than anywhere else, is a large, grey, gravel arena; and in it, breaking the monotonous flatness, a mixed group of *Yucca filamentosa* and *Y. flaccida*. The creamy-white bells of yucca flowers, proudly carried in broad, tapering panicles, are a splendid adjunct, in this plant's case, and the group at Dundonnell flowers with great freedom in most years. This is interesting, because one thinks of yuccas as baskers and the north-west of Scotland is not noted for basking conditions. It seems probable, however, that an open site and the best of drainage are enough between them to make these yuccas flower.

There must be many a gravel sweep in front of British country houses where a central feature of this kind would look well. On a larger scale, I should be inclined to use *Y. gloriosa*, which grows 6 or 8 ft. high, in time, and makes wrinkled trunks like elephants' legs, crowned by a dome of viciously spiky foliage. Not a plant to reel into, in a drunken stupor at dead of night, but just the thing for good, steady owners. Another plant that I should like to see given the gravel treatment is **Eryngium pandanifolium,** with luxuriant, overlapping rosettes of sea-green foliage, spiny along their margins, and 8-ft. flowering candelabras in autumn.

Equally striking (not to say spiking) would be a group of one or other species of the genus **Aciphylla,** the spear grasses of New Zealand. They make porcupine-like, evergreen plants with stiff, narrow, greyish leaves, sometimes margined with gold, dividing into several prongs towards their extremities. They are hardy as long as well drained. Jack Drake of the Inshriach Alpine Plant Nursery, Aviemore, Inverness-shire (a cold spot at the foot of the Cairngorms) offers two species: *A. squarrosa,* which has orange-margined leaves, and *A. colensoi.* If he has run out of these actual species he is likely to have others equally good. These are plants one raises from seed sent direct from New Zealand. They are arresting when they flower in the same way as *Eryngium pandanifolium*; not, that is, for bright colouring—greenish yellow, in this case—but for their noble carriage and branching structure. Both are members of the *Umbelliferae*—the cow parsley family, but don't let that put you off.

In lawns, it is important not to be fussy and crowd in too many incidents. Another horrible lawn practice is to surround each feature with a primly defined circle, square or other geometrical figure. Even if a certain amount of hand-trimming is involved, it is far better to allow the lawn to merge with whatever the feature may be.

Some of the more graceful **bamboos** are especially suitable. You can mow right up to their stems, and if they tend to sucker into the lawn, their straying canes are automatically beheaded. So, invasiveness is no problem, as long as mowing is regular and your summer absences are not too long. *Arundinaria (Sinarundinaria) murieliae* has delicate foliage and an upright habit that well displays its yellow canes, bright green when young. *Phyllostachys boryana (P. niger boryana)* is of more arching habit, and the young green canes change to yellow overlaid with purple blotches as they mature. A very distinct bamboo making a splendid specimen is *Chusquea culeou,* from Chile. A large number of small branches sprout in an arc around the greater part of each node creating, in the aggregate, a bottle-brush effect. The canes and general appearance of the plant are sturdy. It is a shame to crowd this bamboo in with other shrubs or plants. You need to be able to stand back to admire it with a clear field of vision. If you plant more than one bamboo in a lawn, get them well apart or each will interfere with the appearance of its neighbour. At 12 ft., they will be growing into each other before you know where you are. Forty feet will be more like it. There is considerable enthusiasm for bamboos among the gardening public, nowadays, and we have been greatly encouraged since the publication of A. H. Lawson's *Bamboos* (Faber 1968). Mr. Lawson writes with the experience of one who has grown the hardy members of the tribe for ornament, in Devon, for many years.

Bamboos and all the other plants I have mentioned so far should be established in spring—not before April. Grasses too.

Pampas grass is often too large for its environment, when this is a small front garden. On the other hand, single specimens look self-conscious. They need grouping: with three plants I should make an obtuse-angled, scalene triangle. *Cortaderia argentea* 'Pumila' is the dwarfest cultivar so far, 'only' 6 ft. tall in its autumn‘flowering season. Of the 10-footers, make sure you get a good white-plumed strain like Sunningdale Silver. At all costs avoid the 'pink' pampas grass. It does have a pink flush as it is coming into flower but then changes to grey and does not show up at all at a distance.

You could fill in your triangular grouping of cortaderias with lower growing plants having contrasting foliage. *Melianthus major* (see page 90) would be just right if you can be bothered with it, or the large-leaved annual tobacco plant, *Nicotiana sylvestris*. Whatever you choose, it must have the quality of remaining in prime condition right into the autumn, when the pampas grass is having its big moment.

In a smaller-scale setting I should use **Miscanthus** as my grass, instead. The different types all have a fountain-like habit. They mostly grow 6 or 7 ft. tall and flower in autumn, but their dead stems and foliage continue to look handsome and a bright straw colour till mid-winter. *M. sacchariflorus* is exceptionally vigorous and grows to 12 ft., looking like sugar cane. I have never seen this flower, but I love it as a specimen for its foliage.

I have recommended *Kniphofia caulescens* as a foliage plant, but the majority in this genus are grown for their pokers (red hot, yellow hot, white hot, according to taste) and they are such individualistic plants that they look excellent on their own in a lawn setting or associated in a sizable bed with a few appropriate companions. Remember that they are all a little on the tender side, so: spring planting, sharp drainage, protection over their roots in winter with a thick layer of bracken or male fern fronds. To make the most impressive display I would choose a giant poker such as *K. uvaria* 'Nobilis' or Samuel's Sensation, both late flowering (August-September). This is a useful season (unless you are away) at which to have so dramatic a feature in your garden.

The **Cape Hyacinth,** *Galtonia* (*Hyacinthus*) *candicans,* with its loose racemes of waxy white bells, in late summer, works in well with kniphofias. It may not like the positions you choose for it but will sow itself and soon be flowering in the positions of its own choice, which are generally at the edge of a bed. I have never seen veratrums (see page 89) better displayed than in a solo lawn planting.

An idea I should like to put into practice in a lawn is a combined planting of caryopteris, *Lobelia cardinalis* and *Senecio leucostachys.* This would involve a certain amount of work each year, as the senecio is not hardy. The rich blue of *Caryopteris clandonensis* or of *C.* 'Heavenly Blue' would form a new-moon-shaped segment of my informally shaped bed, and above and in the arms of this (for the caryopteris can be kept to 3 ft. if hard-pruned each spring) would rise a 4-ft. stand of the cardinal flower, *L. cardinalis,* with spikes of molten red, insect-like flowers from mid-August to October. Where this abutted nearly on the lawn, there would be a frieze of the silvery senecio, to give light to the lobelias' dark reddish stems and foliage. The senecio would weave its way into these. The lobelia needs frequent splitting and replanting in spring; in some districts it has to be overwintered under glass. From early July onwards it requires the support of twigs. But the thrill the flowers give is worth the effort.

A great many shrubs make good lawn features. My first pick would be the Venetian sumach, smoke tree or wig bush, *Cotinus coggygria* (*Rhus cotinus*), just in its typical, green-leaved form. None of the cultivars with purple leaves are as effective in their flowering as this, when its multiplicity of flower stalks change to pink after the insignificant flowers have themselves faded. Dew seen on this pink froth is such an experience that you'll wonder why you do not spend more time in the garden in the early morning.

You can cover any amount of lawn with a prostrate juniper, without overdoing it; or else with the not quite prostrate *Juniperus sabina tamariscifolia,* rising in horizontal ledges to a height of a few feet. Hovering over a colony of one of these, you could have the Mount Etna broom, *Genista aethnensis,* with diaphanous branches rising to 12 or 15 ft. and transformed into a fountain of yellow in July.

I should also like to try a mixed planting of the **tree peony** species: *Paeonia delavayi,* with maroon-coloured flowers, and *P. lutea ludlowii,* which is clear butter-yellow. These grow about 7 ft. tall and the latter, which is the more vigorous, has a 12 ft. spread. They are not quite abundant enough in their production of flowers to be as showy as one could wish, but their leaves are so very good for six months. Besides they are a good vehicle. Underneath them could be planted colonies of small, winter-and-spring-flowering bulbs, while over them I should grow small-flowered clematis with a late flowering season. The July-to-October-flowering Texensis hybrids are particularly suitable, including the crimson Gravetye Beauty, the pink-flowered Duchess of Albany, the cerise and silver-margined Etoile Rose, among others. The first of these opens to a star-shaped flower, but the others all remain as bells. They can be cut to the ground each winter and thus never become too overwhelming for their hosts to support. One of the cultivars of the spring-flowering *Clematis alpina*—the intense blue Pamela Jackman or the kitten's-eyed Columbine—mixes well with Ludlow's yellow peony.

Now let us consider the case of beds in an open, exposed position that we want to plant up with genuinely labour-saving subjects (which automatically excludes roses): permanent beds requiring attention only once a year, when established, with all the components interlocked to form one unit.

Beds devoted to one kind of plant will be the simplest to manage, although they will lack the interest of variety. Heathers are the most obvious choice here. Some beds could be devoted to the winter and early spring flowerers, others to those with a summer season. Some heathers have beautifully coloured foliage, but the smallness of their leaves and their generally amorphous habit give them no architectural value in a garden setting. This lacuna is normally made good by planting a few junipers of pencil outline—notably *Juniperus communis hibernica*, the Irish juniper—at strategic points among the heaths.

Another ericaceous plant that can be treated like heather is *Pernettya mucronata*. Its leaves, though small, are neat and glossy. It carries showy clusters of large berries that may be white or in various shades of pink and purple. If left alone by the birds, they remain in condition from autumn till summer. This shrub makes a thicket by suckering. It grows 2 ft. tall, and might look out of scale in small beds.

I am not too keen on either of these ideas, myself, but one must keep remembering that the monoculture saves trouble and thought. Entire beds of the larger-leaved bergenias would be utterly weed-suppressing. The elephant-eared *Bergenia cordifolia* has always, until recently, been the most effective in use, but there are nowadays a number of attractive cultivars with flowers of clearer colouring. Such are the German-raised Abendglut, Morgenrote and the white Silberlicht.

The rose of Sharon, *Hypericum calycinum,* is usually relegated to shade but makes a far better showing in the sun. Its only cultural requirement is to be shaved to the ground once annually, in spring: a procedure that also induces freer flowering. Hostas make good beds on their own and do not need shade as long as the soil is reasonably stiff and water-retentive. The showiest in flower are *Hosta rectifolia* and *H. ventricosa*. The variegated types tend to scorch if exposed to too much sunlight. Beds of day-lilies, *Hemerocallis,* can be effective in a free-flowering cultivar and they are no trouble at all to grow, always provided (perhaps I should add) that their beds are free of perennial weeds like convolvulus at the outset.

A bed of interlocking thugs would be rather fun, making no attempt at keeping them separated. If one or other of them went to the wall, its loss would scarcely be noticed. Components might include various periwinkles (which, again, flower better in sun than in shade) and ivies; the pale mauve, starry *Campanula poscharskyana; Ceanothus thyrsiflorus repens*, the most vigorous of several horizontal-growing members of this blue-flowered tribe; *Rubus tricolor*, a creeping non-prickly bramble with glossy evergreen foliage, and *Euonymus fortunei (radicans)* 'Silver Queen' with green and cream variegated foliage in the summer, taking on bottle-nosed pinkish tints in the cold season.

However, if I were planning some permanent beds, my first idea would be to make them large and then to plant with bold groups of self-service subjects that would, in the main, keep themselves to themselves. Provided they were densely leafy from spring till autumn and low-growing, it would not matter whether they were shrubby or herbaceous, evergreen or deciduous.

Herbaceous plants are mainly deciduous, but it would be quite wrong to imagine, on that account, that they are inefficient ground cover. Hostas, for instance, desert the winter scene, but weeds simply do not have time or elbow room in which to draw breath. *Sedum* 'Autumn Joy', of ruby colouring, goes well with the late lavender-flowered *Hosta lancifolia tardiflora* and grey-leaved plants to associate with these are the lower-growing *Anaphalis* species—*A. margaritacea* and *A. triplinervis,* with white ever-lasting flowers—and the filigree-leaved *A. pontica*. And I should like some acanthus in this grouping. I can highly recommend *Acanthus longifolius*; it is soft-leaved yet handsomely dissected and flowers abundantly in every site and season.

This colourful association has brought us up to the 3-ft. level. We had better prostrate ourselves and start again. One of the lowest yet most vigorous of junipers is *Juniperus conferta,* and it has delightfully fresh, pale green foliage. We could build up behind this with *J. sabina cupressifolia,* of rich bay-green colouring (pleasanter, I think, than the better-known *J. horizontalis*) and with the more glaucous-leaved *J. sabina tamariscifolia.* Among these we could associate the dwarf rowan, *Sorbus reducta*. It spreads by suckering and carries pink berries.

A good contrast to the horizontal lines of these junipers could be achieved with a group of *Libertia formosa,* with close-set, narrow, iris-like leaves, but evergreen. Its white flowers, in early summer, appear to be triangular. More colour could be worked into this tapestry with a sun-rose such as *Helianthemum* 'Wisley Pink', of vigorous growth and grey foliage. But it really should be clipped over after its May-June flowering, so as to keep it neat and presentable for the rest of the season. Shrubby potentillas, on the other hand, would need no such attention. If they do require pruning, it can be done in late winter, during the slack season. These cultivars of *Potentilla fruticosa* can be had in white and in shades of yellow and apricot. Low-growing skimmias are another possibility. The males seldom rise above 2 ft. and the one whose flower buds and leaf margins are a deep rich pink all through the winter is particularly decorative. The name to look out for, here, is Rubella. It is sometimes listed under *Skimmia japonica*, sometimes under *S. reevesiana*. It would act as pollinator to a female *S. japonica*, which grows, usually, 3 ft. high in an open situation and carries handsome red, bird-proof berries from September till June.

Various low and dense-growing evergreen cotoneasters could be worked in, especially *Cotoneaster congestus* and *C. microphyllus*. *C. m. cochleatus* is a denser, even lower growing variety of the latter with great appeal. The dwarf, purple-leaved (but deciduous) *Berberis thunbergii* 'Atropurpurea Nana' is good and would contrast well with the glacuous foliage of Jackman's Blue Rue (*Ruta graveolens*). The gorse-like, dense-habited broom *Genista hispanica* flowers in May and is pretty impenetrable.

One way and another, some good situations could be plotted.

Bringing Heather into Perspective

The present-day fashion for growing **heathers** threatens to become a mania. I can imagine the next century's gardeners referring to twentieth-century heatheries in the same sneering tone that we adopt towards Victorian shrubberies.

Heathers are honest burghers, stuffed with resounding virtues. You could call them the backbone and mainstay of the no-trouble garden: evergreen, ground-covering, weed-suppressing, efficient yet quietly pleasing in season and out. They are nothing as individuals. You must mass them and the trouble is that they epitomise the depersonalised plant. All too often they are a cliché and a thumping bore. In the average small garden, a bed of heathers looks thoroughly unsuitable.

They need the wide open spaces, and in a large garden they really can come into their own, but even then more as background material than as protagonists. My favourite heather garden is at Ladham House, just outside Goudhurst in Kent. It comprises a sort of open arena (on sandy soil), perhaps two acres in extent, with a girdle of woodland and park trees by way of background. But it is the incidents, the features growing out of and above the heathers themselves, which are memorable: the shining whiteness of *Rhododendron mucronatum* at the end of May, the gnarled old cistuses in June and the haze of yellow from Madeira and Mount Etna brooms (*Genista virgata* and *G. aethnensis*) in June and July.

I would not say that the heathers at Burford Gardens, in Shropshire, look particularly appropriate in their lush valley setting, but they have been very cleverly combined with clematis. The clematis are of the small-flowered kinds like Minuet, Venosa Violacea, Etoile Violette, Little Nell, Alba Luxurians and Abundance, and they are July to September flowerers which can have all their growth cut back to the ground after flowering, leaving the scene clear for the winter and spring heathers. It is delightful to see clematis like this, scrambling about just above ground level. Another effective autumn association in this garden is the blue of *Gentiana sino-ornata* in front of a late-flowering double pink ling.

Of course there are individual pleasures to be derived from heathers. How delightful, for instance, to see bees working on *Erica carnea* in February. It is winter still, but there you have one of the most palpable signs of spring. I can understand anyone using it as an edging wherewith to mitigate the abominable desolation of their rose beds, for a season. But the rose sticks will not create much of a setting for the heathers.

In April and May, we have the myriads of tiny white blossoms of *E. arborea alpina,* humming with bees and imparting a delicious honeyed fragrance. This is one of the hardiest of the tree heaths. It will grow 8 to 10 ft. tall and, exceptionally, is of sufficient bulk to stand as an individual, becoming craggy and interesting with age. Furthermore it will tolerate shade.

One or two of the cultivated varieties of ling, *Calluna vulgaris,* will bear close inspection. These are the double kinds, already mentioned, with flowers strung out on long spikes, like chains of beads. The pink H. E. Beale and the lower-growing J. H. Hamilton are notable. The only trouble about them is that they are far more attractive in youth, when the spikes are very long, than when older, after the bushes have been clipped over a number of times, and the spikes become much shorter and less distinguished.

To sum up: heathers can be good servants but are dreary and officious masters. If a garden is too big for you, they are a labour-saving way out. If you are unfortunate enough to have inherited a rock garden which is too expensive to have removed, they are a way of obliterating it. And if you have a garden of acres in a rural setting, they can be in their element. But do not go heather-mad and plant them like beds of roses or you will deny yourself most of the fun to be had from gardening.

Colour

Colouring Good and Bad

What we mean by good or bad colouring in flowers is so disput-able that it is obviously safer not to write on the subject at all. But then it has a kind of siren fascination that lures one on. Some people simply have blind spots for certain colours. Orange, for instance, will quite often be anathema to them, regardless of the quality of the orange, the shape of the flower wearing it or the setting in which it is seen. For my part I like all colours if they are what I should call clean, of their kind. The quality of cleanli-ness in this context is not easy to define but I think most readers will know what I am driving at.

Colours also have fashions—and not so much the colour as the word describing it. Thus 'mauve' and 'magenta' are nowadays so unfashionable that the nurseryman dare not use them in a cata-logue description. *Gladiolus byzantinus* is variously depicted as purplish-red, wine-purple and rosy-purple, while the *R.H.S. Dictionary* goes so far as to dub it red. But no one, I think, would in cold blood argue that it was anything other than magenta—a rather beautiful shade (though this is arguable) without too much blue in it.

Of course, it is not just the raw colour, as we may see it in a paintbox or in the mind's eye, that counts. The flowers of *G. byzantinus* are delicate and elegant, not thick and heavy, as in the Grandiflorus types. Likewise the spike and stem are tall, slender and graceful. When it is grown in rough grass, which it can cope with, I defy anyone to cavil at its colouring.

Perhaps it is not so much any particular colour that deserves criticism, as the ways in which nature and man have used it. That dangerous plant, *Salvia splendens*, beloved of parks and public gardens, starts off with a flower endowed by nature with a uniformly blatant scarlet colouring throughout both corolla and calyx, while the foliage is coarse and characterless. Even so, it might be effective in a mixed border if used with discretion, but this is just the way in which you never do see it used. Having reduced the plant's natural stature to a low, compact blob of condensed blossom, man then proceeds to mass it in the bedding schemes with which we are only too familiar.

Unfortunately, many of those who are readiest to sneer at this parks-and-gardens mentality, as it has been called, are delighted at the same offence when it is committed in our larger gardens with Kurume azaleas. I have been re-reading an authority on rhododendrons who was writing about this group when it was just soaring to popularity, after the last war. They are at their best, he claims, in light woodland in great drifts. The word 'drift' occurs repeatedly. He even goes so far as to see 'no reason why the hardiest varieties should not be used in parterres'—a word which sounds more chic than 'beds'. They are, in fact, to be used as a kind of permanent bedding, and this is precisely what has happened. Now the trouble with (or advantage of—according to your viewpoint) many Kurume azaleas is that they are dwarf and dumpy and so crowded with blossoms, in their season, that nothing else is visible. Furthermore their colours include a large proportion of what Kingdon-Ward described as 'sickly magenta or dirty puce'—colours that might look well enough if scattered along twigs like those of *Daphne mezereum*, but which quickly pall when laid on with a trowel.

I admit that my first sight of massed Kurume azaleas thrilled me as much as anyone else. It was something quite new to me then and unexpected. Inevitably our tastes change in gardening. We learn discrimination, but there is no reason to wish that we were born with it. Surely we have all, as children, experienced the wonder of *Prunus* 'Kanzan' in its brief spring glory. The huge generosity of its soft, frilly pompoms were intensely exciting. No one would want to deny their own children the same pleasure by pointing out that this cherry is overplanted; that it is all too frequently seen in the wrong setting; that its pink flowers have too much mauve in them and that this clashes appallingly with the young bronze foliage; that the tree is stiff and outstandingly gaunt in winter while the blossom itself lasts only for a week and is followed by leaves which in outline and colouring are utterly boring.

In Praise of Mauve

It is a sad fact that mauve has long been out of favour. 'Women,' writes Mr. Beverley Nichols, 'seem to have come to the conclusion that mauve does something unkind to their complexions. I trust they will not allow this prejudice to extend to the garden.' But emphatically they do. It seems not to be so much the colour that curls them up, as the actual word. Mauve first came into existence little more than a century ago: an aniline dye obtained from coal tar and described by the dictionary as 'bright but delicate.' What this exact shade is, very few of us know. I was brought up to think of mauve as any colour that was too pink for blue or too blue for pink, yet not dark enough for purple. The word had no pejorative sense to me. In the heyday of its youth, it was clearly the height of fashion. In 1861 the *St. James's Magazine* could write of 'the fashionable and really beautiful mauve and its varieties.' If it would only stage a timely come-back, a whole range of garden flowers could join in the bonanza.

Iris stylosa seems to me the quintessence of mauve at its best, particularly when seen in the yellow light of winter sunshine. Truly, the colour is bright but delicate and much enhanced by the fragile texture and elegant poise of the flower. Such a winning plant is in no need of a popularity stunt. Its adoring public, if called upon to describe the colour, will settle happily for 'rich lavender-lilac'.

Now for a difficult mauve let us consider *Rhododendron ponticum*, a variable plant wherein there is usually a good deal more of pink than in the iris. Most of us, myself included, are inclined to turn from this species in some disgust. The colour is crude, the leaf is dull, the plant is boring. Moreover, the fact that it is widely used as a stock for the hardy hybrids and is much given to suckering adds to our distaste. And yet, one June day, in the woods behind the Bedgebury Pinetum, in Kent, I saw this rhododendron to perfection. Having feasted on conifers to satiety, we looked across the lake to the rising ground behind. Beneath a lowering sky, given to angry spurts of thundery rain, the naturalised ponticum bushes were dark and invisible, and their blossom rose disembodied among the trees, in clouds of mauve—not in huge lumps, but in laminated wisps.

There are two astilbes that are both mauve at its most questionable and startling. *Astilbe taquetii* 'Superba' is tactfully described in the catalogue as 'bright purple-rose.' It is bright indeed, and a splendid plant, at least 4 ft. tall and proudly upstanding; and its foliage—always a strong feature in astilbes—is magnificently wrinkled and indented. The branching panicles are in season at the usual astilbe time in July, with aftermaths in August and September.

A. chinensis 'Pumila' is only 2 ft. high and a genuine late flowerer, from August to October. Again it has an excellent habit and is particularly suited to gardens with a heavy, wettish soil. I find it combines and contrasts very satisfyingly with the golden yellow, black-eyed daisies of *Rudbeckia speciosa* 'Goldsturm'. Both plants flourish in the same conditions and will put up with heavyish shade, if so required.

Then there is that paragon *Hydrangea villosa*, described by one nursery, in an advertisement I came upon, as the only hydrangea that carries *blue* flowers, regardless of soil. In fact, the central disc of tiny fertile florets is very nearly blue, but the large outer florets are a warm old-rose shade and the overall effect is charmingly mauve. This colouring varies very little with soil acidity, in contrast to other hydrangeas, and the species is more tolerant of chalk and lime than most.

A Change of Colour

The way that plants and flowers will change their colour according to such factors as time of year, soil and cell sap acidity, age,
sunlight and so on, has always intrigued me. The subject insinuated itself upon my notice again when I was reading Mr. Graham
Thomas on the Bourbon rose, Mme Pierre Oger. 'When first
open on a cool day Mme Pierre Oger is of a soft, warm, creamy
flesh, and in dull weather may remain so; in sunny weather the
sun warms the petals or portions of them that it touches to a clear
rose, and in very hot weather a really intense colour develops.'
What makes Mr. Thomas so rewarding to read is the combination
he brings to his subject of extensive background reading and
shrewd personal observation, with both eye and nose. One might
have gone on growing Mme Pierre for the rest of one's life
without specially connecting her colour changes with the sun.

The point being taken, I thought of other roses showing the
same manifestation; of Peace, for instance, with its habit of turning pink along the petal margins all through the summer, and of
Autumn, which is always deep orange at its first appearance in
June, but carries blooms of gradually paling colour as the season
advances until, by October, the shade is little deeper than primrose. Probably temperature, as well as the effect of direct sunlight,
has a bearing on these changes.

Now what would Mr. Thomas have to say about *Rosa mutabilis*,
I wondered, turning to the index. At once, of course, I discovered
that I was in the wrong volume, among *The Old Shrub Roses*
instead of *Shrub Roses of To-day*. It is no use having just one of his
rose volumes; you must have all three (*Climbing Roses, Old and
New* being the third) or none; and the trio must not be scattered
in different parts of the house, because inevitably your train
of thought leads you from one variety of rose to another, and
the basic laws of cussedness dictate that you will not have two
consecutive impulses that will be satisfied within the same volume.

Having got into the right one, the index was kind enough to
guide me from R. *mutabilis* to R. *chinensis mutabilis*, this being a
China rose. 'The colour of the flowers is remarkable: they open

from slender pointed buds of vivid orange, flame-coloured where the sun strikes them; on opening they are soft pale chamois-yellow within, while the flame of the bud continues to mark the outside. The second day, after pollinating, they change to soft coppery pink, and on the third day as they wrinkle and fall the colour deepens to coppery crimson. The colours are deepest in hot weather; the countless blossoms resemble flights of butterflies.' And on turning up Masquerade which, by a miracle finds itself in the same tome, we are confirmed in our suspicion that its colour antics are derived from R. *mutabilis*. For China roses grow darker, not lighter, on fading.

It will be noted that Mr. Thomas has here insinuated a new factor to account for the phenomenon: not just the sun and hot weather but pollination, too. There is, perhaps, room for Doubting Thomas here. One should try the effect of removing the stigmata from some opening blossoms of one of these harlequin roses, so that they cannot be pollinated. In which case the flowers that have been treated should not intensify so much in colour as they age, as the untreated.

One is, indeed, familiar with a change of colour, following pollination, in certain other flowers. The honeysuckle *Lonicera japonica* 'Halliana' for instance, which flowers in summer and autumn, opens white on its first evening, but has changed to yellow 24 hours later. *Mirabilis jalapa*, the marvel of Peru, but also known as the four-o'clock plant on account of its habit of opening around tea-time, is white or creamy at first, but quickly deepens through yellow to crimson. Being, essentially, a night-flowerer, like the honeysuckle, the change is again more likely brought about by pollination than by the effect of light or temperature, although physiological changes associated with ageing may have most influence of all.

Another example of a daytime flower whose particular attraction is in its manner of blushing, is the tropical shrub *Lantana camara*, much used in warm climates as a hedging plant (for it is spiny as well as gay), and sometimes in this country for summer bedding. The flowers are gathered into heads rather like a viburnum or a bedding verbena (to which it is related), and there are a great many cultivars in a wide range of colours, but all with the same habit of opening pale—it may be white, cream, yellow or pink, and then intensifying to lilac, flame, crimson, and so on, the flowerheads being darkest at the perimeter.

Why some tulips should have this habit and others not, is a mystery. You know how certain varieties will open uniformly white or yellow, and then develop a pink or reddish flush, first at the margins and then suffusing the entire bloom. Inglescombe Yellow is one of the best known for this; whereas another Cottage tulip, Mother's Day, opens yellow, but changes in the opposite direction to off-white.

White flowers have quite a way of becoming pink before fading. You will often, at the end of May, see what appears to be a pink-flowered hawthorn in a wild hedgerow; only to discover, on closer inspection, that these flowers are at their last gasp, which is the moment when they do acquire a hectic glow. The wood anemone is pink at both ends of its life: as the buds unfold, and immediately before petal-fall. And this characteristic has given its latinised name to one of the handsomest late-flowering Japanese cherries, *Prunus serrulata* 'Albo-rosea', better known as Shirofugen. Pink in the bud, its double, long-stalked flower trusses open pure white but change to mauvish-pink, again at the last. The white-flowered dogwoods are also inclined to turn pinkish; and then there are the hydrangeas.

I do not intend to get bogged down in this genus here, although its colour changes are the most remarkable and varied of any, even to the lurid greens into which previously pink, blue or white flowers will pass on dying. The heavy, white-flowered cones of *Hydrangea paniculata* 'Grandiflora' habitually turn pink at a later stage but the more graceful *H. p.* 'Praecox' goes straight from white to a greenish hue. The favourite old hortensia cultivar, Mme Mouillière, with large white buns, turns pink in sunlight; but where the flowers are shaded, they fade to metallic green. The most noteworthy changes of this type occur in *H. serrata* and its cultivars of which Grayswood is one of the best known. Whereas it thrives in shade, the best colour effects result from placing it where it will receive a certain amount of sunshine. The sterile florets of this elegant lace-cap will then expand to white but quickly flush to pure pink; or perhaps one should describe it as pale red, because the colour includes no blue in its make-up whatever. The flush intensifies until a glowing ruby shade has been attained and finally it passes to deep, dusky red. The whole process covers a period of a couple of months, so that Grayswood's season of beauty is exceptionally protracted. The colour changes described in all these white-flowered hydrangeas occur regardless of and unmodified by the acidity of the soil in which they are grown.

The most interesting colour change in winter is that which manifests itself in many evergreens, as they react to cold weather by turning from green to a kind of purplish hue. You meet this trait in many conifers. The effect can be rather gloomy, as in the ground-covering *Juniperus horizontalis,* whose dark, bluish-green shoots develop purplish tips. But in some cases the purple is delightfully warm-toned, as in the fine-leaved *Cryptomeria japonica* 'Elegans'.

Among broad-leaved evergreens, the habit is most marked in the bergenias. Flower arrangers go crazy over the winter colouring of *Bergenia cordifolia,* but I find its liverish tones rather lifeless and depressing. Quite different are the really brilliant reds that its leaves assume on dying.

It is when a lustrous, shiny-surfaced leaf changes to purple that the most lively impression is made—as with the wavy-leaved *Mahonia aquifolium* 'Undulata', to which the connecting leaf stalks and main veins contribute crimson red. This makes a much larger shrub than *M. aquifolium* itself and has no propensity to sucker. The slow-suckering habit of *Leucothoë catesbaei* makes it a valued ground-coverer on acid soil, yet its thickets of 3 ft. wands, on which the leathery foliage is arranged in two ranks, do not greatly impress in the garden. But in the house it is quite another story. There it can be arranged more tellingly than it naturally arranges itself and its glossy, purple, pointed leaves remain in fine condition for many months.

Cistus corbariensis, with neat, wavy foliage, turns bronzy purple in winter but *C. cyprius* has an equally striking but quite different way with it. From a dark, even lifeless green, the leaves turn a pale lead grey. This is a chilly colour for a chilly season but one cannot help admiring it.

Red in the Border

You can get plenty of warmth into a border without using red at all, and if certain specified colour harmonies are the aim, red may have no place. Most of us, however, mix it into our borders, and we enjoy bold, luminous patches of red, whether of scarlet or crimson shading. Their strength acts as a *point d'appui* for other colours and throws them into relief. Red, moreover, is a sunset colour and takes on a particular richness in the evening light, just at that time when we are most receptive to the pleasures of a garden.

When you come to think of it, there is not a great diversity of red-flowered hardy perennials. In early summer there are scarlet and blood red **oriental poppies.** The former are the more typical, and some people find their colouring blatant or raw. Yet there is surely a wonderful freshness and delicacy of texture about every sort of poppy, and the scarlet of an oriental type is complemented to perfection by the huge black blotches at the base of each petal, and by the velvety-purple blackness of their multitudinous stamens. One of the happiest situations for these May-June-flowering orientals is in a border whose main season will not arrive until July. The scarlet is seen against a setting of many foliage forms, mainly in shades of green. After flowering, the poppies are cut to the ground, and one should see to it that a gap is not left, by growing near them those kinds of perennials that start late into growth but bush out presently. Japanese anemones are good and so are the perennial gypsophilas.

In my own main border, I find there is an almost total lack of red in the second half of June. I could rectify this situation if I set my mind to it, but there are various objections to some of the possibilities. The early-flowering kniphofias are showy and boldly constructed, but are seen at their best on light soils, as also are heucheras. I have never got any sense out of these, except by growing them in rows, like vegetables.

July is dominated by the most scarlet of all flowers, the old-fashioned **Lychnis chalcedonica.** It needs bold grouping and also keeping away from any sort of pink, but it is splendid with white shasta daisies, with pale yellow, blue and purple; best of all, perhaps with its broad domes contrasted by the rich purple spikes of *Salvia superba*. For crimson red at this season you can't beat a voluminous mound of **Monarda 'Cambridge Scarlet'.** The finest **montbretia,** nowadays, is *Crocosmia masonorum,* though it is liable to heavy plundering for the house. Its shading varies a good deal between scarlet and vermilion. Some of the modern border phloxes come near enough to red, and are first rate if you can make a go of them. Somehow, I cannot; they never seem to elude the eelworm for long, and I find the old pinks and mauves and carmines very much easier.

It is, of course, quite unnecessary to rely on hardy perennials for red in your border. Many more gardeners would be growing the **Chilean Fire Bush,** if they realised that in its narrow-leaved forms it is quite hardy. This is *Embothrium coccineum lanceolatum*. It makes a tall but slender bush and its young branches of the previous season's growth are clothed along their entire length with tubular flowers of a fiery scarlet colouring. The soil must not be alkaline but it otherwise has no fads.

There are plenty of **shrub roses** to choose from that will give you red over a long season. You have but to choose a cultivar whose shading suits your tastes and whose constitution will stand up to the rough-and-tumble of border life without your needing to run after it every five minutes with powder and spray. Bonn, Wilhelm and its brighter sport Will Scarlet, would be suitable.

Dahlias can contribute every known shade of red. I dote on Scarlet Beauty—an almost frighteningly powerful colour, but so clear, its blooms shaped with classic simplicity.

While thinking on this subject, I turned with interest to Gertrude Jekyll's red section in the plan of her famous hardy flower border, described in *Colour in the Flower Garden*. She used pokers a good deal and poppies, also crimson hollyhocks at the back. These will not grow for me: the rust kills them, but on lighter soils they seem to get away with it and they are good in industrial-smoke-polluted areas. Most of her reds came from annual and bedded-out plants, however: nasturtiums, for instance. I use them, too; the only problem is to keep them from taking over the entire border. Cannas are excellent in a good year and their foliage can always be relied upon. Gladioli she had in a thin, curved strip some 12 ft. long. Some gladioli are not clumsy, it is true, but they become a wreck too quickly and irrevocably. At the front she had neighbouring groups of the scarlet *Salvia splendens* and the crimson cockscomb, *Celosia*. I should not care about that; both have such hideous foliage, and no artificial flower could look more synthetic than the cockscomb. I should incline towards scarlet bedding verbenas, with which to 'bid the rash gazer wipe his eye'; their foliage, though reminiscent of a stinging nettle's, it not unpleasing.

Planning a Yellow Garden

Yellow is a controversial colour. People shy away from mauve as a word but are perfectly content to grow the majority of mauve flowers provided they are discreetly described as lavender or lilac. With yellow it is the colour itself that tends to frighten them. There are many keen gardeners who have to let you know, as soon as gardens and plants start to be discussed, that they are not prepared to tolerate yellow or orange flowers.

There is little we can do for them, but as regards the rest of us we are all aware that yellow is apt to be the tail that wags the dog, in our borders, especially in late summer. There are so many yellow composites in bloom, just then, each of them tempting, individually. But if we yield too often, we know that the garden will become yellow-heavy.

The answer is to go all-yellow. The longer I garden the more strongly it is borne in upon me that the contrasting of complementary colours, such as blue with yellow or pink with grey, is no worthier an object than the association of colours that are near to and distinct, one from another. Try, for instance, associating a pure red flower with another red flower having a touch of blue

Plate 21. As long as its level can be limited by an overflow, a pond affords the opportunity for marginal planting with many subjects that have no excessive moisture requirements, but are seen to special advantage when leaning over or reflected in water. Here, by the margins of quite a small pond in the Scottish National Trust gardens at Inverewe, Ross-shire, are candelabra primulas, irises such as the pale yellow *Iris forrestii* and the purple *I. versicolor* (while any of the sibirica, chrysographes and kaempferi types would be equally happy), and the unusually arresting *Rheum alexandrae* (in the foreground). This carries spikes of dock-like flowers interspersed by large greenish-white bracts. It is not difficult to grow but seems to flower more readily the further north you go.

in its make-up. 'What's this?' you ask, 'what are those two doing together? They should look ghastly; why aren't I loathing them?'

Well, it does not matter why; the fact is the team-up works. If we have our yellow sunflowers, golden rods, yarrows and rag-worts all mixed up with phloxes, hydrangeas and michaelmas daisies, we shall get terribly self-conscious about balance and the quarelsome overbearingness of yellow. But if we get all the yellows, including also cream, together, most of these worries will simply melt away.

There are still, admittedly, certain harsh shades of mustard yellow that we shall have to use discreetly. **Achillea filipendulina** (*eupatorium*) 'Gold Plate', for instance. This 6-ft. yarrow has an invaluable quality in the bold, horizontal lines of its table-top flower heads. At the more manageable 4-ft. level, Coronation Gold performs the same office, but we gardeners are still waiting for a medium to tall-growing achillea that has the soft, tender yellow colouring of the 2-ft. *A. taygetea*. It will come. Meantime, what shall we grow next to our Gold Plates? Shall it be the spires of cobalt-blue delphiniums? Certainly not. The contrast is effective but utterly crude.

It is far better to use tall yellow mulleins instead of delphiniums. And if your splashes of yellow are in danger of becoming too aggressive, they are easily leavened, say, with the creamy plumes

Plate 22. Santolina neapolitana, in the bottom left hand corner, is the only permanent plant (or shrub) in this picture and it is severely cut back each spring to keep it neat and to prevent flowering. The other material (shown in its setting in Plate 24) was planted in late July to follow achilleas, campanulas and delphiniums. The brilliant red Cardinal flower, *Lobelia cardinalis*, is hardy with me but if there is any doubt about it, can be overwintered bedded into a cold frame. It can then be lined out in spring and moved into its flowering quarters (when the soil is damp) just before flowering begins. Weaving through it and hiding its legs is the inestiminable *Senecio leucostachys*, planted out from 3½ in. pots and also featuring in Plate 5. Behind these is the half-hardy *Ricinus communis* 'Gibsonii', a purple-leaved form of the true castor oil, raised from seed sown in a cold frame in April.

of *Artemisia lactiflora* or with the limy yellow bracts of the latest flowering spurge, *Euphorbia sikkimensis*. Not to mention the innumerable possibilities among foliage plants: shrubs, for the most part, with leaves that start bright yellow and gradually become suffused and softened by green.

As I see it, a yellow garden will be wonderfully varied: there are so many qualities of yellow, and none will fight. Furthermore, it will show up in the dusk almost as luminously as a white border, yet with none of the latter's flatness by day. I would hazard that white flowers and blue flowers need contrasting colours to do themselves justice; but pinks, reds and yellows are each sufficient to themselves.

I thought at first, for my own convenience, of dividing this subject into trees and shrubs on the one hand, herbaceous perennials and bedding plants on the other. It is just how people tend to segregate material in their own gardens but is, when you come to think of it, lazy-minded, because many of the most successful associations are made by combining herbaceous material with shrubs. For instance, I have a group of the 7-foot-tall **Inula magnifica** (*I. afghanica*) in front of and underneath the filmy branches of *Genista aethnensis*, the **Mount Etna broom.** The bright shade of yellow is exactly the same in each, but whereas the broom is diaphanous, all stem and tiny flowers with not a leaf to its name, the inula is a rank-growing composite with enormous leaves and a huge candelabrum of daisies that are each 5 or 6 in. across, and are anything but coarse since their long rays are fine-spun and spidery. The result of matching colour but contrasting texture is very effective.

We might start off with these two as a basis for a summer scheme. Obviously it will be a great advantage in any yellow garden to have dark backgrounds. These might be of evergreen hedges. Equally they could be of deciduous trees and shrubs, now in heavy summer leafage, the yellow seen as a kind of luminous oasis in a sombre setting. Next to the 15-ft. broom we might have a large mound of **golden elder,** *Sambucus nigra aurea.* It needs full sunlight to develop its best colouring, which is retained through the summer, yellow touched with green. Or, if it were shady, we could have that other elder with elegantly cut foliage, *S. racemosa* 'Plumosa Aurea', which retains its colouring well without much sunlight, and is less inclined to develop necrotic brown patches in these conditions. It is, indeed, happiest in the more sunless north.

We are envisaging a hefty grouping at the moment, and I should like to work in a plant of *Populus serotina* 'Aurea', the **golden poplar,** treating it as a shrub by hard pruning each winter. Here again, its fresh greeny yellow colouring is retained right into autumn, and the poplar leaf has that delightful way of fluttering even in the lightest airs that is a substitute to the ear for the soothing monotony of running water.

Reverting to our central broom, it occurs to me that we could grow a climber through its branches that would extend its July flowering season into September. Probably **Clematis tangutica** would be most appropriate, its tiny butter-yellow lanterns followed by fluffy seed heads, but *C. rehderiana,* with straw-yellow bells, would make a change and one would appreciate its cowslip scent. Or we could have a honeysuckle—perhaps the green-and-yellow-veined **Lonicera japonica,** 'Aureo-reticulata' or the glamorous June-flowering *L. tellmanniana* with apricot-coloured trusses. Give your broom a couple of years' start before imposing on it this added burden.

Talking of climbers, I should like a pillar of the large-leaved ivy, *Hedera colchica dentata* 'Variegata', in this scheme. Grown up a 10 to 12-ft. pole, it would make a splendid vertical evergreen feature when mature.

Elder and poplar, inula and ivy all have broad, bold leaves, so let us have for contrast a large group of the zebra grass, *Miscanthus sinensis* 'Zebrinus', its long green strap leaves cross-banded with yellow. The banding is brightest when this grass is sited in full sun, but it grows tallest, to 7 ft., in partial shade.

I can see, now, that it would be easy to have foliage as our dominant theme but, turning aside from that temptation, a large group of half a dozen plants, spaced 5 ft. apart, of **Hypericum patulum** 'Hidcote', would be very suitable. It is the finest hardy shrub-hypericum for general planting, and flowers non-stop for four months. Next, some dahlias. The acid, greeny yellow of Glorie van Heemstede will fit in admirably next the grass and the St. John's wort.

We have got rather a lot of dark green in the dahlia and hyperi-

cum foliage, so a grey-leaved shrub (of which the majority have
yellow flowers) will be a leavener. Given the scale we are working
on, in which nothing so far is less than 5 ft. tall, I shall have
Phlomis fruticosa, the **Jerusalem sage.** It makes a vast spreading
specimen, in time. My 20-year-old plant is 9 ft. across and full of
interesting bumps and hollows. Its branches tend to break under
heavy snow. There is nothing quite like the dusky yellow colouring of its hooded flowers. And, somehow, mulleins seem to go
well with this. I think the 8-ft. **Verbascum olympicum** is my
favourite. Self-sown seedlings always do the best, so we must
not be too fussy as to their exact placing. The grey, felted leaves
of *V. bombyciferum* would be good, too. There is no reason why
we should not have them both together.

So far we have considered our yellow garden only in its summer
aspect and on a pretty generous scale. It could equally well be
catered for at that season using small-growing plants with nothing
taller than 5 ft. However, I have no intention of investigating all
the possibilities. By way of a contrast, however, let us allow ourselves, in our yellow garden, one bed for winter effect, catching
the low rays of sunshine that is itself of yellow quality and will
hence add lustre to the theme. Again I should hope for a good
background against which to set the spires of one or two tall-
growing **conifers.** *Chamaecyparis lawsoniana* 'Aurea Smithii' is the
brightest of these, in winter, growing to 40 or 50 ft. by 10 or 12 ft.
across. *C. l.* 'Stewartii' is similar and almost as good. For a
broader-based, less tall cone, say 18 ft. by 12 ft., *C. obtusa* 'Crippsii'
is outstanding with a very pretty and graceful habit.

One of the advantages of these yellow cypresses is that the first-
year foliage is offset by the second-year foliage behind it, this having by now changed to green. They therefore, in a sense, provide
their own background.

For a narrow golden spire, I should fall for *Juniperus chinensis*
'Aurea'. On the other hand, if a broad, rounded bush only 6 ft.
or so tall is required, I can strongly recommend *Thuya occidentalis*
'Rheingold'. This is nearer to the real colour of gold than any
plant mentioned yet, and in winter it becomes touched with
copper and bronze while yet retaining an appearance of freshness
and vitality.

To form a lowish groundwork, 5 ft. high, much more spreading, but compact and bright yellow right through the bush, there is the yew *Taxus baccata* 'Semperaurea'. This, though a compact grower, is for general effect in a fairly spacious setting. In a special place where you can admire it at close quarters, *Chamaecyparis obtusa* 'Tetragona Aurea' (most of these lovely conifers labour under the most dreadful pseudo-botanical nomenclature) will never cease to give you little shocks of pleasure. Quite apart from its colouring, which varies from cream to gold, its growth is at once feathery and yet also encrusted like a moss or lichen. This, too, will grow 5 ft. tall and rather more across, but slowly.

The obvious broad-leaved **evergreens** to grow in association with these conifers are the ones with variegated foliage, notably *Ilex aquifolium* 'Golden King', an almost prickle-free holly that is wonderfully luminous; *Elaeagnus pungens* 'Maculata' ('Aureo-variegata') which always looks its brightest in winter, and *Griselinia littoralis* 'Variegata' which, instead of having hard leaves like the last two, is of smooth and soapy texture, oval in outline and coloured in shades of yellow-green, blue-green and cream—mainly nearest the margin. It will grow 8 or 10 ft. tall in time but should not be exposed to the coldest winds.

One or two of the yellow-variegated forms of *Euonymus japonica* will look well, too, especially as they are so glossy, and the green in them will make for a telling contrast in a generally yellow setting. If this border had a large bulge or promontory in it one could make a feature (in not too cold localities) of spiky variegated forms of New Zealand flax, *Phormium tenax*, and of *Yucca filamentosa* and *Y. gloriosa*.

As regards flowering material, we can have the Chinese witch-hazel, *Hamamelis mollis*, and its sulphur-yellow form, 'Pallida', and a groundwork of winter aconites, *Eranthis hyemalis*, to be followed by crocuses and the less coarse-growing Narcissus such as *N. cyclamineus* and its cultivars February Gold and March Sunshine.

I might exclude the deservedly popular *Mahonia japonica* (*bealei*) with its strings of pale yellow, lily-of-the-valley-scented flowers, opening in succession all through the winter. Of course one must have it somewhere (preferably in shade), but the shrub's general appearance is dim, with matt, lustreless green foliage.

But in a spring planting I should want *Mahonia aquifolium* 'Undulata', which has glossy foliage that always looks cheerful, and clusters of bright yellow berberis flowers in April. This associates well with a fairly early tulip such as *Tulipa fosteriana* 'Golden Emperor'. The single *Kerria japonica* with a groundwork of Munstead polyanthus in cream and yellow shades, is a pairing that never fails in its impact (unless the birds strip them) and is especially useful in cold heavy soil in a darkish situation. To these we can add doronicums. They will grow anywhere, but bleach less and have a longer season in shade.

There is a huge range of daffodils to choose from, but I should concentrate on those with rich, butter-yellow colouring, like the jonquils, and the pale primrose-yellow of miniatures like W. P. Milner (a trumpet) and the hoop petticoat *N. bulbocodium citrinus*. This, too, is the season of the ranunculus tribe: buttercups and celandines in their double flowered forms; kingcups (*Caltha palustris*) single or double, do not need a pond margin, if the soil is moist; globe flowers—various *Trollius* cultivars—are in season from April till June and again are happiest in moist soils.

Plants with Grey Foliage

To the unsophisticated person, plants with grey foliage are just plain dull. Confronted with grey or white, he says, 'I like a bit of colour.' It is interesting how the taste for grey increases with the degree of sophistication, reaching its apotheosis in those exquisite creatures who can exclaim that they adore all the greys. Throw them in a handful of hosta leaves for good measure, with a few fasciated abnormalities, and their exaltation will know no bounds.

I do feel, for my part, that an all-grey border or an all-grey garden is a little bit flat—tonally, that is, not texturally, of course, for the wide variation in leaf form among grey plants is one of their strong points. One can get a contrast of colour with perpetual-flowering pinks, whose grey or glaucous foliage blends with their surroundings. Another natural for the grey border is that old cottage-garden favourite, **Lychnis coronaria,** with silvery, felted leaves and dazzling magenta flowers—a magenta without too much blue in its make-up. And a grey setting suits it to perfection. I should never be able to resist, in a garden of grey, adding splashes of intense colour such as the yellow and apricot spires of *Eremerus bungei* and its hybrids or the flaming turks caps of *Lilium* 'Maxwill'. The opportunity for setting off their brilliance in such cool surroundings is too good to be missed on puristic grounds.

Many of the grey plants belong to the daisy and sage families; But whatever their family, they all prefer full sun and sharp drainage. Their felted leaves allow them to withstand high wind and low rainfall, but most of them are of Mediterranean origin and, alas, are none too hardy. Those gardeners with light, free-draining soils have the fewest disasters.

For use in a roomy border, the **cardoon**, *Cynara cardunculus,* is an improvement on the globe artichoke. They are close relatives, but the cardoon has a larger, more deeply incised leaf. Its flower heads are smaller—too small and spiky to eat—but more numerous, and are borne on a titanic structure which rises to 8 ft. and is a magnificently impressive sight before, during and even after flowering. Established clumps are hardy, but young, single-crown plants are more vulnerable. The offsets which you plant from artichokes and cardoons in spring, initially make large but lush and watery plants from the one crown, and these are rather frost-tender. Subsequently, if it gets through its first winter, the central crown proliferates, and the smaller, subsidiary offsets thus produced are less lush but very much hardier. So, once you have an established group of cardoons in your border, it is as well not to disturb it for at least the first 20 years.

Turning from the largest of the large to the smallest of the small, for the very front of the border, **Artemisia schmidtii** 'Nana' comes through any winter ordeal with sublime unconcern. It makes a grey-green mound of filigree foliage, especially enchanting when it has trapped a sprinkling of raindrops. It is a herbaceous species and encounters its main hazard in spring, when the young shoots are just beginning to extend. If house sparrows take a fancy to it at this time they can easily kill a plant outright, and many losses that are ascribed to lack of hardiness should, in fact, be laid at the sparrow's door, or nest, rather.

Sparrows have a special fancy for grey foliage in the nesting season.

A grey shrub whose attractiveness varies in and out of season is the fairly recently introduced **Ballota pseudodictamnus,** of which we can confidently say that it is hardy when established, although it may get severely bitten back by a really prolonged frost. It is at its most pleasing in spring and early summer, with round, soft-woolly leaves and chaplets of green calyxes making bobbles along the flowering spikes. The washy mauve flowers are nothing in themselves and the plant presently gets a little dusty looking and will need cutting back in August, giving it time to make new shoots before the winter. You really need more than one plant (three or four, in fact) to make a worth-while unit.

The best known of all grey-leaved shrubs, **Senecio laxifolius** (frequently confused with the similar *S. greyi*) is often not given the best treatment, and is allowed to become scrawny and full of bare patches. For one thing it must have full sun: like all the greys, it will develop its palest colouring and most compact habit when allowed to bask. Then, from time to time, it must be cut back into the old wood. If you do not care about its flowers, the best cutting-back season will be early April, and you can do so every year. It will soon re-clothe itself in young shoots and will then look comely till its next cut.

But I happen to like the flowers of *S. laxifolius.* They are not at all the same colour as ragwort, as is sometimes held against them, but several tones lighter; they are considerably larger, too, and their great sheaves make a very jolly display in June, preceded by a ravishing promise of silvery buds. The flowering is brief and you must do your pruning after it, cutting back into thickish wood behind the flower trusses. The shrub will then look threadbare until the autumn, but will probably flower very little in the following year and will therefore need no pruning at all.

S. lanata, the Woolly Willow is a rare native from mountain rock ledges in eastern Scotland. It makes a compact, 2 to 3 ft. shrub with rounded leaves that are particularly silvery when young (and the male 'pussies' are a charming extra, then) but continue to look well right into autumn. It seems to be easier to please this shrub in northern gardens than down my way and it is altogether a relief to find a grey shrub that is so out-and-out hardy.

Scent

Scent and Sentiment

There are some flowers that we expect to be scented; if they are not, they are out. Others, of which we do not demand this quality, may surprise us by producing it. 'Where does the scent come from? It cannot be that gladiolus,' we say, while the gladiolus indulges in a quiet smirk at our expense.

Show a red **rose** to anyone with the slightest vestige of a sense of smell, and he will automatically put his nose to it. Lacking scent, it may still make a name for itself as an exhibitor's flower, but it will touch nobody's heart. A red rose is not just a nice arrangement of sumptuously coloured petals. It embodies all that we have ever known and felt about roses right back to our first childhood garden. White roses arouse no expectation of scent, but neither do they involve their beholders. Before the cold chastity of a Virgo, it is easy for head to rule heart.

Roses are subject to more intensive breeding for new varieties than any other flower, and there is no way in which the quality of scent can be so quickly lost sight of and hence lost. Yet, just because a devoted public has the words 'roses do not smell like they used to' monotonously on the tip of its tongue, this statement is and will always be quite untrue. Admittedly we have a good number of scentless roses among us, but this is nothing new. Certain categories of roses always were deficient in this respect. I sometimes even feel a trifle irritated when a rose I admire for its beauty is brushed aside as utterly worthless by someone to whom I point it out, merely because it is not scented. Had I been indicating a large-flowered clematis, say, the same person would have judged with unbiased eyes, simply because he was not bringing his nose into play.

But he is right to be fussy about roses, and the same prejudice could profitably be extended to those many flowers that have lost their scent by default. The **clematis** itself is a case in point. Quite a number of clematis species are strongly scented: *C.*

montana of vanilla; *C. flammula* of meadowsweet; *C. rehderiana* of cowslips; and *C. heracleifolia davidiana* of I know not what, but something very strong indeed, hailing from the perfumery department. And there are others. Most interesting, perhaps, from the breeding viewpoint, is one of the parents of an important group of the large-flowered hybrids, namely *C. fortunei*. This double-flowered clematis, introduced from China in the early nineteenth century, was already a hybrid of unknown origins, but clearly with close affinities to *C. florida*. It was used again and again in the early hybridising of large-flowered clematis, and it was scented. Had any stress been laid on this quality when the early crosses were made, we might now have an exciting range of scented, large-flowered hybrids. As it is, *C. fortunei* has long since disappeared, and about the only scented clematis of this group left in cultivation is Fair Rosamond: scented not very strongly, but most agreeably 'between primroses and violets,' as it was described when first it appeared, nearly a century ago.

What a tragedy befell the florist's cyclamen, when it was developed. Derived entirely from *Cyclamen persicum*, without the aid of any other species, the potted cyclamen as we know it is the result of patient selection of the qualities that the breeder thought worth while. One cannot help admiring a well-grown specimen. It is massive, with great waxy blossoms and thick, leathery, dark green leaves, and exudes an atmosphere of opulence akin to the gloxinia's. But then, if you have seen a well grown specimen of the original *C. persicum,* your heart will surely be lost to it. Admittedly, the white or very pale pink colouring with a magenta circle at the mouth is not startling. But the leaves are beautifully marbled; the flowers, with their twisted, pointed lobes ('gazelle's horns' is the Arabic name for them) are gracefully poised; and the scent from one plant is overwhelming, whereas a whole greenhouse full of the standard type of cyclamen would smell of nothing more than that generalised odour of plants that you always do get in a greenhouse.

Petunias, too, are in danger at the breeder's hands. And let us never forget that his hands are ours, because it is ultimately for us, as consumers, to set his standards. Petunias have always had a delicious scent (particularly in the evening) in certain shades, particularly the blue and purple. Somehow this has managed to survive the large-scale breeding that has been going on in the petunia world, but it can only be a matter of time before it finally vanishes. One scarcely ever sees mention of scent in petunias written about as a quality worth fostering, and it is almost never mentioned in catalogues.

Scents Moral and Immoral

My one-time music teacher, Kenneth Stubbs, who was also an expert gardener, used to classify flower scents into those that are moral and those that are immoral. The distinction, when you come to think of it, is quite clear. Moral scents include all those warm, foody, daytime smells, like coconut-scented gorse, clove carnations, vanilla *Azara microphylla*, mignonette, lupins, wall-flowers, stocks and thyme.

The immoral kind reserve their main strength, appropriately, for evening and night-time. To give them their botanical names is to divest them of all magic. Reminiscing on frangipani-laden, tropical evenings is evocative enough, and circumstances would seldom require the precision of *Plumeria acutifolia*-laden evenings. But what nursery would supply a night-blowing cereus on demand? Thornton's painting from *The Temple of Flora* shows a gorgeous white cactus bloom against the perhaps too parochial setting of an English church-tower, whose clock hands are point-ing to midnight.

Often there is no helpful alternative to a botanical name and we must resign ourselves. The summer-flowering *Eucharis* looks like a large, pure-white narcissus, except that its stamens form projections on the corona like the points on a tiara. In *Pamianthe peruviana,* the corona is much enlarged, while the petals them-selves are narrow and spidery. Both are wonderfully fragrant, but stove plants, requiring a minimum winter temperature of 60° or 65° F. However, the nearly-related *Pancratium maritimum*, from the Mediterranean littoral, is nearly hardy and just as fragrant, flowering in spring. Bulbs are sometimes procurable and, if given a really well drained and sunny position, as in a south facing, raised border, would be worth trying outdoors anywhere in the south or east.

Stephanotis has usually been considered a stove-house climber, and it doubtless flowers most freely in stove conditions; but a friend has been surprisingly successful with it in his sun-room, where a temperature of not less than 50° F is maintained, and the plant has been flourishing for five or more years. He also goes in for gardenias and tuberoses in the same room. It is wise not to get too sentimental over a gardenia plant. This is an evergreen shrub that can and will grow very large in time, but is much freer flowering when young and still manageably small. Besides, there is a limit to the number of open gardenia blossoms that the human frame can tolerate at close quarters. **Tuberoses** (*Polianthes tuberosa*) are reasonably cheap but nearly always virus-infected and the tubers do not last well after the first year. Best to acquire them afresh early each spring. They are ugly plants, with untidy, stringy foliage, and so might just as well be raised out of sight in a warm greenhouse and then picked when at their best. The scent is overwhelming, but it is pleasant to be overwhelmed, now and again.

Many immoral scents are borne by perfectly hardy plants, including our own native butterfly orchids and wild honeysuckle. These are night wafters but *Osmanthus delavayi*, with a scent very similar to the orchid's, is powerful by day, being at the height of its season in April. Each twig carries several score of pure white, tubular flowers, so that a large bush in bloom is almost as impressive to see as to smell. But it is also a nice plant for its neat, evergreen foliage, and you can maintain a comely habit in it by lightly clipping the bush over immediately after flowering. This also has the effect of making it flower twice as freely in the next spring. It likes a sunny position and a good soil, otherwise it sulks and puts on little growth. Hard winters set it back, but only temporarily.

Fragrance in Winter Flowers.

It always comes as a pleasant surprise that so many hardy winter-flowering plants should be scented. What insects can they hope to attract at that season, whereby they may be pollinated? Presumably the answer to this one is that things were different at home. Either it was so cold there in winter that flowering was delayed till spring, or else it was so much less cold that pollinating insects were on the wing a'plenty. And even with a climate like ours, some of these winter-flowerers do sometimes contrive to be pollinated and, subsequently, to ripen good seed, I shall refer to this point on considering the individual plants in question.

Some of them flower over such a long period that they embrace several seasons. Such are the violet and the primrose. I can find primroses in our woods, where they have recently been coppiced, in every month of the year. This, in Sussex, must be a different, more optimistic strain than you find wild in the north, where they seldom, if ever, bloom until April and May.

Scented violets do not grow wild in my part of the Weald, but, in the garden, they are seldom flowerless. And anyway the violet scent is transmitted through the whole plant, leaves, stems and all, so that one is never without it, flowers or no flowers.

Get a bunch of common snowdrops in a warm place and they are fragrant as newly extracted honey. This is, in essence, a February flower and there are bees about again by then. These snowdrops always set a heavy crop of seed. Not so the autumn-flowering type. They flower well for me in October but never set a fertile pod. Perhaps they are inherently sterile.

'Have you ever smelt *Crocus longiflorus*?' I asked a friend who had never heard of it, let alone its scent. I picked her a bloom to sniff. Unfortunately my ploy fell flat. It was a chilly, though bright, November morning and the crocus was not smelling that day. In January we have *C. chrysanthus* 'Snow Bunting', which has the strongest honeypot scent of all.

I always associate the **winter heliotrope,** *Petasites fragrans,* with the winter walks we used to be made to take as children. It was a roadside diversion along various bits of verge we passed and, again, it grew on the cutting banks in which our nearest railway station was situated. Grows, I should say, I suppose, for petasites is no easily eradicated weed. It should never be planted in the garden except (and this is a good place for it) on a well segregated rubbish dump. Needless to say, it is in no way related to real heliotrope and the sickly scent of its wan mauve flowers is nothing like cherry pie either. Still, it does flower in January, wasting its sweetness on the desert air, and we, as desert vagrants, are grateful.

Viburnum fragrans has the irritating habit of making its principal flowering effort in autumn, before its coarse foliage has been shed. Further clusters of blossom do occur spasmodically over a long period, however, even into April, by which time the flowers and their stalks are far more elongated than heretofore, and take on a quite different appearance. The scent is of almonds. My bush, which I have scrapped, fruited very rarely, but it did on at least one occasion. In its place I now have *V. bodnantense* 'Dawn', a showier hybrid with *V. fragrans* as one parent and *V. grandiflorum* as the other. In a mild climate, this last species will be the best of the bunch, but it is unreliable. I lost mine in the wet winter of 1960. Its buds and even the flowers are very pink and it has transmitted a good measure of this quality to the hybrid.

Some people's plants of **Mahonia japonica** are already flowering in October and their season lasts for six months. Their lily-of-the-valley fragrance is something very special to have around in winter, and the strings of pale yellow flowers are quite charming to look at. This shrub is tolerant of all soils and it is hardy but is usually most successful in a partially shaded position. I have known specimens thrive in full sun but, more often, they go a bad colour if fully exposed. No regular pruning is needed but you will find, after a number of years, that this and other mahonias make long, vertical shoots on which a good deal of bare wood is exposed. You can cut these back quite mercilessly in April, as soon as flowering is done with. They will break from the old wood and flower with undiminished freedom in their next season.

Most important of the scented winter-flowerers (and it must be admitted that it is even more important for its flowers than for its scent) is the **Chinese witch hazel**, *Hamamelis mollis*. We have two bushes, both over 30 years old, and they are about 7 ft. tall and rather more across. They are never likely to grow much larger, as I cut large branches from them for the house just before Christmas, each year, where they soon open their clusters of dark knobbly buds into their characteristic, spidery yellow blossoms.

These shrubs look handsome in the garden against a dark background and the frost never spoils their display, so they can be sited in quite exposed positions. But by bringing liberal supplies indoors, you can not merely observe them comfortably with your eyes, but also savour their unique fragrance, which will waft more freely under house conditions. In a warm room, however, the display will last for not much longer than a week and you'll be tempted to gather more branches, and then more again. I must warn the reader that there is a danger of carrying these plundering raids too far, for the Chinese witch hazel is reluctant to make new shoots from old. Therefore, however artistically or discreetly you make your cuts, you will find, on returning to the bush for the same purpose a year later, that the mutilated branches are, in most cases, exactly as you left them. Now and again a new shoot will arise, however, and thus start a new branch, and it is not unusual for strong new shoots to start up from the centre of the bush, near ground level.

Less than most members of its family is this shrub lime-shy. Certainly it is worth attempting on any but the thinnest of chalk soils, and if it sends out distress signals with poor growth and prematurely yellowing leaves, it can be treated with that admirable antidote to lime-induced chlorosis: iron sequestrine (marketed by Murphy's). Another deficiency that used to show up on my plants as a premature browning (scorching) of the leaf margins, I corrected by applying wood ash and, as this did the trick, I assume that a shortage of potash was the trouble here.

All Chinese witch hazels have to be grafted, which is a very great nuisance and ensures that demand invariably outpaces supply. A keenly interested gardener whom I have with me now, told me that he once tried grafting the witch hazel on to the wild hazel but that it did not take. He said he had got the method from a book. This is where those common, cosy English names that we apply to plants can let us down with such a crash. *Hamamelis* is not remotely related to the wild hazel, *Corylus avellana*, and the application of the word hazel to both is merely on account of a superficial resemblance in leaf shape. *H. mollis* is, in fact, grafted on to seedling stock of the American species, *H. virginiana*. This takes two years to germinate from seed, under normal conditions, and another year to grow large enough to be used as stock for grafting. Fortunately, in after life, it rarely misbehaves itself by suckering.

I have never seen fruit on *H. mollis* myself, but correspondents from as far apart as Devon and Edinburgh tell me that theirs seed regularly, so it must be a question of procuring a clone with fertile sex organs. My Edinburgh correspondent's (Mr. J. S. Russell) experiences will be worth quoting, for one rarely finds reference to this subject in books. 'The seeds are sown in clay pans whenever ripe (generally end of December) and left in an open frame outside until the following autumn when they are transferred to a cold frame. Germination, generally in the region of 75 per cent., occurs in the following March. The plants are true to type and flower when about six years old.'

If you have room for only one witch hazel, do not be content, as a substitute, with *H. japonica* or with any species other than *H. mollis*. The others have their own charm but are either less effective or lacking in scent or both. The best of the *H. mollis* variants is Pallida, with paler, clearer yellow petals than the type, showing up better at a distance. I must admit, though, that *H. japonica* var. *zuccariniana* is very pretty with bright lemon yellow flowers and more than usually twisted petals.

Among the many winter flowering shrubs of coarse habit and boring appearance in summer is a group of **bush-honeysuckles.** They should be sited out of the way and used mainly for picking. I thought I had been rather clever in planting *Lonicera fragrantissima* under a winter cherry. Not many shrubs thrive beneath a cherry's canopy, but this one does. Unfortunately, it never flowers there, unless it happens that the previous summer has been exceptionally warm and ripening. Rather than move this lonicera, which, after all, fills a difficult space with evergreen foliage, I bought a plant of *L. purpusii*, and tucked it away, but in full sunshine. This is a hybrid and with the rare quality of excelling both its parents: *L. fragrantissima* and *L. standishii*. It is freer-flowering than either and will start up in every mild spell until spring The flowers are carried in pairs, and are quite small,

Plate 23. Sheffield Park gardens, in Sussex, are famous for their autumn colouring. Dozens of plants of the deciduous *Nyssa sylvatica*, from the south-east U.S.A., were planted at the beginning of the century. Here a specimen is shown doing its stuff. Sometimes nyssas turn yellow rather than red; often they drop their leaves without colouring. As the tree has no other claim to admiration, it is suitable only for large landscape gardens. But this picture does show how deciduous trees and shrubs with bright autumn colouring are displayed as flatteringly as maybe against a dark background of coniferous trees and evergreen shrubs.

white, but with such a heavy, heady scent, akin to that of *Daphne mezereum,* that a few sprigs are as many as you need in any ordinary-sized room. The leaves have mostly dropped off, at flowering time, and it is easy to strip the remainder from gathered pieces.

The **winter sweet**, *Chimonanthus praecox,* has a spicy fragrance that is basically far more agreeable. This is another large-growing shrub of sordid appearance in its summer dress. Fortunately it strips for action, and is usually at its prettiest by Christmas. Frost kills opened blooms, but a succession open until February. A sheltered, sunny position is advisable, although the shrub itself is hardy.

I have known impatient gardeners to throw out their winter sweet after five or six years of waiting in vain for flowers. I admit to experiencing a certain relish as I point out that, had they waited one more year, they would probably have been rewarded with blossoms both then and increasingly every year thereafter. Seven years is the average waiting period; the time a young plant needs in which to make vigorous growth before settling down to its main business.

Winter sweets are best left unpruned, so far as possible, otherwise you encourage the production of watery young shoots at the

Plate 24. Two photographs showing the same part of my Long Border of mixed shrubs, herbaceous plants, annuals etc., the first taken in late June, the second on 10th October.

The primrose yellow *Achillea taygetea* is dominant in the top scene, with the magenta-flowered bloody cranesbill, *Geranium sanguineum* on its left. Behind are plantings made in the previous autumn of *Campanula persicifolia* and the Pacific hybrids delphinium, Percival, a seed strain with white flowers and a black eye or 'bee'. The shrub rose Perle d'Or is seen top left. It has miniature flowers on a large bush and produces two big flushes.

In order to maintain continuous interest in this important border, I lift the achilleas, campanulas and delphiniums after flowering and line them out in a spare plot, bringing them back in late autumn. Meantime their place is taken by other annual or perennial plants (see caption to Plate 22). The cranesbill is cut right down in mid-season and is seen flowering a second time in the lower plate. Many of the hardy cranesbills will behave in this obliging manner.

expense of older flowering wood. When picking for the house, you should take care not to leave snags, through which the dread coral spot fungus can gain entry. It has a weakness for this shrub and is liable to kill large portions of it.

Some winter sweet bushes fruit very freely and, if you sow their seeds fresh, in September, they will germinate almost immediately, the youngsters looking much like beech seedlings. But you can get inferior stock this way, carrying flowers that are twice as small and insignificant as they need be. Take seed, if you can, from a bush that is known to flower handsomely.

Jasmines the Year Round

From the gardener's viewpoint, **jasmines** as a group have much in common with the honeysuckles: some are climbing, others not; some are scented, others odourless; some are winter-flowering, others children of the most swooning summer evenings. Indeed, there is no season when jasmines are not active.

The winter jasmine, *Jasminum nudiflorum*, opens the first of its flowers in October, before the leaves have fallen, while the last stragglers appear in April. But it is in the full tide of its blooming in December. A well grown specimen trained across the wall of a two-storied building is a magnificent sight; each of its several hundred, wand-like strands, wreathed with some 20 yellow blossoms. Few gardens are without this plant and, more often than not, it is a neglected, scrubby feature, full of dead wood. It is not a true climber, but scandent like a climbing rose or a bramble, hoisting itself up and through the branches of other shrubs. So, if you are not giving it a wall to itself (and it will thrive on walls of any aspect) it looks rather nice filtering through a wisteria. But it is equally happy on the flat, and I would then associate it with the stiff, bracket growths of *Cotoneaster horizontalis,* whose leaves become crimson in November just when the jasmine is turning to gold.

Remember that this shrub likes to be fed just as much as any other, and it should be pruned regularly each April by shearing back all those shoots that have been flowering through the winter. This will stimulate the plant into producing a generous new crop of its green wands on which to flower in the following season. How the nurseryman ever manages to sell this species is a mystery, because every strand that happens to touch the ground, roots at the point of contact within a few weeks, and these self-layers make welcome presents.

J. primulinum is an opulent cousin of the winter jasmine. The flowers are half as large again and most come double—a kind of hose-in-hose effect, one flower within another; the colour is the usual strong yellow, and there is no scent. This is a reasonably hardy shrub, but needs a sunny south aspect, and will then flower in April. It never makes anything like such a good show in the open as it does in a cool greenhouse. There it will flower a month earlier, and with stunning abandon. Being vigorous, it is better to restrict the roots by growing it in a fair-sized tub or strong wooden box, rather than in a bed.

This species is often confused in garden literature, even by those who should know better, with *J. polyanthum*—largely, I suspect, because their names begin and end with the same letters. There are few more intense thrills of anticipation than that occasioned by seeing a plant of this, laden with its clusters of pale pink, sharp-pointed buds, just as they are about to unleash their almost palpable fragrance on the ambient air. Again, it is for the cool or even the cold greenhouse, as long as it does not get so frosted as to lose its main crop of flower buds. These develop early in the new year and expand into clouds of white blossom around February. *J. polyanthum* is most usually cultivated in a large pot, its twining shoots being trained around a framework of three or four canes. After flowering, it should be pruned back severely, otherwise it will get quite out of control. Alternatively, if you can be bothered to strike cuttings, annually, in late spring, they will have made strong plants by the following winter and the old stock can be discarded. Sometimes this jasmine grows like mad but refuses to flower, even though it may be root-bound in a pot. I have had this experience with it myself but, rack my brains as I may, have been unable to puzzle out the cause.

Our common summer jasmine, *J. officinale,* has much the same habit of growth and manner of flowering, and the same wonderful fragrance, strongest in the evening and at night. But, of course, it is hardy. Its larger-flowered variety, *J. o.* 'Affine', never flowers as freely at any one time, but has a four-month season, from July to October. Its growth is far more rampant—embarrassingly so in many situations. But where you can spare the space, I recommend planting this jasmine with a *Clematis montana* and letting them fight it out together. Their vigour is well matched. They will cover almost anything you put in their way, and you will enjoy the vanilla scent of *C. montana* in late spring followed, after a brief interval, by the jasmine's powerful contribution. No regular pruning will be possible—only a severe hack-back of everything within sight every ten years or so, with the consequent loss of a season's blossom on both shrubs.

The hybrid, *J. stephanense,* is a twining climber of moderate vigour, flowering only for a few weeks at midsummer, but an extremely pretty soft pink colour and just as well scented as it should be.

I have a soft spot for the sprawling but free-standing shrub, *J. humile*. It is reasonably hardy and grows to about 6 ft. All summer it carries clusters of soft yellow, slightly scented flowers, and these are followed by shining black fruits, so that in early autumn you have a combined effect of flowers and fruit together. *J. parkeri* is like a miniature rock-garden version of *J. humile,* and only a foot high. My plant lost no time in dying on me; and, as you seldom see mature specimens of this jasmine, the suspicion lurks that it is tricky.

Temperament among the Daphnes

Looking back over the years, it is daunting to think of how many **daphnes** must have died in my garden. Luckily for my ego most other daphne enthusiasts have shared the same experience. This beautiful genus has thus acquired a reputation for being captious and when a specimen dies we are apt to shrug our shoulders and say 'Oh well! It's a daphne. What can you expect?', as though the finger of fate were ever pointing in that direction and nothing we could do would deflect it. We are almost certainly wrong.

The commonest disease of daphnes is caused by the fungus *Marssonina daphnes,* which defoliates a plant, often quite early in the season. Repetition of this stripping act is so weakening that an affected plant can easily be killed over a period of three years or so. But we can intervene. Two or three applications of a copper fungicide at fortnightly intervals, in spring, when the young foliage is expanding, should gain control. As dead leaves can harbour the disease, they should be collected from underneath the bushes and burned. I have been particularly troubled with the disease on *Daphne mezereum, D. odora* and *D. pontica;* not on *D. tangutica,* but it seems to have a pretty wide host range within the group.

Sudden death in a daphne could be caused by the honey fungus, *Armillaria mellea* (see page 358). *D. burkwoodii* is typical of a naturally short-lived species (hybrid, actually) that can be expected to die fairly gradually towards the end of its term.

For anyone with even the remnants of a sense of smell, daphnes are indispensable. *D. collina* is only faintly scented, but nearly all the rest of those in cultivation are heavily endowed with this property, though its quality varies greatly. When I was staying in the Swiss Alps one summer, my landlady declared that the scent of *D. cneorum* was actually poisonous, and would not allow a sprig of it to enter her house. There does seem to me a kind of malignant undercurrent behind its overt sweetness—such as could perhaps give one a headache at persistent close quarters.

The scent of *D. mezereum* has the same heavy, heady quality, but is delightful to meet as a whiff in the garden. This is undoubtedly the most popular of all daphnes, partly because it is the first to flower, and partly because the dense wreaths of pinkish-purple blossom along its leafless stems are very effective. Plants may live for 20 years, and I know one owner of *D. mezereum* who used to bring his daphne with him whenever he moved house, without the plant objecting in the slightest, although as a group daphnes are bad movers. None of the planted mezereons in my garden are alive today; but the race is kept going by bird-sown specimens, which seem happiest when they come up in rather shaded places, as under a yew hedge or overhanging *Cotoneaster horizontalis.*

In some districts, greenfinches develop a habit (which forthwith becomes an insatiable appetite) of eating this daphne's seeds while yet unripe and green. They strip the lot and no fruit is set. This has happened to me, and also to Miles Hadfield in his Birmingham days (as recounted in his fascinating book *One Man's Garden*). After he had been without daphnes for a number of years, a chance seedling turned up and the greenfinches, now of a generation that had forgotten, left it alone.

D. *odora* is another of the heavy-scented brigade, and scarcely later in its flowering than D. *mezereum*; but its laurel-leaves are evergreen and the flowers are carried in terminal clusters—rich purple without, whitish within. It is reputedly hardier in the variety with yellow-edged leaves called Aureo-marginata. Shelter from the coldest winds is its only requirement. In the south it can be flowered well in shade, but in the midlands and anywhere north or west of these, D. *odora* needs all the sun it can get and is even then apt to be shy, for lack of ripening. It is one of the easiest to strike from half-ripe cuttings with a heel, in July, so a good queue of replacements can always be assured in case of accidents.

The foliage of D. *odora* whether variegated or plain is really no great shakes. Far more pleasing is the rich evergreenery of our native spurge laurel, D. *laureola*. It is quite common in chalk and limestone woodland but I have never been on the spot at the right time of day (which is at night) to analyse and pass judgment on the scent of its little green flowers. Similar but an improvement as a garden plant is D. *pontica*. This is a handsome bush, 3 ft. high and more across, clothed in rosettes of broadly rounded, dark green leaves. The spidery, pale green flowers open in April and May and are so abundant that they do make a distinctly pleasing visual impression but their fragrance is their outstanding asset. Next to D. *burkwoodii*, which is in a different category, it is the pleasantest and most soothing of all daphne scents. The plant should be sited at some spot where you are sure to pass on returning home from an evening out. Then it will come to meet you, stopping you dead in your tracks as also in your thoughts, with its sweet message.

I think D. *tangutica* is the easiest and most fool-proof of this tribe. Its hardiness is such that winter's onslaught makes no impact whatsoever on its evergreen foliage. The bush grows quickly and may be 4 ft. high by 7 ft. across at maturity and it seems to be unaffected by daphne troubles. The leaves are a little boring, but inoffensive. The bush flowers first in May and should be sited in a sunny, open position if a really telling display is to be obtained. Each shoot has a terminal cluster of half a dozen blooms, greenish purple on the outside, white with a hint of green and purple within. The scent is good and not in the least cloying. There is a small second crop on the young shoots in summer. The large, orange-red berries are striking. Each contains one seed, and this will germinate quickly if sown fresh.

D. tangutica may be a mere geographical form of *D. retusa*. The latter is a slower growing, denser bush, seldom reaching the dimensions of the former but having the greater dignity of one who is never to be hurried.

D. burkwoodii is a hybrid usually sold as the clone called Somerset. It is a fast-growing, short-lived shrub, deciduous, tricky to propagate (from cuttings) but so good when seen at its best that it is difficult to go without. At its best it will be a dome-shaped specimen, 3 ft. tall and covered in May with clusters of palest pink blossom smelling of pinks.

The creeping evergreen *D. blagayana* is supposed to be easy if you realise that it likes to have its prostrate branches weighted with stones so that they can root as they go along. It has terminal clusters of wonderfully fragrant, pure white flowers in spring. It is said to be good in shade. I make these remarks obliquely as it has shown its dislike for me and all my works in the traditional daphne style.

Strength and Weakness in Buddleias

Buddleias are in the top flight of second-rate shrubs. They all grow exceedingly fast and most flower from the word go, so they are a boon to the impatient gardener. Their very speed, however, denotes an inevitable flimsiness of structure which gets by, in summer, when they are fully dressed, but is sadly skeletal in winter. But these fragrant plants are indispensable.

They are usually pot-grown and can hence be planted at any season but as some are not out-and-out hardy, spring is the best time for getting buddleias established. The most typical butterfly bushes—cultivars of *Buddleia davidii* or hybrids with this as one parent—associate well with herbaceous perennials in a roomy border. Flowering at the ends of their young shoots from mid-summer onwards, they have very much the habit of herbaceous plants, and when the border is being done over, in the autumn, you can shorten the buddleias' branches by at least half, while you are about it. This makes them more presentable and orderly. Their pruning can be completed in spring by shortening these same shoots of last year's making to within an inch of the base of each. Actually, I often do the whole pruning in one go, in late autumn, because I find my buddleias are none the worse for it, but in harder climates than ours this might be dangerous were a bad winter to ensue. Each gardener has got to learn from experience in his own garden.

If I express an opinion on which are the nicest buddleias to grow, it must be understood that this is a very personal matter and the reader is welcome to disagree. The most popular *B. davidii* cultivar at the moment is, I should guess, Royal Red—actually a reddish-purple shade. I was thrilled when I first met this but am now utterly bored. There is a matt lifelessness about its colouring and texture that makes it a tedious life companion. A newish one, Black Knight, is very, very dark violet, but the shrub has an impossibly coarse and leggy habit. The white cultivars such as White Profusion, are splendid at their best, with large spikes, but when a white flower changes to brown without shedding its petals (and all buddleias have this unpleasant habit) it shows more than in any other colour. Think of white lilac or of *Aruncus sylvester*.

The straightforward, richly coloured Fromow's Purple and, equally, Ile de France are good, though not new. Better than any of these I like Glasnevin Blue, mainly on account of the bush's comely, spreading habit and of the slender elegance of its flowering spikes. The colour is quite a nice deep mauve. There is no reason for insisting on a dark colouring, and I consider Lochinch as fine as any buddleia that has yet walked our gardens. Its leaves are grey and the flowers, gathered in substantial trusses, are clear lavender. After a long trial in my garden, it is thumbs down for *B. fallowiana* 'Alba'. Its leaves are very pale and silvery, which is an asset, but the flower trusses are no use at all. They are slender, cream-coloured, each flower having an orange eye. The general impression is dirty, made dirtier still from the fact that by the time the flowers are opening half-way along each spike, those at the base have already changed to brown.

All these buddleias look the better for being dead-headed immediately after their first flush, if you can get round to it, and they are thereby encouraged to flower again, a little. This job gives some of us violent hay fever, but we can escape our fate by choosing a moment when the bush is still drenched from rain.

The semi-evergreen *B. globosa* makes a particularly large and ungainly shrub, quite untowardly disreputable in its off-seasons. It flowers on its old wood, in early summer, but will not flower at all if pruned in autumn, winter or spring. The only possible time is immediately after flowering. After these harsh words, I must admit there is something endearing about this shrub when it is covered with its clusters of tight orange globes, and they are deliciously scented. There is a hybrid between this species and *B. davidii* called *B. weyeriana*. It combines the worst features of both parents in a sickly orange, pink and mauve vomit.

The popularity of *B. alternifolia* has greatly increased of recent years, I fancy, and it is indeed a very lovely creature when seen at its best. There are two disconcerting traits in its nature: first, it resents root disturbance at planting time, and may show its dis-approval in the usual way—by dying. Second, it is extremely vigorous and may demand far more room than you were pre-pared to allow. Again, this is a shrub that flowers, in June, on shoots made in the previous year, and so can only be pruned immediately afterwards. I remove whole branches, to the tune of perhaps one quarter of the bush. You ultimately make life easier for yourself by allowing this species only one main stem, growing it as a staked standard, right from the start. It will flower most freely in a year following a warm summer, and is then alive with blossom carried on long, wand-like strands; the usual mauve and with the typical butterfly-bush scent, yet never visited by butter-flies. In *B. a.* 'Argentea', the small, lance-shaped leaves are an attractive soft grey, and there is every reason for growing this form in preference to the type-plant.

B. colvilei, at midsummer, carries loose trusses of exceptionally large flowers, each an inch across and coloured rose red. Against a wall the shrub is evergreen and earns its position by its large and handsome leaves. This is just as well, for it is shy flowering in its early years. In milder districts it can stand in the open as a free specimen and may reach tree-like proportions, but is then a scraggy object and pretty well deciduous.

Late-Summer Scents

The weather in August is often docile without being fiercely hot. On some days the sun breaks quickly through a dense early-morning mist. At the same time our mulberries give a sleepy heave, as a first breath of wind stirs them, and the only violent branch movements in the garden are caused by bouncing sparrows. On other days it is moistly cloudy but still quiet—a kind of weather gardeners can enjoy, since the light is gentle and flowers look well beneath it. Either way, the garden exhales an abundance of delicious scents.

The annual carnations are good wafters, once they get going. All the colours, even the whites (which are so drearily odourless in the florists' soulless brand) contribute generously. I always have odd plants of mignonette scattered about the garden at strategic points and sometimes grow a few in pots, which I can move around. 'Does mignonette ever smell like it used to?' I was asked rather querulously by one elderly visitor, as though the Bomb, the cost of living and a Labour government must between them have put an end to all such pleasures. Well, it does; but you never quite know when. Sometimes its spicy fragrance reaches you most powerfully by night; at others, when the sun is on the flowers. All you can do is to wait for it, because nothing comes of sticking your face into the plant. Always grow the commonest sort of 'unimproved' mignonette. Those of more robust and up-right habit or bolder colouring are less fragrant.

Petunias smell strongest in the evening, like their relatives the nicotianas, but the bedding verbenas belong to daytime. All except the pure scarlet strains are well scented. Stocks, too, are daytimers; the night-scented brand has quite a different quality, with something of almond essence in it. Most varieties of the modern sweet pea need to be gathered together in large numbers before they yield appreciable fragrance. I was much struck, a few years ago, by a hedge of purple sweet peas growing in the Northern Horticultural Society's gardens at Harlow Car, by Harrogate. Their flowers were small and without the large wavy standard petal and open wings of the modern strains, but the scent was of a voluptuous richness such as one had forgotten a sweet pea

could possess. This was the old-fashioned Grandiflora type of
60 years ago, before the modern Spencer varieties had monopol-
ised the market. They are sold as a mixture, both seeds and plants,
by Unwins of Histon, Cambridge.

Of the shrubs, *Hoheria sexstylosa* is radiant throughout August,
with pearl-like buds and white star flowers among gleaming
foliage, piled up in billows to a height of 15 ft. It has the characteristic honey scent of other hoherias, and the flowers make a
particularly flattering background for the newly emerged brood
of red admiral and peacock butterflies, with which it is popular.

Anyone with an acid soil can grow the sweet pepper-bush,
Clethra alnifolia, which carries spikes of warmly fragrant, small
white flowers in late summer. The bush likes moisture. It then
grows 8 ft. tall and gradually spreads by suckering.

Better than the scent of the few roses that are flowering at this
between-seasons period is the stewed-apple fragrance of the
sweet-briar. I have a seedling near a garden seat and I prune it
hard every year so that it is stimulated into strong growth from
spring till autumn.

Lonicera japonica 'Halliana' is much more inclined to waft by
day as well as by night than are most honeysuckles, such as the
Late Dutch. The hair-oil fragrance of *Clematis heracleifolia
davidiana* is powerful on some days. Spartium is always good; the
hebes that are related to *H. salicifolia*—Miss E. Fittall, Hidcote
and Midsummer Beauty—are very sweet. Spiciest fragrance of all
is given off by the common myrtle, *Myrtus communis*, in its August-
September hey-day. It is like an etherealised version of the goodly
smell of crushed myrtle leaves.

The smell of hydrangeas is seldom mentioned. It is neither
pleasant nor unpleasant; a sort of vegetable aroma, slightly acrid
and quite insistent at times. I enjoy it. Phloxes, which look so well
with hydrangeas, are the most bountiful of the herbaceous plants
for scent at this time.

I have always been puzzled by a globe thistle that I originally
acquired from a friend's garden solely on account of its scent
being strongly reminiscent of carnations. This is *Echinops sphaero-
cephalus,* a six-footer with ugly foliage and undistinguished grey
flower heads. It has never given off the same scent since I have
had it. But it is not unusual for flowers to smell differently at

different times and in different places just as vegetables can vary in their flavours.

Special Situations

Some Seaside Shrubs

I frequently have this particular pistol aimed point-blank at my head—will such-and-such a plant stand salt-laden gales? When I do not know, my favourite escape is to refer my inquisitor to J. R. B. Evison's *Gardening by the Sea* (Pan Piper 6/od.). If, on the other hand, I am asked to recommend plants—usually shrubs— for seaside planting, I am in a stronger position, for there are a number of seaside stalwarts that one has observed again and again when visiting the coast, and many of them are such good value that it is a pleasure to grow them inland, too.

There is, for instance, the **sea buckthorn,** *Hippophaë rhamno- ides,* often colonised on sand dunes to stop them drifting. It is quite one of the loveliest of silver-leaved shrubs, slowly developing into a small and interestingly shaped, gnarled tree. The foliage is narrowly willow-like, and is deciduous, but in winter the female plants retain their unique-looking, gleaming orange berries for many months. As sea buckthorns are nearly always raised the easy way, from seed, it is difficult to buy by sex, as one would wish, for one male could serve a larger number of wives. What you can do is to plant a small mixed colony and hope that a number of berry-bearing ladies will be included. But Treseder's of Truro, Cornwall, do offer sexed plants, and they are certainly worth the extra price put on them.

One of the handsomest evergreen shrubs for seaside use (and it is hardy in many inland areas too) is **Griselinia littoralis.** The young plant is at first inclined to look skinny, but it is reasonably fast-growing and makes an excellent clipped hedge, or else can be used as an unclipped windbreak, eventually growing 12 or 15 ft. tall at least.

I think the common old evergreen **Euonymus japonica** tends to be underrated. It is usually seen in a formal hedge but I like it best as a large, free-growing shrub. Whatever its shape, an evergreen leaf cannot be uninteresting if it is highly polished, as in this case. I would go for a golden-variegated form and if parts of it reverted to plain green I should not worry, for it is pleasant to see this shrub with alternating green and variegated patches.

The easiest, hardiest and most commonly planted **daisy bush** is *Olearia haastii*. I can think of few drearier shrubs. It can grow large, in time, but always remains thick-set and dumpy. The white flowers are certainly carried in abundance and at a useful time, in August, but only for a week or two, after which they turn a venomous brown. But this species' real trouble is in its little privet leaves, which are sombre and sooty.

When we touch upon *O. macrodonta,* we are suddenly lifted on to quite another plane. In some maritime districts such as Cornwall and the West of Scotland, it grows gigantic, even to 20 ft., and is much used for hedging and wind-breaking, having the convenient amenability of allowing itself to be pruned hard back into old wood, if necessary, or, equally, of remaining comely if never pruned at all. Even 10 miles inland as we are, it needs a reasonably frost-sheltered position and is unlikely to exceed a height of 7 ft. or so. The leaves are a gentle grey-green, in colour, broadly elliptical and edged with mock prickles, as though aping a holly, but actually soft to handle. The white daisy flowers make a voluminous and jolly display, in their season. There are thousands of them, but they are well enough spaced for one always to remain conscious of them being neatly and symmetrically formed as individuals.

The most exciting olearia is *O. semidentata.* It is less hardy than the last but a first-rate seasider. When really well suited it makes a 10 ft. bush in all directions but in the majority of gardens one can plan for something of no more than 3 ft. Its elliptical leaves are grey underneath and pleasing enough but the daisies are the real thrill: the largest of their tribe, about 2 in. across with rays of a strong mauve shade and a rich purple disc. The last is a most unusual and captivating feature. The daisies are borne singly and open over a months-long summer season.

'And then, of course, there is **Senecio laxifolius,**' I say, expecting a series of brisk, affirmative nods from the interlocutor, who is questing shrubs to furnish a wind-battered seaside garden. Sometimes, however, there are no nods; merely an 'Oh yes,' and it turns out that everyone is not, after all, familiar with this indispensable—even after I have tried them with the other popular name by which it is known, *S. greyi*. It should be in every garden, and I have discussed the merits and treatment of this shrub on page 312.

An awed hush must prevail when we mention the dignified and aristocratic *S. rotundifolius*. This can be considered hardy only when within sight and smell of the sea. It succumbs in my garden, if unprotected, so I have now developed a routine of lifting my plants in autumn, potting them up and overwintering them under glass or in a dimly lighted cellar. When more than 4 ft. tall, the plant is wrapped around in its border position with heavy polythene sheeting, this being tied into and kept rigid against strong canes. The inside of this snuggery is then stuffed with old male-fern fronds, and they are lifted off the top of the bush during really mild spells.

The leaves of this species are tough and stiff like old leather, glossy olive-green above and pale fawn beneath and around their rims. They are broadly oval, and 4 in. long by 3 in. across, when fully grown. It is such a striking shrub that everyone notices it. *S. elaeagnifolius* is similar but possibly even better, with slightly more elongated leaves, enhanced by sinuous margins. But there is a good deal of confusion between these two species.

These senecios are New Zealanders, and so are the **hebes**, the shrubby veronicas. With the accent on sea-worthiness, I would choose *Hebe dieffenbachii* for its foliage; and three similar hybrids, Miss E. Fittall, Hidcote and Midsummer Beauty, for their flowers. See page 433 on hebes.

Like all the **brooms**, *Spartium junceum* has to be pot-grown and can be planted at any time. It is very reliable on the coast and gives better value than any other broom, having the largest flowers, the sweetest scent and the longest season of flowering, from late June till September. True, the shrub is gawky, but there can be a certain appeal even in this defect. Certain flowering shrubs that easily blow apart in our inland gardens are yet renowned for their sea-worthiness. The tree lupin, *Lupinus arboreus*, is one and the tree mallow, *Lavatera olbia* 'Rosea' another. Both are really shrubs, of course, and grow about 5 ft. tall.

Gorse is a familiar coastal wilding, and the double form, *Ulex europaeus* 'Plenus', is particularly worthy of garden space where the soil is light and poor. I have never seen gorse form such a solid mass of yellow as where its young shoots have continually been nibbled back by rabbits—a point worth remembering by rabbit-ridden gardeners, though it will be advisable to give the plants a rabbit-free start with a circle of wire netting, until there is a basis of woody growth that will preclude your shrubs being nibbled into eternity.

Holly is another wind, salt- and rabbit-resistant shrub. There is an area of shingle near us, on the coastal boundary between Kent and Sussex, called 'the hollies' on account of its curious, sporadic colonisation by these shrubs in 10-foot-tall lumps that slope gradually upwards on their windward side but rise almost sheer on the sheltered north-east face. There is a huge selection of delightful ornamental hollies of which every gardener is likely to want one or two specimens, if not a complete wind-breaking outfit.

Frustrations of a Chalk Garden

Most of us can find plenty to grumble about in the nature of the soil on which we garden. Either it dries out or it never dries out; or it is full of rocks and stones or it sets like concrete. And if it is not the soil it is the wind we catch or ghastly frosts in every month of the year. The number of gardeners about who are ready to spin a non-stop tale of woe is fantastic, but the only ones for whom I do occasionally feel more than a grain of sympathy are those who have to cope with chalk.

This is odd, in a way, because when you think of our natural flora, the most exciting and beautiful communities, including a long list of orchids, frequently occur in chalk woodland and on chalk downland. But in a garden you are, to an extent, up against it.

For one thing there is excessively free soil drainage. This is not so serious as on acid, sandy soils, like the Bagshot or the Folkestone sands. These are highly infertile whereas chalk soils are quite the reverse, but they do mop up all the organic dressings you apply: the farmyard manure, the garden compost, the leaf-mould, peat, spent hops, road sweepings, sewage sludge and all other similar oblations, with alarming speed. You cannot let up for a minute. And then, the soil in a chalk garden habitually looks horrid. The moment it dries—and it dries in a moment—it turns a livid, pale grey colour that is thoroughly unappetising.

Two steps need to be taken to counter this situation. An adequate and willingly used irrigation system is more than ever important for one thing, and you need to be more than usually alert to the importance of keeping the soil covered with vegetation.

As chalk turf is so very beautiful, and comprises many of the finest grasses—the delightful quaking grass, *Briza media*, among them—as well as the gayest flowers, I would, in any suitably rural setting, give a large part of my garden over to rough grassland, mowing it only two or three times a year. In your borders, shrubs need to be planted so as to give close cover, and herbaceous plants in large groups, and with little space in between groups. If you want to include annuals and bedding plants, it becomes more than usually necessary not to let them starve in their boxes, to plant them out betimes and to keep them well watered for the first few weeks so that they have already made good ground cover by the middle of June.

Of course, what first comes to mind when we think of chalk gardening are all the plants—shrubs in particular—that we shall not be able to grow, because of the soil's alkalinity. None of the *Ericaceae*—rhododendrons and heathers and allied genera—with the exception of the winter-flowering heaths and of the arbutus tribe; no camellias nor meconopses, excepting the Welsh poppy. This deprivation is shared by most lime soils, but there are extra aggravations on the chalk. Lupins are out of the running; even delphiniums can develop a hectic yellow colouring to their foliage, although this does not preclude their cultivation.

Hydrangeas will be pink or red flowered, never blue: no great worry in that, but their foliage will often suffer, and expensive applications of iron sequestrine will be necessary to correct jaundice. The lovely *Hydrangea villosa* is one of the few that puts up gladly with chalk.

And there are other shrubs that are liable to suffer; not in the first few years, perhaps, but in middle life, just when they should be settling down to give of their best. Among these must be numbered the Japanese quinces, usually called 'japonicas'; the evergreen types of *Ceanothus*; some of the *Cistus* tribe and a great many roses. Curiously, the majority of climbing roses seem to be happy enough on chalk. So do the larger and more vigorous-growing shrub types, such as the rugosas and hybrid musks. But the majority of floribundas and nearly all the bush hybrid teas—even the robust Peace—are liable to succumb. Their leaves turn yellow, they lose vigour and fade out.

It is silly to fight to grow a costive plant when there are, even on chalk, so many willing and trouble-free alternatives. Nearly all the viburnums are hilarious on chalk, and so are the buddleias, deutzias, philadelphus and many other huge tribes, as well as such winners as *Osmanthus delavayi*. Peonies, both herbaceous and shrubby, are out-and-out chalk-lovers, as was so amply demonstrated by the doyen of peony growers and breeders, the late Sir Frederick Stern, in his chalk garden on the Sussex Downs. Here, too, he bred and grew glorious specimens of *Magnolia high-dowensis*, with huge, pendent white globelets offset by crimson stamens. Only a few magnolias can be fully relied upon on chalk.

The kniphofias (which I find tricky on clay, whose water-retentiveness works against winter hardiness) are splendid chalk plants and there is a wonderful range of heights, colours and seasons of flowering, among them. And all the grey-leaved fraternity, whether shrubby or herbaceous, are at home in a sunny position on chalk, revelling in its very dryness. So, for the same reason, do many bulbous plants from the Mediterranean and Middle East, as also from South Africa, including crinums and agapanthus.

Perhaps, after all, we need not be so very sorry even for the chalk gardener.

Plants for Light Soils

Gardening on clay, as I do, there are some herbaceous plants that I scarcely touch. But for anyone living on freely draining lime or sandy soils, they present no trouble at all, as long as they are handled at the right times of year.

Pyrethrums are typical of the sort of plant I mean. On light soils, you expect to meet them in every other garden; they are stalwarts of the old herbaceous border. But they abominate soils where the water hangs around them in winter, and if you should be so incautious as to lift, split and replant old clumps in autumn, at the start of their dormant season, the chances are that you will finish them off completely, whatever the soil. In early spring, on the other hand, just before they have started to make extensive growth, is an excellent time to be getting busy with pyrethrums. Or you can leave it till just after they have finished flowering and split them up in early July, along with the bearded irises. That will give them a nice slice of the growing season in which to get re-established.

Botanically speaking, pyrethrums belong to the huge genus *Chrysanthemum*. Their flowers may be single, yellow-eyed daisies, semi-double or double, and they come in a gay range of vivid pink and red shades. Their stems, on a healthy, well-nurtured plant, grow to 3 or even 4 ft., and they make splendid cut flowers. On the reverse side of the medal, they are floppy things and need discreet but efficient support, if being grown for garden effect. As they are stemmy plants this is not so easily given. They die ungracefully towards the end of June and the only possible treatment then is to cut them down to ground level, which leaves you with a large hole in your border during the important summer months.

If your garden is large enough to include a May-June border as one of its features, then pyrethrums will comprise an important ingredient along with irises, poppies, peonies, lupins, geums and veronicas. If not, then they are best relegated to a picking plot. There is a lot to be said for splitting and resetting them every year, in well manured ground. They will then reward you with a sub-sidiary crop of blossoms, invaluable for cutting in their autumn season.

In the same genus are the **shasta daisies,** cultivars of *Chrysan-themum maximum*. As border perennials that are also suitable for cutting, they take over from pyrethrums in the July season. No one, however, has ever yet succeeded in suffusing natural blood into the shasta daisy's cheeks and they are all dead (or nearly dead) white. When people say they do not like white flowers because they are funereal, this is the sort of white flower they are thinking of. However, the market knows what constitutes a good cut flower, and gets over this little prejudice by dyeing them—usually pink or pale blue. The result is distinctly pleasing.

Nevertheless, the shastas have their place as white flowers in the border, and they are manageable on clay soils. But they give of their best if split and replanted at least every other year, and spring is the obligatory season for this operation with the less hardy cultivars such as Esther Read. This shasta, with its neat, fully double white flowers, is the florists' favourite and it is also a splendid border plant: barely 2 ft. tall, requiring no support and providing a substantial autumn crop if the first is dead-headed. However, it has to be added that the autumn flowering tends to weaken the plants' capacity for overwintering successfully.

The yellow eye of single shasta daisies livens them up considerably. If you want a straightforward single with a large, bold flower on a 4-ft. plant, go for Everest. If you like the ragged effect of fimbriated rays (as though someone had been at them with scissors), then Phyllis Smith.

A disadvantage in the ranker growing shastas is the plant's dead-greenness, particularly before flowering. For this reason it is wise to exclude them from an all-grey-and-white border. They make it too heavy, and white phloxes have the same tendency. Shastas associate much more happily with scarlet *Lychnis chalce donica*, purple *Salvia superba* and yellow asphodels.

If you are one of those who have read about capsid bugs but never been able to pinpoint them in your own garden, single shasta daisies will give you your chance. Capsids are shy insects, and they dodge out of sight (for they are fast sprinters) on the approach of a hostile shadow. But they love to sit on the daisy flowers on a sunny day and, being green, they show up well against their white and yellow background. This is a formidable pest that feeds on plant sap. It can prevent or ruinously distort the flowering of fuchsias, dahlias, caryopteris, perovskias and many more, as well as shastas themselves. One should spray with Dicofol.

Another genus of composites that likes conditions of very free drainage is **Gaillardia**, and, again, its perennial members (all derived from *G. aristata*) should be planted in spring. Like heleniums and rudbeckias, gaillardias have daisies in which the rays are basically yellow but may be overlaid to a greater or lesser extent with bronze. This reddish-brown colouring tends to form a zone at the base of the rays, but in Mandarin, for instance, the entire ray is bronzed, right to its tips. The disc, moreover, is always a dark purplish colour, which makes a change from the usual yellow of daisy eyes. The great merit of perennial gaillardias is that they continue flowering for many months; their main defect is a thin, stemmy habit. They are the reverse of ground-covering but, being only 2½ ft. or so tall, are hardly worth supporting.

Rudbeckias will flourish on most soils, but the closely related **Echinaceas** must have it light. I find them hard to please on Wadhurst clay, but when I grew them on chalk they showed their satisfaction by self-sowing freely. The main botanical distinction separating *Echinacea* from *Rudbeckia* is the obvious one that the rays in the former are purple (or white) in colour, but yellow or brown in the latter.

E. purpurea is a sturdy, self-supporting perennial, 4 ft. tall, and a generous grouping makes a telling feature. The central disc is globular and prominent: the more intriguing because its dark colouring is offset by a spangling of bright orange anthers. There are some worthwhile modern cultivars in which the dusky purple of the rays has been improved, by selection, to brighter, clearer shades. White Lustre is an attractive albino.

Then, **scabious**. There are more than a dozen cultivated varieties of the perennial *Scabiosa caucasica,* which is evidence enough of this plant's popularity. But, again, it is happiest on light soils, and established plants should only be disturbed, for splitting up and increasing them, in spring. There is an endearing quality in the scabious flower that touches us even in comparatively insignificant, wild species. Doubtless the pincushion effect is largely responsible. But *S. caucasica* is showy by any standards and although never pure blue, near enough to pass for blue, while the white and lavender-coloured cultivars are valuable too. Valuable, but mainly as cut flowers, I always think. As border plants, these scabious will never let you down completely; they carry a continuous succession of flowers from June till October. But there are never enough at any one moment to be out-and-out effective.

There is a charming and little known perennial scabious that would give pleasure to a great many gardeners. This is *S. gramini-folia*. It grows only 18 in. tall. The mauve pincushions are about an inch across and freely produced, but it is the plant's silvery foliage that gives it a special quality.

Some of the **sages** are regrettably on the borderlines of hardiness. A light soil tips the balance in their favour. One such is *Salvia argentea,* a biennial that is grown for its wonderfully white-felted, broad, silky leaves. I cannot get much sense from *S. uliginosa,* ineptly named because, far from preferring a boggy situation, it is seldom seen at its best in this country except on the lightest (though well-manured) fare. It will then make a forest of 5-foot-tall stems, crowned, in autumn, with short spikes of light blue flowers. And they really are blue, not just euphemistically so. *S. ambigens* is a deeper, more intense shade but just as pure. I do manage to keep this species (which is tuberous-rooted) going, but my main trouble with it, again, is from capsid damage.

Kniphofias, the red-hot pokers, vary in hardiness considerably, the oldest cultivars being pretty reliable anywhere, but a light soil wins more than half the battle in the cultivation of the more exciting kinds. It is better not to disturb healthy, established clumps; they can be left for many years. But if you do want to propagate them by division, spring is the moment.

Health in the Greenhouse

The mood in most of my friends' greenhouses is distinctly sad. The plants look unhappy—not through any deficiency in kindness on their owner's part but, quite simply, because they are growing in too dry an atmosphere. Their leaves are matt and lustreless, hanging with a kind of pinched brittleness. And the owner's trouble is that, not knowing what a healthy plant should look like, he does not realise that anything is seriously amiss.

It is the standard designs of greenhouses and their fittings that are largely at fault. They do not help you to set about things in the right way. Greatest of bugbears is the slatted bench. Most of us need some sort of staging on which to set our pots and boxes at a convenient height. Wood slats are said to allow the plant all-round ventilation. So they do, but they also make it exceedingly difficult to combine good ventilation with the high humidity that is desirable for luxuriant growth from March to October.

The arrangement that best suits the plants, I find, is a strong framework of staging, say 3 ft. from front to back, on which are laid sheets of asbestos or of corrugated iron. It is best for these to be not quite watertight, so that they allow the passage of excess water. Over them is laid a layer of fine gravel: the staging needs a 2-inch-wide lip to contain this. I use the $\frac{3}{16}$ horticultural grit (see pages 57-8) that comprises the 'sand' in John Innes composts but has a variety of other uses. The substance must be coarse enough to allow the free passage of water but it must also be fine enough to enable you to stand pots level on it without difficulty.

Now, as to the paths and the floor under the benches: usually there is far too much concrete around, and this, again, is conducive to a dry atmosphere. You can water it, but it dries out again too quickly. I recommend a gravel or grit path, contained by an edging of wood to prevent it spreading under the staging. Under the staging itself I should leave the natural earth of the ground that the greenhouse is covering. For cleanliness and to get an even cover on which to stand pots under the bench, spread another layer of grit or fine gravel.

This space under the benches is extremely useful. You can stand arums here and boxes of geranium cuttings, whose light requirements in winter are very low. And you can store boxes and pots of all kinds of dormant bulbs and tubers: hippeastrums, achimenes, dahlias, cannas. In summer, when requirements for storage space are at a minimum, I allow ferns to take charge under the staging. These are all self-sown wildings: bracken, hart's-tongue and male ferns. Their greenery in summer provides a valuable reservoir of humidity. In winter I cut them all away, because at this season excess humidity is undesirable, and anyway I need the storage space again.

We have now reached a situation in which not only the soil in your plant pots is holding moisture, but also the entire floor of the house and the benching. As the house heats up by day, these areas will all be contributing water vapour. The red spider mite is an excellent indicator of whether the air in your greenhouse is damp enough. If it is, you will never be troubled by this pest (except on *Datura suaveolens*). But if not, then the mites will build up, especially in summer, to a vast population. This is a minute, very pale yellow, almost colourless creature (of the spider family), just visible to the naked eye and usually found crawling about on the undersides of leaves—particularly soft leaves like the peach's, the primula's or the passion flower's. You can gain control with a chemical such as azobenzene, but it is far more sensible not to give the pest its chance.

The humid atmosphere of the greenhouse that provides ideal growing conditions should never be allowed to become close or stagnant. It should be combined with freely circulating air. Another frequent fault in greenhouse design is failure to provide enough ventilators. Amateurs often imagine that they are doing something rather clever by whacking up the temperature in a greenhouse, especially if it is, for instance, a sunny October or March day when the contrast between inside and out is especially marked. You had far better err a bit on the side of too much air than too little and that is true of every season. Prop your greenhouse door open, by day, whenever the weather is mild and the wind not howling through it at 20 knots. And do not automatically shut down at night. From April till November, there are far more nights when you should leave on generous ventilation, in a cool greenhouse, than not.

If the plants are all in moveable containers, it is a good plan to have a complete turn-out of greenhouse contents each summer —say for a couple of months from mid-July. It is quite warm enough for nearly all of them outside, at that season, but you do need a sheltered and handy position on which to stand your pots. Then you can give the house a thorough clean-out, washing the glass and turning the grit on the staging. You can shut it down so that it bakes inside. This catches on the hop any pests that might be building up, and the shift gives you the chance to attend to all your plants individually as you handle them, which you might otherwise fail to do if they never had to be moved. Some will want re-potting. With others it will be enough to peel off dead foliage, remove the old (probably green) surface layer of soil (prodding around among the top-most roots with a pointed, wooden label) and thereafter top-dress with fresh potting compost.

From late October till March, the main hazard in your greenhouse will be from excess humidity. Only water your plants when they are dry but when you do water them, make it a thorough dose that will soak its way right through the pots. 'Plenty but seldom' is the recipe, not 'little and often.'

The grey mould fungus, *Botrytis cinerea*, which appears as a fur coat on stems and leaves, can be a great scourge in winter. Go over your plants at frequent intervals and remove any dying or infected leaves, otherwise the trouble can rapidly spread and polish off large numbers of susceptible plants such as *Mimulus glutinosus* and gazanias. If you are overwintering autumn-struck cuttings of plants such as these, under glass, those that were struck latest will be in the softest and most vulnerable condition. In some cases it will be better to strike them earlier, say in July, so that the plant is already tough and well established by the winter. In other cases, like bedding verbenas or *Helichrysum petiolatum*, where rotting is no great danger, and the later they're struck the better, October will be soon enough.

Another way you can help young rooted cuttings through the winter, under very cool glass with only enough heat just to keep the frost out, is by overwintering them in the pots in which they were struck. There will be, perhaps, 7 cuttings in a 3½ in. pot. The cutting compost is light and free-draining, which will be all to the good. Pot them off individually into John Innes No. 2 in March, when they can make use of the extra nourishment. If this job is done in autumn, when the days are getting shorter and colder, the plants cannot make use of the stronger mixture but, on the contrary, will be more susceptible to rotting.

Paradoxically, botrytis, although a mould, is often most serious on plants that are dry at the root. So, in winter, keep the plant's foliage as dry as you can but the roots moist—except for succulents, that is, which can go without water for several months, especially the cacti.

Clay pots dry out very much more quickly than plastic. Do not on that account, go all out for the latter so as to save yourself trouble. Plants that are simply being grown on might just as well be grown in plastic containers but those that will be used for display in their growing pots *look* so much better in clay. This is a point which many gardeners and nurserymen ignore.

Troubles from botrytis will be far less likely in a greenhouse whose minimum winter temperature is maintained at around 45° F. Remember, though, that the expense of heating doubles for every extra five degrees you demand. Of course you will insist on the extra heat in a conservatory, where you will want to be able to relax, and enjoy yourself quite apart from your plants' preferences. But where a greenhouse is mainly being used to bring plants on, either for the house or for the garden, then it is surprising what a vigilant gardener can do with no more heat than will exclude frost. And so cheaply.

Coming to Terms with a Lawn

Pep articles on lawn management are normally considered appropriate by the horticultural journalist in search of fodder at certain times of the year, especially spring. If he has no garden of his own (and it's surprising what a lot of them haven't) he's in a happy position for telling others exactly what they should be doing or resolving to do, without fear of recoil. Unfortunately I have a garden, a good deal visited, in which the lawns were hastily prepared on high-quality clay sub-soil, over 50 years ago.

I also have bitches. Now dogs are selective, or sporadic, shrub-killers, but bitches attack the turf. I have tried to train mine to favour the rough grass, but when this begins to lengthen, they resent its dampness against their bellies (being dachshounds, whose bellies the grass is not long in reaching). You can dilute the lethal potion by following up with a watering-can, but that works only when the girls make attended sorties on limited and planned occasions, not when they are living half their days in the garden, as in the summer months.

Each of us has his own special lawn problems, and they are legion. The more you care, the worse and the more numerous the problems become. One of my keenest and most skilled of gardening friends can turn a completely blind eye to weeds in his turf. He is, I should say, a happy gardener. But I do find his plantains obtrusive and, after all, they succumb most readily to a dose of selective weedkiller; more promptly than daisies by far. However, he points out that they would leave a nasty gap.

If I knew more about their different species, I should write at length on the mosses of lawns. There are mosses for every condition, not just for acid lawns with poor drainage. Even on free-draining, chalky soils there are mosses to meet the situation. All of them are beautiful, and so wonderfully soft and spongy to tread on. It is what visitors from the Continent most admire in English lawns; that and the fact of being allowed to walk on them at all.

Then there is the nice question of whether to consider clover a weed or not. Of course the lawn nut must, but what about the ordinary chap who wants a bit of time left over to spend on his borders? You have to be a persistent nagger to rid yourself of wild white clover, so why not rationalise a little and dwell on its virtues? A small, neat leaf; stoloniferous, carpeting habit; imperviousness to drought; nitrogen-fixing root nodules; forage for bees. It all adds up, and some gardeners welcome a situation they feel it beyond them to oppose, and deliberately sow clover seed on the patches that are still free of it. But, like most forms of life, clover is cussed and it seldom makes a uniform sward.

How fascinating to scan the lawns by torchlight, on a dewy night, and see their teeming earthworm population all laid out, dew-bathing presumably. Approach your beam to any individual worm, and it suddenly shoots underground, for its tail always keeps contact with the hole from which it emerged, and can pull it back into safety with remarkable agility. Worms aerate the soil. Badly drained at the best of times, I reckon that my own lawns would seize up if deprived of their worm cohorts. On younger, more carefully prepared lawns, worms are a doubtful asset and their casts are very much more obtrusive.

Most worm-killing agents bring their victims writhing to the surface, where they have to be swept up and disposed of; a gory ploy. Lead arsenate has the great advantages of killing the worms underground and of being persistent over several years. This is what I use in my frame yard where I have pots standing. Worms in pots stop up the drainage and frequently kill its contents, so something has to be done about it. A disadvantage in lead arsenate is that it is sometimes and inexplicably ineffective. Also, it is poisonous.

I have only touched on, not tried to cover the troubles attendant upon lawn management. There are few greater garden pleasures than the contemplation of a perfectly kept lawn, but it must be someone else's and not your own, otherwise you are only too painfully involved in the work of upkeep. I remarked in a letter to a friend in Wareham who keeps the finest turf I know of anywhere, that this involves more labour than a similar area of intensely gardened borders. 'How right you are,' he replied. 'Apart from anything else, I have had to spray at least five times for cortisium and fusarium apart from moss and fertilisers. Wish I could chuck it but directly one gives up the lawns all go to hell.' Of course, he does not really wish to chuck it because, after all, the results are superb and I take off my proverbial hat to any perfectionist in any department of gardening, even the cultivation of exhibition chrysanthemums. Only leave me my peace.

Grand Colonisers on the March

There are many plants that gain entry into our gardens by reason of some wheedling charm yet turn out, once established, to be in-eradicable weeds. Still, the charm remains, though the gardener's jaundiced eye can no longer appreciate it. It might be an idea, for a no-trouble enthusiast starting a garden from scratch, to plant entirely with these terrifying but beautiful rampers. In no time, the garden would be fully furnished, and the furniture could fight out its destiny without the landlord caring a fig for the outcome. Of course, the neighbours would have something to say.

These plants are sometimes described in nursery catalogues as grand colonisers. They spread either by seminal or by vegetative methods: seldom both ways simultaneously. An outstanding exception to this general tenet is **Campanula rapunculoides.** Above ground, it sets seeds by the thousand, and they are so small and light that the wind can carry them to considerable distances. Underground they make thin white rhizomes that creep into and through every adjacent group of plants, and are practically impossible to extract therefrom. Economically described in the seedsman's catalogue as having 'bluish-violet, drooping funnel-shaped flowers,' no notion of its other propensities is conveyed, and danger of deception is increased by the similarly named *C. rapunculus.* This is the perfectly innocuous biennial rampion, whose fleshy white roots we can eat in winter salads; or, if we leave the roots alone, we can admire sheaves of purple bells on slender stalks in the following summer.

Among vegetative spreaders, the **polygonums** have earned themselves the worst name, and they include two or three species that possibly take the prize as giants among hardy herbaceous perennials. *Polygonum cuspidatum* is one such. It is sometimes mistaken for a bamboo and sends up 10-ft. canes, annually. A froth of white flowers is carried in autumn and the red-brown stems, though dead, look handsome throughout the winter. One way of containing this sort of plant, as also the more exuberant bamboos, is as a lawn specimen, where you can mow right up to and all round it, decapitating any young shoots that have strayed into the turf. But your mowing should be regular. At Hampton Court, there is a hedge of it on the far side of the canal. Sited where it can get into no mischief, anyone can enjoy this unusual hedging plant.

Some of the **spurges** are surprisingly invasive, especially on moist soils. In dry conditions, *Euphorbia sikkimensis* may be quite difficult to establish and keep going. With me it grows 7 ft. tall and each year extends underground by about a foot in all directions. I just have to be firm with it, and chop round with a spade. *E. griffithii* is even more enterprising, adept at elbowing (or nosing) its way through crowds. In every situation, it should go far. The cultivar that has been attractively named Fireglow, is sometimes claimed to be less inclined to stray. Only slightly less. Its flower colouring is very good but its foliage is not so interestingly tinted as in some other cultivars.

When I read that *Geranium nodosum* was a 'valuable coloniser for any shady place,' I planted it under some magnolias. I have a weakness for geraniums but this one's flowers, described as 'cool, lilac-pink,' offended my sight as a most villainous and dirty magenta. That one plant had not been established for more than six months when I set about eradicating it, and the job took three years to accomplish.

Among rock plants, the innocent looking **Veronica filiformis,** with its candid, baby-blue eyes, is really the most dangerous felon. It is an overground runner, so you can see what it is at, but, as in a nightmare, you are helpless to do anything about it. This speedwell's favourite trick is to get into your lawn, where selective weedkillers have little effect on it, and then to spread itself by small pieces breaking off and getting picked up on the mower's roller. From its new site it makes a fiendish invasion of borders on the opposite side from its original station. It is only too true that you should look on every plant gift from however well-meaning a friend, not as a gift horse but as one of the Trojan breed. For either the plant itself may turn out to be an invader (which was why your friend had some of it to spare for you), or else the invader was lurking unnoticed among the roots or stems of its harmless host. This is invariably the way ground elder gains access to a garden. It is a weed of cultivation, not found in new gardens, but always introduced. All new plants from unexamined sources should be regarded as quarantine suspects for their first season.

4. Facts, Failings and Contradictions

The Fallible Plant

Why Don't They Flower?

At many points through this book I have touched on the subject of why plants will sometimes flower (and, in some cases, fruit) freely, sometimes poorly or not at all, but I want to gather a few of the threads of this fascinating but baffling subject together, here. Before going into details it is, I think, possible to pin-point certain prevailing themes. There is heredity, for one. With certain species of plants (e.g. *Kolkwitzia amabilis*) we know that there are good and bad flowering strains around. Then there is climate. Abundance of sun, abundance of rain or a combination of the two, at key seasons or in key sites (your garden has its micro-climates) will promote flowering in many plants. Frost damage may prevent it. Soil: some plants tend to flower more freely on well drained rather than on water-holding soils and *vice versa*. Mechanical factors: if birds, insects or other creatures consume some vital part of a plant, it may be unable to flower. Physiological factors: these are closely linked with climate and nutrients, and there are cases of a plant 'exhausting' itself with heavy blossoming and fruiting in one year to the detriment of the next year's crop. The age and maturity of a plant comes under this heading, too.

Unfortunately I cannot write with the authority of a trained plant physiologist, because I am not one, but I can write with the experience of a trained and reasonably observant gardener.

I have already said a good deal on **heredity** as it affects freedom of flowering with special reference to *Magnolia grandiflora* and its precociously flowering clones Exmouth and Goliath (pages 80-1). And I have commented on the fact that perennials grown from seed tend to mature more slowly and later than those that are propagated from cuttings. Enough on that.

Climate has many influences. We are not surprised that plants should flower most freely following a hot summer, but the effects are sometimes so delayed that we may ascribe the result to some other factor. As I mentioned (page 135) *Zephyranthes candida* flowers best in a hot summer. It flowers in August and September and is mainly affected by the weather immediately prior to its flowering season. A boiling June and July will have the desired results. *Iris stylosa* (properly *I. unguicularis*) shows its reactions to a summer baking or the lack of it in its winter flowering season. But the Australian bottle-brush, *Callistemon subulatus* (*C. citrinus*), which flowers in early July, is mainly influenced in its generosity by the weather of twelve months earlier.

Hollies flower, unnoticed, in May but it is their fruiting that we care about, in the following winter. The flowering of a female holly (the males flower freely every year, but that is of no interest to gardeners or flower arrangers) depends partly on the ripening influence of the previous summer or summers; partly on its state of 'exhaustion' following the production of a heavy crop of berries. Other things being equal, you would expect a hot summer one year to result in generous flowering and fruiting the next. But if the hot summer coincides with a year in which the holly is fruiting heavily anyway, it may be in no fit state to do the same again in the next year.

Perhaps it is perverse in me to start by citing the holly, which is of mere aesthetic and superstitious concern to humans, rather than fruit trees (apples, pears and plums) which touch us nearer the heart—in the stomach, to wit. The irritating habit of biennial bearing so often evidenced by certain varieties may be caused by too heavy cropping in one year being followed by a rest in the next.

Such behaviour is founded on what the physiologists call the carbohydrate/nitrogen ratio. Concentrations of carbohydrates (sugars, starches) in a plant promote favourable conditions for flowering and fruiting. A high concentration of nitrogenous compounds, by contrast, promotes vegetative (leaf and shoot) growth.

Heavy flowering and fruiting exhausts the reserves of carbohydrates in a plant; inhibits, in it, the initiation of new flower buds for the next season (and perhaps for the season after, too) and results in barrenness until reserves have been built up again. The sun and hot weather aid and abet the build-up of starch and sugars in a plant. Rain and manuring with nitrogenous fertilisers promotes growth at the expense of carbohydrates and hence of flowering. A balance needs to be achieved between the two, if the ideal of a vigorous and healthy plant that also flowers and fruits abundantly, is to be attained.

Where lilacs are concerned, I have already pointed out that the effort of over-prolific flowering is in itself so exhausting that a rest-year must be expected to ensue, even if you promptly remove the dead heads so that the shrub is not obliged to fruit. With rhododendrons, on the other hand, matters may be rather differently arranged. Some of the most popular, ultra-hardy hybrids will flower freely every year, no matter what the weather and whether you remove their spent blooms or not. Many of the choicer species, however, do have a biennial-flowering habit. Each flower truss has one, two or three leaf buds immediately below it. They are noticeably inhibited by flowering and break into later and feebler growth than shoots borne on branches that are not flowering. It is generally reckoned—though I have not heard of anyone proving it experimentally, and have doubts myself—that the dead-heading of most rhododendrons is very well worth doing (awkward and tedious though the job is, on a large bush) in order to promote freer flowering in the following year.

The effects of climate, sunshine and summer temperatures are also evident in the behaviour of the same shrub when grown in Sussex (say) or in Sutherland. *Camellia japonica* and its cultivars are normally grown and flower freely in the shade, in south-east England. But in north-west Scotland their most promising site will be against a sunny, south-facing wall. Otherwise they just do not set flower buds. The same goes for forsythias and, to an extent applies also to lilacs and bearded irises. They all tend to be more costive in the north. *Daphne odora* is another such plant, free flowering in sun or in shade in the south and in East Anglia, but when you get into the Midlands, even, it has to be considered a shy-flowerer, demanding every scrap of sun and heat available.

In young shrubs, the carbohydrate/nitrogen ratio is low and

this often results, not unexpectedly, in strong growth but little or no flowering. This is not altogether to be deprecated because one wants a shrub to build up a good, bulky framework. If it starts flowering too freely at an early age, it may remain a runt to the end of its days. However, gardeners include a good many impatient people who cannot bear to contemplate a waiting period of 6 or 8 years before a young shrub settles down to flowering. They should steer clear of the large-leaved and most exciting rhododendrons and of many other shrubs such as winter-sweet (*Chimonanthus praecox*), kowhai (*Sophora tetraptera*), *Magnolia kobus* and some wisterias, notably *Wisteria floribunda* 'Macrobotrys'.

Nutrition of young shrubs is a matter deserving some thought. The thoughtless gardener tends to starve them. But it is possible to overfeed, too. Not only can this promote soft, lush, frost- and wind-susceptible growth, but it can needlessly delay flowering. This is why I recommend growing *Cotinus coggygria* (*Rhus cotinus*) and *C. americana* (*R. cotinoides*) in a lawn. In a well-manured shrubbery they may grow too strongly and coarsely either to flower or to colour up attractively in the autumn, for many years. As lawn specimens, however, they are automatically subjected to the strongly inhibiting influence on their growth of the grass turf.

A wisteria's coming of age may also be needlessly delayed by too vigorous growth in its youth. Pruning checks growth and vigour and it is standard practice with a wisteria to spur back its young shoots to within an inch or two of the base in July, each year. The fact of doing this job in the middle of the wisteria's growing season acts as an additional check. Summer pruning is also widely practised, with the same end in view, on fruit trees.

An over-vigorous tree can sometimes be encouraged to grow less strongly and hence start flowering and fruiting, by bark-ring-ing. A strip of rind is removed from right round the tree trunk. If this strip is too wide, the tree will be killed (see the next chapter), so it is a case of playing with fire. A half-inch-wide strip, such as can heal over in the course of one season, should not be exceeded in most cases.

Root pruning has the same end in view. A trench is taken out from round the base of a non-productive shrub or tree at a dis-tance of 4 or 5 ft. from its main stem, and its roots are severed with a sharp spade. It is usual to do one half of the circle in one winter and complete the other half in the next.

Or you may confine a plant's roots (in a pot, for instance), so as to check its growth. Fig trees are often grown in a confined root run so as to bring them on to fruit at an early age. A greenhouse climber like *Jasminum polyanthum, J. primulinum* or a bougainvillæa will be less rampant and flower better if their roots are confined in a pot or box.

Another growth-checking, flower-and-fruit-promoting gambit, practised on wisterias and on many crops (notably tomatoes) is the application of potash fertiliser dressings, while withholding nitrogen. The potash has the desired effect of inhibiting the plant's uptake of nitrogen, and it is the nitrogen that is making it grow too lushly.

The act of taking cuttings largely prevents the uptake of nutrients, and especially of nitrogen, in the cutting material, until it has made roots and become a plant. There is temporarily a high carbohydrate/nitrogen ratio in such shoots and this often causes them to flower. I regularly take cutting material in July or August from a 10-foot-tall bush of *Elaeagnus pungens* 'Maculata'. This bush has never flowered in its life (as it is grown for its foliage, this is no serious matter). But the cuttings invariably flower in their propagating frame in the same October-November. The flowers are quite insignificant but so sweetly scented that they draw attention to themselves in this way. *Daphne odora* behaves in like manner. Newly rooted cuttings that were struck in July will always flower in the following March, but the young, strongly growing plant will not flower again for two or three years after that.

Some plants flower much more freely in a sunny site in your garden than they would in shade. Periwinkles and the Rose of Sharon (*Hypericum calycinum*) are often recommended as ground cover in shade; the elephant-eared *Bergenia cordiflolia*, likewise. But if it is flowers you're after, get them into the sun, where they will also do their ground covering every bit as well.

Many bulbous plants derive from hotter climates than ours: notably from the Mediterranean, the Middle East and from South Africa. In this climate they tend to get, not only too little sun, but too much moisture in their resting season, when they do not want any moisture at all. This is why we plant them in a hot spot and in soil where they get the freest possible drainage. A raised bed is often a good place for such as these. Then we can hope to see them flowering rather than merely leafing or even rotting away.

But there are other bulbs from cool temperate regions that can take or even need a great deal more moisture. When a cold winter is followed by a thumping good daffodil season, you will hear people say the daffies seem to have enjoyed the snow. In fact it was decided how well or badly the daffies would flower, way back in their previous growing season when they were storing up supplies in their bulbs and laying down flower buds. My own unsubstantiated observations suggest that if they get abundant moisture in May, this more than any other factor will promote free flowering in the next spring. The snakeshead fritillary is a native of water meadows and I have noticed that this, too, flowers best in the spring following a wet spring. In a succession of dry springs, flowering is very poor indeed and the bulbs dwindle. The same could be expected to happen where they were grown on a light sandy soil instead of on the water-holding clay or alluvial stodge that they prefer.

Severe frost in winter will no more prejudice subsequent flowering than will a slight frost in spring. Even two or three degrees in April or May can do a vast deal of harm, both seen and unnoticed. Seen damage will be to rhododendrons and azaleas in flower. Unseen, to early flowering clematis, for instance. If your *Clematis montana, C. alpina* or *C. macropetala* fail to flower well in late April and May, the chances are that their young flower buds were caught by frost at that most vulnerable moment when the leaf-, flower- and shoot-buds (they are all rolled into one) first expanded in late March or early April.

Hydrangea shoots and branches often survive the winter only to be caught on the wrong foot in spring. Their buds tend to unfold rather early and will then be unable to put up any sort of fight against a late frost. The unobservant gardener will only begin to realise that something is amiss when no flowers appear in July and August; merely a superabundance of foliage.

Some plants stop flowering when they get old and woody. Such are the dianthus tribe and the sea thrift (*Armeria maritima*). You must start again with dianthus by taking cuttings, and with the thrift by pulling an old plant into pieces and pushing these into the ground. So too with heucheras. The popular purple-leaved plum, *Prunus cerasifera* 'Atropurpurea' also tends to stop flowering in old age. I have never had the chance to experiment on such a specimen but should like to try the effect of lopping the tree all over. This is a dangerous performance with plums and cherries, as they are subject to dire bacterial and fungal diseases. The safest time for the operation would be in spring, as growth was being renewed, and one would treat the wounds with a protective wound dressing such as 'Arbrex'. If the tree remained healthy it could be expected to make strong young shoots on which it would flower in the following spring. Regular pruning of this kind, immediately after flowering, is what one normally practises on bush prunuses like *P. triloba, P. cistena* and *P. tenella* in order to make them produce abundant young shoots on which to flower in the next spring. *Osmanthus delavayi* is a similar case, flowering 3 or 4 times as freely in the next year if encouraged to make an abundance of young shoots by clipping it over immediately after flowering in May.

Congestion (and consequent starvation) is a factor that may limit or prevent flowering, particularly of certain bulbs. *Scilla peruviana* needs splitting and replanting every third year or so, and bulbs such as *Zephyranthes candida* and *Sternbergia lutea* do need dividing from time to time. Some of the *Narcissus* tribe are subject to overcrowding, but, if naturalised, their replanting is really too big a task to tackle.

Damage to dormant and expanding flower buds by birds often completely prevents flowering of many trees and shrubs, especially in rural areas. The *Prunus* tribe are particularly susceptible and this is widely recognised. But the non-flowering of other shrubs frequently fails to be ascribed to bird-pecking, although it should be. Japanese quinces, weigelas, kerrias, mahonias, wisterias (every year in my garden) and viburnums of the *Viburnum carlesii* type are all stripped by birds at various times and in sundry places. With viburnums, the blackened, charred-looking remains are generally ascribed to frost damage or to an unidentified disease, but it is them birds again. Either move to the suburbs or stop growing the susceptible shrubs. Bird repellents are of limited efficacy, so far; black cotton works sometimes but often not at all.

It is worth a trial. 'Scaraweb' is good if you can bear the sight of it.

Capsid bugs often prevent their more susceptible hosts from flowering, in particular *Caryopteris* and *Perovskia*; also fuchsias. A tarsonemid mite has, in the last ten years or so, been increasingly on the rampage among the most popular group of Novae-Belgiae asters (michaelmas daisies). They, too, are prevented from flowering. The R.H.S. finds that spraying with the chemical Dicofol is effective, but I am quite happily giving up growing these plants altogether. Mildew gets worse on them from year to year and verticillium wilt is a frequent and lethal disease among their ranks. They flower for a very short time in autumn and look terribly boring all through the summer. So, one way and another, I have few regrets. There are still plenty of unsophisticated asters that are easy to grow and have an unforced charm that the 'improved' cultivars have lost, with their emphasis on being showy.

There still seems no explanation for the non-flowering or capricious flowering habits of certain plants. *Gentiana acaulis* (now *G. excisa*) is the most notorious case in point. We all know it likes a sunny aspect but after that it is anyone's guess. In some gardens it flowers like mad without any sort of coddling or propitiation on the owner's part; in others it just grows with never a flower to be seen. In that case you can try it in different parts of the garden and if none of them suit it, go blithely without and take your pleasure from admiring other gardeners' spring gentians or, better still, from a trip to the Alps.

Mysterious Deaths

When a plant dies in your garden, how do you react? Do you re-enact one of the historic tragic roles: Medea, Phaedra, Werther, Macbeth? Do you lash out? Or do you, with a glazed, all-passion-spent-expression, merely comment that plants invariably die on you, anyway, and that you only have to look at one for it to wilt forthwith? Or perhaps you gleefully rub your hands and say 'Good. Now that's made room for a mandragora. I have been longing for the excuse to get one for years.'

For myself, I have more or less reached this last state, but I do dislike a plant dying without my being able to pin-point the cause. It leaves an uneasy sense of incompleteness. Every death should be rounded off with a diagnosis—otherwise who knows but what 'they' may not be at work? And it will be only a matter of time before they strike again.

There should be abundant circumstantial evidence to guide you to a diagnosis. Here is a list of eight primary possibilities:

(1) Disease
(2) Pests
(3) Frost
(4) Drought
(5) Drainage and drains (a subtle distinction will emerge)
(6) Soil alkalinity
(7) Bad treatment somewhere along the transplanting line
(8) Brown Fingers

Let us examine these in turn, remembering that it is total death we are talking about, not disabilities, however crippling. We must keep the subject within bounds.

First and foremost, then, **diseases**. Certain plants are subject to recognised and sometimes killing diseases. For instance, wilt disease of clematis or leaf blotch of hellebores. But of far greater importance are the diseases that attack a wide range of plants. Most widespread and serious of these is the disease without a name caused by the honey fungus, *Armillaria mellea*.

Writing of it from the R.H.S. Plant Pathology Department at Wisley, Miss Audrey Brooks says that, occurring every year regardless of weather, this is one of the most troublesome fungus parasites, 'as it can kill old and valuable trees and shrubs, and can also attack herbaceous and bulbous plants. We have received specimens of *Ballota pseudodictamnus*, camellias and also daffodil and tulip bulbs affected by this root parasite as well as the more common host plants such as privet, roses and rhododendrons. On average one letter a day is written on the subject of the Honey Fungus, and the advice we give is that all plants affected by this trouble should be dug out, together with as many of the roots as possible. The soil in the area should then be sterilised with a 2 per cent. solution of formalin, or should be changed completely.'

Do not imagine that this is a disease that will pass you by. Especially in established gardens it will strike sooner or later. In my own garden it has killed a number of old orchard trees. They always say, for this reason, that an old orchard is the worst of sites for a new garden. But there are three other areas in my garden where honey fungus is rife and it would be very difficult and laborious to get rid of it. In each case a tree was the original victim and thereafter became a source of infection because the fungus can perennate on any bits of tree root that are left in the ground.

The most tiresome area of infection, with me, is in the top section of my Long Border—a mixed border of shrubs, herbaceous plants, bulbs and annuals. Two old apple trees stood in this part of the border and started the trouble. I have, as a result, lost a hibiscus, a deutzia, a succession of *Euphorbia wulfenii* plants, an entire patch or *Iris graminea* and a number of other victims that I have mercifully forgotten about. Only when I occasionally come upon a cache of old labels is it brought home to me how frequent and extensive my losses are. I believe that this fungus also carries on a running battle with my Japanese anemones and with *Astrantia maxima.* Running is the literal word, for these both spread by underground rhizomes and the disease never quite catches up on them.

It is true that you never know what will go next but, by the same token, you do know that much will be spared, which is why I have never confronted the enemy. I keep planting and hoping that what I plant will be immune. There is very little definite evidence of reliable immunity. Some practised gardeners claim that magnolias are spared, but I do not set much store by that.

The easiest way of recognising this fungus is from its fruiting bodies in the autumn. They are not necessarily produced, but when they are, you know what you are up against. These are tufts of toadstools, typically the colour of darkish heather honey. They usually come up from the ground. Another recognisable feature, at any season, are its 'bootlaces', by which the fungus spreads and perennates. Look for these black, bootlace-like growths on the surface of dead bits of infected wood (but underneath the bark). Sometimes they are obvious; more often not.

Another killer is *Nectria cinnabarina,* the coral spot fungus. Its fruiting bodies appear as a rash of small, cushiony pustules, coral red in colour, covering the dead twigs and branches on which the fungus has been sustaining itself. It can be very pretty. This fungus is always with us, and spends most of its time feeding on dead twigs such as pea-sticks. But from dead tissue it can spread to live, and then the trouble starts. It is especially prevalent on redcurrant bushes. As redcurrants fruit on spurs set close to their old wood, we prune them by cutting all their young lateral shoots back to a stump, within half an inch of the base. However cleanly we perform this operation, each cut inevitably leaves a snag that dies; and as dead snags are the invariable points of entry for the coral spot fungus, it is not surprising that the redcurrants' multiple invitation is sooner or later accepted. First one branch dies, then the whole bush. You can cut a dead branch out and hope thus to stem the infection, but, in redcurrants at least, it seldom does.

Some shrubs seem particularly prone to attack, and a special watch should be kept on these, cutting out infected wood as soon as it dies, and always cutting back flush with a live branch, never leaving a snag. The winter sweet, *Chimonanthus praecox* is a frequent victim and so are the judas tree, *Cercis siliquastrum*, the dwarf buck-eye, *Aesculus parviflora* and also *Elaeagnus pungens*. Figs and spiraeas such as *Spiraea arguta* are also easily infected, but never too seriously, because they grow from a stool; if one branch dies, others can sprout from ground level to take its place. The fungus works above-ground only.

Silver Leaf disease, caused by the fungus *Stereum purpureum*, is most commonly noticed on plum trees or bushes such as *Prunus triloba* and on morello cherries; sometimes, also, on apples and commonly on the Portugal laurel, *Prunus lusitanica*. It is also quite frequent on laburnum, poplar, rhododendron and many other trees and shrubs but does not necessarily show the very characteristic and easily recognised silver leafing. If you can cut out an infected branch before the whole bush or tree has become infected you may save the day.

Bacterial canker carries away many a cherry tree. It is difficult to do anything constructive about bacterial diseases in general, as they are not controlled by spraying. Fire Blight of pear trees, hawthorns, cotoneasters and other shrubby members of the rose family has lately become endemic in this country, but is serious only in the hotter south-east and in hot summers. It is still a notifiable disease. I have yet to see it but my friends from the Ministry tell me I should have no trouble in recognising it. I hope

I shall not have to, but neither shall I keep my eyes shut. Soft Rot of bearded (and other) iris rhizomes is caused by a bacterial infection. You notice the foliage turning brown, often at flowering time, and can confirm the source of trouble by the revolting smell of infected rhizomes. Whole clumps are not necessarily involved and you must get rid of the diseased plants, or parts of plants and start the healthy pieces off again on clean ground.

A number of soil-borne fungus diseases cause annuals to die suddenly in the middle of their growing season. An off-the-cuff list of victims in my garden that have caused me secondary anguish would include zinnias, tithonias, China asters, annual rudbeckias, *Gilia rubra*, lobelias (*Lobelia erinus*) and cleomes. Rotation of crops is undoubtedly the simplest solution, here, though you will never be quite free of these troubles. Hardy primulas (including polyanthus) often die of root rots caused by one or other of two fungi with a preference for them. Another perennial that is often 'took sudden' by a soil-borne disease (usually in the middle of its summer growing season) is *Dimorphotheca barberiae,* the hardiest perennial of this South African tribe. When you see the plant ailing, take cuttings quickly and, when they have rooted, plant them out in a different place.

Pests more often maim than kill, but there are too many exceptions for that statement to be established as any sort of rule. Leatherjackets (the larvae of crane flies or daddy-long-legs) build up into plague populations in some years and they eat plant roots; or they will eat through the collar of a newly planted-out annual and destroy it overnight. They are terrors with the beautiful perennial Cardinal Flower, *Lobelia cardinalis.* Their worst damage is executed in spring and early summer when they are at their largest and most voracious.

Ants often kill plants—even quite large shrubs—simply by their disturbing presence in the soil in very large numbers. They can make rock gardening and gardening among paving stones difficult because they are so difficult to get at and destroy, here. They respond to a variety of insecticides but are much more resistant than most insects. Some gardeners find that the Japanese ant-killer (a liquid of undisclosed constituents) works like a charm; others find that, like most charms, it does not work at all.

Moles, too, destroy by loosening plant roots or even by lifting them right out of the ground. I do not advise messing around with old wives' remedies. If you feel you must rid your garden of them, call in your nearest pest control firm (the same outfit usually deals with rats and mice) and they will lay earthworms dipped in strychnine in the mole-runs.

Deer, hares and rabbits can all be lethal, especially serious when they eat the bark off trees in wintry weather. A circle of bark removed from a tree will kill it.

You will protect your plants from **frost** if you think they are worth it (I have mentioned one method for *Senecio rotundifolius* in my seaside shrubs chapter), or you will overwinter cuttings under glass of recognised susceptibles and let the parents take their chance in the garden, or you can let your plants take their un-protected chance in the garden and just fill the gaps with some-thing else if and when the necessity arrives.

It is worth mentioning that when a shrub sheds all or most of its leaves, following a shock like transplanting or frost, it has a high chance of recovery. The leaf-dropping is a defence mechan-ism and cuts down on transpiration at a time when the roots are in no fit state to replace water losses. If, on the other hand, the leaves die while still on the tree or shrub, then it is probably a gonner.

Drought, like frost, has delayed-action effects, especially on trees and shrubs. It may kill or maim a small plant quickly enough but large specimens often fail to show distress until the following winter, by which time it is too late to do anything to save them. Do become irrigation-conscious. It pays over and over again. In my garden, there is a topiary yew in the shape of a peacock but the peacock has for some undiagnosed reason died, while its supporting plinth (all part of the same plant), right down to ground level, has remained in good health. Many visitors love this dead peacock more than anything in our garden and it provides them with a wonderful talking point. If they see it in the spring, they sagely remark 'Ah! we can see the frost has hit you.' If in autumn, '*You've* suffered from the drought, we can see.' A versatile bird.

Badly drained land on which the water lies without getting away in certain seasons, is death to the majority of plants. Some, such as lilacs, are especially susceptible. If you are starting a garden

on heavy land it is really essential to put in a comprehensive network of land drains, at the outset. Even on quite a steepish slope,
clay soils can get waterlogged unless drained.

It is surprising how often faulty sewage disposal will not be
noticed or, at least, not be remedied by its owner until the
effluent has killed a number of valuable shrubs. I can think of
several cases where this happened to keen gardening friends of
mine—always heavy smokers, however, and happily unaware of
the pong that assailed me as a non-smoking visitor.

The remainder of my selected killing factors can be quickly
despatched. If you try to grow calcifuge plants on limy soil, their
leaves will turn bright yellow and the plants will die.

On the subject of planting and transplanting hazards, I have
already written extensively (see page 11 *et seq.*) and as to brown
fingers, why, this is the unfortunate condition of some people who
should never have been made to garden. Everything they touch
is handled and treated in the wrong way. There is no sympathy
between them and plants, no sort of affinity or understanding.
They are almost as much to be pitied as are those other unfortun-
ates who would make splendid gardeners but lack the opportunities.

Green fingers is our expression for a kind of applied intelligence;
an interest in how living things tick. To the man with brown
fingers, a plant might just as well be inanimate, and by the time
he has finished with it, it is.

The Fallible Gardener

Popular Gardening Fallacies

People tend to believe what they read. There is a certain seal of
authenticity about the printed word, and anyway it is much less
trouble to accept someone else's dictum than officiously go out
of your way to prove each point for yourself. Authors are themselves the most shameless plagiarists, and so mistakes get quickly
established as traditions, and traditions are very hard to break.

I remember being surprised on first reading that *Clematis
orientalis* was scented. Whoever initiated this observation possibly
had his wife standing behind him as he took that first fatal sniff,

only it was she that was wearing the scent, and not the flower. Something of the sort can so easily happen, and it would not have mattered except that this man was a gardening author, and nearly every subsequent authority who has come along with books or articles on clematis seems to have done just sufficient homework to have equipped himself with this cosy titbit of misinformation.

It is mainly to exorcise my own guilt pangs that I am airing the subject here. Writing in *Country Life* on moisture-loving plants that yet will not tolerate total immersion, I cited *Iris kaempferi* as being particular about good drainage during its dormant season. Well, I mean to say, this is the pap on which all gardeners have been reared. *I. laevigata* goes under water; *I. kaempferi* stays above. It is as simple as that. How should I dream of querying a fundamental law? And yet, before the print of that article was dry, came a letter: 'I am so interested in your remarks in *Country Life* this week, about *Iris kaempferi*.' That was a suspicious beginning; no one bothers to write to you expressing interest unless he is about to refute what you have written. I braced myself. My correspondent, in fact, found that the only way she could persuade this iris to flower and to flourish, was by holding it forcibly under water in the depths of winter until it stopped screaming for mercy. After that it never looked back. Even when every fish in the pond (there were two) died of cold and starvation, the iris just went on singing hallelujahs night and day.

So I boxed up three good roots and launched them on my pond, with a little chant of benediction. The box duly sank, and its contents grew lustily till the autumn, when they became dormant. They never re-appeared.

Then, in another garden, I was shown some white *I. kaempferi* growing happily under water in a lake, where they had flourished for many years, only they were not *I. kaempferi* at all, but *I. laevigata*. It was a simple case of mistaken identity. 'Aha!', I thought, 'I have you by the heel', and wrote scathingly in my weekly column. Whereupon my fair correspondent sent me a photograph of her beastly iris and some leaves, which have features distinguishing the one species under discussion from the other. Hers were *Iris kaempferi*. This was too sickening and I have been in a sulk about it ever since.

Another question on which dogmatism abounds is the depth

at which bulbs should be planted. I dislike being told to plant a bulb 6 in. deep, because the clay is not so very far down in most of our garden and it seems to me that bulbs will get better fare if they are near the surface. Those bulbs that like to be deep have ways and means of reaching down to their desired level, however superficially we may plant them. Many tulips, for instance, send down what are known as dropper bulbs, to a depth of 9 in. or more. *Tulipa kaufmanniana* is a notable example, here: if you think you will move an established group, the tulip will have the last laugh, because it has already sent some of its bulbs to a lower level than you were prepared to dig.

Other bulbs and corms make special fleshy contractile roots. These roots are of annual formation and duration. As they die, they shrink, and in shrinking they draw the bulb down to a lower level. This is a particularly necessary provision in the case of corms (such as crocuses and gladioli), because new corms are made on top of the old. Without some compensatory provision, they would soon find themselves at the surface. Indeed, on certain rather light, loose soils, this does constantly happen. Presumably the contractile roots are unable to get a purchase on the open-textured soil around them, with the result, experienced by a friend who gardens in north-west Scotland, that his bulbs are always lying about on the surface.

The moral seems to be to plant deeply on light soils but shallow on heavy.

One autumn, I was consulted about a choice of flowering shrubs to plant for shelter as well as colour at one end of an exposed new swimming pool. The owner said she would prefer evergreens because of leaves blowing into the pool. I had to point out that evergreens shed as many leaves in a twelve-month as deciduous shrubs. In fact, when you came to think of it, deciduous shrubs would be a better bet, in such a case. One would expect the pool to be used from May to September, and evergreen shrubs would shed more leaves in this part of the year than deciduous. Evergreens, in fact, are shedding in every month, but tend to be moulting most freely in late spring, as a compensation to putting on fresh foliage at that season.

There are many fallacies with regard to watering. 'Once you start watering you have got to go on', they say. In fact, one thorough soaking administered in a dry spell is certainly much more valuable than none, just as one equivalent fall of well-timed rain would be. 'It is dangerous to water while the sun is on the plants' is another hoary old let-out for the gardener. If the sun is mean enough to come out after rain, what then? One or two woolly-leaved hydrangeas may get scorched and the white parts of the variegated *Hosta crispula*. That is the sum total of casualties.

'Never water calcifuge plants with hard water'? On this, I can only say that from my own and other people's personal experience irregular doses of hard water do not seem to matter. In fact it is better to give the plants the water they need and to worry about its hardness later. In particular is this the case with pot plants, normally watered from above. Your rain water supplies have run out; your precious orchids are in need. By all means, give them hard tap-water then.

I find that lime very rapidly gets leached out of pot soil. I use the John Innes composts for all purposes. We mix them ourselves and the turf for the loam is skimmed off a field next to the potting shed. Now, our local soil is only slightly acid. Wherever they may be grown in the garden, hydrangeas that could be pink or blue, according to soil acidity, are pink. And yet, when I grow them in pots, in John Innes No. 3 compost to which $2\frac{1}{4}$ oz. of lime (calcium carbonate) has been added to each bushel, the flowers come lilac or blue, denoting an acid soil. So I never trouble to omit the lime from the compost recipe, whatever I may be potting: *Lilium auratum, L. speciosum,* newly rooted azalea or camellia cuttings. Whatever it may be, they all get their stated dose of chalk, and none of them mind it, because it is so soon washed away in solution.

Even among experts there is a complete divergence of opinion on the question of whether you should reduce the branches of a tree or shrub that has been moved, and that has sustained root damage in the process. I know very well where I stand on this one, but the other viewpoint is, to quote the author of a fairly recently published book, when discussing the transplanting of deciduous trees, as follows: 'If the root ball appears fairly intact, it may well be advantageous to shorten all growths by about a fifth. If the roots are rather damaged, I would be inclined to leave all growths uncut for the first season and prune rather more heavily the following autumn. If the roots are damaged, the plants will not be able to exert enough strength to make new buds and new growth until the root system has been re-established, and this is best done by leaving the aerial portions untouched.'

The way I would re-word the last sentence and the argument it puts forward is as follows: if the roots are damaged, the balance between roots and shoots has been upset. Until the tree has replaced its lost roots, it will be unable adequately to supply with moisture and nutrients its present complement of branches. These should therefore be considerably reduced, on planting, so that there are no more branches than roots.

And that goes for any tree or shrub, deciduous or evergreen, that is being moved, quite apart from the pruning treatment it may anyway require in order to shape its branches. It will re-establish more quickly if the roots have less top-hamper to cope with than they well can, rather than too much.

Brief mention of one last fallacy, my particular *bête noire*, that clematis should have lime added to the soil in which they are planted. This is quite unnecessary. The myth arises from seeing our native *Clematis vitalba* growing wild on limy soils. Clematis do equally well on a wide range of soils, both alkaline and acid. What really matters to them is moisture and feeding. Thus, acid sandy soils and thin chalky soils both, for the same reasons, tend to make clematis culture tricky, because they are low in humus and clay content, and readily dry out. Adding lime to the soil of your flower garden will not hurt the clematis, but it may hurt something else—a camellia, perhaps—planted near it either then or years later, long after the reason for putting in that mortar rubble has been forgotten. Keep your lime for the vegetables.

5. Seasonal Highlights

Winter

The Recurrent Theme of Winter

At no time in the cycle of the seasons do you get that feeling of 'here we are again' so strongly as in winter. For one thing it is very quiet; there are few interruptions or distractions. Friends and visitors keep away—probably they don't want to be shaken from their illusion that in your garden it is always summer. Relations stay indoors.

It is in my rose garden that winter predominantly holds court. Enclosed by hedges, this area is isolated and, whereas it becomes stiflingly hot in summer, in winter it collects more frost and snow than anywhere. But one can usually prune and peg the roses. In doing so, I always try (being a moderate sybarite) to chase the sunlight. Until about 10.30 a.m. this scarcely counts, but by 11 a.m. it is quite palpably warming, if you get yourself into just the right place. It seems a pity to have to go in to lunch at the best moment in a winter's day, because by 3 p.m. the sun is already failing.

We hear and read a lot about the garden in winter but, speaking for myself, it gives me little actual pleasure. Nearly all pleasurable thoughts are in looking forward, in noting bulbs pushing through, the number of dormant flower buds on shrubs and trees and so on.

Anything that flowers in winter is very welcome, of course, but mainly with the idea of bringing it into the house. A handful of evergreens look well in the garden: the bay trees, the fatsias and the golden holly, for instance. But there is almost too much evergreen in my garden with its extensive architecture in yew hedging and topiary. Yew, we are always being told (and I have frequently said it myself) makes a sober and dignified background setting for borders of gay flowers. But where are the gay flowers? No, the yews in winter would look glum indeed but for one saving grace, and that is their irrepressibly cheerful contours. They have tried to imitate the man-made masonry of bricks and stonework, but have failed triumphantly. Always they will bulge or lean or spread into comfortable obesity, and the result is hilarious, giving the lie to all serious pretensions.

Still, I should really prefer a landscape garden at this time of year; to be able to look from my drawing-room window, as at Scotney Castle, down on to the wonderfully soft yet varied colouring of deciduous tree tops, trees of typical Kentish wood-land, and beyond to a grassy hillside set with a scattering of ancient-looking Scots pines. Is there a tree with more character, at maturity, than this?

Or to have water—a lake that really was a lake. Even at my own modest pond-side I derive more satisfaction, in winter, from seeing the carmine dogwood stems and their reflections, than from any other garden feature. When the water is frozen over, the effect is ruined and the dogwoods become less than half themselves, but for most of a typical English winter, the water remains ice-free. The sun comes out between the depressions, and the whole scene vibrates with light and colour.

The dedicated flower gardener should never yearn for an open setting and a view. Not for himself. All his efforts must be aimed at cutting down the devastating effects of living on a windy island. This is what has happened and it still happening in my garden, perched on its south-west-facing hill-side. I have recently planted another eight Leyland cypresses, to windward of us. We add and add and the trees grow and grow, so that little of the countryside remains to be seen even in winter, let alone in summer. What does remain are views of the half-timbered house, the oast house, the barn with the glow of its vast tiled roof and of other old farm buildings that were worked into the garden framework—views of these from the garden in the flattering light of low winter sun-shine. For these we might well be envied. The buildings are full of warmth. In slate and millstone grit country, a comparable view might be chilly, but its inhabitants will have the compensation of mountain scenery and rushing streams; perhaps even of a natural rock garden, the only kind worth having.

Conifers for Winter Colour

Conifers have many moods. In spring their young foliage is sometimes as fresh as anything that season can offer and the 'flowers' of a larch and of certain spruces and firs, such as *Picea likiangensis*, are in astonishing shades of red that are a delight to gardeners and flower arrangers alike. In summer, the glaucous-leaved types are at their most persuasive and the young cones of the firs (species of *Abies*) vary in colouring from pale ice, through dove and mauve to rich navy blue. In autumn we see many cones at maturity and the deciduous conifers take on bright tints before leaf-fall.

But it is in winter that we are most inclined to turn to conifers for comfort, and they will not let us down. Their mood is quite different then, however, and a main fact to bear in mind is that blue-leaved (glaucous) conifers reflect everything that is most chill and foggy, leaden and glum from the sulky skies and muffled distances so characteristic of the season. Thus the variety of Lawson's cypress called 'Allumii', popular for hedging, looks particularly dismal in its dark, blue-green garb, and so does Triomphe de Boskoop, although admirable during the growing season. It can grow quite quickly into a 50-ft. cone-shaped column, with a pleasantly loose, informal habit, and the young shoots are only a few shades deeper than duck-egg blue.

Yellow cypresses, by contrast, are at their most attractive in winter, but it must be admitted that they do owe much to their sombre companions. Background is all-important to this lively colour. I know of only one supplier listing *Chamaecyparis lawsoniana* 'Aurea Smithii', namely Four Winds Nursery, Holt Pound, Wrecclesham, Farnham, Surrey. There is a fine mature stand of this at the National Pinetum, of which I must say a word at this point. It is located at Bedgebury, in South Kent, between the villages of Lamberhurst, Flimwell and Goudhurst, and was started in the 1920's when it was found that the collection at Kew was suffering from London's proximity. The Bedgebury collection is now reaching maturity and has created its own special landscape. Despite the fact that it does not advertise itself, it attracts some 50,000 visitors and their dogs, annually. But the place is always open and it is easy to choose one's time to miss the crowds. I am lucky enough to live only 12 miles away, and often slip over there, particularly in winter. The last time, it was February and snowing, but one is sheltered among the trees. In autumn, there is an extraordinarily rich assortment of fungi, among the trees, many of them edible.

C.l. 'Aurea Smithii' is markedly the brightest, in winter, of the yellow cypresses, and makes a graceful spire. Failing this, *C.l.* 'Lutea' and *C.l.* 'Stewartii' are also good, and commonly offered. *C. obtusa* 'Crippsii' is of a brilliant yellow-green on the outside of a bush; the second-year foliage turns plain green and makes for contrast behind the yellow. This conifer is pleasantly feathery and of a more spreading, though neat habit, 18 ft. by 12 ft. at the age of 30 years.

The cypress-like tree that is universally admired when viewed across the middle lake in Sheffield Park Gardens, Sussex, is actually the golden form of the Chinese juniper, *Juniperus chinensis* 'Aurea'. It is superbly backed by a twin Monterey pine, *Pinus radiata* (*insignis*), and this is the ideal background colour in the winter landscape, for the pine's foliage is dark yet lustrous and responds rewardingly to a touch of winter's sunshine. In a smaller setting, a pine that would contrast just as markedly, yet is of uncommonly cheerful bottle-green colouring, is *P. sylvestris* 'Viridis Compacta'. It makes a large bush rather than a tree, being dome-shaped and clothed with foliage right down to the ground.

At Bedgebury I have noted, with some surprise, that *J. chinensis* 'Aurea' is little brighter, in winter, than *J. chinensis* itself. The latter is a male specimen, and the club-shaped, fawn-coloured knobs of next spring's 'flowers', then thickly scattered over the whole tree, are an unexpected and pleasing feature.

If a juniper can look like a cypress, it is not to be wondered at that a cypress can resemble a juniper; and so it is with *Chamaecyparis thyoides*, though it is broadly columnar. In 35 years it has grown at Bedgebury not quite as many feet, and is some 12 ft. wide. The foliage is minutely scaly, slightly glaucous and deliciously aromatic when bruised. It is adorned with thousands of beige, button-like cones, each only $\frac{1}{8}$ in. across, but so numerous as to be effective. This cypress has the outstanding merits of extreme hardiness and tolerance of wet soil conditions. It must be reckoned a fairly slow grower, but gardeners are all too much inclined to choose specimen cypresses that will attain their ideal bulk within as few years as possible. After that, they will either grow too large or have to be clipped, which spoils the appearance of many of them, or have to be scrapped.

However, we can return to our yellow theme *Cupressus macrocarpa* 'Donard Gold'. It has outstanding qualities in a reasonably mild climate or a sheltered position. Its tiny leaves and slender branchlets give it an air of elegance and refinement that are rather unexpected in so rank a grower. By the time winter has got under way, it is pale green, not gold, but this colouring is blithe and fresh in its season. For those in a hurry, this makes a good pot or tub plant, but weep no tears when it outgrows its station, for this is the inevitable price that must sooner, rather than later, be paid. A winter exhibit in the R.H.S. hall showed a 2½ ft.-tall specimen that looked nicely in scale in a 7 in. pot and another ditto ditto, 7 ft.-tall in a 15 in. diameter tub.

For other ideas on yellow conifers for winter effect I must refer the reader back to 'Planning a Yellow Garden' (page 304).

A really tall conifer but particularly economical of lateral space is the incense cedar, *Libocedrus decurrens*. It can grow to 60 ft. while remaining only 6 ft. across. Overhead wires should be one's main worry, when siting it. Its bright yellow-green leaves are arranged in a kind of loose rosette formation of fan-like fronds.

Many conifers make good ground-cover, but for a lively colouring in winter I should go for *Juniperus sabina cupressifolia*, which is bay green even in the coldest weather.

Evergreens

For half the year the nurseryman has uphill work in making casual sales of deciduous trees and shrubs. Shorn of leaves, a plant looks half its summer size, and the impulse-buyer's imagination is not up to visualising it at other seasons. 'I do like to have something to look at in the winter,' the cry goes up. So it has to be an evergreen.

Now the majority of evergreens, and especially those with broad leaves, come from warmer climates than our own. Our climate is temperate enough, in all conscience, and allows us to grow a wider range of plants than is possible anywhere else at such high latitudes. But even so, we have to expect cold wintry spells from time to time, such as many of our favourite evergreens are not accustomed to in their native haunts. The great trouble is that an evergreen is never as fully dormant as a deciduous plant. A constant interchange of water and nutrients between roots and leaves has to go on the year through. If the ground becomes frozen, water supplies to the foliage are cut off. The leaves hang limply in a desiccated condition, which may be further aggravated by cutting winds and, if a plant's natural activities are thus suspended for too long, it will die.

The nature of the beast, as I have thus far outlined it, has a number of implications for the gardener. It is mostly his evergreens that he will need to protect in winter. By wrapping their branches around in polythene, he can create a microclimate of moisture-saturated air that the wind's worst efforts will fail to dissipate, and by packing bracken and similar lagging about its stem, while at the same time allowing the polythene to reach down to the ground, he will materially reduce the frost's capacity for penetrating the earth at that point.

This plastic bolster, then, is the 'something to look at in the winter' that our impulse-buyer is yearning towards. The alternative, should his evergreen be hardy enough to survive without protection, is all too frequently a shrub, say a rhododendron, with matt green foliage of numbed appearance, hanging limply curled up throughout each frosty spell. Nothing could look more dejected. Snow presents further hazards, its branch-breaking weight being the most obvious. But if not immediately knocked off, it will congeal and freeze on to evergreen foliage, with destructive results.

Not all evergreens have the advantage of leathery leaves. Let a few winter gales assail the more fragile of them, and they become so bruised and tattered that, from Christmas till Easter or later, one could wish that they were not evergreens and had voluntarily shed their foliage at an earlier stage. When evergreens do shed their leaves, it usually seems to be at the wrong moment for the gardener. He grumbles enough at the deciduous fall of autumn, but at least he can gather up and dispose of this lot all in a matter of eight weeks at the end of the garden's growing season, and will be free to attend to other things for the next 44. Loud and bitter is his lament, then, when May brings with it, not merely the expected ice saints with their festival of late frosts, but a leaf-fall festival by the evergreens, which somehow never fails to take him by indignant surprise. The larger and the more imposing the evergreen, the greater the fall; and if it is a bay tree or, worse still, an ilex (*Quercus ilex*), some gardeners would rather chop it down than be confronted by this annual insult.

Having fallen, evergreen leaves become everbrown. You some-times hear it said of plane and Spanish chestnut leaves that they never rot down, but this can be seen as an obviously coloured exaggeration, when compared with the persistence of bay or holly. There certainly is a tendency to overdo the evergreens in some gardens, with a depressing effect for much of the year.

However, although they are liable to disappoint us in winter, and especially during frosty spells, yet there is much comfort to be derived from some of them, and after all we do not usually get frost for as much, even, as half the duration of the three coldest months.

The view from the window near which I sit writing, is domin-ated by an enormous **bay laurel,** of tree-like proportions. It was here before the garden was made, early in this century, but it is not mere sentiment that endears it to me, nor even the fact that it grows within striking distance of the kitchen stewpot. The yellow-green of its foliage is reinforced by the yellowness of winter sunlight. Its branches stand out like plumes from the main body of the tree—so that, particularly when sunshine follows rain, it has an air of sparkling and self-assured grandeur.

Those who grow bay laurels as clipped hedges or in formal shapes, have no conception of their naturally sunny disposition. For one thing, a clipped bay is usually attacked by scale insects. They secrete a sticky honeydew on which black moulds grow, so that the host plant looks, and is, thoroughly unhappy. Unclipped bays never get this trouble. Then again, the clipping of any large-leaved shrub has a noticeably mangling effect on each individual leaf. For this reason none of the bushes that we loosely term laurels should be allowed to bear 'the marks of the scissors.' They should be given plenty of space and encouraged to grow in a natural 'luxuriancy and diffusion of boughs and branches.'

While the bay, *Laurus nobilis,* is the true laurel, there are several other species with a higher claim to the title in popular parlance. *Prunus laurocerasus,* the cherry laurel, is usually either clipped or crowded in, but a very handsome creature when given its chance. Its large and rather pale green leaf has a lustrous surface that is lacking in the bay, but is one of the most helpful attributes in giving an evergreen a cheerful appearance. Lacking it, and having besides, a very dark leaf, the laurustinus, *Viburnum tinus,* would be sullen indeed, did it not carry its crops of white flowers, pink in bud, throughout the winter.

All the evergreen viburnums tend to be on the glum side, with *V. rhytidophyllum* in a nadir of depression. This shrub arouses a great hate in many gardeners. It has a large, laurel leaf, felted underneath but glossy and densely wrinkled along all its many veins on the top. These leaves tend to hang vertically throughout the winter, even when it is mild. The shrub is often planted under trees, where it can exist but looks particularly dejected. Its flowers are normally a dirty white, but in the variety Roseum they are dirty pink, which makes a change. I would not bother to write all this about *V. rhytidophyllum* did I not think that, despite its faults, it can be a fine shrub. It needs grouping; it needs plenty of room, in an open position so that it can form a large feature, 15 ft. tall by, say, 25 ft. across. Then the foliage will look really rather distinguished for much of the year, and it will carry huge crops of clustered red berries in August, changing to a no less remarkable jet black as they age, with a telling mixture of red and black berries in each truss during the intermediate period.

The Portugal laurel, *Prunus lusitanica,* has smaller leaves than the bay's, and they are very dark. It is not at its best in winter but again, given space in which to develop, makes a beautiful specimen and is spectacular in late spring with its white blossom massed in candle-like spikelets. It has a particularly good variegated form. The leaves are margined in cream and the young stems and leaf stalks are a deep, glossy red.

Another large group of laurels comprises the many forms of *Aucuba japonica.* When Keats wrote in 1819 to his sister Fanny about how he would like to put a globe of gold-fish before a 'handsome painted window and shade it all round with myrtles and Japonicas,' he was possibly thinking of this shrub, then rising to popularity. Aucubas have achieved a return to favour, thanks to a well merited re-assessment by the flower arrangers. Their misfortune is in being shade-tolerant. You nearly always see them growing scraggily under trees, or else clipped, in town gardens. Neither condition does them justice. I have yet to see a really well grown specimen.

Perhaps the chief merit of all the **arbutuses** in winter is in the warm red colouring of their trunks—a feature that becomes distinctive as they reach maturity. Conspicuous enough in the strawberry tree, *Arbutus unedo*, it is far more accentuated in the hybrid *A. andrachnoides,* of which *A. unedo* is one parent. And then we have *A. menziesii,* with its beautifully smooth-barked, rufous trunk and branches. An excellent fast-growing small tree, this, for a sheltered position, but not always easy to establish. There never was a more ticklish shrub for resenting disturbance. I have had two unsuccessful tries at it. You can raise it quite easily and quickly from seed, but must never attempt to prick the seedlings out. Discard all but one and plant this straight from its seed pot to its final site at an early age.

The strawberry-like fruits of *A. unedo* colour up in November and are very exciting and decorative, coming as they do at the same time as its flowers for next year's fruiting. But specimens often remain barren throughout their lives. This must be a question of strain rather than company, because a singleton arbutus may sometimes be a heavy cropper.

Hellebores

The **Christmas rose,** *Helleborus niger,* would generally be reckoned easy to grow, but you have only to talk to a random selection of gardeners about their experiences to find that this plant is curiously variable. In some gardens it gives no trouble, while in others there is not a place to suit it. Yet it lays down no rules for our guidance. In a general way, all hellebores like lime, but I would never recommend the addition of lime to any part of the flower garden, as it is poison to so many good plants. And even the lime-lovers, including hellebores, seem to get on well enough without it under garden conditions. Neither is shade necessary to the Christmas rose, though it is a useful plant to be able to grow under trees or along a north wall. It certainly likes fertile soil and, as one would expect of a woodland plant, it revels in humus. One cannot go wrong by adding large quantities of peat or leafmould to its site before planting. Old clumps are best split up in spring, if you want to increase them; but there is never any need to disturb them. The nurseryman's normal method of raising stock is from seed, and the young plants so obtained can be moved at any time from September to May.

The commonest type of Christmas rose does not flower until the New Year or even February. Its stems are on the stumpy side, and it is a common practice to cover the plants with cloches, both to prevent mud-splashing and to draw them up a bit. Cloches are not beautiful objects, and there is something to be said for growing Christmas roses in a row in the kitchen garden, purely for cutting. *H. niger* 'Altifolius' really does flower at Christmas, and may in fact be anything up to a month earlier. Its stems grow a foot tall without encouragement and its flowers are large, but pure white: there is a purplish flush on the undersides of the sepals.

When we speak of Lenten roses, we mean the softer-stemmed, herbaceous types with nodding flowers and an infuriating unpredictability as to whether they will take up water when picked or not. Taking a hint from Sybil Emberton (*Garden Foliage for Flower Arrangement*), I have prepared myself for quoting her way of getting over this little difficulty, by trying it out for myself. It works. You boil the stem ends for about 20 seconds and then make a shallow slit with a sharp-pointed knife from the top of each stem (just below a flower) to the bottom. Then give the hellebores a spell of several hours' total immersion (in a bath or sink). And that is it. Thereafter, they will not blench even in the warmest living-room.

To the same clan belongs *H. atrorubens*. It is very easy going and seems to thrive on neglect. I have it under a wall where the sun never reaches it. A little overhead protection as from an overhanging deciduous shrub, is desirable for these soft-stemmed mid-winter flowerers, otherwise a severe frost can dish their display. This one is always flowering by Christmas and quite often before the end of November. The flowers are borne in clusters, opening in succession, and each bloom is 2 in. across, a beautiful soft purple with only a hint of green. With its precocious habit and easy temperament, the only reason I can think of for not seeing this species in gardens more frequently, is that it is slow of increase and therefore not a good nurseryman's subject.

The main flush of blossom from Lenten roses is borne from February till April, and a number of species are involved, notably *H. orientalis* and *H. guttatus,* the latter contributing a rash of purple spots towards the centre-base of each sepal. As their old foliage looks tatty and disreputable at flowering time, it is as well to cut it all away just before they bloom.

The flowers vary in colour from green-tinged white, through green and greeny-pinks and purples to purple itself and in cultivars like Ballard's Black, to a very dark shade indeed, against which the crowds of pale-anthered stamens stand out like spots of galactic light. Among hellebore collectors, these dark ones have competitive significance but they are not as telling in the garden as some of the slightly paler shades. *H. abchasicus,* for instance, although variable, does often produce a rich and sonorous reddish purple colouring. The blooms of these Lenten roses are up to 2½ in. across and established clumps are effective as well as charming.

Neither the Christmas nor the Lenten rose can boast about its foliage, but this is the chief glory of *H. corsicus* and of *H. foetidus,* which are both low-growing, evergreen shrubs. I never can make up my mind which of the two I prefer and, indeed, they probably look their best when grown as ground cover in broad adjacent drifts. They will tolerate quite heavy shade and are thus of great service in unpromising conditions. The nine or so leaflets of *H. foetidus* spring from an arc-shaped base and make a long-stemmed fan with a three-quarter-circle sweep. They are a very deep but lustrous green. In *H. corsicus* (which is now correctly *H. lividus* subspecies *corsicus* but was *H. argutifolius* for a few years and heaven knows what next) the foliage is somewhat glaucous and is trifoliate, with the two large, outer leaflets pouched on their lower side like a pelican's bill. The leaf margins are expressively described in my British flora as spinescent; theirs is a kind of mock-spininess.

Both species are usually flowering by January. Their very pale, melting green inflorescences are in particularly marked contrast to their foliage in *H. foetidus.* In severe frost you would expect this fleshy growth to be destroyed and, for the time being, it goes limp and sad, but always picks up with the arrival of milder weather. The green bell-flowers of *H. foetidus* become edged with maroon as they age, and are beautiful as well as interesting. The larger, saucer-shaped flowers of *H. argutifolius* are a uniform light green, which shows up well. Neither species is long lived and they suffer from a destructive leaf-spotting fungus disease which works back into the stem and frequently kills them. But they self-sow generously, so there should always be youngsters coming on if the ground is left reasonably undisturbed.

Both the shrubby hellebores and the Lenten roses are splendid under deciduous trees and shrubs. They associate well with *Narcissus cyclamineus* and its hybrids, with scillas and ground coverers such as the foaming white *Tiarella cordifolia*. Also with evergreen ferns.

Spring

I am often asked of a plant, by people who are wondering whether it might be worth getting for their own gardens: 'How long does if flower for?' If I say: 'For a good month,' in a tone of warm encouragement, they feel all right; but if I say: 'Perhaps three weeks,' in a noncommittal sort of voice, they look dubious. Yet the truth about the majority of spring-flowering trees and shrubs is that they last in beauty for one week only. Almond, plum, cherry and apple blossom come and go with alarming fleetness, each leaving us with another 51 weeks of waiting for its return; and yet we do not look at the matter like that at all. For when they burst into our consciousness and are vividly with us, their presence carries us forward to spring's next revelation and then the next. There is no time for regrets at this season, or second thoughts or cool evaluations of a plant's rent-paying capacity.

Suburban Trees and Shrubs

My friend said: 'I have just planted another laburnum. They tell me it is suburban, but I adore laburnums.' I was wholeheartedly on his side. With a cool background of large park trees on the fringes of his garden, the **laburnums** will show up to perfection. It is common to denigrate this tree as suburban, but the fault is with its unhappy architectural setting, not with the plant. It is not even like some cherries, for instance, that seem too self-conscious and sophisticated to look appropriate in the country-side. Plant it in the country, and the laburnum seems more naturally rural than a weeping willow.

One is apt to forget what an interestingly shaped tree the laburnum makes, when mature. This, I think, is especially true of the Scotch laburnum, *L. alpinum*. I noted that for many miles along the A94, north-east of Forfar, in Angus, this tree is inter-planted with others of a larger kind, and makes a decorative yet sturdy accent. I was so interested in the individual form of each tree that the quality of my driving probably suffered a bit. It was June and the laburnums were flowering, but what struck me then, as at other times, was that the pendant 'golden chains' accentuated the structure of each branch, but that their length—whether long or short, was an irrelevance.

We all tend to plant those varieties with the longest racemes, such as *L. vossii* and *L. watereri*. Yet in maturity and old age the tree, with its thick, squat trunk and short jointed, gnarled branches, dominates, and its flower pendants can be quite stumpy without disappointing.

One of the commonest suburban plantings that we notice in May is laburnum with lilac and pink or red may. And a first rate combination they make, for not only do the colours associate well: there is also a pleasing contrast between the laburnum's falling stalactites, the lilac's rising cones and the flat-topped clusters of may blossom. Features such as these, however often repeated, can greatly mitigate the boredom of suburban housing.

Not so **forsythia,** worse luck. We have had a bellyful of this shrub by mid-April and it is a relief when its leaves at last expand and begin to subdue yet another epidemic of the yellow peril. If we only had a preponderance of whitewashed buildings in this country, forsythias would be ten times improved. But the shrub has intrinsic faults quite apart from its setting.

There is no elegance or character of any sort in its structure. Its crude *exposé* of colour is undiluted by foliage. And in its most popular cultivars the flowers are packed into such congested lumps that it is like being asked to swallow a helping of cornflour pudding. Of course there are forsythias and forsythias. The primrose yellow, early flowering *Forsythia ovata* is sweet, and I like the slender wands of *F. suspensa*. And any forsythia in a good setting can be strikingly handsome, but one has to be careful. For instance, you often see an excruciating combination of forsythia and the deep pink flowering currant, *Ribes sanguineum*.

The archetypal suburban tree is the **flowering cherry**. This often modifies and graces its setting very charmingly—especially the less flamboyant, early flowering kinds such as *Prunus yedoensis, P. conradinae, P. subhirtella, P. sargentii* and the hybrids Okame and (similar but even better) Kursar. And the double flowered form of our native gean, *P. avium* 'Plena', makes a splendid tree when allowed the necessary space for its full development.

If you are intending to plant one or two cherries in your garden, there are a number of points to look out for. First, tree shape. The ubiquitous double pink Kanzan (*Prunus serrulata sekiyama*) is unpleasantly stiff, as a rule, with an obliquely ascending branch system whose outline becomes softened only at maturity. Shimidsui (*alias* Oku Miyako), on the other hand, tends to be of lamentably weak growth, whereas *P. avium* 'Plena' makes in every way a magnificent specimen, but could easily outgrow the space available to it. The one thing you want to avoid, with cherries, is cutting them about, thus giving easy access to the bacterial and fungal diseases that are liable to affect them.

Another question is tree form. Most people prefer to buy a standard, but they would often have done better to settle for a bush. All cherries are grafted on a selected strain of the wild gean. The vigour of stock and scion is seldom matched. One or the other will grow the faster, and the result is an increasingly ugly lump at the point of union. On a standard, this point is at the top of the trunk, and it is clearly visible, but on a bush it is only just above ground level and will scarcely be noticed. The bush will grow into a tree in course of time, and the fact that it has a number of stems is of little moment. Where garden space is limited and a columnar tree with little lateral spread is required, the semi-double, soft-pink-flowered Amanogawa cherry will nine times out of ten be the professional's recommendation. Well, the flowers are pretty, for a few days, and the tree does what is expected of it, but the branch system is thick and ungainly and becomes ever more markedly clumsy as a specimen matures.

Then there is the question of flowering time. The winter-flowering *P. subhirtella* 'Autumnalis' may flower at any time between October and April and certainly gives best value in its length of season, although frost may spoil its winter's efforts. All the spring flowerers can be expected to be out and over in a week or 10 days, but they do between them offer a reasonable spread of season from March till May.

P. sargentii often opens before the end of March. It is the loveliest pink cherry, I think, but also the most ephemeral: its single flowers are out and over in a matter of six or seven days. Undoubtedly, double-flowered cherries give more value for money than single; the former hold their petals for several days longer. But, as a compensation, *P. sargentii* is the most reliable of all cherries in its display of brilliant early autumn colouring.

Time of flowering also decides whether you are to see the blossom on almost naked branches—as you will with an early flowerer—or mixed with young foliage. The young leaves may be green, slightly bronzed or rich copper, according to variety. A copper leaf coupled with a pure white flower is superb, and this you get in Tai Haku, perhaps the finest hybrid cherry of all, with enormous single white blooms and making a shapely tree. You also get it in the species *P. serrulata spontanea*, which has quite a different appeal, as you would expect in a wilding, but is as fresh and charming as possible.

Bronze coupled with a strongish pink flower can be a little disconcerting. *P. sargentii* gets away with it; for one thing the leaves are still very small when the flowers are at their best and, for another, the shade of pink is clean. In Kanzan, however, the flower is a distinctly bluish pink, and this does clash with its purplish foliage. The creamy-yellow-flowered Ukon also has a bronzed setting—delightful in this case. It is a nicely shaped tree when mature. On examining its semi-double flowers at close quarters you may be surprised to discover that there is actually no yellow in them at all; only some flecks of green that, mixed in with white, give a sulphur impression.

One of the characters distinguishing the latest-flowering cherries is the very long flower stalks that they develop. This is just as well, for the foliage is fairly widely expanded by then, and the 6 to 7 in. stalks ensure that the flower clusters are nevertheless well displayed. Latest of all and one of the finest is Shirofugen (*P. s. albo-rosea*), with coppery foliage and double flowers, pink in the bud, opening white and then changing to pink again It is often at its best in the second half of May.

This, then, and the double gean, would by my choice for a double white cherry, Tai Haku for a single white, or *P. s. spontanea* where unassuming informality was desired; and *P. sargentii* for a single pink, or Kursar where a smaller tree was required. For a double in this colour I should choose Ichyo (*P. s. uniflora*). Only semi-double, its deep pink buds open to softly shaded flowers of a particularly good shape, wide and disc-like, with a clean, open centre.

But bethink you, before going cherry-mad, of the damage that bullfinches can do to many of them—Kanzan is usually exempt— if you live in the country. Remember that many cherries have large oval leaves that cast a heavy shade and are of boring appearance throughout the summer. Their branch systems in winter are thick and clumsy in outline. And remember, finally, that cherries are among the greediest of trees with far-reaching roots that are close to the surface. Few plants thrive beneath them. So many gardeners plant ornamental cherries that there is a strong case for enjoying their plantings when they are in a state to be enjoyed and dispensing with them and all their drawbacks in your own garden.

Magnolias for Spring Planting

With their large, bold blossoms so proudly displayed, **magnolias** are undoubtedly the most glamorous and effective of all shrubs or small trees and there is room for at least one specimen in every garden. The polluted air of industrial towns does not worry them in the least and they are tolerant of a wide range of soils although some are calcifuge.

April is the best month in the whole year for planting and establishing magnolias. They have fleshy roots which are apt to rot away in winter, following an autumn disturbance. But in spring they can quickly make good any damage done to them, but do remember to keep your young plants well watered until they are thoroughly settled in. The other point to remember about these fleshy roots is that they strongly resent being dug around. You can easily kill a large and mature specimen by digging over the ground near it. Feed, then, entirely with surface mulches of organic material like garden compost, and forbear prodding about with a fork. One reason for magnolias making such excellent lawn specimens is that they are automatically undisturbed here. It would be as well, however, at least in the early years, to keep a circle 5 ft. across, round your magnolia free from turf and you could plant small bulbs and hardy cyclamen here.

Outstanding as a lawn specimen and making a sizeable tree in time, is *Magnolia soulangeana*. This is a hybrid and varies a good deal in habit and colouring so that a number of cultivars have been named. Typically it makes large goblet-shaped, whitish blooms stained purple near the base. They open on naked branches in April and are really exciting en masse. Everyone stops to look. This magnolia will tolerate a fair amount of lime in the soil but nothing approaching raw chalk. It flowers at a reasonably early age. The handsomest and most striking cultivar is Lennei, which is deep pink over all the outside of the bloom, and is more broadly globular than *M. soulangeana* itself. The habit of Lennei is different, too, making a large, sprawling shrub rather than a small tree. It flowers, principally, in May. Rubra (previously known as Rustica Rubra) is slightly more puce-stained than the type-plant but looks a bit grubby, being neither one thing nor the other. The albino form *M. s.* 'Alba' is a good plant and often sold as a substitute for *M. denudata*, to which, however, it cannot hold a candle.

M. denudata is undoubtedly the finest white magnolia, growing into a small umbrella-shaped tree only 12 or 15 ft. high and covered in April with pure white, broad-petalled, waxy blooms that are strongly lemon-scented. It dislikes lime.

The best beginner's magnolia is *M. stellata*; it flowers when still quite a baby bush and can take its place with other shrubs in a border. Its first blooms will often open before the end of March and it is as well to site it so that the display is unlikely to be spoilt by wind and frost. The flowers themselves are smallish and spidery, blush-pink in bud opening to white; very prolific and giving a succession of blossom over a long season. It tolerates some lime, but not too much.

M. kobus, to which it is closely related, is excellent on chalky soils. It makes a large tree and is regularly smothered, when mature, with white blossom but takes 7 years or so to reach flowering size. One of the best magnolias for the smaller garden and valued, too, by flower arrangers, is *M. liliflora* 'Nigra'. The bush does not grow too large, it flowers from an early age and the blooms are elegantly shaped with tapering petals and a rich wine-purple colouring. This, again, is April-May flowering.

There is a group of several species and hybrids with down-facing, bowl-shaped flowers that open with the young foliage, in the last part of May and in June. Probably your best choice here will be the hybrid, *M. highdownensis,* which is also good on chalk. Its blooms are 5 or 6 in. across and have an eye of maroon red stamens and a good scent. If you want a magnolia for a shady position near trees, the similar *M. wilsonii* will be at home, while *M. sieboldii* is almost as handsome in September with its purplish seed pods and brilliant red seeds as in early summer when flowering—again white with a dark reddish centre. These will take about 4 years to settle down to flowering. It is not quite as hardy as some.

The Brooms

In May the common **broom** stabs our woodland clearings and decks all the waste places where it can get a footing with flashes of brilliant yellow. In Scotland in June it is even more spectacular, covering acres at a time with an astonishing display, while emitting a curious acrid smell that wafts into your car as you drive through it.

The gardener on acid soil is indebted to the wild broom, *Cytisus scoparius* (*Sarothamnus scoparius*, as we should call it) for its parentage of many popular hybrids, but they also derive from it a scraggy habit and a short life. The Scoparius hybrids are best used in the garden as expendable stop-gaps among more permanent plantings. Neither surprise nor tears should be wasted on their sudden departure, if they have given us 4 or 5 years of pleasure in the meantime. But always make sure, when buying them, that they are growing on their own roots. Nowadays this will usually be the case, for they are normally raised from cuttings. But if grafted on laburnum seedlings, their life is disastrously short. The irresistibly pretty brooms grown as standards, which you see at the Chelsea Flower Show, are always so grafted, however, and will die suddenly and inevitably within only two years.

As to the scraggy habit of ordinary bush brooms, there are two ways of countering this. The first is to accept it—to let the plant grow as it will, but to supply it, in any but the most sheltered positions, with a stout stake for its entire life. The other possibility is to get busy at the right moment each year with shears or secateurs. Immediately after flowering, cut all the long, wispy green-stemmed shoots of the previous season's growing, back by half. This helps to keep the shrub neat, but it is still likely to need a stake.

There are many seductive varieties, but if you are making your choice at the show bench, where the flowers are seen at close quarters, remember that those which include two or more colours may be interesting in detail, but will probably give a muddled effect when viewed at a distance in your garden. Self-coloured flowers will make the strongest general impression. One other point to remember about the Scoparius hybrids is that they are seldom happy on chalk or lime soils. But there are other types not sharing this objection.

Cytisus praecox, for instance: here is a broom with many good qualities, chief of which is its compact habit. It makes a rounded, well-furnished bush some 4 ft. tall, and seldom needs support. The small, primrose-yellow flowers are borne in their thousands; they have a pungent, sour smell. This broom, itself a hybrid, now has several offspring with the same good form but in different colours. Gold Spear is rich yellow; Zeelandia is lilac coloured, and Hollandia is reddish-purple.

Although *Cytisus praecox* seeds freely, you cannot be certain that the seedlings will come true. One of its parents is *C. albus,* the Portugal broom, the only species having white flowers. Despite its untoward gauntness, this is a most endearing shrub, 6 to 8 ft. tall and decked in showers of tiny blossoms, discreetly but sweetly scented. This one is easily raised from seed. The seedlings vary in their habit, and it is generally possible, by picking out the most compact among them, to equip yourself with reasonably shapely specimens.

C. kewensis is another hybrid with the same primrose colouring and the same smell as *C. praecox,* but the blooms are slightly larger and are borne on foot-tall sprays arising from a prostrate plant. It is thus ideal for cascading over ledges and dry walls. With the years, it covers an extensive area, but its thin growth is the reverse of weed-suppressing. It looks well, in its season, with clumps of *Viola cornuta* in its typical violet colouring.

If you buy or are given a pot of the florists' genista, properly *C. canariensis,* at Easter, it is well worth planting it out in a sunny sheltered place, once the first flush of its deliciously scented yellow spikelets is over. By the sea and in other mild areas it will often survive a succession of kind winters, growing 5 ft. high and as much through; but, even if it is to die in its first cold spell, it will in the meantime, have continued flowering for you right through the summer and autumn, and its greenery is fresh and far leafier than the average broom's. It roots remarkably easily from soft cuttings, and these, if struck in early summer, can be overwintered as nice young plants in a heated frame.

The most obvious ways in which the genus *Genista* (the other big group of brooms) differs from *Cytisus* is that the former's flowers are always yellow and that the plant can be spiny as in the petty whin, *G. anglica,* a native plant of heathland whose main function would seem to be in spoiling an otherwise pleasant picnicking spot. It is so petty that you have sat on it before realising your mistake. *Cytisus* are often yellow but may be other colours, and they never prick. A further difference, of some cultural importance, is that whereas many *Cytisus* are short lived, most of the genistas will go on and on for upwards of 30 years.

The largest of them is also the best. *G. aethnensis,* the Mount Etna broom, often looks like a small tree, 15 to 20 ft. high, with very slender branchlets drooping at their tips. The plant is virtually leafless, and there is thus nothing to mask or mitigate its display, in early July, when it is transformed into a shimmering golden fountain.

In its native habitat, on the slopes of Etna, *G. aethnensis* has to endure ferociously strong winds. Even on the fatter soils of our gardens, it is often root-firm and may need no staking. Perhaps the one drawback to the Mount Etna broom is that it does not start being impressive for quite a few years. It will flower when very young, but takes some time (like most of us) to achieve an important bulk. *G. cinerea* and *G. virgata* (the Madeira broom) would be more suitable for impatient gardeners. They are rather similar; very free flowering right from the start and make substantial 10 to 12 ft. shrubs with a midsummer season.

Genistas also abound in prostrate species; ground-huggers suited to rock gardens, dry wall ledges and paving that does not get trodden on unduly. *G. pilosa*, another native species, is well worth a place in the garden. Its strand-like shoots never rise more than 2 to 3 in. above the soil surface but cover an area of many square feet in course of time. It flowers in May. *G. januensis,* the Genoa broom, grows in the same sort of way, but its dark green shoots are winged and this gives the whole plant a much firmer-textured appearance. The flowers, in May and June, are dazzling, in great pools of yellow. Mr. Harold Hillier has planted it extensively on his fascinating rock garden, near Winchester. The rocks form escarpments on a slope, which is fairly conventional, but having mounted this you find yourself on a plateau of pebbles from which the rocks arise in occasional outcrops, and plants like this broom bask with evident complaisance. One gets a feeling of spaciousness that is quite unusual in rock gardens, where general effects are much more commonly swamped by a mass of detail.

Genista lydia has become famous of recent years. Coming from south-east Europe and Syria, it is not quite hardy in every circumstance; but it generally managed to pull through even after the 1963 winter. It makes a grand display in June, and the fascinating thing about this broom is the impression created by its sickle-shaped branchlets. On the flat, it is about one foot tall by an indefinite number of feet across, but when it finds itself near a vertical surface the shrub rises to 3 or 4 ft. It lives only 6 or 7 years.

Dyer's greenweed, *G. tinctoria,* is a pleasant, deep evergreen shrub of loose growth, about 2 ft. tall, common on wasteland whether of chalk, sand or clay. It has long been used for its yellow dye, particulary in conjunction with woad, to give a green wool. There are several garden forms, of which the double Plena is the showiest.

The most popular prickly broom is *G. hispanica,* growing into a too, too solid and compact evergreen shrub of smug appearance. But whereas single specimens look dreadfully dumpy, they can be nice when run together and forming a low, 3-ft. hedge. An annual

trim with shears immediately after flowering is its only requirement. The flowers are carried in tight bunches at the top of short
stalks, in May. They last for little more than a week.

Brooms are usually pot-grown and can therefore be planted at
any season. Exceptionally, James Smith Ltd. of Matlock, Derbyshire, grow theirs in the open ground. Often the *Cytisus* plants
received are 2 or 3 ft. tall but they do not move at all too badly,
although they may die back quite a lot from the tips, to start with.
Once established they cannot be moved. Their roots are too long
and coarse. They all like an open, sunny site.

Early Flowering Herbaceous Plants

There is a particularly fresh and charming group of herbaceous
plants that flowers in April and May. However much we may
tend to spread the work of splitting and planting the general run
of herbaceous subjects during the winter, we should deal with
these early flowerers betimes, since their period of dormancy is
just coming to an end in late autumn, when it is beginning for
most other plants.

The dark-purplish shoots of **Mertensia virginica** will be seen
pushing through in early February, but the plant is active long
before·this. Its roots are tuberous and, after a few years, will
become congested with a tendency to rot, which can be arrested
by gently cutting up the crowns in autumn, leaving at least one
tuber attached to each of its white growing points. This is one
of the most spring-like of spring flowers, like a pulmonaria with
all the coarseness eliminated, its fresh soap-smooth foliage
crowned at 18 in. by flowers and buds that combine pure azure
with flecks of pink and mauve. Around the time of its flowering
I always search among my clumps for self-sown seedlings.
If pricked out into a seed box forthwith, these will make large
plants by the autumn and will flower well in the following spring.

Dicentra spectabilis, known variously as bleeding heart, lyre
plant, Dutchman's breeches, lady's locket and lady in the bath,
is another rather fleshy-rooted plant that needs attention once in
a while, if it is not eventually to fall into a rotting decline. Dig up
your old clumps in autumn and then scratch your head while
deciding what to do next. The case is not nearly so clear as with

mertensia. First you must search out the growing points, which are pinkish in colour when well developed; but some are no more than white pimples, and they are scattered about the top of the rootstock in a confusing jumble. A sharp knife has got to be inserted so as to keep some roots attached to each group of shoots. If you find yourself left with almost rootless shoots, these can be potted up and brought on in a closed frame. Shootless roots, on the other hand, are worth bedding into a spare patch, as they do occasionally, though not reliably, make new shoots out of nothing. But all good samples from your divisions can immediately be re-planted as a new group for flowering next spring. Again it is worth looking for self-sown seedlings in May, and bringing them on somewhere so that they are not crowded out.

Ranunculus aconitifolius 'Flore Pleno' is a **buttercup** with mounds of perfectly formal, double white flowers, known as bachelor's buttons or fair maids of France. In this the white roots radiate starfish-wise from a disc-shaped crown. There is no tendency to rotting here—only a waste of the plant's potentialities, if it is allowed to grow too congested; for the young starfish try in vain to peer out from under the parental skirts. It is easy to pull the interlocking units apart. However, you must first get your original plant, which may be a little expensive, as, easy though it is to grow, its increase is never rapid enough for the nursery-man to be able to satisfy demand. And, naturally, this ultra-double flower sets no seed. Never be fobbed off with the single-flowered type-plant, which is scarcely worth growing once you have seen the double.

The double form of one of our three commonest wild butter-cups, R. *bulbosus*, is incredibly beautiful, but seldom seen. It is low-growing—no more than a foot tall—and the flowers are substantial, some 2 in. across and packed with petals all agleam with the lacquered surface peculiar to buttercups and celandines, and shading from rich yellow at the flower's margin to pure green at the centre. Plants can be killed if attacked by root aphids, which are white and very fond of this buttercup.

From buttercups to daisies: **Doronicum plantagineum**, the leopard's bane, is known in a variety of cultivated forms, but I find 'Miss Mason' usefully early and reasonably dwarf. It likes frequent splitting and replanting; and so, when grown in a border, is probably best broken up and removed to the vegetable garden as soon as flowering has ceased, in June, and brought back into prominence in November. But when naturalised in fairly rich moist soil under trees, where the rough grass is not so rank as to compete, doronicums will carry on for years without attention.

Summer

Peonies

Wherever you may read about **peonies,** whether in a specialist nurseryman's catalogue, in gardening articles or in books, the emphasis is the same and phrases such as 'of the easiest culture'. 'labour-saving' or 'the ideal no-trouble plant' are repeated time and again. However, my impression from my own garden and from the remarks of many other gardeners is that peonies are not as easy as they used to be. In the old days you could plant your clumps in well prepared ground and then virtually forget about them except for an annual top-dressing of manure. As long as you did not allow a colony to become ruined by the encroachment of bindweed or some other perennial weed that cannot be extracted from the peony crowns, they would last in good health for 25 to 30 years without disturbance and without ever failing to carry bountiful crops of great satiny blooms.

But nowadays only too often one hears of failures, in both the shrubby and the herbaceous types. The latter, in particular, are subject to blindness at an early, vestigial stage, their flower buds just shrivel up and fail to develop further. Their reasons for this behaviour are still obscure and no satisfactory remedy has been found. Another trouble, often but by no means always linked with blindness, is peony wilt disease (in no way connected, let me hasten to add, with clematis wilt, wilt of asters or hop wilt) caused by the fungus *Botrytis paeoniae*. Once it has gained a hold, this keeps up a running attack from spring to autumn. It disfigures the peony foliage, causing it to wither prematurely and robbing you of the autumn colouring that you would otherwise enjoy in the lactiflora hybrids. And if it gets into the main peony stems, as with those of my *Paeonia emodi* it often does, quite early on, the entire shoots collapse, flower buds and all.

Obviously, the earlier in the season the rot sets in, the more damage is done, and we do make a practice now of going round all our peonies about the middle or end of March, when their new shoots are 4 to 6 in. long, giving them a protective spraying with a copper fungicide (you can use it on your daphnes and willows at the same time). And it is worth repeating this a few weeks later, when more foliage has expanded. The pathological pundits also say that all dead and diseased debris should be removed, cutting down the stems of herbaceous peonies to below ground-level. In practice I find this impossible, because even in early autumn the next year's buds are already prominent and hard up against the last inch of old stem, so that you cannot completely remove the one without damaging the other.

Tree peonies, even the toughest species such as *P. delavayi*, are also subject to wilt disease, which may kill a whole branch down to ground-level or merely work back from dormant buds and affect side branches. These you have to cut out, but it is very hard to know just how far back you must cut to be rid of all infected material. *P. delavayi* has the additional drawback, as a source of inoculum, of not shedding its old foliage in autumn. It hangs on in an unsightly manner, and even if it is snipped off leaf by leaf, a bit of leaf stalk will remain behind. This makes hygiene difficult to practise. Fond though I am of this species, I have cast out my oldest specimen, because it was losing so many branches, and although the plant was reacting as best it could by throwing out strong young shoots 3 or 4 ft. long, from low down, it was losing the battle. When you dig out a peony, it seems small wonder that it should be a martyr to disease, for its roots are thick yet fleshy and of an almost spongy consistency. The whole plant, indeed, is soft, even though woody, and seems to invite infection. And what a curious smell it has when wounded: like a sort of rancid pepper.

The other vigorous shrubby species that is commonly planted these days is *P. lutea* in its variety *ludlowii*. This was introduced from Tibet in 1938 and was shortly accorded a jubilant acclaim. For it was far superior to *P. lutea* itself, with an earlier flowering season and larger blooms, of the same brilliant yellow and held facing outwards, so as to be easily appreciated, even amid its luxuriant foliage.

Further experience suggests that the Emperor's new clothes

were diaphanous after all. *P. lutea ludlowii* makes a very large shrub, 7 ft. tall by 12 ft. across and, except when used expressly as a space-filler in a large garden where much space has to be filled, is scarcely worth it. For the size of the shrub, the flowers are, frankly, not large or numerous enough; they make little impact. In itself, however, the foliage is handsome, being deeply lacin-iated, and it has a great pull over *P. delavayi* in shedding its leaves cleanly, in autumn, very often all at once in a matter of one blustery day.

Three-quarters of all the peonies grown, belong to the florists' group of lactiflora hybrids. They have received most attention from hybridists and offer the widest range of flower form and colour. These are the latest flowering group, having their main season in mid-June; they carry more than one flower to a stem and thus give some sort of a succession of blossom; and they are pleasantly scented. Also they are admirable for cutting: no other flower at that season gives you such an immediately bold effect and yet without the stiffness of, say, a bearded iris or a gladiolus.

Of the various single- and double-flowered types, it is hard to say that one likes one more than another. Singles for simplicity, naturally. That sumptuous boss of golden stamens looks particu-larly well in a frame of blood-red petals, as in Lord Kitchener, or against the pure white of that old-fashioned stalwart—one of the most prolific of all peonies—Whitleyi Major. And yet a huge double frilly confection such as Festiva Maxima, pure white with little flecks of red near the centre, would invite you irresistibly to plunge your face into it, even if there were no scent and it were known that hordes of earwigs were lurking among the flounces.

The snag about the doubles is their heavy-headedness. They hold so much water and are so slow to dry out, even in June, that thorough twigging is necessary a month beforehand, if their blooms are not to sway to the ground. And, if they are to be culled for the house, they should be gathered before the blooms have expanded and collected water, otherwise the rot sets in.

I think the double-flowered tree peonies—which are the second largest florists' group—are a mistake. They just are not practical. I remember seeing a fine specimen of the double yellow-flowered Souvenir de Maxime Cornu, whose every bloom had, of necessity, been given individual support. Wire rings had been used in this case, and the result was hideous. I cannot understand how gardeners can turn a blind eye to the obtrusiveness of these accessories. And yet the peony had to have support right up to its neck, and its growth is too sparse for this to be given invisibly. A better buy—though one of the most expensive of peonies—is the single-flowered l'Espérance, with wide blooms of a similarly alluring buff-yellow. It does hang its head a little, not from weightiness but because this is its penchant. However, when the bush has gained a bit of height, with the years, this is no drawback.

All the hybrid tree peonies have to be grafted on to pieces of root of the herbaceous types. Whatever their price, they are small and fragile when they come to you. On the rare occasions when I buy one, I ask for early spring delivery because, so often, an autumn-planted specimen just fades away without having shown any sign of life, and then you have all the argument and worry of whether the little victim was on its way out before its arrival or faded away on meeting its new owner. Plants imported straight from Japan are, as you would expect, even more subject to these hazards than the home-raised article. Plants that have been received in autumn are safer potted up and kept under cold glass, for the winter, than committed direct to the garden. When you do plant them out, make sure that the graft union is well below the soil level so that the scion is quickly enabled to make its own root system.

The old-fashioned double crimson peony, Rubra Plena, that one associates with the cottage gardens at the end of May, is the only one of the *Paeonia officinalis* group that is commonly seen, although the dirty pink/white Mutabilis is also occasionally encountered. Maurice Prichard's used to stage some most exciting cultivars of this type at the Chelsea Flower Show, only they never seemed to have any stock and have now, alas, gone out of the business. Grandeur has single dark red blooms with golden anthers. Anemonaeflora Rosea is deep pink with a central cushion of enlarged golden stamens and there were others. The trouble is that they are slow of increase and it will always be difficult to build up sufficient stocks to satisfy the inevitably heavy demand of a public whose appetite has been whetted by a show display.

It is sometimes hard to locate a source for the more out-of-the-way but exciting single-flowered peony species. Yet, where plants are unobtainable, it may be possible to get seed, most probably from Thompson & Morgan of Ipswich. Raising peonies from seed is a most satisfactory occupation. As long as the seed was not shrivelled and hence no use in the first place, good results are assured. True, it is a little slow; the seedling takes 18 months to put forth its first leaf, and another two years to reach flowering size, but you get such excellent plants this way. I recently planted a large patch with four- and-five-year-old, home-grown seedlings and can hardly imagine a happier occupation. The tallest-growing and the one having the fattest, juiciest winter buds, was *P. emodi.* The shortest, at only 18 in. or 2 ft. is *P. obovata alba.* Its pure white petals look especially telling against the purple colouring of its young foliage. And then there is *P. mlokosewitschi,* an early-May-flowering herbaceous peony with butter-yellow flowers. Some of my seedlings came translucent pink. The yellow is a rarer colour, true, but the pink gives one ideas of further possibilities. Seed of the other yellow herbaceous species, *P. wittmanniana,* is also obtainable, and it is almost as good as its cousin, though a trifle more wan in colouring.

These single-flowered peonies do want planting in a bit of shade, as against a north wall, otherwise a hot sun at flowering time makes them come out and go over within the week.

Gazanias

Gazanias, like all South African daisies (venidiums, ursinias, arctotis, dimorphothecas, felicias) are the very essence of summer, radiant and fickle, gladdening and maddening by turns. Visitors to the R.H.S. gardens at Wisley on a sunny day in summer or autumn will be entranced by their fabulous collection of gazanias, near the alpine house. These have mostly been obtained by a process of selection of seedlings, made on the premises. Any of us can do the same, for gazanias are readily raised from seed which can be obtained, initially, from one of several seed houses, and the plants will set seed in your own garden, thereafter.

Plants obtained from cuttings taken in the previous autumn, will come earlier into flower—in June—and this will be your method of perpetuating any particular variety that you have fallen in love with. But it is difficult to buy plants. With the exception of fuchsias, dahlias and chrysanthemums, for which public demand is terrific, nurseries do not generally find it worth marketing tender perennials which have to be sent out in May. The customer asks for one plant or two, and the expense is disproportionate.

Gazanias are a bit of trouble. There is no disputing this, but I have been growing them for more than 20 years now, and I plant out about 90 of them in a sunny bed each early May (they will stand a few degrees of frost) and can state from experience that once you have worked out the best routine they take up very little time.

In any case the gazania personality is so strong that you make yourself a willing slave. The plant is neat and clumpy, but the leaves vary greatly from plant to plant. Some are long, lanceolate and green; others may be quite short, pinnate and thickly white-felted. The latter, indeed, are often grown principally for foliage effect. Usually, of course, it is for the flowers. There is no basic gazania flower colouring. They may be cream, primrose, lemon or chrome yellow; apricot, vivid or deep orange; brown, beige, purple or crushed strawberry-pink. And at the base of each ray there are markings in contrasting shades in which black predominates, but often including spots of startlingly brilliant green.

They are exceedingly fussy about weather and, even if the day is hot throughout, insist on strict trade union rules by shutting up at four o'clock. A closed or even a half closed gazania flower is practically invisible, and distinctly depressing if you do happen to see it. There is no moodier flower, but when they do relax and bask, you will want to fling off your clothes and bask in sympathy.

No plant could be of easier cultivation, with the one rider of their not being hardy. They will grow happily on all soils, light and heavy, and are never attacked by pests or fungal disease. Of course, their position must be open and sunny, but they will take any amount of wind and are unaffected by salt spray on the coast.

In autumn, you must think about propagating the varieties that are worth saving. Lifting and re-potting old plants does not work, but it is easy to take cuttings of non-flowering shoots. You pull them off with a heel and then trim this clean with a razor blade. If the leaves are long and floppy, you can shorten them by one third, also with the blade. Should the shoot have a flower bud, tweak it out.

You can get about nine cuttings into a 3½ in. pot, using an open cutting compost, and this goes into a close frame. Bottom heat is unnecessary and a mist propagator is undesirable, since (as is the case with most hairy-leaved or woolly-leaved perennials) the cuttings tend to rot away if kept excessively damp. Some of the outer leaves on each cutting are liable to die, and should be peeled off before their rotting spreads to the rest of the shoot. Give them air as soon as they can take it without flagging unduly.

I used to make my cuttings in the second week of September and pot them off individually about the end of October. However, this is space-consuming and I now find it even more satisfactory to make my cuttings in the last days of October. When they have rooted, in December, the pots are transferred to the open green-house bench, where they remain till March and the cuttings are only then potted off individually, into a cold frame, being ready for planting out six weeks later. If short of space in spring, you can plant them out direct from the pots in which they were rooted, but the plants take much longer to grow into nice fat specimens, that way.

The roots of gazanias have a way of clinging tenaciously to the pot sides and bottom, and you are liable to leave much root behind, when turning them out. If you make sure that the entire ball of soil and roots is wringing wet, before you attempt the operation, the chances are that you will accomplish a painless extraction. They stick less to the sides of a plastic pot than to clay. Best of all, you could use a composition pot that rots away after a few weeks, or a soil block.

Are Lupins Worthwhile?

Most gardeners have an affectionate feeling for **lupins.** They take us back to our childhood. Their warm but peppery smell is nostalgic. Their plump spikes seem to be asking to be patted with the flat of one's hand. They are popular with bees, are gay, colourful and, together with oriental poppies, are among the first recognisable heralds of high summer. Furthermore, they flower at a useful time for the average gardener, just after he has had to throw out the spring bedding but before the mainstays of summer have got into their stride.

Why, then, should I ask whether lupins are worthwhile? Because their display lasts for only a fortnight and that is not very long for a perennial that occupies a good deal of space. And then, for the rest of the summer, the plants look more or less a wreck. You can dead-head them and let the old stems carry a few side-spikes, later on, but they never look up to much and commonly become mildewed as the season progresses. Alternatively, you can cut the plants to the ground after flowering—undoubtedly the best policy with the aforementioned poppies, but weakening to lupins, which are anyway rather apt to seek excuses for dying on us. The modern Russell lupin is a fine, upstanding plant with bold spikes in a tremendous range of straight or bicoloured shades, but somewhere in its ancestry is the blood of an annual species, and the improved lupins of today are inclined to be short-lived.

What I am saying, really, is that wrecks in the border are something we can accept in September but shall swallow less readily in late June and July. Furthermore, to be thoroughly enjoyed, lupins really want to be grown in masses, not just spotted about here and there. How can we square our love of the plant at its best with it becoming a liability in the garden at its worst?

In a large garden or in public parks, the solution is not too difficult. You can plant your lupins in special beds either on their own or with shrubs and other early-flowering perennials—they do contrast wonderfully with oriental poppies, I must repeat—and then either forget about that part of the garden later on or replace them with something else. Before siting lupins in a small garden, however, do consider whether their appearance from mid-June onwards is not going to be rather too dear at the price.

Really, I believe that the happiest solution, although it does involve extra work, is to treat them as biennials. Sow your seeds in April, line out the seedlings in a spare plot and, by the autumn, you will have large plants for transferring to their flowering positions. After flowering, throw them out and replace with summer bedding sown about the last week of April. In this way your efforts will be rewarded by a double display from one piece of ground and the fact that lupins are apt to be short-lived will be neither here nor there. But you will still need to have a garden large enough to include that spare plot.

Even if you are treating them as perennials, it is as well to sow a few seeds each spring so as to have strong plants with which to replace any old ones that are looking weary in the autumn. Autumn is the only time for planting lupins; spring is too late, as they come into growth very early and never get properly established if moved after the new year. You can buy plants of handsome named varieties, but I would never go to this, as it seems to me, unnecessary expense. You can grow such excellent strains from seed, in a range of thrilling colours. When people say their lupins have 'reverted', what has actually happened is they they have allowed their old plants to self-sow. These seedlings grow strongly and gradually oust their parents but, being unselected, are not themselves of such good colouring. As this process goes on, they get near to the wild blue type-plant of their early ancestors.

Like all plants with thick, fang-like roots, lupins prefer the sharp drainage of light soils. However, be warned against growing them on chalk because, light though it is, it brings on acute chlorosis. The lupins' leaves turn bright yellow and the plants fade away.

Lupins generally grow 4 ft. tall at flowering time and it is a question whether one should support them. I never do. Sometimes an untimely gale or wind with rain, knocks them all over the place at the climax of their flowering, but more often it is fairly quiet around the turn of May and June, and the lupins proceed in triumph.

Easy Primulas for the Summer Garden

Many **primulas** are specialist's plants but many others are for all of us, if we will obey a few simple, basic rules. A typical and particularly useful group are the candelabras, growing anything from 18 in. to 3½ ft. tall and with flowers arranged in tiers (whorls) along naked stems (scapes). They love moisture and are especially appropriate in damp woodland or by stream sides, but they can be fitted into most gardens, provided their moisture requirements in the growing season are not neglected. However, they will not stand being waterlogged or flooded in winter, when dormant. The candelabras' season lasts, according to their several species, from April to July.

Most are great self-seeders, and you do want to be a bit careful about letting them do this indiscriminately, because (unlike *Campanula persicifolia,* for instance, which scarcely ever looks out of place, wherever it may sow itself) they can look rather weed-like when scattered around and aré always most effective in the mass. Another point against self-seeding is that the candelabra section as a whole are promiscuous. They interbreed readily and the progeny can assume repulsively livid, dirty complexions. A point in favour of growing these primulas from seed, every now and again, however, is in order to regain virus-free stock. The virus diseases from which they suffer are not transmitted through the seed. You can often spot this trouble by a noticeable reduction in leaf size and plant vigour, combined with uncharacteristic, toothed leaf margins.

Primula japonica is one of the earliest candelabras to start flower-ing, and two of the best coloured cultivars are Miller's Crimson and Postford White. It is wise to keep these well separated, in the garden, so that they cannot interbreed. Nearly all inter-mediate shades, in this species, are grubby pinkish mauves. Another fault in *P. japonica* is that the flowers quickly scorch or bleach.

P. pulverulenta is typically a brilliant, deep rosy magenta; obvious, perhaps, but effective, and well offset by the coating of white farina on its stems. If you cannot take this colour you will certainly get pleasure from the Bartley Strain, in which the flowers cover a range of pale, pastel salmony shades. These are all three-footers. At half their height is a Pulverulenta strain called Red Hugh, that comes surprisingly true from seed and is as rich a colour as the 3-ft. Inverewe, but plants are apt to be short-lived and to require frequent renewal. Inverewe itself is spectacular when seen in drifts, being a brilliant and clear but by no means harsh red. Not everyone stocks it so I will put in here

Plate 25. Above, Crown Imperials, *Fritillaria imperialis,* with yellow or orange flowers in spring.

Below, Lenten roses are hybrids of *Helleborus orientalis* and other species and have a long season early in the year.

that it is listed by Jack Drake of Aviemore, Inverness-shire, although he comments that demand usually exceeds supply.

P. chunglenta is a hybrid between *P. chungensis* and *P. pulverulenta.* It is 3 ft. tall, and although pinkish-orange may sound dangerous on paper it is here most pleasing in actual fact. *P. chungensis* is one of several pure orange primula species, but not the best. For a small setting I should choose the petite *P. cockburniana,* a brilliant deep, clear orange and only a foot tall. Of the same colouring but rather larger in its parts is *P. aurantiaca,* also noted for its stems and flower stalks being dark and red-tinged. *P. bulleyana* is an obliging three-footer, fairly late-flowering and usually encountered somewhat hybridised in pleasant apricot shades. However, it has sometimes been crossed with *P. beesiana* (a nasty magenta) and with *P. pulverulenta* to give an extraordinary jumble of clashing colours—mauves, yellows, pinks, oranges and apricots. If you want an eyeful of colour, these should supply the desired knockout punch. Partial though I am to many mauve and magenta shades, I find *P. burmanica* quite repulsive too; it has dense heads of large, crude-mauve flowers, each with a yellow eye; very effective.

For a clear butter-yellow flower on a graceful 4-ft. stem, it would be hard to beat *P. helodoxa.* I think it looks marvellous in front of blue anchusas. But in many gardens, including my own, it tends to die out unless you are constantly re-planting it. *P. prolifera* is similar and said to be easier but I have not got round to trying it.

These candelabras, on which I have so far concentrated, are the best known of the larger, late-flowering types. As easy to cultivate, however, are most members of the Sikkimensis section, and they have the outstanding merit of exhaling, in the evening, a strong, airborne scent. This is delicious and not in the least sickly. Their funnel-shaped flowers are carried in one large, crowning umbel, after the style of a cowslip. Indeed, they are often known as giant cowslips, but not very appropriately in other respects. Even their scents are of entirely different orders.

Plate 26. Above, Pinus ayacahuite has foot-long cones set among elegantly drooping needles.

Below, Abies homolepis has navy blue young cones.

Best known, most easily grown, largest in leaf and stoutest in stem is *Primula florindae*. Its flowers are typically clear yellow, and well over 100 can be packed into one umbel. They open in succession, so this primula's season is a long one, extending into August. The leaves are heart-shaped and lush, but put out pathetic distress signals the moment they run short of moisture. However, they are no slower to regain their vitality once a good soaking has been administered. None of these bog primulas are suited to gardens without some form of irrigation, except in a few excessively wet outposts on the fringes of the British Isles. Beds and borders that are desperately soggy for three-quarters of the year can suddenly turn hard and caked in a midsummer drought, just when primulas are in fullest leaf and at their thirstiest.

P. sikkimensis, which gives its name to the section, is yellow too, but of much slighter habit and with svelte, elliptic leaves. But you might just as well have done with it, I think, and settle for *P. alpicola* in its full colour range. It can be soft yellow, too, but also fresh, pure white, and covers a range of mauve and purple shades, all in quiet tones in unexceptionably good taste. It is really surprising how seldom one sees this primula, which has no drawbacks and whose evening fragrance is particularly good.

P. capitata is a reliable late flowerer, but of slighter build than those so far considered, and only 1 ft. tall when in full bloom. It is a mealy plant, carrying dense heads of quite large, lavender-coloured bells. This is very easily raised from seed, and so (provided the seed is good) is *P. viali* (*P. littoniana*), one of the most extraordinary and arresting of all primulas. So extraordinary is it that most people, seeing it for the first time, fail to recognise it as a primula at all, unless they happen to spot the leaves. After a very late start in spring—which will send you all of a twitter, thinking that winter has done for it—*P. viali* is in its prime in July, with elegant, 1-foot-tall spikes, shaped like a red-hot poker's. The illusion is the more marked for its red colouring, before the flowers expand, this colour deriving from the calyx segments. The corolla is mauve, and it overwhelms the red, but a half-opened spike combines bright red in its top portion with mauve in its lower. The effect is beautiful as well as weird.

If summer's tail-end is not too mouldy, this primula sets good seed in abundance; but the best time to sow it is not as soon as ripe—small seedlings being tricky to bring through the winter months. Sow it and all your other primulas in March and April. The tendency always is to sow far too thickly, the seed being minute and there is a strong impression in the sower that nothing will germinate. When a thousand or more seedlings materialise in one moderate-sized pot, competition quickly becomes acute, but you can save the situation by pricking out at an early stage. Neat fingers and a readiness to handle tiny plants are great advantages here.

All those primulas that make multiple crowns can be increased by division. This includes the entire candelabra and sikkimensis sections and is the only way of keeping a good cultivar, such as Inverewe, true to type. Division is best carried out in the growing season and as soon as flowering is over. In this way (as with bearded irises) the plants are enabled to get re-established before the dormant season. Choose your moment, if you can, to coincide with a rainy spell.

One fault I notice with informal plantings of primulas, even in a woodland setting where they should look at their most informal, is that they often give the appearance of having been bedded out. True, they have been, but you want to disguise the fact. Do not follow your paths or your stream beds with regular parallel ribbons of primulas. Let the planting bulge in natural re-entrants and narrow at other points—maybe where a shrub encroaches. Primula planting is not a military exercise; you are not bedding out squads and platoons. As I wrote of daffodils, if every plant is put in at the same distance from its neighbour, you will end up with a series of straight, diagonal lines, however little you intended to. So vary your spacing. And do not interplant your primulas with (for instance) meconopses as one might plant tulips with forget-me-nots. Again, the bedding cliché is out of place and it is more effective to get your primulas and poppies into separate but adjacent groups with, perhaps, just a little overlapping and intermingling.

Evening Primroses

Anyone with the remotest interest in gardening will know what is being talked about when the vernacular for the genus *Oenothera* is used; but, as is so often the way, the common name is thoroughly misleading. **Evening primroses** are not primroses, and only some of them open in the evening. They do, however, all have certain similar and recognisable features: a regular, bowl-shaped flower; colouring that is either yellow or, less often, white; and finally, descending to the subjective, a cheerful, welcoming mien.

Almost too welcoming, at times. My earliest memories of *O. biennis* are of having the end of my nose plastered with its yellow pollen, through savouring the fragrance of its newly opened blossoms. This is the most familiar of all the evening primroses: a biennial making, in its first year, a rosette of narrow strap-shaped leaves; in its second, a slender, rather weedy-looking flowering stem up to 3 ft., carrying a seemingly endless daily succession of 2-inch-wide yellow blooms, from early evening till morning, one or two at a time on each stem. The flowers open intriguingly, in a series of visible jerks, which can be precipitated if sprayed upon, at the magic hour, from a watering can. This species naturalises in rough places, and I particularly connect it with the dunes of that Mecca for lovers of wild flowers, the Royal St. George's golf links at Sandwich.

As well known is *O. erythrosepala* (or *O. lamarckiana*), another biennial, but much stronger growing, with broader leaves, a stature of 4 to 5 ft. and flowers at least 3 in. across. Once you have got it in the garden, you are unlikely to lose it; but it could not be called a serious weed. Again, it is pleasantly scented.

Another nocturnal evening primrose is *O. acaulis,* but it is uncommon. It is a low, herbaceous perennial with dandelion-like leaves (hence its synonym, *O. taraxacifolia*). The large white blossoms are about 3 in. across and show up well on summer nights, but also last into the following forenoon, finally changing to pale pink as they crumple up and fade.

Their scent is of a cheap and cloying brand of soap. It is a nuisance that a quite different and inferior species is being currently marketed as *O. acaulis*. Though I do not know its correct name, I have grown this one and thrown it out. Its yellow blooms are 2 in. wide, and they do not open till after dark. Moreover, they have faded by the time any normal person claps eyes on them the next morning. Indeed, I have been assured that they often wither by 5.0 a.m. Both the true and the false *O. acaulis* are technically stemless, as their name implies, but their perianth tube is 4 or 5 in. long and hence gives the appearance of a stem, much as you find it in crocuses. The seed capsules are clustered at ground level.

Deservedly one of the most popular of its tribe is the glamorous *O. missouriensis*. It is a prostrate, sprawling herbaceous perennial, hardy if not waterlogged, and making annual stems that ramble for about 15 in. in every direction over the soil surface. So it is excellent as a front-line plant where required to break the hard edge of paving. In winter it disappears completely and is easily destroyed by the officious and unwary. The bright yellow flowers are 3 in. across and look spectacular adorning such a low plant. They open early in the evening and last for nearly 24 hours, but are scentless. This species' alternative name, *O. macrocarpa*, spotlights an unusual feature: its enormous seed-pods with flanges like the wings on a mortar shell.

Even more effective as a mat-former is *O. tetragona riparia* (syn. *O. riparia*), but in many ways it is a very different plant from the last. It is hardy and perennial and makes dense, basal rosettes of narrow foliage in winter. In early summer the flowering stems rise to a height of 9 in. or a foot; but as soon as they start flowering, the first shower or heavy dew brings them to the ground, where they form a pool of solid yellow over the next two months. Individually the flowers are quite small but very numerous; and this is where the name of 'evening primrose' gets us into trouble and has to be explained away, for the flowers are strictly of the day, expanding in the morning and shutting up at night. The most telling way in which I ever grew this plant was in a ribbon on each side of a straight path, backed by a dwarf, purple-flowered lavender hedge. Unfortunately the ground became oenothera-sick. What this means, in fact, is that oenotheras are subject to attack by the same strain of stem eelworm as infects herbaceous phloxes, and when this happens the plants die out.

There are many modern named varieties of oenothera, with stiff, self-supporting stems a foot to 18 in. high, that make excellent and showy border plants with day-flowering habits. They are yellow-flowered, but in Fireworks, for instance, the buds are red, while in *O. cinaeus* the young spring foliage is ruby tinted.

On our clay, I have never made a success of *O. speciosa,* which is not fully hardy, but when it is at home it is charming, with slender 18-in. stems carrying 2-inch-wide white blossoms that age to pink. If happy, the plant spreads quite rapidly by underground rhizomes. It is worth trying on freely draining soils.

Border Phloxes

August is a testing time for herbaceous and mixed borders. It becomes clear, as the month progresses, whether we are going to witness a rapid and early disintegration, with unfettered colonies of mustard yellow sunflowers and golden rod taking charge of the autumn scene, or whether a plan has been at work that will allow the border to develop and 'set budding more and still more later flowers for the bees.' The countryside tends to look its worst at this time of year, with masses of tired, dusty, caterpillar-riddled foliage. The more reason, it seems to me, that our gardens should be gay oases.

Herbaceous **phloxes** are not always the easiest of plants to grow successfully, but there is nothing to touch them in the late summer border (except dahlias, perhaps). It is easy enough to get your cool background shades and interesting shapes in the August border, but you really do need heavy splodges of colour to set them off. For this reason I do not mind phloxes of the most screaming pinks, mauves and magentas. All these will tone in perfectly happily, as long as those mustard yellows I was mentioning are kept under control.

The names of most of my phloxes are unknown to me. Much the safest way of introducing a fresh variety of phlox into your garden is by begging a piece from an obviously flourishing clump in some other garden; but, naturally enough, it will usually come to you without a name. I have always been unlucky with phloxes I have bought in. The charms of a modern variety seen on a show stand leave one more clueless than with most plants as to its garden-worthiness. It should, but may not, be self-supporting, and its flowers should be able to stand up to a reasonable degree of adverse weather without bleaching or bruising too badly or being prematurely knocked off by heavy rain.

But the greatest hazard when acquiring a new phlox is that you may be introducing the dreaded phlox eelworm with it. There will be no joy in phloxes for you where this pest is present. It is a microscopic creature that inhabits the stems and leaves of phloxes and of oenotheras. When these disappear, the eelworms remain in a resting state in the soil around infected plants, and re-invade young tissues on their reappearance in spring. Although you can never see the eelworms, you can soon learn to recognise their presence by the plant's peculiar reaction to eelworm attacks. The young phlox shoots and foliage become puckered and distorted and—an infallible indication—some of the leaves on stunted shoots become reduced from their normal oval shape to a mere green thread.

There is only one course of action: the infected group must be dug out and burnt and no more phlox must be planted on this site for three or four years. There is a saving factor in this tale of destruction, however. The eelworm never invades the plant's roots, and, as phloxes can be propagated very readily from root cuttings, you can elude the eelworm as I have already described (page 68).

Phlox paniculata, the wild type and principal parent of most of our herbaceous phlox cultivars, is a wonderful garden plant, and smothered in August with delicate mauve blossoms on airy panicles of a lightness and grace that have been quite lost in the course of hybridisation. Its only drawback is in growing (on my soil) 5 ft. tall, and needing to be staked. One way out of this trouble that can be adopted with most over-tall herbaceous perennials is to decapitate the young shoots in early summer when they are about half grown. Remove the top six inches or even a foot. They will flower a week or ten days later but will be sturdier and self-supporting. The drawback to this wheeze with a phlox is that its domed panicle is one of its conspicuous assets. Stopping the young shoots means that you get a number of small panicles from each stem instead of one big one, and the small panicles have less individuality as units.

Another dodge that can be put into operation on many perennials, I also had to use one year on this phlox, when the plants at the front of my main group grew taller than those behind. To prevent this happening again, I simply lifted and immediately replanted the front plants (without splitting them) in the autumn, when I was overhauling the border. This form of root pruning sufficiently reduced the plants' height in the next season without affecting their freedom of flowering.

Phlox paniculata has a nice albino form and there are other interesting by-ways among the border phloxes if you look out for them. For instance, *P. maculata* 'Alpha'. Instead of broad, domed panicles, *P. maculata* has them narrow and columnar, which makes for a completely different massed effect. Alpha is a nice pinkish-mauve, flowering in July, while *P. m.* 'Mrs. Lingard' is pure white, 3 ft. tall. A really lovely thing. At one time *P. paniculata* was frequently crossed with *P. divaricata* and the hybrids were called *P. arendsii*. They have large flowers on dwarf plants and are early, being at their best in June. Not many remain in cultivation but perhaps the finest is Elizabeth: pale blue with a dark eye, and only 2 ft. tall—which is just as well because its stems are slender and weak. But this is a beauty and looks well associated with the pale lemon corymbs of *Achillea taygetea*.

Border Giants

Garden literature tends, nowadays, to assume that nobody has room for a large plant. Hybridists and nurserymen take the same view. Among the michaelmas daisies, for instance, you have to turn back to an old variety like Climax before you can hope to find a seven-footer. Very few herbaceous plants are listed as growing higher than 5 ft. This is partly because nurseries are usually on poor, sandy soils, and their plants never attain any great height; partly, also, because to list a plant as growing higher than 5 ft. puts the average customer off.

However, there are a lot of gardeners, like myself, who do still enjoy a large border. And whether this is a one-sided affair, say 15 ft. from front to back, or whether a large island bed, we do need some big stuff in it. The sad fact is that there are very few really worthwhile tall herbaceous plants. Considering that they have to make 6 ft. of growth in as many weeks, it is not, I suppose, surprising that they are often of coarse and weedy appearance and, in the sumptuous growing conditions of a well-nourished border, only too liable to outgrow their strength and flop helplessly.

I would not gladly exchange my clay stodge for a free-draining, drought-prone sand or chalk soil; but the latter do have a welcome stiffening effect on tall herbaceous plants. I am very fond of **Rudbeckia** 'Herbstsonne', with its oil-smooth foliage and its lemon daisies with a fresh green central cone. But its weak-kneed ways have beaten me, and anyway one had to see it from an upper-floor window in order to enjoy its flowers properly. But on light soils that can be adequately watered—for it has a great thirst—this cone-flower is a reasonable proposition.

The **plume poppy**, *Macleaya (Bocconia) cordata*, is apt to sway over from the base with me. I had avoided growing this plant, chicken-heartedly, until a few years ago. Like a number of other fleshy-rooted perennials, it dislikes being moved and takes a year to settle down, but tends to ramp thereafter. But the wide-awake gardener should not be deterred by a trifling matter of this kind. All the same I have now, with considerable effort and deep digging over two years, got rid of (or nearly got rid of) it, after all. Although mine was sold to me as Coral Plume, which is a warm colour rather like the incense plant, *Humea elegans,* it turned out to be a washy thing and its season was too short.

I have persisted in avoiding **Crambe cordifolia,** although it makes a strong bid for one's affections at its midsummer best. It is then one mass of tiny white blossoms, from top (7 or 8 ft.) to toe. But its dark heart-leaves are coarse and, after flowering, you are left with a huge hole.

Vernonia crinita and *Eupatorium purpureum* both look intolerably weedy, to my eyes. The old **tree scabious,** *Cephalaria tatarica,* is well behaved with me and never sets a seed, though there is a fertile strain that self-sows abundantly. Its branching inflorescence rises gracefully yet sturdily to 7 ft. and I have a soft spot for its flowers, although their greenish-yellow colouring is rather too subdued. **Hollyhocks** are ideal for those who can grow them without rust disease becoming a nuisance. I tried getting over this by growing annual hollyhocks, but although they attain the required height and include singles and doubles in a good colour range, their leaves obscure the blooms. Also they get rust!

A plant that really comes into its own on heavy soil is **Artemisia lactiflora.** It cannot abide a drought. Growing to 6 or 7 ft., it is one of the few tall herbaceous plants that are absolutely self-supporting. Its creamy plumes associate charmingly with anything you care to put nearby. We have it, in one place, next to

Thalictrum dipterocarpum, another moisture-lover that will grow
6 to 8 ft. tall, with enormous panicles of its delicate mauve
blossoms, but less than half as high on arid ground. That old
cottage-garden plant **Chrysanthemum uliginosum** (once known
as *Pyrethrum uliginosum*) is fond of wet places, too. Its white,
greeny-yellow-eyed daisies, each about 2 in. across, are fresh and
pleasing, coming as they do in early October. It grows to 7 ft.,
but no border can take much of a plant that is a passenger throughout the summer and early autumn, and needs good support.

The **cartwheel flower**, *Heracleium mantegazzianum,* is truly
rigid and never in need of crutches. Ten or more feet tall, each
of its main platforms is said, by the *R.H.S. Dictionary*, to consist
of up to 10,000 flowers. I should have enjoyed watching the man
who made this estimate setting about his task. But certainly, it
seeds all too freely for most parts of a tamed garden.

Probably the most architectural of all herbaceous plants is the
cardoon, *Cynara cardunculus*. It is first cousin to or, maybe, even
blood brother of the globe artichoke, but the former's leaves are
larger, more deeply cut and, I fancy, greyer; the candelabra-like
inflorescence rises to 8 ft. (instead of the artichoke's 4 ft.), is much
more branching and has smaller, more prickly heads—all the
better for looking at, but painful and unrewarding to eat. I cannot,
in my garden, escape supporting the cardoons, and it is a difficult
job. You need stout stakes of 2 in. diameter, and it is hard work
knocking them in, because once the cardoon leaves have expanded,
the ground beneath them, where the stakes have to go, gets hard
and bone-dry and remains so till autumn. Furthermore, even
tarred twine round their stems is not strong enough to last the
season out. Insulated telephone wire is the answer.

Foliage Effects with Shrubs

If there is a dearth of giant herbaceous material of sufficient merit
to deserve a place in large borders, at least there are a number
of soft-wooded shrubs that can often be treated rather like herbaceous plants in order to contribute an exotic, even a tropical,
touch.

The idea of growing **Paulowina tomentosa (imperialis)** entirely for its foliage is well established. It is readily raised from

seed. The young plants are set 4 ft. apart and pruned back each winter to within a couple of inches of the base of the previous season's shoots. When growth is resumed, only one shoot is allowed to develop on each plant; this will reach a height of 10 or 12 ft. in a season, and be clothed with specimens of its furry, heart-shaped leaves, which are 2 to 3 ft. across. Obviously the site must not be exposed. The effect is a trifle extraordinary, but opulent in a recherché vein that depends on size and form rather than on size and colour. Leaves of this solidity would contrast particularly well with a clump of fine-leaved bamboos such as *Sinarundinaria nitida*, or a tall grass of the *Miscanthus* tribe. Another tree that can be treated like a herbaceous plant in exactly the same way as paulowina is *Ailanthus altissima* (*A. glandulosa*), the tree of heaven. This has pinnate leaves that may grow 4 ft. long, by this pruning method. Even more interesting in the same sort of style is the stag's horn sumach, *Rhus typhina* in its cut-leaved form laciniata.

Such plants are surely more dramatic than the dowdily pretentious hardy **palms** one sees in holiday resorts. These are *Trachycarpus fortunei* (better known as *Chamaerops excelsa*) with evergreen fan-shaped leaves. When young and no more than 4 or 5 ft. high, they can look pleasing and I should not be against recommending them provided you were strong minded enough to chuck them out as soon as they were past their first youth. Most often you see them as gaunt trees with hideous, thick furry trunks surmounted by bundles of old, unshed leaves and finally a tuft of live ones that is quite out of scale with the obesity that has gone before. The great thing about trachycarpus is its extraordinary hardiness.

Of the **maples,** I had never cared about the green-and-white *Acer negundo* 'Variegata' until I saw it treated as a shrub, against a good dark background. As a tree, it seems always to revert to a dull, plain green plant, but any such tendency in a shrub is easily thwarted. The golden variegated and pure yellow-leaved forms are equally effective. Another acer that would set this one off well is the reddish-purple-leaved variety of the Norway maple, *A. platanoides* 'Schwedleri', and it will take similar treatment. It must be remembered that if you severely prune a shrub that normally grows into a tree, every year, its constitution is inclined to become gradually weakened and replacements will be necessary from time to time.

Other vigorous maples with handsome foliage may be treated in a like manner, as may **poplars**. A good yellow form of the silver *Populus alba*, is Richard's variety (Richardii) and the silver poplar itself is no less effective. A poplar that has recently come into prominence as a regularly pollarded specimen is *P. candicans* 'Aurora', whose young foliage, up till midsummer, is strikingly variegated in pink, green and cream.

As a flowering shrub that responds to a severe annual pruning, the form of the Canadian **elder** called *Sambucus canadensis maxima* is most satisfactory. At a height of 7 or 8 ft. it carries its thousands of creamy flowers in handsome flat-headed umbels up to 18 in. across, from July to October. After flowering, its intricate network of flowering stalks turns to blackcurrant purple, over which the ripening berries are spangled like beads on a hair net. This shrub needs and deserves a lot of space. It radiates a mood of expansive prodigality.

The elder tribe is altogether a good quarry. For its foliage, the golden elder, *S. nigra aurea* contrasts particularly well in an open sunny position with a heavy purple shrub such as *Acer platanoides* 'Goldsworth Purple' (alias Crimson King); with a purple-leaved *Prunus* like *P. cerasifera* 'Nigra' or with *Corylus maxima* 'Purpurea', the purple-leaved hazel—all cut hard back annually or biennially. With these could be associated a group of willows of quite restricted growth: *Salix alba sericea,* with leaves like silver fish. I should also want the golden catalpa, which again is far less vigorous than its green-leaved counterpart.

Deciduous Trees in Summer

Glancing across any piece of countryside in August, one is impressed—even oppressed—by its uniformly heavy aspect. Deciduous trees are in their summer doldrums. Many have settled into a sullen, broody greenness that is not greatly lightened even by an interesting leaf shape. When we are planting trees for ornament, our choice will be guided by many factors—shape, size at maturity, winter outline, bark texture, spring blossom and foliage, autumn colouring and so on. The question of their appearance in summer is liable to be brushed aside, yet we have to live with them in this state for one quarter of each year.

Any given species of tree will probably make its annual growth in one of two ways: either it will rapidly put on its new shoots to their full extent in early spring, and spend the rest of the leafy season in maturing them; or it will make continuous extension growth throughout the summer months, so that its extremities are young and springlike till September. Most indigenous trees, and many more besides, belong to the first category; it is they that tend to pass through a boring period. Horse chestnut, wych and English elm, sycamore, beech, hornbeam, lime and even the British oaks are pretty tedious from July to September, though individual oaks often create a second spring in July by unfolding an aftermath of young foliage. This happens when the first crop has been devoured by caterpillars.

Some, in this category, get away with it by the light and airy quality of their leaves—notably the ash, a tree of contrasts if ever there was one; so uncompromisingly stark in its winter outline, with branches that remain thick right to their black tips; but diaphanous and feathery in summer, never casting a deep, glum shade. The walnut is rather like this, too. Its pinnate leaf is of a tougher quality, but cheerfully coloured, while the pale grey bark on trunk and branches is never quite out of sight.

The **Chinese pagoda tree,** *Sophora japonica,* is dark in colouring by late summer, but with a pinnate leaf composed of some 13 leaflets, it remains light and shimmering. Sophoras do flower at maturity, but one plants them for their other qualities. Maturity is not attained for 30 years, if then. August is their season, when they have one, and the ground beneath is littered with a carpet of spent flowers like grains of rice: a common sight on the Continent, but rare in Britain.

Of the pinnate-leaved trees, by far the freshest-looking is the false acacia, **Robinia pseudacacia.** As you drive through town, suburb or countryside, you can pick them out instantly at a considerable distance, because of their pale green colouring and the fountain-like arrangement of their foliage. The robinia is hardy but its branches are brittle, and its one requirement is a reasonable degree of shelter from the fiercest winds. So it is an excellent tree for town and inland gardens.

Poplars, including aspens (*Populus tremula*), can never look wholly dull, whatever their colouring, because their long leaf stalks ensure that the slightest breath of air will set them in motion. The black poplar, *P. nigra,* is not otherwise very exciting, except as a food plant for the caterpillars of some interesting moths; but the golden poplar, *P. serotina* 'Aurea' is a wonderful plant. The copper of its spring foliage changes to euphorbia yellow and then to a gay lime green, retained till autumn. Given the space, I would plant it against a purple beech. Grey poplars, *P. canescens,* are exquisite, too. The undersides of their leaves change from white to grey, as they age, but the trees' growth is of the continuous variety, and so there are always more pale young leaves coming on.

Although the common lime is dull, once it has finished flowering, in July, the **weeping silver lime,** *Tilia petiolaris,* remains a constant delight. Not only do the branches of this very large tree weep, but so do its leaves, hanging on long stalks and twisting in the breeze to reveal their pale grey under-surfaces. Grey-leaved trees can never bore. Thus, the **white willow,** *Salix alba,* is one of the pleasantest of its enormous tribe, in August, while, on a smaller scale, the **willow-leaved pear,** *Pyrus salicifolia,* is even more charming. You always see this in its weeping form.

Of the few deciduous conifers, larches become very dusty-looking. The dawn redwood, *Metasequoia,* keeps on growing all summer, but is fairly dark-leaved. Of similarly feathery appearance but far fresher is the swamp cypress, *Taxodium distichum.* It is one of the finest of all specimen trees, but more on this anon.

A few deciduous trees earn their summer keep by flowering late. **Catalpas,** with their great open panicles of whitish blossom, are worth growing only for this. The tree is clumsy, the leaf coarse, but the flowers certainly are a thrill. To bloom well, the tree needs a good baking. Because, too, the branches are brittle, this is ideally a town plant. **Koelreuteria paniculata** flowers in late summer, with panicles of yellow blossom, less conspicuous than the catalpa's but on a pleasanter tree—broad-headed and with bold, pinnate leaves. It can easily be grown from seed, but you need to choose a strain that produces flowers of a reasonable size: they can be squinny little runts.

Chile in the August Garden

The glory of our garden in August (sharing the palm with *Hoheria sexstylosa* and *Hydrangea villosa*) is a tall slim column of **Eucryphia nymansensis** 'Nymansay'. It is robed in white from top to toe, and so densely that one is only just conscious of its evergreen, leathery foliage. The flowers begin to expand at the end of July, and it is as though the shrub were encrusted with hundreds of butterfly chrysalids, from which the perfect insects are emerging, first with limply drooping wings but soon expanding, as they dry, into great white silky textured sails.

These flowers remind people of Christmas roses or of a white Rose of Sharon. Each is 3½ in. across, composed of four broad petals and a boss of some 200 stamens, tipped with red anthers. Even at the moment of opening, the bud seems incredibly small. The sepals form a cap, much as in an oriental poppy, and when this has been pushed off, the expanding trick takes place. The flowers send out a honeyed fragrance and are beset with bees throughout the daylight hours. When the wind and rain are at their most persistent, the visitors are all strong-winged bumble bees, but the honey bees join in as soon as the screws are loosened a bit.

This plant is a hybrid between *E. cordifolia* and *E. glutinosa*, both hailing from Chile. Nymansay is reasonably hardy in the south and west of Britain, but difficult in the midlands. It should be given as frost-free a situation as possible. In a frost hollow, its young growth will be repeatedly crippled, and it will never make a shapely bush. After the bad winter of 1962–63, my specimen lost most of its foliage but was otherwise undamaged and flowered as well as ever that summer. But some of my gardening friends lost theirs. The older the shrub the better become its chances of survival, but one has to start somewhere. The natural habit, which can be encouraged by restricting a specimen's growth to one leading shoot, is columnar. I planted mine when it was about 6 in. tall, in 1950, and it is now 18 ft. high by only 4 ft. or so across. So it is really an ideal specimen for the small garden. In time it may reach to 40 ft. or more.

Why do we not see eucryphias in every suburban front garden, hen? There is, apart from hardiness, a snag. My Nymansay had been 8 years growing before it started to flower, and although it has been more regular than clockwork ever since, eight years is a long time for an unsettled populace. Neither can you take a short cut by planting a large specimen, for large specimens intensely resent being moved, and will sit and scowl at you mutinously, for year upon year. A small plant put out from a pot in spring, will get away in fine style, however, and you can feed and mulch it generously. The roots are right at the surface, so you should certainly not dig about it. Cuttings of the current year's shoots can be taken in September, in pure grit, and, being slow to root, should not be potted off until the next spring. Even then, they are apt to die without apparent cause, and they should be kept shaded until thoroughly settled.

Most eucryphias dislike lime, but Nymansay is exceptional, and it derives its tolerance from the *E. cordifolia* parent. Now, if there is one thing I have against Nymansay, it is the frowsty appearance of its foliage in the non-flowering months, but particularly in winter, after half of it has been shed. But *E. cordifolia* is of a much more distinguished build. Its growth is chunky, its evergreen foliage lustrous, and it flowers when quite young. But it is less hardy. What, then, of the other parent, *E. glutinosa*? This is the hardiest of the lot. Its pinnate foliage is pleasingly shaped; it is deciduous, and its leaves change to marvellous orange and red shades before falling (if you have a good soil for these autumnal conflagrations). It must have acid soil, though, and there is another possible drawback. Seedlings often give rise to plants bearing double flowers, and the flowers of a double eucryphia are nearly always a hopeless mess (quite apart from a general loss of refinement) because, being too full of petals, they rot as they open. Before buying, ask your nurseryman if he raised his stock from seed, or vegetatively from a single-flowered specimen.

E. glutinosa is not a precocious flowerer, and neither is its hybrid when crossed with the Tasmanian *E. billardieri* (better known as *E. lucida*). But this hybrid, called *E. intermedia*, is a good shrub and should certainly be grown, if you are of a settled,

Plate 27. *Hebe* 'Midsummer Beauty' is a shrubby veronica with long, lavender-coloured scented spikes carried from summer right into midwinter.

sedentary disposition and not on chalk. It is evergreen, and the leaflets are quite small, giving the shrub an air of pleasing elegance. Furthermore it flowers from late August onwards, which is after those so far mentioned, and extends the eucryphia season.

How to Choose Hydrangeas

We all know that from July onwards there are not so many flowering shrubs to choose for the garden. Our mainstay, then, are the **hydrangeas**. That rather makes it sound as though we have to restrict ourselves to a diet of bread-and-butter, with no jam or cake to liven things up till spring comes round again. But I do not regard hydrangeas in that light at all. For me they are a favourite shrub that happens to flower at a most convenient time when other shrub favourites have retired from the scene.

There are hydrangeas for all tastes. The mop-headed hortensias are undoubtedly the most popular, but they are regarded, in refined circles, as crude, blatant, obvious, coarse, vulgar. In that case I must have something of all those qualities myself. I do not like all these hortensias at all times and in all places, but they have a tremendous luxuriance and vitality that one cannot help admiring. I know you see them in every suburban front garden in every seaside resort but they somehow manage to transcend their banal surroundings. They refuse to stay primly in beds but bulge and spill over, as if they had just risen like a yeast loaf.

The wild types of hydrangea are known as lacecaps and typically have flat heads consisting of a central area of tiny fertile florets and an outer ring of large, showy sterile florets. These are generally considered, by the general public, to miss it, but are the only kinds worth growing, according to the sensitive (but self-conscious) man of taste. In choosing your hydrangeas you will be steered, according to the sort of upbringing you have received, either towards the showiest mop-headed hortensias, or towards the comparative elegance of the lacecaps. If you like both

Plate 28. *Above,* the young foliage of *Veratrum nigrum* is followed by 6 ft. panicles of near-black flowers.

Below, the stripy Zebra grass grows 7 ft. tall and flowers, as here, in October.

types, that gets us no further and we must consider the other most important factors in respect of choosing. These are: hardiness, vigour and flower colour.

Many hydrangeas, alas, are none too hardy. Those that are best suited as pot plants are often the least reliable in the garden, so that many disappointments arise from the flowering hydrangea that was a present in a pot and which you subsequently planted in the garden. The trouble about the less hardy hydrangeas is that they never let you know just where you stand, by dying on you. What happens is that they grow luxuriantly all through the summer, making masses of sappy, leafy growth from ground level. These shoots never ripen (i.e. toughen, harden) enough to carry them through the winter. They get frosted right back to the ground and the process starts all over again in the next spring. If the shoots made in the summer can be carried alive through the winter, they will flower in the following summer. Otherwise not, or very little.

So you must choose your varieties accordingly. An experienced nurseryman will be able to help with advice on hardiness but a great deal depends on your garden and even on different parts of your garden, some of which will be colder and will collect more frost than others. You can, at the least, help yourself by not planting your hydrangeas till spring. Make sure that you buy a plant that has 2 or 3 woody branches on it. These branches will become woodier still, in your garden, during the plant's first summer and will have a decent chance of surviving their first winter. Having cleared that hurdle, its chances will become rosier each year as the shrub's bulk builds up and its old branches get tougher and more frost-resistant.

Second, vigour. If you are an impatient gardener (the chances are 50 to 1 on) you will buy the hydrangea that grows fastest into a good sized shrub. It fills its allotted space and this was insufficient because, being an impatient gardener, you planted it too close to its neighbours or to a path. What next? You cut it back. But in cutting it back you remove all its flowering wood. It reacts by making a mass of sappy young shoots and they probably all get frosted. No flowers. We are back where we started.

Now, some hydrangeas are of much dwarfer habit and slower growth than others. So, again with the helpful advice of an experienced nurseryman (a pretty girl in a flowered apron at the garden centre will not be any use to you on this sort of occasion), buy your hydrangeas so that their potential growth equates with the space you want them to fill.

Never prune your hydrangeas by shortening their shoots back (except for some of the *H. paniculata* group and one or two other white-flowered species). The only pruning should be by thinning out. You crawl under your bush, in March, until you are near the middle of it and then you cut out its weakest old shoots right to ground level. Over a period of many years, the average hydrangea needs to renew itself. By cutting away its oldest and least vigorous branches you admit light and space to the centre of the bush and encourage the development of a few (not too many) new branches.

Now hydrangeas are hungry shrubs. They respond to good feeding. Give them a mulch of bulky organic manure or compost in the winter and a feed of general fertiliser (at 4 oz. to the sq. yd.) in spring. Never feed them in the summer or you will encourage soft, frost-susceptible growth at the tail end of the growing season. You want to encourage growth in early summer, but ripening in late summer and autumn. Of course, all hydrangeas are thirsty. I say 'of course' because the shrub makes its needs so obvious, its flower trusses wilting and looking pathetic and reproachful if short of water. No one with any feelings will let thirst go unquenched.

Colour variations in hydrangea flowers are so extraordinary and so capricious, even as from one part of a bush to another, that my advice, for anyone's peace of mind, is to accept them all, or nearly all, and to enjoy what comes. However, there are inevitably some colours that we prefer to others.

Let us forget about the whites for the moment. Among coloured hydrangeas, the tendency is for flower colouring to vary according to the acidity of your soil. A flower that comes red on alkaline soil will be violet on a very acid soil and something in between on neutral soils. A flower that comes pink on alkaline soil will come blue on very acid soil and some shade of mauve where the soil is slightly acid or neutral. This is irrespective of variety. If you say to a nurseryman 'I want a blue hydrangea' he can sell you one with a name like Bluewave, but cannot guarantee that the flowers will come blue in your garden. 'All right,' you say, 'I'll buy one that's flowering in a pot and that definitely is the shade of blue I want.' You do so, but next year your paragon flowers pink, in your garden. People either find this easy to understand or quite impossible, so I shall not labour the reasoning.

It is very easy to change the colouring of your hydrangea's flowers from blue to pink or from violet to red. All you have to do is to add lime to the soil and make it alkaline. Thus, with the dwarf red-flowered variety Westfalen (dwarfness always goes with the deepest colouring), a pure red is generally agreed to be more attractive than a purplish hue. If your shrub turns purplish you will give it lime to change it back to red.

To make alkaline soil acid is practically impossible. Those who live on chalk or lime and want a blue hydrangea had best grow it in imported, acid soil in a tub and water it with soft rain water.

On soil that is neutral or slightly acid, producing mauve flowers in your hydrangeas, you can hope to make them blue by feeding them with iron and aluminium salts. You can buy blueing powder together with dosage instructions from Boots or from various garden sundriesmen: Joseph Bentley of Barrow-on-Humber, Lincs., has a 'Hydrangea Colorant' that 'changes pink hydrangeas to exquisite blue.'

On too alkaline a soil, many hydrangeas grow unhappily and show their distress by turning yellow in their leaves. Matters can be improved by watering them with Murphy's Iron Sequestrine.

You cannot change the colour of a white hydrangea, but there is a normal tendency for the flowers of white hydrangeas exposed to sunlight to turn pinkish or even red, as they age. In shade, they turn a curious and metallic green, on ageing, and this also holds for coloured varieties. But the weather needs to be good, while this is going on, in autumn, otherwise the entire flower head will rot, as it ages, instead of taking on those seductive hues that are so valuable to flower arrangers.

Finally, a few suggestions on varieties, according to your needs. If hardiness is of the first importance, then you must be content with certain of the white-flowered hydrangeas. *Hydrangea paniculata* has domed heads with large sterile white florets mixed with a fuzz of white fertile florets. It has several variants: *H. p.* 'Praecox' flowers in July and is very informal and pretty and requires no pruning but it does die ungracefully and the shrub looks horrible in autumn. *H. p.* 'Floribunda' flowers in August with elegant cones of mixed fertile and sterile florets. It can be pruned quite hard, like a common buddleia, in spring, and still flower well at the ends of its new shoots. *H. p.* 'Grandiflora', the most popular in this group, has large conical heads of all-sterile florets in September. These heads are particularly large if the bush is hard pruned. There is no need to prune if you do not want to but the shrub may grow 8 or 9 ft. tall. *H. cinerea* 'Sterilis' and *H. arborescens* 'Grandiflora' are lower growing with bun-shaped heads of white, sterile florets on 3 to 4 ft. bushes. These again are very hardy and they do well in sun or in shade. They combine well with border phloxes and, at the Northern Horticultural Society's gardens at Harlow Car, near Harrogate in Yorkshire, they are effectively associated with the spires of bright yellow loosestrife, *Lysimachia punctata*.

Of the large-headed hortensias, (forms of *H. macrophylla*), there are many famous names. Some standard varieties that are a good deep pink on alkaline or neutral soil but change to vivid blue (sometimes too vivid and electric a colouring, to my way of thinking) on acid, are Europa, Générale Viscomtesse de Vibraye, Altona and Hamburg. The last has very large florets and grows, normally, only 3 or 4 ft. tall but needs shelter. Mme Riverain is a washed out, common looking pink thing in ordinary soils but can turn a pretty pale blue under acid conditions.

Westfalen, already mentioned, grows only 3 ft. tall and is a deep, rich red as is Ami Pasquier. Mme. E. Mouillière is a splendid white hortensia, with a very long flowering season, its flower heads developing from new wood and from old and opening in succession until the first frosts.

The strongest growing and most obliging lacecap is Bluewave —pink with me but no less loved for that. It grows 7 ft. tall in a reasonably sheltered position and flowers from early August into autumn. Bluebird is a month earlier and delightfully frothy, blueing readily but charming even when mauve. Its habit is twiggy and it grows only 4 ft. tall. Lanarth White is good in full sun and has interestingly pale green foliage. Its sterile florets are white but there is an admixture of blue fertile florets. In most parts of the country the bush grows to only 3 or 4 ft., but in mild areas it becomes a giant.

H. acuminata 'Prezioza' is a recent break with small bun heads opening very pale pink and changing to red—regardless of soil acidity. It should be grown in full sun to obtain the best colouring. The foliage on this and on Bluebird changes to carmine in autumn and retains its colouring for many weeks.

Some of the rough-, hairy-leaved hydrangeas make beautiful shrubs of the lacecap type with rosy lilac flowers. Far and away the best of these—the finest thing in my garden in August—is *H. villosa*, but you must have it in the best clone, and as it has no distinguishing clonal names, this may be tricky. The plant does not like too much wind and it hates a late spring frost, but is not otherwise difficult and makes a big shrub, 8 ft. high and 10 or 12 ft. across, for which due allowance must be made. I have it on the north side of an 8 ft. wall.

Autumn

The Cone-bearers

Everybody loves a fir cone, and many cannot resist improving on nature by pepping them up at Christmas time with silver or gold paint. Cones are beautifully constructed and satisfyingly shaped and there is far greater range of types among them than is generally realised.

Most typical of the popular notion of a cone is the **pine's**. Our native Scots pine, *Pinus sylvestris,* has cones only 2 or 3 in. long. Nevertheless, it used to amuse us, as children, to make a posy of tiny flowers in a ripe cone. One soaked a dried specimen in water until its open scales had almost closed—for these cones react strongly to dry and wet—and then inserted the flower stalks into the slit above each scale. When the scales had completely shut, they held the stalks firmly in position.

A large pine cone is, of course, much more exciting. The maritime pine, *P. pinaster,* has rather fat cones up to 6 or 7 in. long, and these are the sort that are most commonly used to decorate fire grates in summer. This pine is hardy anywhere in the south and is particularly useful on poor, sandy soils and near the sea; not much use on clay, however.

The stone pine, *P. pinea,* is principally admired, throughout the

Mediterranean, for its quaint and picturesque umbrella shape, but the cones are substantial and enclose large, nut-like seeds with edible kernels, called *pignons*, in France, and much used in cooking even in this country. I sowed a batch of these, gathered high up in Lebanon, in 1954, and the young trees gave me their first cones with viable seed, from which I have raised a second generation, in 1968. The cones are quite large and on the plump side but their scales do not readily open, in this climate, and have to be artificially heated, whereupon the cone falls to pieces but you get hold of the nuts. My trees are perfectly hardy (1962–63 proved that) but not very wind-firm and I am sure the secret here is to plant the seedlings out at an early age before their roots have become pot-bound. They transplant extremely badly unless pot-grown, however.

The Monterey pine, *P. radiata* (*insignis*) is a particularly good shelter tree in milder districts and near the sea. It makes a broad, spreading specimen of pleasing outline, is remarkably quick growing, adding as much as 3 ft. to its stature in a year, and its foliage is at all seasons an exceptionally bright and cheerful green, unless scorched by winter frost-winds. It is one of the commonest pines that are noticeable for their habit of holding on to their unopened cones year after year, so that they are still present on quite old branches. The other is the bishop pine, *P. muricata*. This again makes a very decorative specimen and looks well in a group. Its trunk and branches develop a handsome, rugged appearance at quite an early age. It is hardier than *P. radiata* and will stand a good deal of wind buffeting. Its cones, which are about 3 in. long, have a prickle at the tip of each scale, which makes them uncomfortable to handle, and they are so firmly fixed to their branches, even when they have been ripe for years, that it takes a real effort to wrench one off.

In the conifer lovers' bible, Dallimore and Jackson's *Handbook of Coniferae* (lately revised and now costing 8 guineas), we are told that the cones often remain intact on the branches for 30 or 40 years, the seeds being liberated by forest fires, after which there appears a good ground covering of seedlings. It seems a drastic device for ensuring procreation. Before man was present to initiate frequent forest fires, the pines must have got a bit tired waiting for a happy strike of lightning, to start one. If you want to get at the seeds of one of these close-fisted pines that are reluctant to open up their scales, you should either put them into a low oven at about 110° F. or close to a hot fire, for a couple of days. It is surprising how this heat treatment does not destroy the embryos.

Some of the most desirable pines for garden ornament have 6- or 8-inch-long thin, silky-textured needles, whose very softness causes them to hang in elegant sprays and to catch the light as viewed from eye level. Even a quite young specimen, clothed with branches right down to the ground, is a delightful feature. And, from about the age of 12 or 15 years, they can be expected to carry their clusters of exceptionally long and exciting-looking cones.

The best known, because it is most often exhibited at R.H.S. shows, is *P. ayacahuite*, with cones a foot—even 18 in.—long but this species is not to be recommended for general planting, since it is subject to the crippling blister rust disease. *P. wallichiana* (also known as *P. griffithii*) is to be preferred. Although its cones seldom exceed a foot in length they are glamorous enough for most of us. These two species when growing near each other in Westonbirt arboretum, gave rise to an excellent hybrid, *P. holfordiana,* bearing splendid cones. It inherits a rust-resistant constitution from its wallichiana parent.

The silver firs, species of **Abies,** are the most splendid cone-bearers, because they carry their cones proudly upright, like candles, on the upper sides of their branches; also because they are often very large and because they are, while immature, most exquisitely coloured. But—and there are a lot of buts about them, as about so many good things—many do not start coning until quite mature trees, and then only near the top of the tree, so that you really need field glasses and a good, pliable neck, before you can properly admire them. No use thinking you will have a nice close look at them when they drop off, because the habit of all the *Abies* is to shed their scales separately, when ripe; the entire cone disintegrates.

However, some species cone when quite young and close to human level. The best miniature species from this angle, is *A. koreana*. The cones are only 2 or 3 in. long, but gathered together in plentiful colonies, and they are bluish-purple with buff banding, when young. A tree may start coning when only 4 or 5 ft. high and seldom reaches more than 20 ft. in this country, so is suitable for quite small gardens. You can sometimes buy seed from Thompson and Morgan (Ipswich) or plants from G. Reuthe of Keston, Kent.

A friend in Wester Ross has two youngish specimens of *A. spectabilis*, and his attention was first drawn to their fruiting by the grieve's wife asking if he had seen the 'navy cones.' They are really a brighter and more attractive colour than navy blue, but blue they are. The colour, in this context, seems incredible till you get used to it, but is quite common in the immature cones of various *Abies* species. This one is none too hardy in Britain as a whole. An easier species, with cones of the same colour, is *A. homolepis*, the Nikko fir. Again it carries them on reasonably low branches but all the silver firs are temperamental cone-bearers, with frequent off-years.

Cedar cones are barrel-shaped and not unlike those of *Abies* in their manner of disintegrating when ripe, also the way they sit on the tops of the branches, but at quite low levels, so as to be easily admired. Indeed they are admirable, and a pale glaucous colouring while unripe. The closely related larches have much smaller cones but they persist on the branches and are useful for house decoration. When young, in April, they are tiny but a sumptuous red shade that contrasts dramatically with the pale green foliage.

Many forms of **Thuja occidentalis** carry their tiny, ⅛-inch-long, elongated cones in such vast numbers that they transform an entire tree. In September, before they are ripe, they are yellow-ish in colour and would make delightful material for the flower arranger. So would the young green or glaucous cones of **Lawson's cypress**, *Chamaecyparis lawsoniana*, in such free-coning forms as Allumii and Triomphe de Boskoop and many more. These are of globular outline, only one third of an inch across but in hordes around the margins of the fan-shaped branches.

Deciduous Conifers

You may say that among the main advantages of conifers is the fact of most of them being evergreen. But the few common deciduous conifers have outstanding merits as ornamentals, and some of these—notably their autumn colouring—they owe to the very fact of being deciduous.

Few trees will make a handsomer or more distinctive specimen than *Ginkgo biloba,* the **maidenhair tree**—when it is happy. Its curiously fan-shaped leaves with their central cleft, smack of the archaic, and we learn with a sense of fitness that this tree is known in fossil form and is the survivor of an earlier style of vegetation, with none but very distant relatives in the plant world of today.

In autumn the ginkgo regularly draws a climax of attention to itself by changing to resplendent golden yellow before shedding its foliage. One can think of magnificent examples up and down the country all over Britain, and it is tolerant of a sooty atmosphere in industrial settings. Yet one does also see many examples, perhaps 30 to 50 years old, which have never got away. They just stand around looking pinched and depressed; lichens accumulate on their bark; year after year they make tufts of leaves from the same gnarled old spurs, but little or no extension growth. The fact is that a ginkgo must, in order to do itself justice, have really good growing conditions. If, for instance, you can place one on the site of an old vegetable garden that has been deeply dug and generously dunged over many years, the maidenhair tree will get away to a flying start and never look back. A site where generations of pigs have rootled, and the docks and nettles reach mammoth proportions, would equally be congenial, but a lawn of fine bents, fescues and such-like poverty grasses would not.

Ginkgos are easy enough to buy and are perfectly hardy trees, but much nursery stock is imported, and this has often been grown on an inert matrix of peat and sand with a high water table and all nutrients added. Extraordinarily rapid and soft growth results, and the shrub or young tree is so charged with moisture that it cannot be reckoned hardy until it has been grown for a year in more ordinary conditions. Some British nurseries will do this, and you are then perfectly safe in planting in autumn, but it is otherwise safer to take spring delivery.

When your ginkgo arrives you will find, most likely, that it has no main stem but several branches of more or less equal strength arising shrub-like from the base of the plant. It is up to you to train it as a tree with one trunk, and this will be the case with any tree that has not been purchased, specifically, as a standard. Very often more than half the young tree will need to be cut away so as to get it on one leg, but it is best to minimise the shock by spreading this operation over a period. On arrival, then, you can make a start by deciding which stem is to be developed as the trunk, and immediately cutting out the tips of all the shoots that might otherwise compete as leaders. During the growing season you will continue the process by reducing these unwanted shoots, until, by the end of the first year, you have your plant on one stem. Subsequently, as this increases in height, you will first reduce and then remove the lowest lateral branches, thus gradually developing a trunk up to the required height of 6 ft. or whatever it may be.

It is easy to propagate the maidenhair tree from cuttings of young shoots taken in July or August, with a heel, and set in a cold frame. I find it amazing that this simple method should go unmentioned by every work of reference I have turned to, including Dallimore and Jackson, Bean's *Trees and Shrubs Hardy in the British Isles*, and the R.H.S. *Dictionary*. All mention seed as the basic method, but seed is seldom produced in this country—the tree is dioecious and most specimens are male.

The other tree known in fossil form and, indeed, only in this form until its dramatic discovery in 1945 as a living tree in China, is the **dawn redwood**, *Metasequoia glyptostroboides*. Metasequoias have been widely planted since their introduction some 20 years ago, and they are evidently extremely easy-going and attractive deciduous conifers. Their leaves are arranged in two ranks, like a yew's, and they change to a fine rust colour in autumn. The tree, moreover, has no fads but grows happily in any soil. I take a couple of potfuls of half-ripe cuttings in mid-August each year, and they are nicely rooted two months later.

We do not yet know what individuality of character will show up in the mature tree grown as a specimen. I find it hard to believe that it will be quite as attractive as the **swamp** (or deciduous) **cypress**, *Taxodium distichum*, of the south-eastern United States. In this corner of Kent and East Sussex, taxodiums were, for some obscure reason, widely planted as individuals in lawns some 80 years ago. In every case that I have seen, whether the tree was held to one trunk or allowed to branch low down, the results in maturity are singularly beautiful. No other deciduous tree that I can think of retains so fresh and bright a shade of green right into late summer. And its airy foliage changes in October to a really brilliant russet.

The tree is noted for its pleasure in waterlogged ground that may be inundated for a part of each year. But it is said to be safer to plant a young specimen on a slight mound, if the site is wet. from which it will reach down to the water. The tree will also thrive under normal soil conditions. In hollows where late spring frosts cut its young growth back, its development may be retarded until, after a few frost-free springs, it has succeeded in pushing its head above the danger level.

Taxodiums are famed for the knee roots that they throw above ground level when growing in a wet place. There are some impressive colonies of these, looking, I thought, something like termite villages—in the garden at Syon where the great garden centre now reigns. Bean, in the 1914 edition of his book, mentions these 'fine examples' and they must surely be even finer, today, for there are no signs of deterioration.

Larches were a good deal planted as ornamentals, 70 to 100 years ago; lamentably seldom nowadays. There is much pleasure to be had from these maturing specimens at various times of the year. In spring, their foliage is the freshest of fresh green: in autumn it changes to bright yellow, contrasting particularly well, it seems to me, with the blue-green of adjacent Scots pines. They could be planted alternately to make an avenue. Larch foliage holds till the very end of November. I was much taken, recently, with an accidental association of *Clematis vitalba* climbing into the lower reaches of a maturing larch. The Old Man's Beard was at its most silvery, the larch at its warmest yellow, the colouring being intensified by November sunshine.

A full-grown larch has something of the cedar about its lines, though it remains pyramidal for longer. My only criticism (if it would but heed me) is that it has perhaps rather too many of its more or less horizontal branches and that these are apt to look a bit disorganised, pointing in different directions and criss-crossing. It is of the European larch, *Larix decidua* (*L. europea*) that I have been writing. Since the war, the Japanese larch, *L. leptolepis,* has been much in vogue for commercial planting. How the tree looks when full grown, I do not know, but its winter aspect has great appeal inasmuch as the young twigs are bright red—pale beige is its European counterpart.

Larches have greedy, surface-feeding roots (they need good drainage, incidentally) and they grow too large for the average modern garden, but there is still scope for planting them along boundaries and in the policies. Future generations will be grateful.

Hardy Fuchsias for the Autumn

Autumn initiates the wettest, windiest season of the year, and it sees the final break-up of the flimsier components in the garden scene. Yet the season seldom fails to provide some of the most glorious weather of all: the light is soft, the whole countryside glows, and the garden is more than ever a place in which to linger, since we know that lingering will be out of the question for many months hereafter.

Whether or not you are in a great hurry to start overhauling your borders at this season will depend on how successful you have been in keeping them in good shape up to this moment. Gardeners who are autumn-minded can often contrive to be surrounded, still, with a wealth of flowers in early October. Their best friends are not so much those plants that begin to think of blooming only now, but those whose season may have started back in July or even earlier.

Fuchsias are a wonderful stand-by in this context, although their use as hardy plants has but recently begun to be seriously exploited. Of course, the frost question cannot be ignored. I am not thinking so much of winter frosts, but of the early autumn breed such as may already have blackened the dahlias, fuchsias and other like plants in certain unhappily sited gardens, by late September. Each gardener will know what to expect in this line and will make his plans accordingly. My own garden is on a slope near the top of a hill and we seldom get frost before the last week in October; often, of recent years, not till well into November.

Fuchsias tend to flower more and more profusely as autumn advances. Damp, cool conditions are what they like. Capsids feeding on their growing tips are a major obstacle to their flowering in the earlier part of the season, but these insects disappear from the scene about mid-September, allowing the fuchsias to burst into renewed growth and a prodigious wealth of late blossom.

They fit well into so many parts of the garden. Although technically shrubs, their habit when treated as hardy plants is largely herbaceous, and they blend equally with other shrubs or with herbaceous plants in any kind of border. Dwarf types like Alice Hofman, Tom Thumb and Display can be used as edging plants or to give late colour in a rock garden. The most vigorous will make internal hedges, while any large-flowered variety, whether hardy or not, can be grown in tubs and ornamental pots.

The most vigorous hardy fuchsia is *Fuchsia* 'Riccartonii', with small red and purple flowers. In a hard winter it will get cut to the ground, but can make 5 or 6 ft. of young growth in a season, and therefore deserves to be much more widely planted as a hedge, and not only in the west country, where we are most accustomed to seeing it thus treated. F. 'Molinae' (also called F. *magellanica* 'Alba') with pale green foliage and palest pink flowers, is equally vigorous, but tends to start flowering rather late if it is killed back in winter. When it can make a permanent, shrubby framework of branches, however, it will begin its flowering season in June or even earlier.

F. 'Gracilis' is slightly depressing, but its variegated form, Versicolor (or Tricolor) is one of the best of all garden plants. Its foliage is constantly changing colour between ashen greygreen to bright pink, either in streaks or along stems and veins, the colour being most intense in spring and again in autumn. And its flowers, with drooping red calyx segments, are abundantly produced. Strongest growth is made from the base of the plant, and it is therefore best to cut it right down each spring, as growth is being renewed, even if the old wood is still alive. It will make 4 ft. shoots in a season. The plant's only fault is a tendency to revert to plain green, and any such shoots must be wrenched out as soon as they appear, in late spring.

Of the large-flowered hardies the full tale has yet to be told. Indeed it never can be told because climate varies so much even from one part of a garden to another, let alone from one garden to the next, that we can never be sure which fuchsias may prove hardy with us until we have tried them out. They should be planted in late spring and a few cuttings taken in autumn so that if anything befalls the parent we shall not remain bereft. Once we are assured of the parent's hardiness, however, all precautions can be thrown to the winds.

I never give my fuchsias winter protection, apart from not cutting down the shoots of the more doubtful kinds till spring. But in harder climates it is wise to plant the crowns rather deeply and to mound them over with grit each early winter.

Among the large-flowered types one of the showiest and most reliable is the double purple and pale pink Lena. In a normal year it starts to flower in mid-June, and carries on without interruption for the next four or five months. Princess Dollar, in carmine and double purple, is astonishingly abundant. The waxy carmine flowers of Phyllis are obliquely held on sturdy shoots 2 to 3 ft. long. Mme Cornelissen, in red and white, is very upstanding, to 3 ft., while Chillerton Beauty (pink and mauve) is densely bushy. Uncle Charlie is a great favourite with all that know it, with a long lilac skirt in widely overlapping folds and a carmine calyx whose segments roll back. Tennessee Waltz is very similar and equally hardy, but the calyx stands out horizontally.

Dahlias in their Prime

More often than not, there is a certain relief when summer is over. It so seldom lives up to our exaggerated expectations. But autumn is a season of which nobody ever expects or remembers much and it can thus spring on us frequent and pleasant surprises. By September, dahlias are at last allowed to bloom without those tragically intoned words: 'What, dahlias already!' being heard. **Dahlias** should nowadays be regarded as belonging as much to summer as to autumn, especially the dwarf bedding types. Still, September sees their culmination—the time when they have at last concealed their stakes, when they are most valuable in stiffening a garden that might easily dissolve into an amorphous froth of michaelmas daisies, and when the mellow quality of autumn sunlight best suits their warm colours.

Dahlias are now available in such a varied assortment of flower forms and plant habits that there is no justification for sweeping them aside with a dismissive gesture as vulgar or clumsy. We are chiefly indebted to the powerful influence of the flower-arranging movement for new dahlias that have completely broken away from the exhibitor's stereotyped notions of what constitutes a noble, prizeworthy bloom. Most of the flower arranger's requirements, such as a long, strong stem without need for disbudding, and an elegant, graceful bloom of only moderate proportions, are precisely those that will also best suit the gardener when he wishes to gain the most telling effects from dahlias in association with other plants. Anyone who is interested in dahlias as garden plants should try, in autumn, to pay a visit to the R.H.S. trials at Wisley, where standard varieties of accepted worth are grown alongside new varieties that have yet to make a name for themselves. The latter are *sub judice* and are consequently labelled with a number only. This should not put the visitor off, however, for he has merely to leave a note of the numbered varieties that interest him at the office, and he will be informed, at the end of the season, of their names and the stable from which they emanate.

These dahlias are grown, for convenience, in a large block on their own. But it is about as easy to translate the effect they would create into your own gardening terms as it is impossible to do so by merely seeing cut blooms in the mammoth trade exhibits of flower shows. Take their foliage, for instance—almost always a weak point with dahlias. Often it is far too coarse and obtrusive, but in a variety such as Firestone, a brilliant scarlet semi-cactus, the leaves are quite finely divided and really rather nice.

The old so-called peony-flowered variety (I could never see the resemblance), Bishop of Llandaff, has blood red flowers but is particularly noteworthy for its finely dissected purple foliage. There are now quite a number of dahlias with interestingly bronze-tinted leaves.

Among the dwarf, $2\frac{1}{2}$ to 3 ft. bedding dahlias, I greatly fancy Gertrud Lachmann, with anemone-centred blooms of a light, black currant purple. There are several of these anemone-centred bedders. They are like singles, but with the disc florets much enlarged, like a honeycomb, and of the same colouring as the outer rays. Single dahlias have a charm of their own. There is a nice named white single called Weisse Orchidee, sometimes translated, for our benefit, into White Orchid. It grows 4 or 5 ft. tall and the margins of its ray petals are inrolled, creating an overall spikiness in the bloom that takes the eye.

The waterlily type of decorative dahlias are special favourites with flower arrangers. Fully double but with comparatively few, broad and widely spaced petals, they are exceptionally graceful and can now be obtained in a comprehensive colour range.

Hebes

Hebes are the shrubby veronicas. It is sensible that they should have been separated from the main veronica tribe, because they comprise a distinct group, and all come from New Zealand or thereabouts. Some people have an unshakable dislike of hebes. It is always interesting to inquire into the foundation for this kind of prejudice: usually it stems back to some early association. In this case I suspect a link with uncomfortable seaside lodgings and virago-like landladies; equally, with the rigours of seaside boarding-schools (so healthy for the children).

Essentially seaside shrubs, the commonest and most indestructible hebes are also the most boring, with dull oval leaves and white or washed-out mauve flowers. But having once put these behind you, the range and beauty of the remainder leads from one enthralling discovery to another. Hardiness, or the lack of it, is certainly a major obstacle; and should you go hebe-mad, the gaps in your borders will be frequent and alarming. But most of us inland gardeners, provided we do not live in a frost hollow, can contrive to cope with most of the hebes we should like to grow. Two survival factors are strongly in their favour: they nearly all root extremely easily and they grow extremely fast.

When one is siting tender hebes in the garden, they should be given a sunny place and not be exposed to north and east winds. But they are blessed with terrific fibrous root systems, and will stand up to south-west gales complacently, so that a position near an exposed south-facing wall is ideal. Their fibrous roots also allow you to move hebes around even when in full growth, at the height of summer. So, if you keep some of the showy types in a cosy reserve plot from autumn till June, they can then be given a heavy soaking, lifted and used as bedding plants to replace something with an early flowering season.

Some of the hardiest hebes are extremely attractive and among these I would place the curious 'whipcord veronicas' with scale-like leaves that seem to disguise them as some kind of cypress. *Hebe cupressoides* is one such and makes a sufficiently formal 3- to 4-ft. shrub to be used like a juniper as a corner-piece or a tub specimen. Its leaves are blue-green and a trifle dusty looking. The whole plant gives off a wonderful aromatic fragrance which is detectable even in freezing weather. The flowers are tiny little skimmed-milk, blue-white things, but carried in a great cloud in their brief early-summer season. They are really rather charming.

H. *armstrongii* is another of the whipcords, but with slightly larger scale-leaves and it is of a golden-green colouring that is specially warming in winter. This grows to about 3 ft. H. *salicornioides* 'Aurea' (still among the whipcords) is not by any means golden but it is a very yellow-green, and always looks cheerful even in the dreariest winter weather. It grows slowly but surely and makes a low 15-inch-tall, ground-covering shrub such as associates excellently with winter flowering heathers. So does H. 'Edinensis', of similar habit but with bright green foliage making a dense hummocky shrub of great individuality.

The whipcord hebes are not the only ones grown mainly for their foliage. Waikiki and Mrs. Winder are both cultivars that flower only half-heartedly but make nice specimen bushes, about 2 ft. tall, with lanceolate leaves of strong purple colouring. Mrs. Winder is particularly striking.

Many hebes are grey- or glaucous-leaved, and some of these are popular shrubs for the rock garden. H. *pimeleoides* 'Glaucocoerulea' has sharp-pointed little leaves. In H. *pinguifolia* 'Pagei' (long known as *Veronica pageana*), the grey leaves are rather broader. Both have white flowers of no great merit. The bush that came to me as H. *glaucophylla* (but I would not like to guarantee the correctness of its naming) is bolder than the last two with broader leaves but still blue-grey and its spikelets of white flowers in June and July are large enough to be a welcome feature. That is a plant for the front of a mixed border.

Autumn Glory is an old favourite with purple foliage. It is seldom without a flower but its first and largest crop opens from silvery buds to violet blossoms in July. This makes a sprawling, front row shrub and once in every 4 or 5 years you must be severe and cut it hard back in April, thereby sacrificing a year's blooming but restoring order. Purple Queen is another very old one, with larger, rich purple leaves and violet-purple flowers. It grows upright to 2½ ft. or more and is good in a sunny but sheltered position but not so hardy as those so far described.

Although I have included the hebes for discussion in this autumn section, yet it must already be clear that many are valuable either for their flowers or for their foliage in summer and winter and even in spring. The most beautiful but, alas, one of the tenderest of all hebes is *H. hulkeana,* which flowers in May. The shrub is nothing to boast about, either for its habit or its foliage but the pale mauve flowers are carried in large loose panicles of ravishing freshness and innocence. This is certainly a species worth struggling for. It does well near the sea (it grows wild on sea cliffs in New Zealand) and can also be coaxed into a mood of reasonable compliance against a sunny south wall, inland. It sprawls and grows about 2 to 3 ft. tall. *H. fairfieldii* might be described as the poor man's hulkeana. It seems to be a hybrid with *H. hulkeana* as one parent and it looks very similar but makes a shorter-jointed, dwarfer, less sprawling shrub with smaller leaves margined in purple. The flower panicles, too, are smaller. This appears to be a hardier plant.

The presumption that no gardener will want to consider a plant that is not trouble-free or labour-saving has always struck me as thoroughly tedious and unimaginative. Headfortii is another hebe that will die on you if you turn your back on it in winter, but then perhaps you will not. It is low-growing and makes a neat, horizontally branching shrub with obovate leaves, and it flowers in May. The colouring is a good rich mauve but the individualistic thing about it is that these flowers are borne on multiple, branching spikelets. And their earliness is unusual.

H. macrantha flowers in late May or early June and has the largest flowers of any hebe. They are white, carried on a lowish shrub of undistinguished form and foliage, but hardier than you would expect. These flowers are quite something, and no hebe enthusiast will want to go without *macrantha.*

Bowles' Hybrid flowers most freely in June and is very good at its best but, in this case, slightly *less* hardy than one expects, and the shape of a bush can be spoilt by its losing a number of branches in winter. At its comeliest this makes a perfect 2-foot-high dome of small, lanceolate leaves which are utterly obliterated by the wealth of pale mauve flower spikes in their season. Unless you subsequently dead-head, the bush's vigour is seriously impaired.

The hebes you are likeliest to see in coastal plantings, in Britain, are *H. brachysiphon* (syn. *H. traversii*), *H. dieffenbachii* and *H. salicifolia*. The first of these has small, evergreen leaves on a neat, ball-shaped shrub growing about 5 ft. high and covered with spikelets of white blossom in June. But it is really one of the great hebe bores; formal yet devoid of personality. *H. dieffenbachii* needs to be grown in great banks and boskages (it makes a splendid wind-break) and can then be impressive but is not for the small garden. Its leaves would be unimpressive except for their arrangement in four tiers, and this does give them character. Flowers are borne on large, mature bushes only. They are in 2-in. spikelets, very pale mauve but pleasing.

H. salicifolia has narrow willowy leaves but no special identity as a bush. However, it carries its long, thin flower spikes with terrific abundance. They are a very washy mauve but deliciously scented. It sows itself all over the place, including on and in old walls.

This is the most important parent of a group of three similar but useful and beautiful cultivars; beautiful when flowering, that is, but nothing to write home about in their off-seasons. They are Midsummer Beauty, Hidcote and Miss E. Fittall. Really there's not much to choose between them. They are moderately but not out and out hardy (not as tough as *H. salicifolia*); they make very large bushes (when not set back by frost) 7 or 8 ft. tall by up to 12 ft. across and they flower abundantly with 6 inch-long spikes of a sufficiently strong mauve shade to be effective, and they are scented. Hielan Lassie has this same sweet scent but it is a tighter bush, up to 6 ft. high with leaves half the size, and much shorter but numerous flower spikelets; a deep mauve, fading, and carried most freely in June-July. If the early winter is mild you can often pick flowering sprigs of Midsummer Beauty in December and January.

Now on to the showiest but tenderest hebes; again with a tremendously long flowering season especially if their dead heads are removed. There is a good deal of confusion in their naming and much synonymy.

The most exciting colouring is possessed by Simon Deleaux, with bold flower spikes in a striking shade of crimson. Evelyn is a bright and striking pink on a more compact 2 to 3 ft. bush than some, here. Gauntlettii is in roughly the same colouring. The leaves are smaller and the shrub is a bit hardier. La Séduisante has rich purple flower spikes on an upright 3 to 4 ft. shrub with purplish, glossy leaves. As the leaf shape in this section is rather a dull oval, on the whole, one appreciates the compensations of good colouring and finish, as in this cultivar. Alicia Amherst (or Veitchii) has rich indigo flower spikes but its large green leaves are too voluminous. Carnea has narrowish leaves and pink flowers but an improvement on this is the fairly modern Great Orme, with long, slender spikes that are deep pink on opening and fade so that each spike develops a characteristic two-tone effect. The leaves are willowy; the bush grows to 3 ft. and is not too tender. I must fit Cranleighensis in here because, although its pink flower spikes are on the small side, they can in a mild season go on right through the winter, developing their intensest shading in February. This grows to 6 ft. and is only moderately hardy. Last, *H. andersonii* 'Variegata'. This is grown mainly for the wonderful green-and-primrose variegation of its large, soft leaves. Young plants are frequently used and abused in the bedding schemes of public parks and gardens. But if you can bring the shrub through the winter, it has far more character in its second and third years and carries welcome crops of deep mauve flower spikes.

Lastly, there are the two hebes commonly bedded out and used in window boxes in London: *H. franciscana* (syn. *H. elliptica*) Blue Gem and its variegated form 'Variegata'. They have smallish markedly rounded leaves and extremely little personality. Exceptionally frost-tender, they are scarcely worth the private gardener's attention.

Berries to Feast the Birds

Any country dweller who plants a berrying tree or shrub with the notion that he will derive weeks, even months, of pleasure from it at the fall of each year, must be a townsman by training. In our towns and suburbs one may, indeed, be amazed to see cotoneasters that are still laden with fruit right into the spring. But in the country, *Skimmia japonica* is one of the few red-berried shrubs that normally defies the birds' inclinations and, presumably, their digestions also. Hollies are not their special favourites, and holly berries will usually survive Christmas. I have known them hang on till June.

If we are not to enjoy the display of berries, we can at least train ourselves to enjoy them vicariously, by watching the birds at table, and we may feel that it is worth planting for that pleasure. My window overlooks a *Cotoneaster horizontalis* and this provides the pleasantest of distractions when birds alight on it. One is entertained at the difference in eating methods between the blackbirds, who gobble the fruit whole (later distributing the seeds over all the garden) and the greenfinches and house sparrows, who swallow the seeds but spit the pulp out from the sides of their beaks. And I was interested to see a pair of bullfinches, one day, eating in similar finch style. I had not seen them taking an interest in berries before.

What I am always hoping and watching for is one of those flocks of waxwings that are so much in the news and in my friends' gardens some years. But, brimming over with their favourite cotoneaster food though this garden is, the word has never yet got around to them. Yew berries are another of their pleasures, and a friend in Wester Ross has twice had the vast female yew, which is such an inspiring feature in the centre of his garden, hung with waxwings. The yew's fruit is charming—a soft pinkish-red shade with a bloom on it—but is seldom borne in sufficient quantities to make a striking display. But the slow-growing, fastigiate Irish yew, which is always female, is short-jointed in its habit and hence carries its fruit in a dense array that can be arresting: the more so, as Irish yews are often left unclipped.

Any kind of regular cutting is liable to reduce a shrub's fruit-bearing potential. *Cotoneaster lacteus* is an exception. This is an evergreen with greyish-green foliage and a drooping habit. But, given a little help at the outset, it can be trained to form a high hedge. There is a famous example in the botanic gardens at Glasnevin, on the outskirts of Dublin (and others, more recent, in the R.H.S. gardens at Wisley). The young plants were set 18 in. part and their leaders each tied to a cane, until they had reached the required height of some 8 ft., the laterals being pruned to obtain the necessary bushy growth. At maturity, the hedge merely requires one annual clipping, with secateurs, in August, during which all the current season's non-flowering shoots are cut back so as to reveal the berries hanging in clusters behind them. The whole hedge is thus transformed, in the autumn and early winter months, into a spectacular sheet of red fruit.

The handsomely fruiting varieties of spindle seem to crop best, in many cases, if planted in couples, so as to obtain thorough pollination. Thus, a plant of the wild spindle *Euonymus europeus* can be placed in discreet association with its more glamorous cultivar, Red Cascade. Another prolific fruiter of an excellent coral-pink shading is *E. phellomana*. A favourite with me is *E. sachalinensis* (formerly *E. planipes*). It is of coarser habit than the others but, not being imbued with any team-spirit nonsense, gives a good account of itself as a lone specimen. The fruits are twice the size of an ordinary spindle's, crimson coloured and resembling a flower, the way they are divided into petal-like segments. The seeds themselves are coated in red, and, while all this is going on, the leaves change to vivid carmine, even on my clay soil, which does not much favour autumn tinting. If you want to grow spindles from seed, it is necessary to be patient, for they take 18 months to germinate.

An arrangement of cut spindle branches in the house contrasts marvellously, I always think, with the conical clusters of the common privet's black berries. Again, however, you must have access to an unclipped bush—an easy matter on the chalk downs, where privet grows wild.

Autumn Colour in Trees and Shrubs

Britain is comparatively unlucky in the capacity of its native trees and shrubs for changing colour. This is not just a question of our climate being unsuited to the development of vivid foliage. When exotic species, famous for their autumn display, are grown here, they quickly put our mousy indigenous types to rout. But if you say that the dying rusts of oak and beech and bracken are better suited to our style of countryside than the flaming tints of New England, I shall not argue the point.

Still, a garden—even a garden on the grand scale like Sheffield Park, Sussex—is not a mere extension of the countryside into our private domain. One of the garden's principal objectives is display, whether it be achieved with bedding plants, spring bulbs, rhododendrons or autumn colour. In any of these cases the display can be brash or artistic, but discreet use of brilliant colour will give many of the most telling effects. The rich greens and glaucous hues of evergreen conifers are given light and life by the introduction of golden-leaved types or of deciduous autumn-colourers.

Only in very large gardens can one afford to plant trees and shrubs entirely with a view to their fugitive autumn performance. The nyssas (*Nyssa sylvatica*) in Sheffield Park gardens are justly famed, and the variation in colour from yellow to crimson assumed by different specimens is quite extraordinary, but I would not recommend the planting of even one nyssa in the average garden. The leaf shape is dull; the tree is not unshapely but has no particular interest aside from its autumn display, and this is itself capricious and often fails to materialise. *Parrotia persica* seems to me an over-recommended shrub or small tree. Again the leaf is ordinary, the habit of the plant is spreading and space-consuming, while it has the irritating habit of shedding its leaves from the tips of the branches downwards, so that when the bulk of the bush is at its colourful best, its extremities are already bare.

What we mainly require is trees and shrubs that are beautiful for a large part of the year—perhaps with a good winter outline, or strikingly coloured stems and bark, or handsomely shaped leaves—so that their autumn performance can be regarded as a welcome bonus added to more substantial benefits. High on my list of trees I would place *Liriodendron tulipifera* and *Ginkgo biloba*, the tulip and maidenhair trees, both with fascinatingly shaped foliage, changing to clear yellow (though sometimes to bronze, in the former). Most species and varieties of birch are good to look at all the year, especially when provided with an evergreen background. As to their autumn contribution, I best like W. H. Hudson's description of birch leaves on a large expanse of lawn. 'One day in early November the south-west wind blew and carried thousands of small yellow heart-shaped leaves over the green expanse, making it beautiful to look at. By and by the gardener

came with his abhorred brushwood broom and swept that lovely
novel appearance away, to my great disgust. Then the blessed
wind blew again and roared all night, swaying the trees and tos-
sing out fresh clouds on clouds of the brilliant little leaves all over
the monotonous sheet of green, and lo! in the morning it was
beautiful once more. And I stood and admired it, and it was like
walking on a velvet green carpet embroidered with heart-shaped
golden leaves. Naturally, when I saw the gardener coming on
with his broom, I cried out aloud and ·brought the lady of the
house on the scene, and she graciously ordered him off.' Hudson
was one of our great stylists.

The American scarlet oak, *Quercus coccinea,* is probably the most
brilliant of its kind, expecially in its variety Splendens, but I like
even better the large, boldly cut leaves of *Q. borealis* (commonly
known as *Q. rubra*), the red oak, which changes to warm rust red.
This is a really tough species and makes a fine tree even in difficult
conditions. In spring, its young foliage is the tenderest yellow-
green.

In some gardens, shrubs that you would not normally associate
with autumn colouring at all flare up unexpectedly; while in
others, like mine, shrubs that are mainly planted for their autumn
display seem not to realise what is expected of them. Partly this
is a question of soil, partly of age. You must always be prepared to
give a plant time to settle down. Shrubs often tend to grow rather
lush in their youth; and this tendency, if not exaggerated, is no
bad thing. If a shrub remains a stunted runt, no more than a few
inches high, it will give you little joy, however brilliantly its 50
leaves colour up each autumn.

My own failures can be ascribed mainly to soil, I think. *Fother-
gilla monticola* is a brilliant and regular colourer when suited. I have
had my plant for nearly 20 years and its leaves invariably turn
brown at the edges and begin to drop off just as they look as
though they were going to colour up first. This specimen cannot
be happy as it is only one eighth the size it should be at its present
age, but it does not take up much room and it never fails to carry
its bottle-brush flower heads in late spring, cream coloured and
honey-scented.

Weigela florida 'Variegata' needs no autumn colouring to make
it worth growing, what with its scented pink funnels in May and

its pleasing green-and-yellow foliage throughout the summer and autumn. But the tantalising fact remains that in certain circumstances its leaves or some of them, at least, and especially if the plant is growing in a pot, do take on a fantastic carmine-pink colouring in a band between the margin and the centre.

I refuse to grow callicarpas; they are so fickle and apt to disappoint. The idea is that they, and particularly *Callicarpa bodinieri giraldii* (far better and more easily known as *C. giraldiana*) should carry clusters of bright purple berries in autumn, but a lone specimen will not and so you group them and still nothing much happens. The leaves of most callicarpa species change to a subtle mauve colouring in autumn. I have only once seen this happen in real life and that certainly was a memorable occasion, the species being *C. dichotoma* (syn. *C. purpurea* or *C. koreana*).

Enonymus alatus, a spindle with curious corky-winged branches, is another shrub that should be played with only by the large-scale gardener. It is stiff and ugly, its fruiting is inconspicuous and its sole claim to fame is a flashy carmine-pink autumn leaf-change that needs the right setting to flatter it.

Most of us should remain content with more mundane material. For instance, *Spiraea prunifolia* 'Plena' is delightful in spring (bullfinches permitting) with wands of little white pom-poms, green in the centre and it can be relied upon in autumn to turn a wholehearted, flaming crimson. Bean, surprisingly, names *S. thunbergii* as a red autumn-colourer, but I have never seen it turn anything but yellow.

Green-leaved shrubs tend to colour more vividly than their purple-leaved equivalents. Thus *Berberis thunbergii* rather than Atropurpurea comes into its own at leaf-fall, but its flowers and fruits being nothing special, I should be more inclined to pick *B. wilsonii*, whose leaf colouring vies with its swags of coral-red berries. And that's one of the good things about *Cotoneaster horizontalis*, the way its dying leaves change to carmine in daring contrast to its pure red berries.

6. Fruit and Vegetable Specialities

Growing Your Own Vegetables

Sales of vegetable seeds gradually fall off from year to year; the demand for allotments and the number of vegetable patches in private gardens also decrease; and one hears the view widely expressed that there is no point in growing your own stuff, and that you can get everything you want from the greengrocer with no trouble and far more cheaply.

When my brother comes to stay, he does a good slice of the cooking and never loses an opportunity for pointing out that it is a waste of time, space and energy to grow your own vegetables. 'The difference between this cabbage and what I should buy at Bristol is that there's twice as much waste on what you have grown.' I could not argue; it was only too obviously true. The slugs had made deep inroads. In fact our cabbages get picked with the slugs inside them, and if not dealt with for a few days (and one is apt to leave a cabbage lying around) the slugs emerge and are found at night crawling around the kitchen draining board.

However, when he saw our leeks, my brother did exclaim that they looked nice. He made no comparisons this time but I knew that he had in mind the market article, more than half of which consists of green leaves with only a very short, blanched stump. In a garden you can do the job properly, taking out a trench wide enough to plant a double row and then earthing them up to get a really long white stem.

Now, even if the nearest greengrocer is a few miles distant, we do not want to grow things that he can supply, of as good or better quality, just to save ourselves the trouble of dealing with him. Luckily there are certain vegetables that we really do not need to grow ourselves. Onions, for instance. Bulbs of these grown in Mediterranean countries can ripen fully and are of far higher keeping quality than what we can produce. And bought celery is excellent. This is a bothersome vegetable to grow oneself and either the slugs or the fly always seems to ruin it. But I do grow **celeriac,** the turnip-rooted type of celery. In season from October till April, it is admirable for flavouring stews and very good, too, as a vegetable cooked in its own right. The swollen root has an awkward sort of exterior, full of crevices, but if well grown, you can peel extravagantly and still have a large white core left for use.

The more you think of it the more apparent does it become that if you are interested in the flavour of vegetables, in having them available over a long season, in deep-freezing them yourself and in being able to draw on a wide and varied range of types, then you must be your own grower. Of course, if you can boast of a little man around the corner who grows everything you need (including wallflowers and summer bedding plants), you are well away. But such little men become increasingly rare: to make a go of it, they need the unpaid labour of a docile contingent of wives and children—unlikely, nowadays.

I often wonder whether I can be bothered with outdoor **tomatoes** (not having the space to grow them under glass). As regards the marketed article, the customer is rightly blamed for a situation where anything sells that looks nice and round, red and rather small. If you complain that it has the consistency of cotton-wool and screws your mouth up, you must add some sugar and not make a fuss. It is a pity, really, that the tomato should be so important an item in our diet, to-day, that we feel obliged to eat it the year round. For those who are prepared to forgo it at certain seasons, the satisfactory situation arises that when tomatoes are cheapest they have most flavour, whereas in spring and early summer, when looking beautiful but tasting their nastiest, they are at their most expensive. Even so, you can grow for yourself, whether under glass or out of doors, a better product than is ever on sale in this country. For one thing, you can choose a thin-skinned variety, such as would be useless on the market, since it would bruise in transit. Some cooks, I realise, make a practice of always blanching their tomatoes before use, even in salads, but this should no more be essential than always peeling an apple or a pear before eating it.

Another advantage in growing your own is that you can starve the plants. A heavy yield is naturally a major consequence to the commercial grower, but inevitably detracts from the flavour. The private gardener is under no such pressure. If he holds back the nitrogenous fertilisers and is content with a moderate or light crop from each plant, both flavour and natural sweetness will be greatly enhanced.

Finally, there is the question of variety. Do you mind how a tomato looks, as long as it tastes ambrosial? Since the average buyer's standards of goodness are based entirely on appearance, the grower has to give first consideration to it. Even we, as discerning eaters, are bound to be influenced by appearances to some extent. For a number of years I grew a yellow tomato. It was very thin-skinned and its flavour was good. But there was no getting away from the fact that, when cooked, it did look anaemic; one would have preferred it to be red.

I have for long considered that the most luscious and flavoursome of all tomatoes were those gigantic, deformed brutes that you see in south European (notably Italian) markets in summer. This is the ox-heart type of tomato. There is now available, in this country, a tomato with obvious affinities to the ox-heart, but of much improved appearance. This is an F_1 hybrid called Davington Epicure, put out by George Roberts of Faversham, Kent. It grows most reliably under glass but is good in the open in a good season. The fruits vary in size considerably, but tend to be large, not infrequently weighing 1 lb. apiece, without any special feeding. They are red, of quite good shape and thin-skinned, and their innards consist of a high proportion of excellent pulp (not in the least cotton-woolly), with very little seed and wetness. The flavour is so good that, when I am taking our dogs for a cross-country walk, I tend to carry a tomato, instead of an apple, as a succulent thirst-quencher.

In a few large centres, greengrocers can supply Webb's Wonderful **lettuces,** but that is exceptional, for this old and famous variety seldom reaches any market. So crisp and brittle is it that it does, literally, fall to pieces in your hands. Now the market likes a tough lettuce with dark green, leathery leaves; a good traveller, in fact. So there is nothing for it, in most cases, but to grow one's own, at least in summer. For June sowing and subsequent growing at a season when lettuces are liable to get parched and to bolt prematurely, I have found the variety Buttercrunch very satisfactory. Its leaves are an unpromisingly dark green and it does not make a proper heart, but neither does it bolt, and it is, in fact, sweet, crisp and pleasant-tasting.

It is now possible to procure seed of sleek, frame-type **cucumbers** that can be grown in the open. The point of growing your own cucumbers, however, is not for looks. However rugged their skins or crooked their fruits, they will cut up just the same. The old-fashioned ridge cucumber is not merely the hardiest for outdoor cultivation; it is also far and away the sweetest and pleasantest kind to eat. There is just one snag about these old ridge varieties. They are not always grown and selected for seed carefully enough. Consequently it is quite usual, if you are growing half a dozen plants, to find that one or two of them are giving rise to bitter cucumbers. They will be bitter while the fruits are still quite young—and once bitter, always bitter. So one should note from which plant a cucumber is being picked and destroy it forthwith, if it turns out to be a wrong'n—or else save its fruit for ornamental purposes, like gourds. Better still, buy seed of Sutton's Baton Vert, which is an F_1 hybrid ridge cucumber, and can never degenerate.

Another instance of the vegetables that you must grow for yourself is the **broad bean.** You will probably have to pick it yourself, too, otherwise it will be brought to the kitchen in that large and leathery condition where every bean needs skinning after it has been cooked. Frozen broad beans that you can buy are small and pretty, but disappointing to eat. But if you have your own deep freeze, broad beans picked at the right moment are among the most successful vegetables for inclusion.

But there is another way of eating broad beans that you can never sample unless you do it yourself. This is by picking the pods when they are only 3 or, at most, 4 in. long, and cooking them whole. They are delicious and unique in flavour, with a slightly bitter tang that heightens their interest and palatability.

You might think it a kind of reckless vegetable infanticide, picking broad beans at such an early age, but it is not so. The broad bean is one of those plants that will continue to grow and to flower indefinitely (unless infested with black aphids). Each plant can set and develop approximately half a dozen pods, but if these are removed when quite tiny, as I have suggested, the plant reacts by setting a further batch. The only loss is in a little time before you subsequently gather the first dish of standard-type beans.

Peas are particularly worth growing, and in quantity, if you can deep freeze them yourself. The marketed brands either have very little flavour or they have an inordinate amount of sugar added. And it tastes like added sugar. A good pea correctly harvested and swiftly eaten or processed has a tremendous store of natural sugar, and does not need it as an additive.

Frozen food has got a bad name for itself. You ask your friends about a restaurant they have visited. 'All the vegetables frozen', they tell you, and this is obviously intended as adverse criticism. The trouble from an intelligent consumer's point of view is that there are too few brands; there is too much standardisation, in fact, and he meets the same brand of the same vegetable over and over again, wherever he goes. Again, what brands there are, are the best available from the processing point of view and perhaps for looks, but not for flavour. With peas, I see no advantage at all in them being very small, in calling them '*petit pois*' and paying more for them; no advantage if their flavour is minimal, which, in the best known brand, I think it is.

Deep-frozen produce has got itself a bad name but it is not the fact of it having been in the freezer that is really at fault, as anyone who has done the job in his own home will readily testify. Deep freeze your own peas and they will give you the greatest joy out of season, retaining almost their full flavour for a year at least. It is just a question of growing a sensible variety like Onward; picking it young, when it will already be quite sizeable yet none the worse for that; then shucking, blanching and freezing the peas as quickly as possible within a few hours of picking.

If you can deep freeze your own peas then you can save yourself the considerable trouble of making successive sowings: early, mid-season, late. Just grow one large mid-season batch; mid-season, because that is when peas will grow fastest and best. Ours come in about the end of July, usually. The great thing then is to be sure that you have all the help you need on the day you need it.

Runner and stringless dwarf beans are also excellent for deep freezing, if not quite as exciting as peas to eat.

Calabrese is the kind of green-sprouting **broccoli** that is widely used for deep freezing. Unfortunately this is a vegetable that really does seem inevitably to lose most, if not all, of its flavour in the freezing process whether it is done by the factory or by you and whatever the variety chosen. It is just a 'for looks' frozen vegetable. But picked fresh it is unrecognisably good.

I wonder, though, how most people do actually pick their various sprouting broccolis (whether green, white or purple)? There was a photograph of a trugful of calabrese in a gardening periodical recently, showing a dozen or so pieces that had been picked with 6 or 9 in. of stalk, off the bottom half of which the foliage had been plucked, leaving it intact on the upper half. This is a gastronomically disgusting way to treat the vegetable. You should pluck the tight flower heads only, with not a leaf among them, and they can be picked straight into a colander, requiring no further preparation. The foliage and stalks you leave on the plant. They will sprout again, to give you further pickings.

Even though a disappointing frozen vegetable, calabrese gives you generous compensation in providing fresh pickings from the garden from August till . . . ? Well, my last pick this time round was on 5th January 1969, but in the coming season I shall grow the late maturing F_1 hybrid variety, Late Corona, that is now on the market (from Unwins of Histon, Cambridge), as well as one that comes in at the normal time.

Actually, I feel sure that I can do better as regards earliness too. From a report of the *N.F.U. Journal* I see that the Scottish Horticultural Research Institute, who are interested in calabrese as a crop for the processor, sow theirs in boxes and transplant into the field. I shall follow suit. We normally sow them with all the other brassicas in an outside seed bed in April, but even down here in Sussex the calabrese never seem to do as well as the other types, germinating more slowly and looking pinched in the early stages, so I will see how a bit of cosseting suits them.

There now seems to be a move to try and breed calabrese with a large, central primary head (like a cauliflower) and relatively few lateral shoots. The F_1 Green Comet preens itself for being one such. From the point of view of processing this might well be a convenience but from the ordinary amateur gardener/consumer angle, plenty of side-shoots produced over a long span are just what's wanted.

Never let your sprouting broccolis bolt incontinently. You cannot always help them getting ahead of your requirements: a few days away from home may bring this about. But at least go over the plants at the earliest opportunity and pick off the heads that are running to flower. This will double the cropping season and the fact is particularly noticeable with purple-sprouting broccoli in spring. An early-maturing variety will come in towards the end of March, in most gardens and seasons. If kept conscientiously picked over, it will remain productive till late May.

Bolting **sprouts** are the other great stand-by in spring: not just the top central rosette of foliage but every young shoot that develops on your old plants. They do not taste in the least of sprouts, by then, but are delicious greens. Newly developed strains of brassicas are often the best, because they have not had time to lose their uniformity. Once distributed, a new variety tends to go downhill. The expense of maintaining a pure strain is more than the seedsman can afford. Irish Elegance is still a beautiful, firm little sprout, cropping over a long season. The best bet, however, is to back any F_1 hybrids you see listed, because in their case seed production is very carefully controlled each year, and there is no falling-off of quality.

If you want a **potato** with any personality you must grow your own. It probably is not worth bothering about the maincrop varieties and anyway an early potato that has been harvested in good fettle will last the season through till the following May. People's ideas about what constitutes the ideal potato, vary greatly so it is best to let them try out the different kinds for themselves and not advise them. I find Duke of York suits me and it likes our heavy soil. It is a firm yellow-fleshed early and also keeps.

It makes all the difference to your crop if the plants get at least one heavy watering at the key moment when they can make best use of it—early or mid-June, for most of us. It requires a terrific natural rainfall, at that season, to give them what they need, and artificial irrigation is usually the answer.

Potato blight, caused by the fungus *Phytophthora infestans,* is an old enemy that can be guaranteed to make an appearance each July. Where early potatoes only are being grown, there should be no need to put on protective sprays *if* you remember to cut off, remove and burn the haulm the moment you see (or smell, for the disease has a strong odour) blight appearing. Then your tubers, which will be quite large enough by then, will be safe and you can harvest them at your leisure.

I never thought I should want to grow **chicory,** but I have done this year and am glad. I would not so much mind the imported article being more expensive than hitherto, but I do expect to be able to buy really fat chicons, which keep well and on which there is little or no waste. A lot of the chicory we see on sale, nowadays, is of poor, spindly quality.

The seed was sown in the open ground in May, the seedlings were thinned and had made handsome plants by the autumn. I rather expected and feared that they would have enormously deep and vulnerable tap-roots like seakale or parsnips, but no; although fleshy they were stump-rooted and hence easily dug up and easily accommodated at the next stage. Nevertheless, I shortened them a bit.

For forcing them I have pressed into service the ornamental tubs that are used for pelargoniums and the like, in summer. I packed about 15 chicory roots into each and worked old potting soil in among them. In order to get the headroom for covering the crowns with 9 in. of sand, I fitted a sleeve of thin wooden slats round the edge of the tub. With this covering you get nice bullet-shaped chicons, not blown things.

The first tub for forcing was put on our dark cellar stairs in late November and I was amazed at the quick results, compared with seakale. I am now on the 3rd tub at the end of March and the 4th cropping should see me through to a new outdoor lettuce season, following a March sowing under cold glass.

Globe Artichokes

The **globe artichoke** is becoming increasingly popular in this country. It is funny how people's attitude towards it as a food varies. Some will tell you that they cannot be bothered and that artichokes are too fiddling to eat and a lot of fuss about nothing.

This is because they were never brought up to it, and, indeed, it is unnerving to watch a novice's attempts at eating one. He takes an unconscionable time to achieve nothing at all, tries to consume the wrong parts and gets his teeth choked with the tough, hairy bits that would later have been the artichoke's flowers. Now, botanically speaking, the edible parts are the base of the bracts, (which have to be sucked individually or in groups) and the large, fleshy, disc-shaped receptacle: the *fond d'artichaut*. Artichoke addicts seldom bother about the leafy bits; they quickly peel these off, pull out the disc florets with one tug, and get to the heart of the matter, the receptacle. On these we gorge. No question is heard of a surfeit of artichokes; day after day we sink our teeth into their juicy cores, to emerge after each prolonged guzzle, triumphant and refreshed, yet keenly anticipating the next set-to.

Well, then, artichokes are easily grown, but they take up a lot of space for the crop they produce, and with even one addict in the family you need a minimum of two dozen plants, spaced at least 3 ft. each way. But they are the handsomest of vegetables to grow, and their foliage covers the ground so exclusively from spring till August that weeds are no problem for a large part of the year. April, or the first half of May is the time to start a new bed. Never grow seedlings. The result is a horrible hotch-potch, most of the progeny being as prickly as a cardoon. Neither is the purple-headed artichoke a good culinary variety. You should grow one or other of two famous cultivars: Vert de Laon is like an explosion, the bracts all outward pointing; Camus de Bretagne is like a football, with incurving bracts. As regards flavour and freedom from prickles, there is nothing to choose between these two. The former is slightly the hardier, but the heads of the latter are a shade easier to pack into a saucepan.

You buy what are termed 'rooted offsets'; material that may be better known to you as Irishman's cuttings. They are obtainable from Thomas Little at Church House, Smeeth, Ashford, Kent. They have been (and, if you are doing your own, they should be) shorn of all their leafage so as to prevent loss of moisture by transpiration and to give the small roots the best chance of becoming established without heavy demands on them for water supplies. The offsets are planted as shallowly as you dare, so they have a purchase on the ground, and the slightly bulbous leaf bases should still be visible at the soil surface. You should water them in well and keep watering them generously for the next three weeks or so, when new foliage will begin to appear. The earliest stages do look most unpromising but are no cause for alarm. You just keep watering.

In this first season your crop will mature from late July till October. The heads produced are very large and of the highest quality. In subsequent seasons, you can expect your first heads towards the end of June. In really forward years, I have had them in late May, but July will provide the bulk of the crop and by August, except for a few stragglers, it will be finished. Thus it will be seen that, if you want artichokes from June till the autumn (sometimes even into November), it is wise to do some new planting every spring, and to rely on old clumps for early cropping. For any enthusiast living in the colder parts of the country, the best policy would be to detach some offsets from established clumps in September; to pot them up singly and overwinter them under glass, planting out the next spring. Meantime the parent bed could be scrapped in the autumn and dug and manured in readiness for next season's crop.

If you are keeping your old bed going, fruited stems want cutting to the ground, when they have cropped. A billhook is the handiest implement for dealing with their woodiness. This allows light to reach the crown of the plant, where new foliage will develop before the onset of cold weather. It will subsequently get frosted, but will act as a fixing for the straw or bracken that you work in as winter protection. If you do, that is. In bleak, exposed situations, you must, but especially on heavy soils, this kind of material encourages slugs and various rots, and I prefer to do without it.

When my friends complain that their artichokes are blind or are cropping poorly, the reason is invariably overcrowding. When planting, each rooted offset should consist of no more than one shoot. And you must remember to feed the brutes. You can lightly fork in farmyard manure or garden compost around your established clumps, in early spring,—their roots are not too near the surface. Follow up with a dressing of general fertiliser at 4 oz. to the square yard in April.

At the end of 3 years, your old beds should always be replanted on account of this overcrowding and plethora of small shoots that I have harped upon. Really, if one could be bothered, I think it would be best even for South country dwellers to replant every year: you get such magnificent heads. Not having any early crop would be the sole disadvantage, apart from the fag of it.

Seakale

Crambe maritima, better known as **seakale,** is one of those vegetables that you must grow yourself, if you like it, because it scarcely ever appears at the greengrocer's. The wild plant occurs along most of our unbuilt-up shores, and looks like a floral explosion in early summer when its handsome glaucous foliage is surmounted by a cloud of white, honey-scented, cruciferous blossom. Nature's only mistake, here, is in most often setting this white display against a very pale off-white background of shingle or sand. In the garden you can do better, and seakale is worth growing for ornament alone, especially among plants whose main display is in May and June.

Wild seakale likes to grow within striking distance of the tide-line. Its seeds can then be dispersed by the sea itself, and they are not destroyed by salt water. The plant is sometimes mistaken by beachcombers for wild cabbage. I must, on this account, be one of the few people who have eaten, or at least bitten into cooked green seakale leaves. My mother, on some seaside jaunt, collected them and, labouring under the widespread misapprehension that Dame Nature's products must be more nourishing and wholesome than anything a garden grows, brought these 'cabbage' leaves home and cooked them—without, of course, saying anything. Similar pranks are constantly being played by our womenfolk on their innocent men, and always in the hope that it will end in the refrain, made to a fellow-conspirator, 'and he never knew the difference.' On this occasion he could hardly help knowing, having never previously put anything so bitter and stringy into his mouth.

Seakale leaves and shoots must be blanched. They have then, when cooked, a delicate flavour and texture that is not unlike asparagus. It is a useful vegetable to have coming in at midwinter, and a succession from forced and unforced crowns keeps you in seakale till the end of April. Production is a continuous cycle, and I will break into it in December, so as to describe my own methods. When their old leaves have been frosted, the plants are dug up from their row in the garden and dumped on the potting bench for me to deal with.

First I discard any that show signs of Black Rot. This is a bacterial disease that is always lurking. It turns the roots and/or crowns soft and black and is easily recognised by its nauseating stench. Then I cut off the smaller, distal portions of root-pieces that are, ideally, not much thicker than a pencil. They are cut into 3-in. lengths, bundled up in groups of 25, making sure that the top end of each cutting remains at the top, and plunged into grit in the open.

Back to the potting bench. Seakale has thick, fleshy, awkwardly branched tap roots, and the next thing is to shorten these further so that some five or six crowns can be fitted into a 10-in. pot. This is then filled with old potting compost—the crowns just breaking the soil surface—and watered thoroughly. Those pots that are not yet to be forced are left under the potting bench, where it is cold. The others are brought indoors and stood on a tin tray in a cubbyhole under the stairs going down to the cellar. Any house can find some such position, where it is dark yet reasonably warm, say 55° F. All that has to be remembered now is to water when necessary—perhaps once in 10 days or a fortnight. From a potting in mid-December, I am cutting in the first week of February. Other pots are brought in, successively. You can wait for a second cut, from side-shoots, if you do not mind these being thin and spindly. After cropping, the roots are thrown away.

Meantime, by April, the root cuttings that I plunged will have made shoots from their upper, cut surfaces and will be lifting their 4-in. coverlet of grit. They are then lined out at a spacing of about 18 in. in the kitchen garden, but allowing only one growing point to remain on each cutting. The others are rubbed off, so that all the plants' energies are concentrated into producing one fat shoot each. The position must be sunny, and that is about it, apart from keeping weeds down.

The other method of growing seakale is to have the plants in permanent beds, in the open, and to cover them, when blanching time arrives, with inverted pots. Special seakale pots, with lids, used to be easily obtainable and they are so decorative, in a functional way, that it is worth hunting for them at sales. A correspondent informs me that they are still obtainable, new, from Harris Bros., The Wrecclesham Pottery, Farnham, Surrey. You set three or four cuttings close together, only 4 in. apart, so that the pot drops over them, and allow 2 ft. between groups. Natural cropping like this gives you seakale in April, and the plants can be left without resetting for about four years.

The best way to start growing seakale is from pieces of root, but this will be possible only if you know of a private source of supply. You can, however, raise plants from seed, which is on the market. But it takes two years to get a first crop; only one from cuttings. Also seedlings show variability and may, for instance, force at different rates. So you should select the most satisfactory and thereafter propagate it from roots.

Currants and Raspberries

I am no sort of an expert on fruit and am unable to chill the reader's blood by quoting how many million big-bud mites were emerging from each of his blackcurrant bushes on that balmy spring day that he may mistakenly have been enjoying. But as a consumer, and as maker of the family's jams and jellies, my interest is undeniable.

My 16 **blackcurrant** bushes (spaced 6 ft. apart) were twice as many as we, or any ordinary household, should need. Blackcurrants are heavy croppers. Even if the birds strip them of buds in some years—and their tastes do seem to vary enormously in this respect from one season to another—one can usually lay down enough currants from 8 bushes, in the good years, to tide one over. The old variety Boskoop Giant is still the best for the private gardener. It has a thin skin, very large juicy fruits and long bunches. The first two of these factors would be against it, as a commercial variety that had to travel, but this is no concern of ours. A trouble from which Boskoop Giant suffers, when grown under field conditions, is running-off: many of the green fruitlets drop off in May. But in the shelter of the average garden this is seldom experienced.

The blackcurrant's two most serious troubles are from big-bud and 'reversion.' I have always found one annual lime sulphur spray to be wholly adequate in preventing the development of big-bud. 'Reversion,' in which the plant appears to revert to a useless wild prototype, is actually the manifestation of a virus disease. After 15 years it got my bushes at last, and there was nothing for it but to grub and replant, this time with only 8 bushes. One of the signs of 'reversion' is that the leaves become smaller, narrower and with fewer lobes, but the more easily recognised characteristic is that the fruits become quite tiny—first on one or two branches, but presently on the whole bush. Sooner or later, this disease puts an end to the useful life of every blackcurrant bush, so one does want to be on the look-out for it.

Redcurrants are so much more attractive to birds that we have them in a cage with the raspberries. They are lighter croppers than the blacks (especially in their early years), so one needs more plants. I have 10 bushes, now nine years old. At four years they yielded only enough fruit to make 3 or 4 lb. of jelly; at five they bore 17 lb. of fruit between them, which made 18 lb. of jelly the extravagant way: using their own juice only and not adding water. At 8 years they yielded over 8 lb. per bush—more than enough for ourselves and several friends.

Next to birds, the worst redcurrant pest is the caterpillar of the gooseberry sawfly. When this is allowed to build up its numbers unchecked, nothing will be left of the redcurrants' foliage, by August, except a skeleton of leaf midribs—quite a laughable sight, unless the bushes are one's own. Handpicking is possible, if you are persistent and vigilant. The young larvae are gathered together in a clutch, on one leaf, and are easily dealt with at this stage. But fresh batches of eggs are laid over a period of three or four months.

As to **raspberries,** I think every gourmet is agreed that Lloyd George is still streets ahead of any modern variety, for flavour. I remember a fruit-growing friend proudly demonstrating to me how he could roll a ripe berry of the variety Malling Jewel between his fingers, without its changing shape or crushing. It was like a bit of rubber and an excellent traveller, no doubt; also a vigorous grower, a heavy cropper and even welcome as something to eat, if nothing else was available. Lloyd George is squashy and must be eaten within a few hours of picking, but that, after all, is perfectly feasible in one's own garden. It is an acid fruit and needs plenty of sugaring, but the flavour really is superb. Raspberries, unlike strawberries, are very well worth deep freezing. A glut is nothing to get worried about.

Still, there is nothing like the fresh berry and one longs to extend the raspberry's season. Textbooks on fruit tell us that if you prune Lloyd George to the ground in February, then you can gather your crop from its young canes in late summer and autumn. Now this variety will always fruit a little at the tips of its young canes in late autumn, but the weather by then is deteriorating and the flavour is poor. All you do, by pruning out the previous season's canes as above, is to restrict your crop to this miserable late effort. There is no gain whatever.

Next time I plant, I shall include some of the American-raised variety called September. This also fruits on its new canes but, let us hope, earlier than does Lloyd George.

Plums

If **plum** trees regularly fail to set a crop, there are two probable reasons. The first and, nowadays, the likeliest in rural areas, is that birds (mainly bullfinches but sometimes tits) are stripping the buds in winter and spring. They attack not only the blossom buds but peck out the leaf buds also, so that you get long strands of bare wood with just a tuft of leaves at the extremities, where the birds cannot conveniently perch in order to finish their job. Were it not for this trouble, I should by now have grown most of the available varieties of plums and gages and be able to write comparatively on them all, largely from the viewpoint of an ardent consumer.

Birds have made nonsense of plum growing in my garden for rising 20 years, but those who live in suburban areas should not be deterred. They are more likely to run into the second common cause of non-fruiting: one which, when appreciated, is easily forestalled or remedied. Many plums are self-sterile and must be cross-pollinated, when in flower, by another variety having fertile pollen. If you think you will have just one gage in your garden, it may fill your rapturous gaze with a mouth-watering prospect of blossom, each spring, yet never set one fruit, unless some neighbour happens to have provided it with a suitable mate. However, if you really have room for only one plum tree, it is still possible to choose from among a handful of self-fertile cultivars.

Most trade catalogues give a helpful and guiding hand on this subject of what to plant with what, and the Blackmoor nurseries of Liss, Hampshire, print a particularly valuable and comprehen‑ sive table of pollinators. This is, indeed, an outstanding specialist fruit nursery, and I have never received or heard of anyone receiving an unsatisfactory plant from them. Plums and damsons are available in bush form, as half-standards with a 4-ft. leg or as full standards with a 5-ft. to 5½ ft. leg, also as fan-trained trees for wall training. If it is essential to be able to walk about under the tree, a standard is the obvious style to go in for, but in many cases a bush is the answer, because the lower branch system allows for easier picking. Some varieties are naturally of so weeping a habit, however, that like other weeping trees they should be started at the top of a 6-ft. leg. Such are Victoria, Giant Prune, Warwick‑ shire Drooper and Early Laxton.

All plums, gages and damsons, with the exception of the Pershore plum or Yellow Egg and of the cherry plum or myro‑ balan, are grafted. There is no truly dwarfing rootstock, so the main consideration from the gardener's viewpoint is to buy trees that have been worked on a stock that does not sucker immoder‑ ately. Suckering may not matter too much where the trees are growing in turf, and the suckers will automatically be mown off several times in a season, but it is a terrible scourge in cultivated ground. And plums do love to grow in cultivated ground—in a shrubbery or other border, say—because they are greedy feeders, and do all the better for not having grass turf to compete with. Common Mussel is the worst stock for suckers. I have a green‑ gage worked on this that suckers to a distance of 15 ft. from the trunk. St. Julien A is a good stock and, for large trees, myrobalan and Brompton are both satisfactory, suckering with restraint.

In discussing varieties, I shall only speak of those I have grown and known from experience, though there are others, like the recently introduced dessert plum Anna Späth (an outstandingly good pollinator) that I should have liked to have tried.

Earliest to ripen, in late July, is the cooking variety Early Laxton; a pretty, pale yellow, plum-shaped fruit, largely overlaid with red. It is sweet, juicy and somewhat insipid, but very welcome as the herald to a new season. The tree's twig growth is slender and weak. It seldom makes a specimen to gladden the eye.

Next to ripen, in early August, is Rivers' Early Prolific, commonly known as Early Rivers. This is the best ordinary, common or garden plum I know. The fruit is smallish, round, dark purple, a little on the dry side until you get it well between your teeth. The stone is free—i.e., it comes away cleanly from the flesh, and this is always a considerable asset. When ripe (and you can finish ripening the fruit, for the last few days, off the tree) it makes excellent raw eating, and you also get best value from it as a cooker if you delay using it until its full flavour has developed. In the war years, when the bullfinches were presumably away on active service and we had heavy plum crops, we would stew the ripe fruit with sugar in large saucepans with only just enough water added to prevent burning. Then after boiling for only a very few minutes, pour it straight into preserving bottles and seal immediately. Thus the product consisted almost entirely of ripe fruit and sugar and was ready to eat as soon as opened.

It is worth stressing the point that all plums, however they are to be used, whether for dessert, stewing, bottling or jamming, should first be allowed to become dead ripe. It makes all the difference to their flavour. The fruit can safely be picked, up to a week before it would ripen on the tree. Picking should include the fruit stalk with each fruit—otherwise rot may prematurely set in at the stalk end of the fruit—and if the stalk detaches cleanly and comfortably from the branch, you will know that the desired state of ripeness for picking has been reached. The fruit can then be laid out under cover, in a safe place, and sorted over every day or so for the ones that have ripened. The aroma in a room where plums are ripening is quite something.

Wasps are the principal bugbear in the plum season. One of the great advantages in Early Laxton and Rivers' Early Prolific is that they often manage to ripen on the tree before the wasps have developed fruit-eating habits. The 'picking' of a heavy crop can then be done by spreading a dust sheet underneath the tree and shaking.

In mid-August Czar comes in: a large bold-looking dark plum, easily grown, cropping regularly and heavily but a thoroughly dull dog when it comes to it. Ouillins' Golden Gage also comes in then, and it is the first of the spurious gages to ripen. It has a large, round, golden-yellow fruit and does not taste bad if you were not expecting it to taste very good. Many plums of dessert quality or thereabouts have cashed in on the word gage wherewith to sell themselves, but the one and only true gage is the Old Greengage or, simply **greengage,** which comes in at the turn of August and September, but is most often met with a little earlier in the shops as an imported product. Its name in France is Reine Claude. The small round green fruits become faintly flushed with yellow, on ripening. The stone is free, the flesh on the dry side and the flavour is quite remarkably aromatic. It is as exciting as unexpected, in so demure-looking a fruit. Greengage is an unreliable cropper, and there has hence been derived from it the more regular and very similar Cambridge Gage, whose fruits with me are a tiny bit larger and come in about ten days later. It is not quite so flavoursome.

A gage plum that dates back to my earliest memories and that starts ripening in late August but has quite a long season, is Comte d'Althann, not widely offered nowadays but available from George Jackmann and Son of Woking. This is excellent, both as a tree and trained against a wall, where the fruits will grow twice as large. The skin is dark red and the flesh yellow verging on orange, with a distinct taste of honey (not a gage flavour at all).

The late August dessert variety Denniston's Superb is very distinct. It is a reliable cropper and has the useful attribute of being self-fertile, so that you can grow a lone specimen without reference to pollinators. The elliptical fruits are smallish, green, becoming yellowish. The flesh is exceptionally juicy. It is sweet but the skin is bitter and has to be spat out, while the stone clings to the flesh, which is a nuisance.

Bryanston has a good deal of gage in its blood, for it is markedly aromatic. The medium-large, round fruits are yellow, sometimes marked with red dots, and ripen from early to mid-September. They are dryish and the skin is rather tough but this is a worthwhile variety, easily grown and cropping well. Jefferson is similar as to skin appearance and flavour but carries large oval fruits, ripening late August.

Victoria is the most famous dual-purpose plum. Its heavy cropping and the beautiful red colouring of its elliptical fruits are points that sell it. To taste, it is bland and lacking in character but very juicy. I have read that Victoria is less prone to bird damage to its flowers and leaf buds in winter and spring than are most plums, but this is not the case in my garden.

A pleasant late-August plum is Giant Prune. It is designated for culinary purposes only, but I have no trouble in enjoying the ripe fruit raw. A sharp, pungent-tasting plum, this, with large, elongated fruits of typical prune shape with a dark reddish-purple skin. The stone is free. It makes a handsome tree and crops heavily right down to the ground.

The Pershore plum or Yellow Egg is aptly described by its second name. The raw fruit is woolly but acceptable when preserved. I see no point in planting it to-day, however.

Figs in the Open

September sees the ripening of the most luscious fruits that this versatile climate allows to reach maturity without roof protection —peaches, gages and figs. I am a confirmed fig pig, and shall therefore dilate *con amore* upon my favourite fruit.

In a normal year, I expect **figs** here, in East Sussex, to start maturing in the fourth week of August; and a succession of well-flavoured fruits will often go on ripening into the second week of October. When people enviously congratulate you on the fig crop you are going to enjoy, they are usually looking at the hundreds of 2-inch-long fruitlets that would provide a second crop if ours were a Mediterranean climate, but which, in fact, will come to nothing. Those which hang on into the new year should be rubbed off, otherwise botrytis rot or coral spot enters through them and eats back into young branches, killing them. It is on the fruitlets that are already well developed by late spring, that we should pin our hopes.

In some years a high proportion of these drop off in June. This is generally said to be due to water shortage at a time when the swelling fruit is most in need of it, and generous watering is recommended at that season. My own experience does not bear this theory out. I have as yet been unable to correlate June fruit-fall with a particular climatic factor.

There are six fig trees in my garden. Five of them are of the variety Brunswick, and were planted when the garden was made, in 1912, to cover large areas of wall. Brunswick is an exceedingly vigorous variety and has the boldest of leaves, five-lobed with deep indentations and a splendid glossy sheen on the upper surface. Its naked branches are palest grey, beautiful in winter sunshine with the tracery of their shadows cast on the wall behind. The three largest specimens are sited on a 20-ft. wall beneath a gutterless roof, and in some winters they are hung from top to bottom with hundreds of icicles—an extraordinary sight when the sun comes out.

Clearly these figs were planted mainly for effect. Their root-run is unrestricted and the border in front of them is heavily manured (it needs to be, with the figs gobbling up most of what one adds). Nevertheless, they carry generous crops of fruit when conditions suit them—about one year in three. Brunswick is the largest fig you are likely to meet: above five inches long and very juicy. Fruits borne in the middle of a lot of foliage remain pasty-faced and of anaemic flavour. But those that stand out from the surrounding verdure and catch all the sun there is to catch (and fig trees must always be given the sunniest aspect available) change to a remarkable chocolate shade and are pure ambrosia.

Figs need protecting in most (but not all) gardens. In the days before rats became easy to control, they would scour the trees and eat every fruit while still quite green. Squirrels, too, can develop a vicious taste for figs. But against more normal pests, of which blackbirds, starlings and wasps are the chief, I find that 6-inch-square brown paper bags are most effective. Indeed, figs seem to be specially designed to have bags slipped over them and quickly secured with a stem tie. You can feel when they are ripe through the bag and then pick off the fruit, bag and all. Plastic bags are no good, as the environment they create is far too moist and rots the fruit. Brown paper bags are tough enough to be used again and again. Even if they get wet, they can quickly be dried before re-use. True, they serve as dormitories for earwigs, but these do little damage to figs. Only now and again will one walk through the eye of a large specimen and be discovered when you are eating it. Nylon net is more durable than paper and allows rain water to drain away. It can be cut for use into squares.

Bags should not be put in position until the latest safe moment, as they take the sunshine from the fruit. If they are put on just as the fruit is beginning to change from green towards brown you can visit your trees every third or fourth day, according to the weather, and pick off every bagged fig with a reasonable assurance that it will be ripe. Figs never ripen satisfactorily off the tree. They are at their best when on the verge of going rotten, when the skin nearly always splits, longitudinally, in several places.

Our sixth fig tree is older than the century and stands in the open, unprotected, a shrub some 9 ft. high and 18 ft. wide. In the winter of 1940 it was severely cut by frosts, but in 1962–63, in common with all our figs, it did not suffer the slightest reverse. It seldom fails to bear a heavy crop and this variety, Black Ischia, is the one I should recommend for most general planting. I have failed to trace it in any nursery lists, but it is common enough in old gardens. Brown Turkey, another small fig, is easy and prolific too, and readily available. These fruit at an early age and without any root restricting practices being required. The fruits of Black Ischia are smallish, with a long, thin neck, and change on ripening from dark green to near black. The flesh is reddish-purple, drier than that of Brunswick and of a far superior and more marked flavour. In a good year I harvest some 400 figs from the one bush and the birds take twice that number.

The less you have to prune a fig, the sooner it is likely to settle down to the business of fruiting. Every time you cut at it you stimulate fresh vegetative growth; so the great thing is not to choose a variety that is too vigorous for the space it is to occupy. When figs are on a wall, pruning cannot be avoided, but should consist of thinning out rather than shortening back.

If you can conveniently restrict a fig's root-run, it does, of course, settle down to fruiting the sooner. Thus, against a south-facing house wall the foot of which has been concreted, a fig can very suitably be grown in a large tub.

In a Mulberry Shade

When you have spent your whole life in the neighbourhood of a tree, you get to know it with an intimacy that goes beyond the general sort of information on the species that is likely to be found in a textbook. So it is with our pair of **mulberries.**

They were planted in 1912, when the garden was laid out, and stand as sentinels on either side of a broad, paved terrace walk that leads to a series of descending circular steps, with projecting and re-entrant curves. This was all Lutyens's design, and there used to stand, on the paving between the trees, four cubic oak tubs, also to his simple and dignified design. These were planted with *Sedum spectabile*. Once the trees grew up, the tubs had to go, for the whole area became heavily shaded. This pair of black mulberries was set 30 ft. apart; really, the distance should have been 40 ft. at least but the trees are now, in any case, too large for the general scale of their environment. Their span (where they do not interfere with each other) is 40 ft. after 57 years, and their height is about the same. Most gardeners planting a mulberry make insufficient allowance for its eventual bulk, and I imagine that more maturing mulberry trees have been chopped down for this reason than for any other.

The leaves of a mature mulberry are heart-shaped (on young trees, they often have deep indentations, more like a fig leaf) and they vary greatly in size. Well placed ones grow about 7 in. long by 5½ in. wide. Although they cast a deep shade, mown grass never fails to thrive beneath them and I take this to be on account of the very short season in which the full-grown leaves are in position. Leafing has barely commenced by the end of May and is not complete until a month later. Most of the foliage has gone by mid-November. Mulberries are not noted for autumn colour, but if October is calm they do change to a handsome yellow. One tree stands outside my bathroom, whose walls are white, but for a few days each year it could be called the yellow bathroom because, whether the sun is shining or not, the mulberry leaves pervade it with their own light.

A mulberry foible that gets people worried is that the leaves on certain branches will often begin to go pale and slightly yellowish as early as August, whereas on other branches they are still rich green. The fear is that the tree's health has taken a turn for the worse. Our own trees do not behave in this manner every year, but they often do, and I have never discovered that, in the event, there has been any kind of long-term effect. Leaf-fall follows a similar pattern, the branches whose leaves remained dark green in late summer, being the last to shed them in November. When that is over, one breathes a sigh of relief, for the tree is never so beautiful as when stripped. Then, too, you can appreciate the warm rufous colouring of its rough textured bark.

But to most people the chief point about the mulberry is, I suppose, its fruit. I would point out that this is being shed, without intermission, from the end of July until mid-October. The stains do not wash off the flagstones underneath until well into December. For three months, the trees are filled with squawking starlings; with blackbirds too, and with wasps and flies and blue-bottles. The month from mid-June is the only time you can sit in a mulberry shade. Rarely are conditions just right for the maturing of ripe, undamaged fruit that is truly fit for a fastidious human's consumption. Now and again this does happen. The fruits hang on until they are almost black, and can then be transferred from tree to mouth in one smooth gliding movement, with the most satisfactory result. No better combination than sharp and sweet together, so that the palate contracts and tingles while the juice gushes separately from the bead-like fruitlets of which the mulberry is made up.

The first thing, if you want to grow a mulberry, is to find a supplier. In any book on fruit growing the author, who probably knows the last word on apples, pears, plums and all commercial fruits, but absolutely nothing about mulberries, will write on the subject of their propagation something like this: 'The mulberry is easily propagated by cuttings of considerable size which readily root if taken in September and October; shoots, a foot or more in length, root with very little trouble in sandy soil in a cold frame.' Now, if the mulberry is so easily propagated, you would have thought that any nurseryman having access to a mature tree from which to obtain cutting material, would be on to a good thing, for there is no lack of demand. Yet it is only with great difficulty that you can locate a nursery supplier, and then he will very likely have imported his stock.

There are two traps for the unwary customer to which I must draw attention at this point. First, it is not sufficient to order *a* mulberry; you must ask for *the* black mulberry, *Morus nigra*. Otherwise you are liable to be served with a plant of the white mulberry, M. *alba*, which is easily raised from imported seed. But, except as food for silk-worms, the tree has little to recommend it, and its anaemic white fruit is useless.

Second, you must acquire a *female* black mulberry capable of bearing fruits. Black mulberries are sometimes monoecious—that is with male and female flowers borne separately but on the same tree. Friends at Aldon Old Rectory, near West Malling in Kent, inherited a mulberry that carries females almost exclusively on some branches, male catkins almost exclusively on others, and both sexes on yet others. The male catkins enabled the females to set good seed and there were mulberry seedlings growing on an old compost heap when they came to this garden, the heap partly consisting, one presumes, of sweepings from the mulberry.

Much more often, however, mulberries are dioecious, the trees producing either nothing but male catkins (no fruit for the hungry owner) or nothing but females, which can swell and make good edible fruits without pollination, but will not set viable seed. If you happened to buy a mulberry that had been grown from seed, it could easily be an unproductive male, so you want a plant that has been vegetatively propagated from a female.

The tree certainly can be increased from hardwood cuttings. I remember one of my form masters at school having succeeded in doing just this. I have not yet been successful myself. It must be one of those cussed plants that favours the amateur.

Having obtained a plant, everything is straightforward, for the mulberry has few troubles and grows fast on good soil. Usually, the tree has no trunk but develops from a series of branches near ground level. These get heavy in a matter of 60 or 70 years, and have to be propped, but even the propping, if well done, can be reasonably picturesque. The natural habit of the plant is weeping, and in many situations it will be necessary to remove a few low branches almost every year. The wounds never callus over, in this species, and it is very important to protect the scars from rotting, by painting over with a bituminous substance —much more effective than the white lead paint we once used.

Glossary

adventitious. Having a different mode of origin from the normal, as shoots produced from roots.

alkaline. The reverse of acid.

anther. The part of the stamen containing the pollen grains.

bract. A modified leaf growing just below a flower's calyx.

break (breaking). (1) The putting forth of new leaves, shoots or buds. (2) Where, due to virus infection, a flower's typical colouring is broken into streaks against a white or yellow background, e.g. in tulips, stocks, wallflowers.

calcifuge. Disliking lime.

calyx. The sepals as a whole.

carpel. One of the units into which the female part of the flower is divided.

chlorosis (adj. cholorotic). An unnatural yellowing or whitening of green leaves, especially between the veins.

close (adj.). Shut up, unventilated; of a greenhouse, frame or propagating case.

compound. Of a leaf or inflorescence; made up of several distinct but comparable units.

corolla. The petals as a whole.

corona. An appendage coming between the petals and the stamens as in *Eucharis, Pamianthe* or the cup or trumpet of a narcissus.

corymb. An inflorescence of stalked flowers springing from different levels but making a flat head, e.g. *Achillea filipendulina* and other yarrows.

cultivar. A plant which has originated in cultivation, not normally to be given a name of Latin form. Thus, Petite Lemon Drop is a marigold cultivar.

dibber. Pointed instrument, usually wooden, for making holes in soil, in which to plant seedlings or insert cuttings.

dioecious. Having the sexes on different plants.

distal. Away from centre or point of attachment; terminal (opposite of proximal).

family. A group of plants comprising a number of related genera, e.g. Cruciferae, the family of cruciferous flowers like arabis and aubrieta; Compositae, the family of composite flowers, in which many are gathered into heads, as in daisies.

fastigiate. Of upright, columnar habit, occupying little lateral space.

filament. The stalk of the anther, the two together forming the stamen.

genus (pl. genera). A group of species with common structural characters. The name of the genus is, in designating a plant, placed first and has a capital initial letter, e.g. *Chimonanthus.* See species and var.

glaucous. Bluish.

humus. Undecayed organic matter.

inflorescence. Flowering branch, or portion of the stem above the last stem leaves, including its branches, bracts and flowers.

involucre. Bracts forming a structure just below an inflorescence, as in astrantias, euphorbias and many eryngiums.

Irishman's cutting. A cutting detached from the parent plant so as to include some roots.

lanceolate. Narrowly elliptical, tapering at both ends.

lenticel. Opening in bark, admitting air to underlying tissue. Lenticels are clearly visible on young woody stems as spots of contrasting colour, e.g. hydrangea, apple.

monocarpic. Fruiting only once. Monocarpic plants may take one (as in annuals), two (as in biennials), or more years to reach maturity but will die after fruiting.
node (adj. nodal). A point on the stem where one or more leaves arise.
organic. Derived from living material.
palmate (of a leaf). Lobed, the mid-ribs arising at one point, as in a sycamore.
panicle (adj. paniculate). A branched raceme, e.g. *Astilbe.*
perianth, The sepals and petals together.
petal. A member of the inner series of perianth segments, together forming the corolla.
pinnate (of a leaf). Having leaflets arranged on either side of a common axis, as in an ash.
piriform. Pear-shaped.
proximal. Nearest a point of attachment. (Compare distal.)
raceme. A collection of distinctly stalked flowers arranged at intervals along a stem, e.g. delphinium.
rhizome (adj. rhizomatous). An underground stem.
rogue. Inferior plant among seedlings. Roguing is the job of removing rogues.
scape. A long, naked flower stalk arising direct from the base of a plant, e.g. *Hemerocallis, Primula.*
scion. A shoot used for grafting upon a rootstock.
seminal. Of, by or from seed.
sepal. One of the parts that together form the calyx, being the outermost whorl of the flower.
species. A group of individuals which have the same constant and distinctive characters. The name of the species is, in designating a plant, placed second, and has a small initial letter, e.g. *Prunus sargentii. Sargentii* is here the specific epithet.
stamen. One of the male reproductive organs of a plant.
stigma (pl. stigmata; adj. stigmatic). The receptive surface of the female part of a flower, to which the (male) pollen grains adhere.
stock. The rooted portion of a plant to which a graft is applied.
stolon (adj. stoloniferous). A creeping stem, usually resting on the soil surface.
stopping. The operation of pinching shoots back so as to make them break into lateral growths.
turgid. Distended with sap.
umbel. An inflorescence with stalked flowers arising from a single point, e.g. allium, amryllis, astrantia, parsley.
var. Short for variety. A natural group within a species, occurring in the wild; normally given a name of Latin form, and placed next after the name of the species, e.g. *Clematis montana* var. *rubens.*
rubens. var. is frequently omitted, thus: *C. montana rubens.*
whorl. More than two organs of the same kind arising at the same level, e.g. the leaves of *Lilium martagon* are arranged in whorls.
widger. A double-ended, spatulate, stainless steel tool about 7 in. long used for pricking out seedlings, removing small weeds, stirring up the top-soil in pots and boxes, etc.

Index

The figures in bold type refer to pages on which illustrations occur.